The Modern American Novel
and the Movies

The Modern American Novel and the Movies

EDITED BY

Gerald Peary and Roger Shatzkin

WITH HALFTONE ILLUSTRATIONS

Frederick Ungar Publishing Co. / New York

Copyright © 1978 by Frederick Ungar Publishing Co., Inc.

Printed in the United States of America

Library of Congress Cataloging in Publication Data

Main entry under title:

The Modern American novel and the movies.

   (Ungar film library)
   Filmography: p.
   Bibliography: p.
   Includes index.
   1. American fiction—Film adaptations—Addresses, essays, lectures.
I. Peary, Gerald.   II. Shatzkin, Roger.
PN1997.85.M64   791.43'0973   78-4373
ISBN 0-8044-2682-1
ISBN 0-8044-6649-1 pbk.

For my mother and father (R. S.)

In memory of Abraham Goldes
and Kenneth Hemstead (G. P.)

ACKNOWLEDGMENTS

We would like to thank Elizabeth Dalton and the staff of the Wisconsin Center for Film and Theater Research, Mary Anne Jensen, Curator of the Theatre Collection, Firestone Library, Princeton University, the staff of the Theatre Research Collection, New York Public Library at Lincoln Center, and Theo Haynes and her assistants in Multi-Media Services, Alexander Library, Rutgers University, for helping us compile material concerning the adaptations of novels into films. Doug Lemza of United Artists (formerly of Films Incorporated) and Sidney Ganis of Warner Communications procured films for some of our contributors when we had about given up hope; likewise, Patrick Sheehan of the Library of Congress arranged essential viewings for our writers. Special thanks also goes to F. Anthony Macklin, editor of *Film Heritage*, who allowed us permission to reprint several articles from his magazine. Jan Luben-Hoffman and Paula Horvath provided assistance with the preparation of the manuscript. Robert C. Rosen, E. Ann Kaplan, and Karyn Kay were kind enough to volunteer editorial advice, and Daniel Hawkes helped with the Filmography. Stan Hochman and Ruth Selden of Frederick Ungar offered support, sound counsel, and Job-like patience. And lastly, thanks to our contributors, without whose earnest and hard work there would be no book.

PHOTO CREDITS

Contents

Introduction

Did you know that Frank Capra's *It Happened One Night* came from a novella, "Night Bus" by Samuel Hopkins Adams? That François Truffaut's *Shoot the Piano Player* is a transposition of a New Jersey-set David Goodis novel, *Down There?* That John Ford's *The Man Who Shot Liberty Valance* originated in a short story from the brilliant Montana regionalist, Dorothy M. Johnson? And that Ford's most stirring personal symbol in the film, the cactus rose, actually is lifted and transplanted from Johnson's tale?

Such sources are rarely cited by pure "auteurist" critics, and the reason could not be more obvious: here is hard evidence to detract from the popular romance of director as sole Artist-Creator. Critic Peter Wollen's description of the mystique surrounding the composition of literature extends, in toto, to the cult about cinema direction:

> The producer of thought is . . . envisaged as the traditional philosopher, whose thought is the function of pure consciousness, pure mental activity. . . . It is to preserve this myth that notebooks and drafts are so rigidly separated from final versions, so that the process of thought as a dialectic of writing and reading . . . is obscured. . . .
>
> (*Signs and Meaning in the Cinema*)

1

Through this volume, we wish to "un-obscure" the cinema, calling into question the more idealist impulses of "auteurism." The *process* of reaching the film product is the topic of practically every essay—directorial vision tempered by the step-by-step of production. Even if, in some articles, the film director is ultimately honored and granted "artist" stature (see, for example, William Rothman's "To Have and Have Not Adapted a Novel" about Howard Hawks, or Douglas Gomery's "Three Roads Taken . . ." about John Ford, or Michael Stern's piece on *Pylon, The Tarnished Angels,* and Douglas Sirk), the thread remains operative: the film is not "thought up" by the director but is built dialectically from prior texts—a screenplay, of course, sometimes a play version, and, in this case, always a novel by a noteworthy American author.

The act of demonstrating how a novel becomes a film is more than academic exercise and formalist curiosity. It is a tool for political analysis. In studying the maze of artistic decisions made along the way to the final film text, we can begin to account for the *planned* ideological choices within the normally opaque Hollywood cinema, where ideology is so entwined with narrative as to seem "realistic," "natural," unintentional, the way of the world.

On this point: our two volumes on the American novel and the movies may be seen as not only a pragmatic adjustment to the Pure Art of director-as-auteur approaches, which dominate such diverse sources as *Movie* magazine, *Film Culture, Film Comment,* and Andrew Sarris's *The American Cinema,* but also as a friendly corrective to the Buried Ideology approach of those influenced by political theorist Louis Althusser and psychoanalyst Jacques Lacan around *Screen* magazine in Britain and post-1968 *Cahiers du Cinema* in France.

Ideology is "profoundly unconscious" according to Althusser (*For Marx*); "the workings of ideology do not involve a process of deception/intentionality" for *Screen*'s Claire Johnston (*Notes on Women's Cinema*); and "What the camera in fact registers is the vague, unformulated, unthought-out world of the dominant ideology," say the *Cahiers* editors, Jean-Luc Comolli and Jean Narboni ("Cinema/Ideology/Criticism"). Even Peter Wollen, also of *Screen,* rethought his auteur chapter of *Signs and Meaning* for his new conclusion in 1972:

> The structure is associated with a single director, an individual, not because he has played the role of artist, expressing himself or his own vision in the film, but because it is through the force of his preoccupations that an unconscious, unintended meaning can be decoded in the film, *usually* to the surprise of the individual involved.

The key word to note (our italics) is *usually*. While we applaud the entry of psychoanalytic methodology in cinema analysis and agree that much of what has been praised by auteurist critics is really unconscious, unintended meaning, we feel the urgent need to restore to prime importance the ideological constructs (that is, what is *perceived* as ideology) which someone has decided either to place in the film or to omit from the film. To this end we have inserted a special appendix on "The Politics of Adaptation."

There are strong unconscious elements at work in the film of *For Whom the Bell Tolls.* But, as Constance Pohl shows in her background essay in the appendix on the making of the movie, there was also Franco's government as bedfellow of Paramount Pictures, mandating what could or could not be said about Fascism, what elements from Hemingway's novel were verboten. This Fascist-Hollywood pact must be considered, as well as director Sam Wood's own rabid anti-Communism.

There are other clear examples in "The Politics of Adaptation" of how ideological messages from the novel are subverted on screen. Joseph Mansfield demonstrates conclusively in the essay on *The Wet Parade* that MGM took Upton Sinclair's pro-prohibition, socialist-feminist tract and made an anti-prohibition, anti-socialist, anti-feminist movie. *The Wet Parade* is a paradigmatic study because the ideological strategies are so much on the surface. Upton Sinclair never bothered to dress up his politics, to homogenize his polemics with aesthetics; and perhaps that is one of the reasons why *The Wet Parade* is considered a decidedly "minor" novel.

And there are other examples in the main section of this book of subtler pressures (see Robert C. Rosen on Otto Preminger's direction of *The Man With the Golden Arm* and Michael Klein on Dore Schary's screenplay for a movie version of *Miss Lonelyhearts*) where the Hollywood artist stands accused of mucking with the literary text to suit his own conservative impulses. Interestingly, the right and center auteurists tend to offer a different set of anecdotes about embattled directors and the trials and capitulations of the Hollywood cinema—stories of Orson Welles's agony over the debased ending imposed by RKO on *The Magnificent Ambersons* (1942), of John Huston's struggles at MGM with *The Red Badge of Courage* (1951), of Nicholas Ray versus a hostile Society, of Monroe Stahr versus Commerce. These sages fit snugly within Marxist Ernst Fischer's conception of Romanticism: "The writer's and artist's I . . . struggling for existence by seeking itself in the market-place, yet challenging the bourgeois world as a genius" (*The Necessity of Art* [1963]).

If we have returned full circle to auteurism, it is at the least auteurism with a materialist basis, situated within the battle of wills and unyielding ideological pressures of the studio and distribution marketplace. (Although it is "vulgar Marxism" to argue that a Hollywood studio will only allow films supporting the economic base, it is folly to find *no* correspondence between ideological constructs and what are perceived as corporate interests. As Raymond Williams summarized his rebuttal of purely Lacanian-Althusserian "Marxist" approaches to cultural analysis in *Marxism and Literature:* "A Marxism without some concept of determination is in effect worthless.") Inevitably, it comes down to dialectics. The novel versus the studio. The novel versus the director. The director versus the screenwriter, the producer, the studio, or whatever. One ideological intention versus another intention. Or, if you will, intention against intention against the Unconscious. Only a fusion of methodologies can begin to absorb it all.

Director Otto Preminger once proclaimed about his film version of the novel *Advise and Consent,* "I have the right to re-create the characters and the story . . . in any medium. Therefore while the author of *Advise and Consent* is a conservative Republican, I eliminated everything in this book I considered reactionary." Here is a fruitful place to begin an analysis: with directorial intentionality, attempting to discern the clear shifts by Preminger (and his screenwriter) away from what was considered reactionary and offensive in Allen Drury's bestseller. But instantly, another factor is the Unconscious, the unintentional— what remains on screen in *Advise and Consent* that Preminger and Drury unthinkingly share, believing these elements to be nonideological, "reality" itself. For example, despite Preminger's proudly liberal intentions, he uses homosexual lifestyle as an index for decadence, something which, in 1962, most Americans would have taken as "natural" and without ideological purpose, as innocent as Preminger's endorsement of bourgeois marriage as an iconic quick study of "healthiness." In these cases, the Unconscious of one era is discovered to be resonant with ideological implication by the altered Consciousness of another.

Switching keys: in the introduction to our earlier volume, *The Classic American Novel and the Movies,* we discussed the abuse which many literary critics and scholars have felt under the aggressive media onslaught of that ingrate art, the cinema. The discomfort has been experienced, perhaps even more naggingly, by several generations of writers. While cinema theorists argue endlessly whether "auteur" directors can be considered fully individuated, many novelists have felt the need to re-emphasize *their* artistic integrity, by breaking away from the movies. A historic model is Willa Cather, who put her foot down. Upset by the way Hollywood had twice, in 1924 and 1934, mangled her 1923 novel *A Lost Lady,* she made a point to eschew any further contact with the cinema while she lived, and more finally, after she died. She provided in her will that the executors

not . . . release, license or otherwise dispose of my literary properties for any dramatization whether for the purpose of the spoken stage or otherwise, motion picture, radio broadcasting, television (or any other) mechanical reproduction whether by means now in existence or which may hereafter be discovered or perfected. [Quoted in "Why More Top Novelists Don't Go Hollywood," by Lacey Fosburgh, *New York Times,* Nov. 21, 1976.]

Typically, Cather overlooked the fact that the novel itself was a product of the first technological revolution; and that the novel, as Walter Benjamin explained, is a creation of "mechanical reproduction." But, by the time of Cather's death, mid-twentieth century, it was clear that the novel, despite its historically progressive role in championing bourgeois values over aristocratic ones, had staked out a claim to a High Art tradition of its own. And this claim was threatened, in turn, by film. As Walter Benjamin noted in 1936, the social significance of the cinema "particularily in its most positive form, is inconceivable without its destructive, cathartic aspect, that is, the liquidation of the traditional value of the cultural heritage."

This sweeping-under of literature is, understandably, as calamitous and unhumorous to most writers as it was a fascinating and inevitable tide in the eyes of Benjamin. American author Joseph Heller epitomizes the literary backlash against movies: "I can't think of any film ever adapted from any work of literature that I or other people feel has any quality to it that even approaches the original work of literature that was its source." (See Heller's discussion of *Catch-22* on film in this text.)

It must be clear that we are dealing—in Updike, Bellow, Heller, Barth, Malamud, Ellison, Barthelme, Pynchon, Ishmael Reed, to name a few—with a generation of novelists which has complicated its trade with narrative structure, style, language, and self-reflexivity in ways that are not easily "filmable." (Let it be said that our list, however arbitrary, is a modernist men's club; the same description is inapplicable to this day's American feminist novelists, who have emphasized accessibility and narrative clarity over formal experimentation.)

The choices pursued by these novelists must be regarded in a dual manner. They are continuing the progressive evolution of the novel as it came out of Joyce and the modernists of the early twentieth century; yet they are indulging, at the same time, in the conservative impulse to preserve for themselves the role of individualistic Artist in the face of mass age, the epoch of the "novelization" and the serial television novel, from Irwin Shaw's *Rich Man, Poor Man* to Tolstoy's *Anna Karenina*. (The direction they have sought is not unlike the movement away from monumental realism in Western painting discernible after the development of photography. The camera could document reality "better" than the painter, so artists moved on to forms that asserted their independence of photographic technology—postimpressionism, cubism, abstraction.)

Above all, it is television which is omniverous, absorbing novels, resurrecting novels, creating simultaneous phenomena in different media as with Alex Haley's *Roots*, happily confusing history and fiction, bestsellers and Great Books: *M*A*S*H**, *Serpico, The Class of '65, The War Between the Tates,* and *Loose Change,* from book to television series, movie of the week to *Masterpiece Theatre* to *Once Upon a Classic*.

If we need further evidence that we live in a period of unparalleled cultural effluence, in which the mass media have merged with print, let us look no further than a *New York Times Book Review* bestseller list. Taking, for example, the February 12, 1978, paperback "mass market" compilation—the books being sold in the highest volume of any in the land—we can observe the following cross-influences and cross-pollination: Of the nine novels and two nonfiction narratives on the list, two have been released as theatrical movies (*Coma* by Robin Cook and *Looking for Mr. Goodbar* by Judith Rossner), one is in production (*The Shining* by Stephen King), three have inspired television movies (*Roots, The Ghost of Flight 401, The Hobbit* by J. R. R. Tolkien), one concerns the travails of a screenwriter (*Blue Skies, No Candy* by Gael Greene), one is written by a movie star (*Voyage* by Sterling Hayden), and two (*Trinity* and *The Crash of '79*) will probably soon become films because Leon Uris's and Paul J. Erdman's previous works have been adapted successfully to the screen.

However, before the panic becomes epidemic, before we proclaim that the dread dynasty of bookburners, of *Fahrenheit 451*, is today, let us remember that the bestseller list has always been just like this, minus the automatic media tie-in: some good literature, but most decidedly not so good. And if we are in an era of "bi-medialism," where even many literate people seem equally comfortable and conversant with images—photographic and electronic—let us note that fine works of literary quality continue to be written; that publishers continue in business—witness this volume in hand; and that books continue to locate an audience, thanks to you, gentle reader.

GERALD PEARY
ROGER SHATZKIN

Tobacco Road (1932)

Erskine Caldwell

Three Roads Taken:
The Novel, the Play, and the Film

BY DOUGLAS GOMERY

Tobacco Road is a legend of the marketplace, a phenomenon usually described in statistical rather than literary terms. The blurb on the novel's latest printing (New American Library, 1976) illustrates this quite succinctly:

> As a novel which has sold nearly three million copies in Signet editions alone and has been translated into fifteen languages, as a Broadway play with a record seven-year run, and as a movie constantly reshown, *Tobacco Road* is an American classic, heading [Erskine] Caldwell's imposing list of successes.

Overwhelmed by these records, most critics have chosen to analyze *Tobacco Road* only in sociological terms: Why was this artifact so popular in the midst of America's worst depression? The few analysts who have examined the text in any depth have dismissed both the novel and play as "dirty jokes" with appeal to the worst instincts of America's growing middle class of the 1930's; at best it is treated as a minor example of regionalist fiction, far below the quality of the work of Thomas Wolfe or William Faulkner. (See, for example, Joseph W. Beach, *American Fiction: 1920–1940* [1941] and Kenneth Burke, *The Philosophy of Literary Form* [1967].)

However, when the novel appeared in 1932, critics greeted it

9

with respect. None anticipated the flood of popularity ahead. It was the 1934 play version—adapted by Jack Kirkland and Erskine Caldwell—which began this "phenomenon" of popular culture, when an appraisal of the play by Burns Mantle of the New York *Daily News* sparked the sellout run. Mantle lauded the play's important social themes, and amateur sociologists, reformers, and critics heaped on more praise. With an extremely low admission price, the play ran on and on—until 1941. Challenges by local censorship groups against road show performances only created larger crowds. Each new ensemble of actors emphasized to a greater degree the play's comic moments, and this too seemed to spur attendance. Eventually the novel became an all-time best seller largely because of the play's notoriety and subsequent publicity.

Hollywood's moguls could never resist the lure of a Broadway hit. Since the coming of sound, the major studios regularly filmed adaptations of all Broadway's major successes. The popularity of *Gone With the Wind* in 1939 suggested that films about the South could do spectacularly well; the success of *The Grapes of Wrath* in 1940 suggested the public liked softened exposés of "important" subjects. Thus in 1940 Darryl Zanuck, head of production at Twentieth Century-Fox, purchased the rights to the play for a reported two hundred thousand dollars, secured the services of Jack Kirkland, the play's author, to help produce it, and reassembled much of the team which had done so well with *The Grapes of Wrath:* director John Ford, screenwriter Nunnally Johnson, actors Charley Grapewin, Russell Simpson, Zeffie Tilbury, Grant Mitchell, and Ward Bond. In February, 1941, as the drama neared the completion of its New York run, the film premiered to lukewarm reviews. Film critics who valued the play (for example, Bosley Crowther of the *New York Times* and Otis Ferguson of the *New Republic*) argued that the movie failed because Zanuck and Ford had diluted the play's realism and turned *Tobacco Road* into a farce. Using those criteria, these reviewers had a strong case. Determinism motivates Caldwell's original story. The novel is a throwback to nineteenth century naturalism—emphasizing sex, fear, and hunger as the primary human drives. There is a clear progression from the novel to the

play to the film of excising the elements of determinism and sub-
stituting comedy.

The central issue in all three versions of *Tobacco Road* is: will
a poor Georgia farmer, Jeeter Lester, be able to stay on his inden-
tured land with his mother, wife Ada, son Dude, and daughter
Ellie May? The bank, represented by George Payne, threatens
to foreclose. In the novel Jeeter can never secure the necessary rent money. Caldwell devotes much space to recreating
Jeeter's fearful thoughts on this matter. Past experience has
taught him to mistrust banks and loan companies alike, because
all they ever suggest is that he and his family move to the city
and work in the mills at subsistence wages. As an alternative
Jeeter tries to approach his "best" son, Tom—who does not live on
the farm—for the funds; but Tom refuses to help. Death can be
the only solution in this world of economic and even familial
injustice. Jeeter's mother dies first, a victim of technology, crushed
accidently by her new car. In the novel's final chapter, nature
joins the conspiracy. The fires (which Jeeter had always thought
to be a necessary condition for spring planting) sweep over the
Lesters' house and kill the sleeping Jeeter and Ada. At the conclusion, Dude articulates the same ideas about planting as his
father did. The reader can only assume that the same economic
and social forces will destroy Dude, after an unproductive, fitful,
and absurd life.

Such a pessimistic ending does not provide the makings of a
hit Broadway play. For his theatrical reworking, Kirkland kept
the same central problem but created a new structure. The play's
action lasts three consecutive days and does not leap through
time or memory as does the novel. The progression of events is
now a series of comically grotesque revelations about the Lesters,
Jeeter in particular. The economic and social forces become
wholly personalized in the characters of landowner Captain Tim
and banker George Payne.

Now the Lesters are more victims of their own foibles than of
larger socioeconomic forces. These family dilemmas provide the
sources of the play's comedy. For example, Jeeter's second
daughter Pearl, only mentioned tangentially in the novel, returns

to Tobacco Road and plays a significant role in the drama. The comic conflict between Jeeter and Pearl's new husband, Lov, over Pearl's inability to adjust to marriage becomes as important as Jeeter's inability to grow crops. This problem, plus neighbor Bessie's pursuit of Dude, are resolved, and then all these younger characters leave Tobacco Road. The comedy which dominates the first two acts slowly evolves into pathos: both Ada and Grandma die; Jeeter lives on, alone.

If we characterize the structure of the novel as deterministic and the structure of the play as a series of comic episodes with a pathetic ending, then the film moves cyclically from defeat to optimism. This pattern is begun in the film's opening two segments. After the credits, a narrator introduces us to Tobacco Road. The land has fallen fallow, yet the Lesters will not leave. "They stayed on and on. But all they had and all that they were; that's all gone with the wind and the dust." The twelve shots with this narration (and a light melancholy version of "Dixie" in the background) progress from three direct views of Tobacco Road itself to the low-angled view of a decrepit mansion to the dust-covered, aged furniture within the house. It is a sad, mythic portrait of a culture grown old. Yet with the narrator's announcement of "Tobacco Road today," director John Ford cuts to a long shot from a high angle of a wild jalopy coming down the road. In the next shot the car, a runaway from Mack Sennett, crashes the gate of the mansion. A lively banjo provides the musical background. The cycle has begun: from pathos to comedy, from defeat to optimism. The oppressive economic and social forces cannot and will not conquer the human spirit. Refusing two alternatives, the mills and the local poor farm, the Lesters have chosen to remain on Tobacco Road, with its simple life and basic ties to the land.

The five days of the film's action continue the cycle. During the first day, the Lesters, in a wild romp, steal turnips from Pearl's husband, Lov; then all share in the feast. Things seem even better the next day as Peabody, the omnipresent newscarrier of Tobacco Road, tells of Captain Tim's return. Yet Tim's arrival the following day sets up the major problem for the rest of the film. He has not come to provide Jeeter with a needed "grub-

Lou (Ward Bond) courts Ellie May (Gene Tierney), and Jeeter
Lester (Charley Grapewin) steals a turnip, under the gaze of Dude
Lester (William Tracy) and Ada Lester (Elizabeth Patterson). *To-
bacco Road* (1941)

stake" but to accompany banker Payne in making a rent demand. Sister Bessie Rice, might have provided funds. Instead she ran off and married Dude, then bought a new car with all her money. Jeeter prays for a miracle, but he is much too pragmatic to wait for the Lord's help.

On day four, one day before the rent is due, Jeeter persuades Dude and Bessie to go to town to sell some wood to raise the money. He quickly abandons them and seeks a loan. Unfortunately the banker is also his creditor. He exits filled with amazement and bewilderment, but *not* bitterness. Quickly Jeeter decides to steal Bessie's car to raise the needed cash. This venture also fails. On the final day, resigned to the poor farm, Jeeter and Ada begin to hike there, only to be "rescued" by Captain Tim, who gives them a six months reprieve to remain on their own farm. Unlike earlier versions, no one dies. The cycle will continue. Jeeter and Ada go on together, albeit without the children.

As a film, *Tobacco Road* has been lost in the contours of director John Ford's distinguished career. Coming in the midst of his first major creative period, it was immediately preceded by *Stagecoach* and *Drums Along the Mohawk* in 1939, and by *The Grapes of Wrath* in 1940, and it was followed by *How Green Was My Valley* in 1941. Critics since then have only noted how it suffered by comparison. (See, for example, Andrew Sarris, *The John Ford Movie Mystery* [1976].) However, though not a great film, *Tobacco Road* is a provocative transitional work in Ford's career, both stylistically and thematically. It lacks the complexity and unity of his masterworks, but it does exhibit many of the basic elements of Ford's greatest films. Its strength lies in several individual sequences. I shall examine only two in detail, suggesting how a more in-depth study of the film should begin.

The first illustrates Ford's complex use of depth of field, placement of figures and objects in space, and music. The sequence, when Bessie and Dude go to the courthouse to secure a marriage license, begins with a long-angle shot of a sign, the first written language in the film after the credits: *County Clerk/Marriage Licenses.* This at once connotes the city, but also foreshadows the trouble these two illiterates will have obtaining a license. In the next shot Bessie and Dude come from off-screen right. The only sound, the first in the sequence, is Dude's screaming imitation of a car horn, intimating that his sole motivation for marriage is to drive Bessie's car. Ford then cuts to a low-angle shot inside the clerk's office. In the depth we see a desk to the left and framed written documents on each wall. In the room's center hangs an electric light. This is the film's first example of decor from an up-to-date, technological world. As Bessie enters, she glances around as if in an alien setting. Only then does the camera pan slightly to the right to reveal the clerk. In this fairly long take Ford first emphasizes decor, then presents the people.

Ford has now established the stylistic pattern for the sequence. The depth of field and the long takes link people, their actions, and the decor. Thus, when Bessie first stands facing the clerk, the two are separated by the implements of modern bureaucracy—desks, ink wells, papers, and files—while Bessie is framed between the two documents on the wall. Only when the conversation dictates does Ford pan, not cut, to Dude. Ford continues to employ takes with great depth and a long duration for the key ensembles of figures which come near the end of this sequence.

Ford's editing follows a nontraditional pattern. When he employs shot/reaction-shot cutting, he separates the figures completely, and links them only to key aspects of the decor, not to each other. When we first see the clerk, it is from an angle that reveals only the clerk's desk, papers, and books behind him. It completely excludes the persons to whom he is speaking, Bessie and Dude. The next shot is of Bessie and Dude. Directly behind Bessie on the wall is hung a framed document, covering her head almost like a halo. There is no hint of the clerk to whom she is speaking, even though he is only a few feet away.

Although Ford surrounds Dude and Bessie with suffocating objects of the city, while isolating them from the bureaucrats, he provides sounds as reminders of the rural culture and as weapons against separation. To counter the clerk's refusal to provide a license, Bessie blows her ubiquitous pitch pipe and begins "Bringing in the Sheaves." Dude and the clerk's secretary join in. Still in the same shot, the camera moves forward and pans toward the door revealing two women and a man entering the office. They too join the singing. Finally Ford cuts to the hall where the mayor is leaving his office, apparently to complain about the noise. Suddenly the mayor begins to sing and marches in step with the continuing music toward the clerk's door. In the next shot he enters the clerk's office; four men and his secretary follow. Ford then cuts to the clerk, very perplexed and alone, separated from all the others. The next shot presents the singing "congregation" led by the mayor, gathered round the clerk's table. The mayor suggests a second song, "Shall We Gather at the River?," a standard in Ford's films and a melody repeated countless times in *Tobacco Road*. Though traditionally a funeral hymn, here it presents the celebration of rural culture amidst this governmental bureaucracy. Its normally plaintive tone becomes buoyant with optimism, complementing the previous song, "Bringing in the Sheaves," begun by the indomitable inhabitants of cropless Tobacco Road.

A final brilliant long take ends the sequence. It begins with Dude and Bessie, alone in the shot, beginning to sing "Shall We Gather at the River?" Soon a hand emerges in the lower right hand corner of the frame with the marriage license. Ford then pans right as Bessie moves to the clerk's desk to "touch" the pen and make her X. He pans and dollies left following an exuberant Bessie and a willing Dude leaving the office. As the duo pass the mayor, the camera stops, framing the mayor and the others, who sing with incredible zest and spirit. The clerk enters the shot, followed by his secretary with her hands clasped under her chin. The clerk protests; the mayor only increases his volume and nods to his employee. The clerk begins to sing, even more vigorously than the others. Ford ends the take by slowly panning left to capture the rest of the singers. This final shot, almost two minutes in length, links a community of urban bureaucrats and country folk through traditional rural hymns. This unity, however, will last only as long as the shot itself.

This sequence is characteristic of Ford's best work. The camerawork emphasizes the continuity of space and the character's place in this world. In opposition, the shot/reaction-shot editing serves to isolate these same people. Noises and singing both reinforce this continuity and intensify the separation. Certain themes begin to emerge. Dude and Bessie, who know only an oral tradition, have brought a sense of community to the city. Yet the residents of Tobacco Road can never fit into the new world; they must abandon the temporary chorus at the end of the sequence. By using a take of extreme duration to end the sequence, Ford merges secretaries, bystanders, and city officials in song. The hope of a newer world, transcending modern bureaucracy and technology, lies with unification of the people of the earth and their urban opposites.

The above analysis uncovers certain stylistic traits in daylight sequences in *Tobacco Road*. In several night scenes Ford adds to this complex visual pattern another component, lighting. One example occurs when Jeeter prays for the necessary one hundred dollars rent money but warns the Lord that he will take things into his own hands if Providence does not step in to help. When Jeeter is alone in the field, kneeling in prayer, the light creates a faint halo around his head, yet it is subtle enough not to be glaringly symbolic. As he begins his demands to the Lord, Ford cuts to a closer shot in which the light on the old man's eyes creates large shadows on the lower half of his face. Jeeter's moral ambiguity is reinforced by this brilliant split of light and darkness. This dual level carries through in most of the film's night sequences: when inhabitants of Tobacco Road stop to take stock of the precarious state of their existence, darkness cloaks their physical squalor.

The classic thematic and structural antinomies in Ford's best films are garden/desert, past/present, and wilderness/civilization. The above analysis of *Tobacco Road* suggests that the key duality in this film is between the country and the city. The plot begins with Jeeter's fourth unsuccessful trek to sell wood in Augusta. It ends with a temporary miracle in the country by Augusta's Captain Tim, a quixotic figure who feels a sense of duty to maintain Jeeter, his father's tenant. Captain Tim is an exception to the normal lack of urban charitability. The city usually responds positively to those with money, not to those, like Jeeter, who *need* money. The city is not anchored in tradition. Thus the inhabitants of the city can unite in songs of an older culture for several minutes and then presumably resume their normal tasks. The city's rules—recorded in books—and its credit standards are equally rigid. The countryside has few rules, no books, and even encourages theft. It tolerates a much more open morality. Its flexibility enables the residents of Tobacco Road to survive in the fashion of a cooperative. The city, although morally "upright" in word, cannot in fact support such people, and thus accommodates the poor by suggesting they work in the mills.

Ford is at his best when he suggests ambiguity of theme in the same sequence, or even in the same shot. At this time in 1939, Ford seemed to side with the country; the ultimate hope for the future lay, somewhat precariously, with the common people. Later, Ford would go on to rethink his historical priorities in such masterworks as *The Searchers* (1956) and *The Man Who Shot Liberty Valance* (1962). Thematically, *Tobacco Road* is a transitional work in John Ford's career. It demands our attention because it foreshadows many of the elements in the later Ford classics. More important, it stands alone for its several sequences which must rank with the best cinema John Ford has created.

Miss L. Gets Married

BY MICHAEL KLEIN

Miss Lonelyhearts, written in the early 1930s in fast-paced, one-hundred-page, B-film style (a montage of fifteen short scenes), is an elliptic allegory of suffering, loneliness, thwarted idealism, malevolent cynicism, and a need for sanity and security in the "jumble of modern society [that is] bankrupt not only in cash but in emotion." [1] Its bitter and anguished author, Nathanael West, held a mirror up to the contradictions of the period but found no answers in the offerings of the conventional American dream. In producer-writer Dore Schary's 1958 film, *Lonelyhearts,* however, 1950s values of pragmatic compromise and upwardly mobile suburbanite marriage easily resolve the maddening contradictions that destroyed the obsessed figures of West's original work. The calculated shifts of style and meaning reveal both Schary's own compromised philosophy of filmmaking and the conformist cultural ethos of Cold War Hollywood in the 1950's.

Nathanael West worked as a scriptwriter in Hollywood throughout the 1930s on at least thirty films, for the most part minor comedies and B features. His friends in California ranged from established novelists (Fitzgerald and Faulkner) to satiric wits (S. J. Perelman) to the literary left (Farrell, Lillian Hell-

---

[1] Josephine Herbst, "Miss Lonelyhearts: an Allegory," *Contempo* 3 (July 25, 1933), p. 111. She calls it a moral "detective story" whose people are "representatives of a great Distress."

man, Josephine Herbst, Lester Cole). The disparate companion-
ships reflect concerns and tensions that are expressed in his
works. On the one hand West was significantly committed to left-
wing political activities: he was a sponsor of the American
Writers' Congress Manifesto; he was involved in support for the
Spanish Loyalists and for migrant workers' strikes in California;
he became an official of the progressive Screen Writers Guild
and was attending Marxist study sessions at the time of his
death in 1940. Yet West's writing is primarily negative, hardboiled, and satiric. It focuses upon the contradictions of the
period and the limits of romantic idealism without stating any
political or ideological solutions. West explained this aspect of
his writing in a letter to Jack Conroy:

> If I put [in] any of the sincere, honest people who . . . are
> making such a great progressive fight, those chapters couldn't be
> written satirically and the whole fabric of the peculiar half world
> which I attempted to create would be badly torn . . . Remember
> that famous and much quoted discussion about . . . Balzac . . . in
> Marx's correspondence . . . The superior truth in Balzac was suffi-
> cient to reveal the structure of middle class society and its defects
> and even show how it would ultimately be destroyed.

The novella *Miss Lonelyhearts'* fifteen chapters are often
titled allegorically (e.g., "Miss Lonelyhearts and the Dead
Pan"). The unnamed idealistic and alienated male protagonist
writes a Miss Lonelyhearts column for a bitterly cynical newspaper editor, aptly named Shrike after a savage bird of pointy
beak and shrill cry. Miss Lonelyhearts has a fiancée, Betty,
whom he avoids after proposing to her. As the book progresses
Miss Lonelyhearts becomes increasingly drawn into the impossible sufferings of the letter writers: rape victims, cripples, out-
casts, and lonely people. He finally seeks out one of them, Mrs.
Doyle, in a pseudo Christ-like attempt to put even one life in
order. The result is a brief sordid affair which makes him more
doubtful of both the needs of the world and his own idealism.
Miss Lonelyhearts' romance with Betty becomes increasingly
ironic and disoriented. Finally, Mrs. Doyle's crippled, jealous husband discovers her affair and shoots Lonelyhearts.

A good deal of the book is devoted to an extended debate between Miss Lonelyhearts' warped and tortured idealism, his desperate prayer for something better, and Shrike's insistence that human nature is hopeless and irredeemable. The contradiction is left dangling: no solution is indicated to the moral and philosophic questions that have been raised in the book. Neither Shrike nor Miss Lonelyhearts emerges as a signpost of value or a figure whose words have authority.

Fragments of the novel are devoted to the romance between Miss Lonelyhearts and Betty. Betty represents paradigmatic American values: "the country," a gingham apron, breakfast, security, cleanliness, order, innocence. "Her sureness was based on the power to limit experience arbitrarily." Lonelyhearts looks to Betty to limit his pain and confusion, his growing doubt of the world and of the values he has lived by. However, he comes to recognize that she too is a nonexistent ideal. Their relationship becomes a dark parody of American romance. In one chapter Betty takes him out to a farm. The scene begins as a typical idyllic pastoral of young love: "the pale new leaves . . . were beautiful and . . . the air smelt clean and alive." The next day, after a celibate evening in an abandoned farmhouse, nature becomes identified with the death and decay of "rotten leaves, gray and white fungi. . . ." This change in tone signals the end of their ironically Eden-like idyll:

> There was nothing to do in the house, so [Betty] began to wash the underwear she had worn on the trip up. . . . She had her hair tied up in a checked handkerchief, otherwise she was completely naked. . . . He blew her a kiss. She caught it with a gesture that was childishly sexual. He vaulted the porch rail. . . . As they went down, he smelled a mixture of sweat, soap and crushed grass.

A thrush in the forest makes an obscene sound like "a flute choked with saliva" and marks, through this antiorgasmic image, stark and revolting, that their fall is complete.

For Lonelyhearts, Betty's loss of innocence makes it impossible for her to qualify as his salvation from the human pain he must daily confront. But Betty, acidly allegorized as "the party dress," maintains her innocence as a social mannerism. She puts on "her litle girl in a party dress air," "pouts," "screws up her nose," drinks a "strawberry soda," and tells Lonelyhearts she is pregnant. He proposes. "He pleaded just as he had pleaded with her to have a soda. He begged the party dress to marry him saying all the things it expected to hear." They discuss their future home, but the reader knows that their upcoming marriage is a hopelessly inadequate solution to the almost metaphysical horrors of the book. Their relationship becomes part of the morass, and the marriage never takes place.

Miss Lonelyhearts has been filmed twice. In 1933 a version entitled *Advice to the Lovelorn* was produced—a Lee Tracy newspaper comedy with melodramatic overtones. The characters of Miss Lonelyhearts and Shrike were fused into a reporter named Tony Prentis. He follows up a letter written to the newspaper "sob sister desk" and uncovers and solves a murder mystery. The film was enlivened by an earthquake shaking things up in the newspaper office. However, neither characters nor audience was unsettled by any moral or social problems.

Lonelyhearts, the serious attempt to film West's novel, was made in 1958. The producer, Dore Schary, assigned direction to Vincent J. Donehue, and starred Montgomery Clift as Miss Lonelyhearts and Robert Ryan as Shrike. Ryan was a good type for Shrike, having played cold and demonic adversaries in *Crossfire* (1947), *Clash by Night* (1952), and many other films (later he would be Claggart in *Billy Budd* [1962]). Clift introduced a sense of Actors' Studio angst to Miss Lonelyhearts which is consistent with West's nervous hard-edged work.

With the exception of several *film noir*-like scenes in the newspaper office—harsh light and shadow, crosscutting between high-angle shots of Miss Lonelyhearts and low-angle shots of domineering Shrike—the film is devoid of expressionistic equivalents of West's prose. The use of frequent close-ups facilitates the transformation of West's grotesque allegorical figures into "characters." (The result is an internalization, softening, and sentimentalization of the concerns of the book, a muting of the contradictions

Adam White (Montgomery Clift), Miss Lonelyhearts, is seduced by the charms of Justy Sargeant (Dolores Hart). *Lonelyhearts* (1959)

which are always in the foreground of West's prose.) The close-ups also serve as a vehicle for extensive dialogue. In a sense, the film is more verbal than West's novel: Strike's Sade-like dialogues with Miss Lonelyhearts' Marat occupy a much greater proportion of the film, are more coherent, and focus greater attention on the spoken word.

Although in West's novel most of the figures (Shrike, Shrike's wife, etc.) are isolated within two or three fragmented chapters, they appear throughout the film. The role of Lonelyhearts' fiancée has been particularly expanded; she is no longer peripheral to Miss Lonelyhearts' life but relates to him throughout. Her name has been changed from Betty to Justy—a symbolic indication that her privatistic values (home, family) are right or just. Miss Lonelyhearts is also given a new name in the film—Adam White. This is an instructive choice. In the novel, Lonelyhearts is an Adam figure only insofar as he wanders in a fallen state. In the film, he is Adam in that he gains practical knowledge through a loss of innocence. By tempering his expectations, he comes to a realistic accommodation with the nonparadisiacal 1950s world.

Dore Schary, who wrote and produced *Lonelyhearts*, was a controversial figure in Hollywood in the years following the House Un-American Activities Committee investigations (HUAC had cited West posthumously). Schary was a famous liberal who at first resisted the witch hunt, finally succumbed to pressure from the other studio executives, and, as head of production at RKO, was primarily responsible for arranging the "realistic compromise" that led to the "Hollywood Ten" blacklisting. According to Dalton Trumbo in *Time of the Toad* (1949), Schary's decision to side with the blacklist was pragmatic: "he had done it to hold his job." And in *Inquisition in Eden* (1965) Alvah Bessie reports that Schary had given the Writers and Directors Guilds "implied assurances that if they would only accept ten martyrs no one else would ever be hurt." [2]

There is an obvious parallel between Schary's political outlook and activities and the virtues of compromise that are asserted in his revision of *Miss Lonelyhearts*. It should be kept in mind,

[2] Editors' note. Schary has never presented his side of the controversy. His forthcoming autobiography will include a chapter explaining his position.

however, that these values, as well as mystification of the family and personal solutions to general social problems, were a major aspect of the dominant culture in the 1950s. Hollywood films of the period, especially the sophisticated works of producers and directors who cooperated with the HUAC investigations, often endorse such values. For example, *On the Waterfront* (1951), the joint work of "friendly" witnesses Budd Schulberg and Elia Kazan, appears to be a realistic and progressive film about workingmen's problems. However, Marlon Brando's seemingly rebellious actions reinforce establishment values: it is good to inform to the police or government; the Church and the Law, not corrupt trade unions ought to be primary institutions in workers' lives. *Viva Zapata* (1952), another film by Elia Kazan, appears to be a positive representation of a peasant revolution. However, the film implicitly supports McCarthy era notions: idealistic and radical intellectuals cannot be trusted; political activities that aim at getting power to change the social order significantly are doomed to a cycle of corruption, disillusion, and failure.

Schary shaped *Lonelyhearts* with similar rhetorical acumen. For example, Shrike's comments about power-crazed idealists would have likely been perceived, in the Cold War context of the 1950s, as an attack on contemporary radicals. He calls them "the easy answer kids with baskets of bushwah [who] finally harpoon themselves, and then they begin to play God." So the novel's Shrike, an apolitical misanthrope, is converted to a political speechmaker in the film. On one occasion he offers Adam a dour and fatalistic lecture on the danger of nuclear war. Another time he bitterly speaks about the Ten Commandments in words that verge on a critique of capitalism:

> We would stop trade and commerce if we lived up to the first, eighth and tenth . . . don't steal and don't covet. We would not see buildings housing the aged and criminal if the fifth, sixth and ninth were followed . . . The quest for the buck, ruble or franc takes in number two. . . .

But the film disarms the radical implications of these criticisms by having the acrimonious Shrike utter them with too-venomous relish. The film also diffuses radical political concern by removing these comments from the sphere of potential action, confining them to rhetorical sound and fury. If Shrike's bitter denunciations seem potentially subversive, in practice they become fatalistic, pragmatic accommodation. In the final sense, Shrike's vitriol communicates a negative, cynical, and impassive view of human nature.

Yet, the film indicates to us that Shrike is more politically knowledgeable and aware than Adam, whose idealism tends to be naively detached from any specific social content or concerns. Shrike's cynical acceptance of the way of the world acquires additional authority, for the rhetoric of the film recognizes the world's corruption while at the same time establishing a basis for adjusting to it.

When Adam begins to share this jaded view, Schary indicates, in a note inserted in the script,[3] that he acquires a new "intensity." "I do not want to lose my temper again," says Adam. "All I want to do is heal a wound I gave myself before it festers." To which Justy adds, "Well, he says he feels that there's something wrong in him because of what his mother did and then his father." The message is clear: abandon activist idealistic engagement with human social problems, concentrate on your own psychological and spiritual self-improvement; deal with your own guilt and imperfection.

Justy has been changed to a positive character in Schary's film. Her role has been enlarged and shaped by 1950s' cultural images of women. Justy is upwardly mobile and subjects Adam's activist idealism to continual critique. Adam starts as a newspaperman out of a desire to report the truth and do good in the world. When Justy learns about his job she has one question: "What is the salary?" Later, when Adam is despondent at not having risen to a better position (a muckraking reporter; not a writer of a sob sister column), she gives him an Horatio Alger pep talk: "Look at me. I started as a file clerk. In two years I became a secretary."

She constantly chides him for having social and humanist concerns:

[3] A copy of Schary's script is in the Theatre Research Collection of the New York Public Library at Lincoln Center.

Adam darling you can't involve yourself with the problems of the whole world.

You take these letters too seriously . . . (*not impatiently but practically*).

Schary's indication, in notes to the script, that she is being practical and not impatient is extremely significant. Justy is marked as a figure of authority unlike anyone in the novel. Schary identifies "practicality," in contrast to active idealism, as a value to be admired and emulated.

In the film, then, Miss Lonelyhearts is no longer an equal adversary in a debate, but is subject to multiple critiques by *both* Justy and Shrike. Whereas Shrike primarily engages Adam in verbal debate, Justy's critique is often absorbed and reaffirmed in the action of the film. As noted, in the novel Miss Lonelyhearts' and Betty's idyll in the country ended with seduction amid negative images of nature; when Miss Lonelyhearts proposed and they discussed their future house, the event was reductively equated in value to sipping a strawberry soda. However in the film they go out to an idyllic spot in the country where Adam confesses past lies. Schary calls the setting "a lovely knoll," inverting West. Then they drive a new, tail-finned V-8 car (in the book it was a borrowed "old Ford") to Justy's house: a very large, very expensive dream house with a very large front lawn. She forgives him his lies and affair with Mrs. Doyle, and at the end of the film they are, of course, going to be married.

Justy is "young and virginal," but she is also pictured as a symbolic mother and housewife as she cooks and keeps house for her widowed father and three brothers. At no point in the film are her social mannerisms (the party dress, pouting) viewed ironically. Instead they are idealized and affirmed as outward signs of virtue and order. When, in front of a coke machine, Adam tells Justy "You taste good like an orange drink should," it is an allusion to her harmony with certain American conventions, values, and ideals. When Justy tells Adam, "Darling, I'll be your family, let me know your every thought," she does not represent an inadequate or limited sense of order, as Betty did in the novel. On the contrary she stands for an ideal, an individual solution to all the confusion and perplexity that Lonelyhearts feels as a result of his encounters with the problems of the world.

At the end of the novel the cynicism/idealism debate remains unresolved. Shrike is estranged from his wife. Doyle shoots Miss Lonelyhearts. Betty is bewildered. At the conclusion of the film, however, Justy arrives at the newspaper office, asks Adam to "forgive her," saying that she now accepts his proposal and will marry him. Shrike, observing this, begins to mellow. Then Doyle arrives and threatens to kill Adam. Adam speaks very sincerely to Doyle: he admits that his motivation in the affair was neither innocent nor altruistic, accepts responsibility for what has happened, and asks Doyle's forgiveness. He also tells Doyle (who is a cripple and impotent) that he, the husband, must ask his wife's forgiveness for treating her with malice and lack of understanding in the past. Doyle wilts and hands over the gun. Shrike, looking on, completes his change of heart: he takes a rose from a vase and prepares to go to his wife (they have been estranged since her adultery ten years earlier).

The conclusion of the film radiates pragmatic optimism. Acceptance of human imperfection breaks several cycles of adultery, revenge, and estrangement, and prepares the way for multiple personal resolutions in marriage: Adam and Justy; Shrike and Mrs. Shrike, Mr. and Mrs. Doyle.

If Shrike has modified his cynicism, Adam has partly compromised his idealism, opted for an individualistic solution to the problems of the world, acknowledged that he has "learned something" from Shrike that he "has need to test." Shrike now says, "My young friend surprised me however by *bending with the wind* rather than breaking." These were the values that Schary posited during the Hollywood witch hunt. More important, they were a part of the cultural ethos of the McCarthy period, when radical idealism and commitment were not only persecuted but challenged by a negative view of human nature, and by a doctrine of conformity, compromise, and pragmatic accommodation to the injustices and miseries of the world.

They Shoot Horses, Don't They? (1935)

Horace McCoy

The Unreal McCoy

BY PAUL WARSHOW

Charlie Chaplin once thought of making a film from the novel
They Shoot Horses, Don't They? Or so rumor has it, writes
Sydney Pollack, the director of the film, in his introduction to the
screenplay, published in paperback along with the 1935 Horace
McCoy novel. And this is not too surprising. Neither the film
nor the novel is "Chaplinesque," but the basic idea is. Like most
of Chaplin's major films, *They Shoot Horses* is about individuals
caught up in and victimized by inexorable social forces. The
idea of a marathon dance contest as brutally efficient as a machine would naturally fascinate the creator of the assembly-line
sequence in *Modern Times* (1936). And it is not hard to imagine
a Chaplin version of this story: either a silent-style comedy like
City Lights (1931) and *Modern Times* or a more ponderous
talkie like *Monsieur Verdoux* (1947).

The film Pollack and his screenwriters, James Poe and Robert
E. Thompson, have made from the novel is much closer to the
latter. It is an earnest and in some ways pretentious film (unlike the case of Chaplin, where the opportunity to talk became
the main source of heavy philosophizing and didacticism, the

This is a revised version of an article that appeared as "They Shoot Horses,
Don't They?" in *Film Quarterly,* Vol. 23, No. 4 (Summer, 1970). Copyright
© 1970 by the Regents of the University of California. Reprinted by permission of the Regents and Paul Warshow.

few instances of lightness and humor here grow directly out of the dialogue). But it is also powerful, moving, intelligent, and sometimes brilliant.

Pollack's previous 1969 film, *Castle Keep*—surely one of the six or eight most disagreeable filmgoing experiences of my life—was an artificial, forced allegory which could never decide whether it was operating from a realistic base or from one of abstract poetic myth. On either level the film was awful—on one, all sense of time and place was haywire, on the other characters were going around making remarks like "We are civilization"—and the shifts between the two were excruciating. But it is wrong to put all blame on Pollack and to write him off: no one could have made anything but a terrible movie from that screenplay (though a more imaginative director might have made the film a bit more fun).

With *They Shoot Horses*, Pollack found a very different sort of allegorical idea, with much greater potential and, by all appearances, very much suited to his particular talents. Horace McCoy's story is about a marathon dance contest during the Depression and about the down and out Hollywood hangers-on who join it, hoping to win the cash prize and, in some cases, hoping also to be noticed by Hollywood talent scouts. But there is no winner, and all that the contestants get for their often incredible effort and endurance is exhaustion and defeat. (In the film this is sometimes stretched to madness or death.) The marathon merely confirms the hopelessness of the main character, Gloria, who at the end gets her partner Robert (the narrator of the novel) to shoot her in the head.[1]

Both the novel and the film—not only through certain "signals" in the dialogue, but by their structure and by the very force of the material—invite us to take the marathon and its story as something beyond themselves, as an allegory or a metaphor. Yet the marathon is a metaphor almost a priori: one of those natural, organic metaphors which grow out of the common core of our

[1] Editors' note. Jane Fonda (Gloria) later commented, "I realize the shortcomings of the movie. The woman who does realize what is going on commits suicide. No, really something worse: she has a man kill her." (Interview in *Cineaste,* vol. VI, no. 4).

experience. Such metaphors seem obvious when you see them, but they take a certain "brilliance" to discover (and a much greater brilliance to utilize well artistically), and they have enormous potential. It is principally this *donnée*, the best thing about the novel, that the filmmakers have taken over from it. And like McCoy (although quite differently and with much greater success) they have wisely concentrated on developing the realistic drama, letting more general meanings grow out of that.

The most curious thing about Pollack's exceedingly curious introduction to the published screenplay is the compulsion he feels to praise the novel and to deny the obvious truth when he compares it with the screenplay and the film. "The cases are not rare where very bad books have made very good films. . . . But *They Shoot Horses, Don't They?* is a splendid novel to begin with," he tells us, when this is an archetypal case of a terribly overrated novel serving to make a good film. The novel is characterized by superficial, ready-made, adolescent tough-guyism and sentimentality and is written in a prose as vulnerable in its way as the "poetry" of Joyce Kilmer's "Trees." McCoy (by way of his narrator, Robert) is capable of such pseudo-truths as:

> There is no new experience in life. Something may happen to you that you think has never happened before, that you think is brand new, but you are mistaken. You have only to see or smell or hear or feel a certain something and you will discover that this experience you thought was new has happened before.

And McCoy means it—literally. The occasion for this observation is a strange girl's attempt to seduce Robert by crawling under the platform, calling "Come on," and pulling at his ankle. Robert suddenly remembers that when he was thirteen or fourteen, a girl his age named Mabel who lived next door had done "exactly the same thing," calling "Come on," and pulling at his ankle, in this case from under the front porch. Since "there is no new experience in life," we must assume that another girl did the same thing when he was seven, and so on, in an infinite geometric regression.

Pollack goes on to explain how he and one of his screenwriters, Robert E. Thompson, "a man who both loved and understood the novel," translated the book into film terms:

> The stark simplicity of the book is essential to its power. But where Horace McCoy can give an extremely lean character line, relying on the reader to fill in the "backs" and "sides" of a character from his own imagination, a film director's problem is rather different. When a film maker stands a person on the screen, that character has [needs to have?] breadth and depth simply by virtue of being seen, and those dimensions must be filled in with action and dialogue in order for the character not to seem hollow.

Either Pollack is unaware of the kinds of changes he and the screenwriters have made from the novel, and the reasons for them, or he is being disingenuous. Not only are the two parts of the last sentence contradictory, but the whole quotation reflects an unusual view of both the art of the novel and the art of the film. McCoy gives an extremely lean character line, all right, but it is not the sort that encourages the reader to fill in the "backs" and "sides" with his own imagination. The words and actions of McCoy's characters are so unreal, so much the product of unthought-out adolescent attitudes, that they immediately ossify the characters into two dimensions. Our imaginations can do nothing with these characters because McCoy's has done nothing with them.

What the filmmakers have taken over from the novel is, basically, a skeleton: the "bones" of the marathon—of a frenetic marathon dance contest in the Depression in which every character we care about is defeated; the "bones" of Gloria, the despairing heroine whose last ounce of hope the marathon finishes off, and of Robert, the naive partner who helps her die. The filmmakers have taken these main elements, and a few other pieces scattered throughout the novel and have put flesh on them—*not* just by "standing persons on the screen," but by creating and changing action and dialogue—and have very largely transformed them. For example, the attempted seduction of the hero, mentioned above—in the novel a gratuitous bit of sordidness involving a woman who is barely described and whom

Gloria (Jane Fonda) and Alice (Susannah York) resting for the dance marathon. *They Shoot Horses, Don't They?* (1969)

we never see before or after—is clearly the suggestion for an incident in the film which has so much more meaning and depth, and such a different tonality, that it becomes something entirely new. It becomes the attempt by Alice, a fully developed character, to seduce Robert: a sudden, desperate effort to make some kind of human contact and fend off her increasing isolation and, finally, madness.

Alice—the anxious, mannered, vulnerable, would-be actress, whose behavior (like her dramatic reading from *Saint Joan*) is always out of place—is one of the two most successfully created characters in the film (if one discounts that minor incident from the novel, she has been created entirely by the filmmakers). And she is at least as much the creation of the actress as of anyone else involved: Susannah York's often brilliant performance is particularly impressive if one remembers her often excellent performances in totally different roles (such as an ebullient upper-class coquette in the superb television production of *The Importance of Being Earnest*).

One clear index of Hollywood's increasing sophistication is the changes in its villains—away from the person who commits evil simply because he likes to, or because that is his function, toward more contradictory and human characters. The character of Rocky, the master of ceremonies, totally corrupt yet totally without malice, helps make evil interesting again; and Gig Young's performance has depth and control.

Although Gloria is also a character of great interest, I cannot go along with all the praise given to Jane Fonda's performance. "Jane Fonda goes all the way with the part," writes Pauline Kael, "as screen actresses rarely do once they become stars. She doesn't try to save some ladylike parts of herself. . . . She gives herself totally to the embodiment of this isolated, morbid girl" (*Deeper into Movies* [1973]). For me, this is just what she does *not* do. It is true that she (and Pollack) have resisted the temptation to give her even the slightest amount of glamour and that there are many good things in her performance. Nevertheless she tends to make Gloria's despair cute and ingratiating—a mere pose—so that her "suicide" goes beyond shock and surprise into implausibility.

This leads me to the flash-forwards. These flash-forwards to Robert's interrogation and trial for the murder of Gloria seem to have been attacked in every review of the film. In the novel the scene in the courtroom and the death sentence itself, which is interspersed in fragments between the chapters, are in the present, and the marathon is a flashback. In his introduction Pollack explains the change by saying that it seemed essential to have the marathon in the present. I see no objection on principle to flash-forwards, any more than to flashbacks. But here the flash-forwards are a kind of cop-out, a way of making us feel what the story of the marathon should be sufficient to make us feel (or should, at least, contribute to making us feel): the sense of Gloria and Robert's impending doom.

The flashbacks in the film are a different sort of problem. The film opens with a series of flashbacks to a single incident in Robert's childhood (the flashbacks alternate with shots from time-present). We see a small boy (Robert as a child) and an old man watching a horse run gracefully through a field. The horse suddenly falls, apparently breaking a leg, and the old man shoots him dead, as the boy watches in tears. The inclusion of this incident is redundant and literal-minded. The sentence "They shoot horses, don't they?," both as the title and as Robert's final remark, is powerful enough in itself—very powerful indeed—and this scene merely weakens it, not just by being redundant, but by calling attention to the specific shooting of a specific horse and away from the idea which really gives the sentence its power: that there may be justice in putting any suffering animal (including a human being) out of its misery. (If the incident with the horse were developed to the point where we could really feel for this animal, then it might contribute something.) Before reading the novel, I felt sure this incident had been manufactured entirely for the film. It seemed just the sort of bogus opportunity that, in the late 1960s, an insecure Hollywood director, eager to be "visual," would seize upon. It turns out the incident *is* in the novel (as another illustration of the idea that "there's no new experience in life"?), and although it is a mistake there too, and for the same reasons, it is nevertheless one of the few things which the film has changed for the worse. As Pauline

Kael put it, "Oh these movie men, with their misplaced romantic imagery, giving us a wild, beautiful stallion running free before it stumbles instead of Old Nellie, the plow horse that McCoy's hero remembered, who was hitched to the plow when she broke her leg and still hitched to the plow when she was shot."

Set in 1932 (the novel is set in 1935, well into Roosevelt's first term), the film is meant to recall not only a certain period in our history, but also certain *films* of that period, especially the gangster films that Robert Warshow discussed in his essay, "The Gangster as Tragic Hero" (*The Immediate Experience* [1964]). It is no accident that the director whom Rocky asks to stand up in the audience is Mervyn LeRoy [2]: LeRoy's films of the period include *Little Caesar* (1930) and *I Am a Fugitive from a Chain Gang* (1932)—as well as the little-known *Hard to Handle* (1933), whose long marathon dance sequence (perhaps the only other fiction-film portrayal of a dance marathon) probably influenced both McCoy's novel and this film. In fact the film of *They Shoot Horses* seems to aim quite directly at achieving some of the characteristics of gangster films which Warshow emphasized, such as the expression of "that sense of desperation and inevitable failure which optimism [in this case the optimism of the official American culture] helps to create."

If, on the most superficial level, the gangster films demonstrated that "crime does not pay," *They Shoot Horses* demonstrates that "honest" effort does not pay either, or at least that those enticing *shortcuts* to success which are within legality are doomed to failure. If, on a deeper level, the gangster films undercut the promise of preeminent individual success and glory which America seems to hold out, *They Shoot Horses* undercuts America's more basic promise of simple security. Both the gangster films and *They Shoot Horses* tell us that success is impossible, but in the gangster films success is glory and power, whereas here it is simple survival.

[2] In the novel the director is Frank Borzage. LeRoy is a better choice, both because he is better known to present-day audiences and because of the kind of film his name evokes. Borzage's films—like the beautiful *Man's Castle* (1933), which resembles the French poetic melodramas of the thirties—are much less harsh and more romantic.

I have said that the marathon is a metaphor. What, then, does it stand for? On one level—and it is this that endeared McCoy's novel to the French existentialists—it can, like the rather similar myth of Sisyphus, be taken to stand for all human existence. But on another level it is meant to stand for, not any society, nor society in general, but a particular kind of fraudulent society—specifically American capitalistic society—which promises its citizens the advantages a society is supposed to offer, but does not keep its promise; which pretends to provide its citizens with comfort and security, but does not; which pretends to unite its citizens in a common bond and to sublimate their natural aggression toward each other, but which in fact fosters—indeed prides itself on—competition and the carrying out of aggression. (To be sure, no one in the marathon actually murders anyone, Robert's killing of Gloria is outside the marathon and is virtually a suicide. Yet Gloria, because she cannot bear the idea of losing, chooses to ignore that her sailor-partner is having a heart attack. The sailor may be dead—this is left ambiguous—and if he is, Gloria may have killed him.[3]) The marathon is, of course, a *caricature* of America, but in many ways it is a good and accurate caricature, capturing the kind of desperate, frenetic activity which is peculiarly characteristic of this country.

But the film has the power to move and excite us beyond this meaning, because it touches upon a primary experience of every living being: the world's seeming intractability, its deep resistance to our efforts, desires, and struggles. *They Shoot Horses* is in many ways a remarkable film, often brilliant in the writing, acting, and direction; and the entire film has an integrity characterized by the single-minded devotion to a single theme, a single mood, a single point of view. Yet this single-mindedness is also the film's great limitation. Although the filmmakers have

---

[3] This episode closely resembles the episode in *The Wages of Fear* where Mario (Yves Montand) drives the truck over the legs of his friend Jo (Charles Vanel): Mario is afraid the truck will get stuck in the lake of oil and he will not be able to get it out to deliver the nitroglycerin and collect the enormous wage. Jo dies soon after. In both cases, a desperate greed in the main character has momentarily driven out all compassion and morality and caused him to destroy someone he basically likes, someone who only *accidentally* impedes his way.

created a sense of life absent from the novel, they have created only enough life to carry their theme convincingly. There are almost no moments which one feels are in the film for their own sake, for the sake of simple feeling or observation (as there are, say, in Irvin Kershner's *Loving* [1970]). The film is too programmatic and therefore finally (although rather pretentious) unambitious: it is less difficult to achieve a unified vision when the material one is dealing with is without ambiguity or contradiction—and the film's lack of complexity makes much of its defeatism seem facile. One longs for just a moment of the kind of looseness, arbitrariness, and openness to experience which are characteristic of the opposite kind of film, like Truffant's *Stolen Kisses* (1968). But a single moment from *Stolen Kisses* would explode the whole thing.

1970

Postscript 1976: After the above was written, an interview appeared with one of the screenwriters, James Poe, dealing mainly with the evolution of this film (in an excellent book, *The Hollywood Screenwriters* (1972), edited by Richard Corliss; the interviewer was Michael Dempsey). Poe was given co-screenwriting credit in the film itself, but no credit whatever for the published screenplay nor any mention in Pollack's introduction. Poe had tried ever since the 1940s to buy the rights to the novel. He finally succeeded in 1966, wrote a screenplay, got backing, and was preparing to direct the film when the project was suddenly taken out of his hands and given to Pollack, who hired Robert E. Thompson to rewrite the screenplay. Poe's detailed and extensive description of the differences between, on the one hand, his screenplay and conception and, on the other, the final screenplay and the actual film—and his bitter criticisms of the latter—are highly interesting and give a unique and illuminating perspective on the film, including a number of aspects discussed in my article.

Sydney Pollack has now directed nine features, beginning in 1965: *The Slender Thread* (1965), *This Property Is Condemned* (1966), *The Scalphunters* (1968), *Castle Keep* (1969), *They Shoot Horses, Don't They?* (1969), *Jeremiah Johnson* (1972),

The Way We Were (1973), *The Yakuza* (1975), and *Three Days of the Condor* (1976). His career to date bears out the impression one had at the time of *They Shoot Horses*. He is an able, workmanlike director who is anything but an *auteur*. His starting point is always other people's material, and there is no strong unity of themes or concerns in the material he chooses; nor does his work exhibit any strong stylistic unity. His films have varied enormously in quality, and while this largely coincides with the variations in the quality of the screenplays, this is not entirely so: for example, in *The Way We Were* (in my—minority—opinion an extremely bad film), Pollack's lifeless direction blighted a fairly promising script. *They Shoot Horses* almost certainly remains his best film, and by a wide margin.

Pylon (1935)

William Faulkner

From the Folklore of Speed to *Danse Macabre*

BY MICHAEL STERN

As literature and as a film, *Pylon* is an eccentric work. Considered by many critics to be Faulkner's most flawed novel, it became Universal-International's only "art film" of the 1950s. Said Pauline Kael in *Kiss Kiss, Bang Bang* (1968), "It's the kind of bad movie that you know is bad—and yet you're held by it." However, other critics—particularly those with an auteurist bent —count *The Tarnished Angels* among the decade's best films, "among the greatest of all films," according to Robert Smith.[1] William Faulkner is reported to have considered it the best screen adaptation of his work—the only film that he saw more than once.

Set in the 1930s, like the novel, *The Tarnished Angels* is, however, a film that could only have been made in the 1950s. It is a rare example of art and intellect arising from a popular culture that denied the value of both. Rock Hudson in an art film? William Faulkner from the studio that gave us Francis the talking mule and Bonzo the chimp and Ronald Reagan? It is a convoluted journey from the lost generation prose of *Pylon* in 1935 to the *fin de siècle* mannerisms of Hollywood, 1957. To fully understand the complex nature of *The Tarnished Angels* as a film, and the process of its emergence from *Pylon*, we should turn first to Germany in the 1930s; that is, a country still scarred by the war and now verging on complete Nazification.

[1] Robert Smith, "The Tarnished Angels" in *Douglas Sirk—The Complete American Period* (University of Connecticut Film Society), p. 48.

We take this detour to find director Douglas Sirk, who had lived through the remarkable Bavarian Soviet Republic after World War I. Having then established a controversial reputation as a theater director, and associating himself with the Brechtian notion of art as a political weapon and with the dwindling intellectual left wing, Sirk was almost literally run out of German theater by the Nazis. He turned to the UFA film studios which, because of their economic dependence on international markets, were among the last bastions of culture to succumb fully to Nazism. So at UFA, for a few years in the mid-1930s, Douglas Sirk began to develop an aesthetic of melodrama.

Like Brecht (whose plays he had staged), Douglas Sirk had always been intrigued by the concept of America. To a whole school of Art-weary artists, the new world offered an escape from the weight of Culture. "America to us was raw and rough. That was our idea of it—boxing, triviality, banality, killing, and the American melodrama, which *was* the American cinema." [2] The films he made at UFA during the 1930s are filled with American imagery and, indeed, in those films (*Schlussakkord* [1936], *Zu neuen Ufern* [1937], *La Habanera* [1937]) one finds the first expression of a formalized aesthetic of melodrama that was later to appear in Sirk's best-known American films, *Magnificent Obsession* (1954), *Written on the Wind* (1957), and *Imitation of Life* (1959). It is this later, developed aesthetic of postwar, atom-age melodrama that energizes *The Tarnished Angels*.

Sirk first read *Pylon* in 1936. He believed it fit perfectly into his evolving aesthetic of popular melodramas, that is, films with a social consciousness poised on a cutting edge of aesthetic modernism. In this new alignment, developed uniquely by Sirk, each of the *absurd* elements of melodrama—coincidence, fate, accident, self-sacrifice—becomes a vital facet of an absurdist world view. The stylized melodrama becomes an expression of entrapment. Caught between the empty rituals offered by society (see, for instance, *All That Heaven Allows* [1956]) and an apocalyptic vision of the future (see almost any vital film from

[2] Author's interview with Douglas Sirk, *Bright Lights* nos. 6–7. Unless otherwise indicated, all quotes are from this interview.

the 1950s), the heroines and heros of Sirk's films find themselves trapped within the melodramatic plots, offered nothing but a Universal-International vision of happiness as escape from the meaningless rituals that define their lives. Thus, the inherent banality of the genre is turned rigorously into a reflection of a despairing postromantic aesthetic. Sirk said, "Ultimately, of course, there is a pessimistic creed behind these melodramas. Life is the most melodramatic story of all. And God is a pretty bad writer."

Sirk wanted to make *Pylon* as a modern melodrama. "UFA turned it down because it was too American. The after-war quality in Germany was completely different than Faulkner's. In addition there was Hitler. UFA was afraid. "Here in *Pylon* you have men coming home after the war completely at a loss." Sirk's comments call attention to *Pylon*'s uniquely rootless status within Faulkner's *oeuvre*. His energy is diffused within the novel upon drifting souls without a home. The flying Schumanns are detached from the earth, without genealogy, without Faulknerian roots sunk into the soil of Yoknapatawpha County. The novel's unnamed hero is an archetypally rootless man—a newspaper reporter—destined by his very profession to wander on the outside of life. In these characters, in their futile circling of the pylons, and in the aesthetic desperation of the prose itself, Sirk saw a reflection of postwar despair. *Pylon* describes a ritualized, pointless striving, as drained of meaning as the book's reporter, described as "a shadow whose projector had eluded it weeks ago."

A key to this aspect of the book's sensibility is Faulkner's own review of James H. Collins's book, *Test Pilot* (1935):

I had hoped to find a kind of embryo, a still formless forerunner or symptom of a folklore of speed. . . . It would be a folklore not of the age of speed nor of the men who perform it, but of the speed itself . . . producing a literature innocent of either love or hate and of course of pity or terror, and which would be the story of the final disappearance of life from the earth. I would watch them, the little puny mortals, vanishing against a vast and timeless void.[3]

3 William Faulkner, "Folklore of the Air," *The American Mercury*, November, 1935, pp. 371–2.

An art drained of pity and terror, in which the human soul threatens to disappear into a folklore of pure motion—perhaps no better definition could be found for the purely cinematic aesthetic developed in Douglas Sirk's melodramas. He said, "In all my films you have a sense of the vanishing hero. Today tragedy is not possible." In the cycle of dramatic evolution, tragedy is replaced with its predecessor, folklore. For both Sirk and Faulkner, the tangible rootlessness of the airmen was a source of this modernistic folklore. And the totemic pylons around which they raced became a perfect expression of the primal sexuality reemerging out of speed itself. There is a remarkable conjunction of sensibilities on this point, especially when we plot Faulkner's *Test Pilot* review against the archetypal Sirkian melodrama, *Written on the Wind,* which is structured entirely around the hero's utter inseparability from speeding cars, pumping oil wells, and drawn handguns.

The withering away of tragedy into melodrama, or into a folklore of pure motion, is an artistic/literary sensibility that arose in the 1920s and 1930s and found its way into cinema of the 1940s and 1950s. Sirk's and Faulkner's idea of the vanishing hero is most clearly and directly expressed, in fact, in Jack Arnold's *The Incredible Shrinking Man* (1957), one of the 1950s' most unself-consciously evocative films. It is not inappropriate here to recognize the preponderance of human biological mutations in films of the decade. Directly attributable, of course, to fears of the atomic bomb, the distortions also reflect the increasing impossibility of heroism. This was the decade of Jerry Lewis and James Dean and the emerging antihero. The point is that in this cultural context, Faulkner's insight into a new breed of life, with crankcase oil in its veins, takes on a dimension beyond machine-age futurism. The awesome terror Faulkner saw in these machine men is not just for their compulsive taunting of death, but for their absolute alienation from life. It was during the 1950s, as Hollywood classicism began to distend into mannerist excess, that this insight from T. S. Eliot's "The Wasteland" found its way into movies—particularly Douglas Sirk's.

To be sure, almost nobody at Universal studios was eager to make *Pylon* into a movie. Why should they be? Faulkner was decidedly not box-office magic; and *Pylon* was perhaps his least-known and least-successful book. But because in Hollywood success = money = power, Douglas Sirk and George Zuckerman, who had just fashioned the enormously successful *Written on the Wind*, were in a position to get their way. Both saw *Pylon* as a great opportunity. Albert Zugsmith, the independent producer at Universal who had a reputation for off-beat projects (mostly low-budget, culturally disreputable ones) managed to railroad the project through the studio brass, "who thought *Pylon* was a snake." [4]

Of his own interest in the project, George Zuckerman says:

> *Pylon* was my favorite Faulkner novel because it involved a newspaper man—which was my primary ambition at the time (at college in the '30s). . . . I believe the novel put forth a fresh, intriguing and (dirty word) intellectual premise: that among us was a new breed with crankcase oil in its veins . . . the newspaperman's insight, and I never considered dramatizing the novel from any other viewpoint. What he learns about himself is that one who plays God sometimes unwittingly plays death. A Sirk or some open-minded critics might appreciate such things. But Universal's high command in New York, whose eye was always necessarily on the dollar, and whose reach went only as high as "the finger-fuckers in the balcony," decided that I had aspired higher than that. Of course, they were right, and I had to pay for it. . . .
>
> Now the newspaper man here—Faulkner's character in essence—does have an awareness above and beyond the boys in the balcony. All in all the American audience wants a diet of trash and doesn't want the unvarnished truth about the human or the peculiarly American condition. This one in my mind (forgetting Icarus and *deus ex machina*, and leaving such words as *hubris* and *askesis* to my novels) is a true twentieth century drama—the union of the flying machine and man.

The essential difference between Zuckerman the screenwriter and Sirk the director—which describes the *frisson* that energizes *The Tarnished Angels*—is to be found in their visions of Americana. Zuckerman is the teller of folktales, a native American

[4] Letter from George Zuckerman to the author. All quotes from Zuckerman come from this letter.

whose intellect projects Faulkner's world onto the printed page of the screenplay with clarity and dramatic, folkloric logic. His list of credits also includes *Border Incident* (1949), 99 *River Street* (1953), and *The Brass Legend* (1956)—all examples of film as a kind of modern folklore. Sirk's sensibility tends to refract this folklore through an Art-weary, disillusioned classicism. And so the prose that has been clarified, dramatized, and structured by Zuckerman is given dramatic form by Sirk at the same time his European, intellectual vision overlays that form with shadowy visualizations of irony, distance, and "Wasteland" despair. The aesthetic at work here is one of reconstitution—as opposed to translation. The architectural clarity of Zuckerman and the painterly intellect of Sirk make *The Tarnished Angels* into a cinematic rendering of Faulkner's deepest concerns, which are only imperfectly stated in the novel itself. Indeed, this is one case where the film need make no apologies to its source—a fact recognized by Faulkner himself.[5]

In *William Faulkner: A Critical Study* (2nd ed., 1952), Irving Howe criticizes the protagonist of *Pylon* for being "alternately a sentimental, sensitive hero and a caricature." Such ambivalence, he finds, weakens the novel. Indeed, what is the reader to think reading about an "appearance of some creature evolved by forced draft in a laboratory and both beyond and incapable of any need for artificial sustenance . . ."? Faulkner's striving to "spiritualize" his hero's flesh makes him not merely intangible, but simply un-conceivable. He is drunk almost throughout the novel—an excuse for his inability to communicate. And, of course, Faulkner willfully denies him a name. Such evasiveness was not part of Zuckerman's sensibility:

When I first read the book I "cast" Jimmy Stewart as the string-bean, unnamed reporter. At Universal, when I was writing the script, I named the reporter Burke Devlin after Burke Davis, a good friend, a southern newspaperman, and later a novelist and biographer—and as tall and as handsome (and more masculine)

[5] Sirk says, "Faulkner told me himself that he considered it (*The Tarnished Angels*) the best film made from his novels. In fact, he told me that I had improved upon the original." (Entretien avec Douglas Sirk," *Cahiers du Cinema*, no. 189, p. 69)

Burke Devlin (Rock Hudson) protects the boy, Jack Shuman (Chris Olsen), from the taunts of the crowd. *The Tarnished Angels* (1957)

than Rock Hudson. In no way was I consciously writing a vehicle for Hudson. That came later from the front office.

The point is that Zuckerman *saw* the reporter.

But it was not Rock Hudson whom he saw. Yet, strangely, Faulkner liked the casting.[6] And Sirk, too, saw concrete qualities in Hudson that made the character "better integrated than he was in Faulkner's book." [7] Sirk says:

> I wanted to use him as a drab guy with no experience but his shitty job in his drab, shitty office. Then he falls in love with the gypsies of the air. . . . These fliers are trying to leave the prison of society —which was terrible after the war. They think they are escaping into the air. But we are all prisoners, into the final prison, which is the grave, and death. This is something I don't think Rock understood, but for his part, as the outsider, his confusion as an actor helped.

And so the reporter's intangible existence is translated in the film as Rock Hudson's own ambiguous nature as a flesh and blood he-man. By contrasting this very solid (if somewhat artificial) Rock to the fliers and their world, *The Tarnished Angels* turns the novel's aesthetic ambivalence into a dramatic ambiguity.

The implicit irony of Rock Hudson's character—expressed with surprising self-consciousness and artistry in his pompous speech at the end of the film—is only one example of the film's essentially ironic style. In fact, *The Tarnished Angels* is a summary film for that aspect of Douglas Sirk's style most frequently analyzed by critics—his use of mirrors, shadows, reflections, and intermediate representations such as masks and statues. The solidity of Zuckerman's screenplay, and the tangibility of his flesh and blood characters, allows Sirk extreme freedom to undermine and deconstruct the narrative without destroying it. As a result, Faulkner's vision is reconstituted and the film retains a dramaturgical integrity.

[6] Sirk says, "Faulkner adored the performance of Rock Hudson, his talent, his simplicity. He thought that perhaps this was a new Gary Cooper." (*Cahiers du Cinema,* op. cit., p. 70)

[7] John Halliday, *Sirk on Sirk* (Viking, 1972), p. 120.

The shadow existence constructed in Faulkner's prose is created in a visual style, not unlike the riding scene in Alfred Hitchcock's *Marnie* (1964), which depicts and abstracts events. Thus, Rock Hudson is seen as the image of a man, as all of the Universal studio phoniness becomes a mere image of reality. We become aware of an objective reality excluded from the world of the film and a sense of "character" that consistently avoids concrete materialization. The film gives form to that which, in the novel, must remain formless.

The means used are techniques of distancing—that is, wrenching our vision out of the spectacle to contemplate images and dramatic structures. The sexual iconography of the film is a perfect example. Of course, the novel's sexual *pièce de resistance* had to be considerably modified. LaVerne's parachute jump, in a post-coital frenzy, with her skirts blowing high over her head, becomes in *The Tarnished Angels* soft-core titillation, and another example of the film's purposeful aestheticization. Faulkner's spectacle of raw sex is replaced by an abstract image on the cinemascope screen which, because of its horizontal dimensions, isolates the image of LaVerne as a sex object. The optical artifice of the scene brings its nature as a sign with meaning into the foreground. It is like the deathmask, literally bursting into the plot, or the pylons ritualistically appearing. Each is an image that in its purposeful separation from the narrative demands contemplation of its meaning, i.e., its existence. Sirk says that today he wishes *The Tarnished Angels* had been in color because the planes going around the pylons do not stand out enough—not so much optically, but symbolically. He wanted them standing apart from the narrative itself, defining, as do the yellow and red sports cars in *Written on the Wind*, a state of being—the characters' existence.[8]

Sexual obsession is a consistent theme in Faulkner's work. And like Faulkner, Sirk is no stranger to sexually-driven characters, especially those who translate their sense of impotence into a mania for speed and power (see *Magnificent Obsession, Battle*

[8] For a further elucidation of this aesthetic, I recommend a study of the Russian Formalist technique of *priëm ostrannenia*—the device that makes strange. This is a vital figure of Sirk's visualization of melodrama. Here, in *The Tarnished Angels,* the device is used to "theorize" the material and reconstitute Faulkner's metaphysical concerns.

Hymn [1956], *Written on the Wind*). It is the iconography of the film by which this is expressed. There is a dialectic, for instance, between Colonel Fineman (fine man), who is crippled, and the free-standing pylons. Fineman and the pylons form a dynamic foreground-background tension in several frames of the second plane race, providing a direct visualization between his metaphoric impotence and the pylons' eternal metaphoric erection. The uniquely modern contrast between mechanical power and human impotence and diminution is an element of *The Tarnished Angels* that perfectly reflects Faulkner's sense of the special tragedy implicit in *Pylon:*

> We had all better grieve for all people beneath a culture that holds any mechanical [sic] superior to any man simply because the one, being mechanical, is infallible, while the other, being nothing but a man, is not just subject to failure but doomed to it. (The *New York Times,* December 26, 1954)

As an expression of this grief, Faulkner miniaturizes the characters:

> Now the Frenchman came up the runway about twenty feet high and on his back, his head and face beneath the cockpit rim motionless and alert like that of a rat or roach immobile behind a crack in a wainscoat . . . perhaps it was the bilious aspect of an inverted world seen through a hooded lense or emerging in grimacing and attitudinal miniature from stinking trays in a celibate and stygian cell lighted by a red lamp.

The film, on the other hand, compares the fliers in their planes to the airplane carrousel, which, like the rocking horse in *Written on the Wind,* mocks the hero's fantasies of power. Whereas Faulkner shrinks the flier to the size of a roach, the film metaphorically enlarges him so that the plane is like a toy, like the carrousel. Faulkner's characters are animalistic. They reduce themselves, like Roger, to garbage buried under water, to the domain of rats and roaches. The film, on the other hand, gives Roger a hero's wake. In fact, *The Tarnished Angels* was shot as Orson Welles made *Touch of Evil* (1958) next door (also a Zugsmith production), and one might make a useful comparison

between both films' depictions of "pseudotragic" heroes. Both
Roger Schumann and Hank Quinlan are defined by the futility
of their aspirations. Each verges on self-parody, as both films are
characterized by melodramatic irony. But it must be pointed out
that irony is not cynicism. Roger "is reaching for certainty in the
air," Sirk says, "A crazy idea, and a grand one." [9]

As befits the heroes of classic tragedy, the characters of *The
Tarnished Angels* confront their despair with full consciousness.
Willa Cather's *My Ántonia* (1918) serves as a specific reference
point for their failures. "How far I've come since then," LaVerne
laments. The book is a reminder of hope irrevocably lost, of
green fields and blue skies in dialectical contrast to the world of
the film. The introduction to LaVerne reading *My Ántonia* is
cross-cut with scenes of the party next door, thus clearly establishing the contrast. It is later in this scene that we learn of her
infatuation with the liberty bond poster and, in flashback, of
the dice game in which she was "won" by Roger. In short, the
same scene introduces both the ideal world of *My Ántonia*
and the illusory visions and game of chance that have defined
LaVerne's life. The book itself is an object-symbol characteristic
of melodrama—a concrete, tangible visualization of an entire
state of being. Its clarity as a symbol (and, once removed, the
clarity of Cather's prose) is a reminder of just how ideal (i.e.,
unattainable) Cather's world is in the context of Faulkner's. It
is a description of hopes fulfilled, locked within a dark leather
cover. Whereas Faulkner expresses LaVerne's state at the end
of the book in a scurrying flight, disappearing into the world of
flying without hope and without explanation, the film grants her
the heroic stature of trying to go back, however much we and
she suspect that "going back," like everything else in her life, is
only an illusion. Contrast Willa Cather:

> The feelings that night were so near that I could reach out and
> touch them with my hand. I had the sense of coming home to
> myself. . . .

to Douglas Sirk:

[9] *Sirk on Sirk*, op. cit., p. 120.

. . . Everything, even life, is inevitably taken away from you. You cannot grasp, cannot even touch feeling, but only reach its reflections.[10]

It is Sirk's pessimistic outlook that is expressed in the film, thereby reconstituting Faulkner's own sense of the futility that defines the striving of this new breed of human. Thus, poetic prose (the unnamed reporter) becomes cultural mythology (Rock Hudson), and lost-generation despair solidifies into absurdist melodrama. Universal Studios is the reflection of which Sirk speaks—a fake, meaningless world in which life—even the most heroic aspirations—is inevitably formed into mere melodrama. Human feeling is resolved into pure motion, and Faulkner's aim—a folklore of pure motion—is realized. As much as the barnstormers to which Faulkner turned in the 1930s, Hollywood of the 1950s provides, for Sirk, a perfect metaphor for ritualized movement drained of meaning.

The Tarnished Angels is therefore a supremely modern film, poised as it is on the edge of tragedy, using melodrama and its Hollywood conventions to express a dark vision of humankind in the new world. The feeble, shrunken characters conceived by Faulkner in 1935 as children of the machine become in 1957 victims of the postwar vacuum and of the futility represented by the threat of The Bomb. The pointless, drunken flight around the pylons in the book turns into the film's symbol for aspiration, sexual striving, a desperate search for certainty.

German director R. W. Fassbinder (who has modeled some of his films on Sirk's) has characterized *The Tarnished Angels* as an accumulation of defeats. It is melodrama that makes it so. Roger promises to give up flying after one last race and *of course* that is when he is killed. Burke Devlin sees one chance to escape his drab life and *of course* he realizes only that he is stuck there forever. That melodramatic "of course" is a generic reconstitution of Faulkner's vertiginously despairing prose. It is a specific visual-dramatic rendering of the novel's sense of inevitable, chaotic loss.

The central aspiration of the novel—the reporter's desire to

[10] *Cahiers du Cinema,* op. cit., p. 70.

penetrate into the world of the airmen—crystallizes in the film into the individual, separate aspirations of each character. Categorically, each is defeated. Ultimately, that is the meaning of both the novel and film. *Pylon* is about penetration, and perception as penetration. As the reporter moves to the center, it dissolves. He can never get there. The pylon remains as a mocking symbol of his impotence. The characters of the film are irrevocably lost in their own illusions and in the film's world of shadows. By reestablishing a possible escape for them to "real happiness," the film gives dramatic form to the novel's purposeful chaos. Jean-Luc Godard admired Douglas Sirk as a director of "tears and speed." The conjunction of Sirk's melodramatic kinesis and George Zuckerman's literate structure not only materializes the essence of Faulkner's novel, but frames it as well within the modernist aesthetic of melodrama as the last form of tragedy. What Faulkner aspired to, even while reviling it—a folklore of speed—has become a *danse macabre* of cinematic gesture.

The Treasure of the Sierra Madre (1935)

B. Traven

Gold Hat, Gold Fever, Silver Screen

BY STUART M. KAMINSKY

B. Traven's 1935 novel, *The Treasure of the Sierra Madre*, presented a great challenge for John Huston, who both wrote the screenplay and directed the film adaptation in 1948. Like Traven's other work, including *The Death Ship* (1934) and *The Bridge in the Jungle* (1938), *Treasure* is a fantastic, hyperbolic, nightmarish saga, far from a naturalistic novel. And Traven's language is strange, to say the least, grammatical and ungrammatical, formal and colloquial, seemingly at will. On first reading, the dialogue might appear to be "undeliverable."

For example, here is the gold-hatted bandit's angry outburst when Curtin, one of the trio of prospectors, challenges him to prove he is a federal officer:

> Badges, to god-damn the hell with badges! We have no badges. In fact, we don't need badges. I don't have to show you any stinking badges, you goddamned cabrón and ching' tu madre! Come out there from that hole of yours. I have to speak to you.

Or earlier, when the old man, Howard, ridicules his two partners, Dobbs and Curtin, for not recognizing the gold they are standing on:

> Well, tell my old gra'mother. I have burdened myself with a couple of fine lodgers, two very elegant bedfellers who kick at the first drop

of rain and crawl under mother's petticoat when thunder rumbles. My, my, what great prospectors a driller and a tool-dresser can make! Drilling a hole with a half a hundred Mexican peons around to lend you hands and feet! I still can do that after a two days' spree you bet. Two guys! Two guys reading in the magazines about crossing a lazy river up in Alaska and now going prospecting on their own.

In both speeches, the changeable style is that of the tall tale rather than the "realistic" novel. Note the arbitrariness of Traven's choices. Gold Hat's switch to the formalities of "We have no badges" and "I have to speak with you," contrasts with the crudities of the rest of his outburst. In Howard's monologue, there is neither rationale for his contraction in the word "gra'mother" and his lack of contraction elsewhere nor reason for the combination of standard English and dialect in "elegant bed-fellers," a formulation not repeated. And so forth.

But it is this weird dialogue which probably attracted John Huston to the novel in the first place. A teller of tall tales himself, an accomplished writer and lover of the bizarre, Huston took on the same challenge in his later adaptation of *The Man Who Would Be King* (1975). He retained the very dialogue from Kipling's story which was the most difficult and idiosyncratic, e.g., the encounter in Kipling's office when Dravot and Peachy discuss their trip and pact. As for *Treasure*, Huston explained the appeal in 1947:

> Traven's unique, a combination of Conrad and Dreiser, if you can imagine such a thing. His people speak no known language—or an English, at any rate, like none I've ever heard. I don't believe he's German, as rumored, for his style hasn't that Germanic exactness; more like the north countries, possibly Sweden. But he's a powerful writer; when you read him you really take a beating.[1]

Huston asked to meet with Traven while shooting *Treasure* in Mexico, but the reluctant author, who obsessively guarded his identity, promised nothing. However, waiting at the

[1] Philip K. Scheuer, "Huston Aided on Location by Army Life," *Los Angeles Times*, June 29, 1947, p. 1.

Reforma Hotel in Mexico City one morning was a thin little man with gray hair. He handed Huston a card introducing himself as H. Croves, translator from Acapulco. He carried a note from Traven indicating that Croves was the novelist's representative. Convinced that Croves was actually the shy author himself, Huston hired him as technical advisor. Croves was present for all the Mexican shooting and, indeed, he made many suggestions which Huston accepted. As "Hal Croves" told Judy Stone in an unprecedented 1966 interview:

> I, Croves, came and visited John Huston and he asked me questions about certain details. I said, "Here, present it this way." He agreed. He was even applauding. "Great ideas, Mr. Croves!" "The ideas I gave you are according to the sense of Traven because we talked it over months ago. . . . I know exactly what is on his mind." I worked so well with John Huston that he even put me on the payroll of Warner Brothers.[2]

Interestingly, Croves's major quarrel with Huston was over the casting of Walter Huston as Howard, in what became an Academy Award-winning performance. He told Judy Stone:

> I said, "John, he is your father, but not the type." Traven wrote about a man so old he can't even stand on his feet any more but he still has the dream of gold, gold, gold and the gold goes away. Lewis Stone would have been the right type in my idea and I'm sure Traven's. I admit that Walter Huston was great. He deserved the Oscar he received. Lewis Stone would not have been so good. Only he was more like the character Traven had in mind.

Setting: Both novel and film open in the town of Tampico, but Traven devotes a number of pages to the Hotel Oso Negro and its inhabitants, "the scum of five continents," who somehow function and protect themselves in a kind of *lumpen* utopia:

> . . . the girls were safer here than in any hotel which makes a fuss about its moral standing. The women were never molested by men

[2] Judy Stone, *The Mystery of B. Traven,* Los Altos, California: William Kaufmann, 1977.

coming in drunk. By the unwritten law of the hotel and of the men who lived here any man who tried to harm one of the girls would have been dead at sunrise.

. . . It rarely happened that anything was stolen. . . . A thief in this hotel was never afraid of the police or jail. He was only afraid—terribly afraid—of the beating he would receive if he were found out. . . . [A] score of guests . . . would take the thief into one of the shacks and there preach him a sermon which would make such an excellent impression on his mind and body that for the next seven days he could not move a finger or an eyelid without moaning. These sermons had proved so effective that the hotel could guarantee that no theft would recur inside of two months to come.

Huston's film includes two relatively brief sequences in the hotel, but he describes none of the other inhabitants except Howard. Clearly Huston's concerns are not with the social organization of the hotel but only with the protagonists who have bedded down there. (Although Traven's "Bolshevik" sympathies are felt in the novel—as in the passage above—the author of *Treasure* refrains from presenting doctrinaire political positions. True, Traven is antigold and vehemently anticlerical, but what he *does* believe in is never articulated except by inference. Nor is political ideology expressed directly in the movie, despite the levels of allegory about "greed." So perhaps Huston is "faithful" to the book?)

Plot Changes: There is a sequence early in the novel in which Dobbs and a man named Moulton journey into the jungle to find jobs at an oil camp. They are joined by a cowardly Indian. At one point, the trio spend a mad night in a tree, convinced that "a great cat. A tiger, A huge tiger, a tigre real, one of the biggest in the jungle . . ." is after them. The morning proves that the tiger was a burro, "an ordinary ass tied to a tree by a long lasso," and Dobbs angrily claims that he knew it all the time. This comic quest is a prelude to the longer, absurd quest later in the novel. Dobbs, Moulton, and the Indian do not find work and are forced to return to Tampico. John Huston skips past this segment. He combines Moulton with Traven's character Curtin (Tim Holt), introduced later, and gets quickly to the primary relationship with the other partners, Dobbs (Humphrey Bogart) and Howard (Walter Huston).

After Curtin and Dobbs have been cheated of their wages by Pat McCormick in the novel, they corner Pat in a bar and make him pay without resorting to battle. In the film, a brutal fight takes place with Pat (Barton MacLane) nearly beating up the two partially drunk partners. The tables are turned midway, however, and Pat, bleeding and unable to see, pays the men while prone on the floor. Huston's interest in the fisticuffs supercedes Traven's desire for showing Pat as an exploiting capitalist. Huston admires Pat's courage in fighting two adversaries, and he also uses the fight to bring Dobbs and Curtin closer together.

Narrative Technique: Traven often interrupts the narrative for extended parables—always obliquely connected to the main plot. There are three especially lengthy tales, two told by Howard, and one by Lacaud—called Cody in the film and played by Bruce Bennett—the stranger who tries to become a partner with the trio in the mountains.

Howard's first story is about a prospector friend of his, forced to return to a once-prosperous mine and help greedy neighbors get more gold. The second expedition proves a disaster. The point of the story for Howard is that he will know when he has enough gold. Curtin scoffs at the tale: "I don't see any curse on gold." Dobbs deceives himself: "I sure would be satisfied with a certain sum, take it and go away to settle in a pretty little town and let the others quarrel." Director John Huston leaves the story out of the film.

In Howard's second parable, a doctor cures the blind son of an Indian chief and is rewarded with a silver mine. When he is murdered by Indian miners he had hired at slave wages, his wife takes over. She "disappears" after accepting the hospitality of the regional viceroy, who steals the silver. This tale anticipates Howard's behavior later in *Treasure* when he helps cure an Indian leader's son. Howard leaves the Indian village behind to search for Dobbs. He departs without riches, only "the very best horse his host had. . . ." In Huston's movie, Howard acts as honorably as he does in Traven's book, but he needs no parable to motivate his charity.

The third story in the novel takes up all of chapter 12 and is offered by Lacaud, although told in the third person, authorial voice. (This is the most uncanny digression in the novel, for this tale is spun for many pages while the bandits are climbing the mountain to attack the prospectors. As usual for B. Traven, not even impending death takes precedence over a good yarn.) Lacaud offers a vivid episode, about how the bandits robbed a train, murdering countless women and children. For the film, John Huston uses the thread of Lacaud's story but places the train robbery in the present tense instead of flashback and makes it less violent (only four passengers are murdered and these events occur off screen). He also situates the sequence earlier in the film and offers his principal characters, whom Traven had only hear the story, as participants in the events. Dobbs, Curtin, and Howard are passengers on that train helping to fight off bandits; and they get their first glimpse of Gold Hat (Alfonso Bedoya), who will later kill Dobbs. (As in his adaptation of Dashiell Hammett's *The Maltese Falcon* [1941], where Huston excised Sam Spade's important existential digression concerning "Flitcraft," Huston here shuns important material because it is difficult to incorporate visually into the film without recourse to flashbacks or a complex chronology.)

Characters and Characterization: In Huston's film, Gold Hat becomes an archetypal, fairy-tale villain, encountered three magical times—on the train, at the campsite, and when he murders Dobbs. (Gold Hat is *not* one of the trio who kills Dobbs in the novel.) In a brilliant example of transposition, Huston took the "I don't have to show you any stinkin' badges" line, uttered as part of a long exchange between the bandits and prospectors at the campsite, and shifted it to much later, the frightening moment before Dobbs dies. It is the last thing that Gold Hat says (and defiantly) before setting his men on Dobbs.

As for Lacaud: he introduces himself, quite inscrutably, in the novel as "Lacaud. Robert W. Lacaud, Phoenix, Arizona; Tech, Pasadena," and that is all that is ever learned about his past. He is half mad, ultimately harmless, and he is finally left behind to work the mine after the others move onward. In Huston's film, Cody/Lacaud is not crazy. He is a genuine menace to the original two by threatening to reveal the gold unless he is accepted as a member of the partnership—and the men vote to shoot him. Their decision is never carried out because Cody is murdered by the bandits at the campsite. (At this point, Huston attaches a scene which offers more details about Cody. Howard and Curtin search the dead man's belongings. They read his personal letter aloud and discover from his wallet that Cody had a fruit orchard in Texas and left behind a wife and child. This sentimental sequence has been criticized as a lapse in tone for Huston's tough movie.)

Both Traven and Huston love Howard. It is no accident that John Huston picked his father to play the delightful role. And it is interesting to notice how Traven's own eccentric writing style in the narrative passages (and in his philosophical sections) sounds so similar to the dialogue he put in Howard's mouth. It seems fair to conclude that Howard is Traven's surrogate—just as papa Walter becomes the surrogate for son John.

Traven and Huston also have an affection for Dobbs. Though he is frequently recalled as a moral brute and a madman, Dobbs is a highly contradictory character in both works, until his crack-up. He is initially generous with his cash, willing to share it and put up extra money to finance the trip. Later, Dobbs is the one who helps Howard repair the "wounded" mountain. And though Dobbs succumbs to the disease of gold, he is not viewed as evil by Traven or Huston or, for that matter, by Howard, who says—in his last comment on Dobbs in the novel— "Dobbs has lost his head so completely that he can't use it any longer." (In the movie, Dobbs's mental deterioration is shown by his regression to animalism: his clothes fall apart, his beard grows, and his body moves closer to the ground. Several times Bogart straightens himself to reveal his shell of humanness, only to crouch forward movements later. Twice in the film, Dobbs reacts irrationally—and thus, ironically—to charges that he is less than human. When Dobbs believes Curtin has called him a "hog" about money, he throws away the gold Curtin offers him to prove he is a civilized human. Later when Curtin implies that Dobbs is "uncivilized," Dobbs hits him.)

The friendship of the men is explored seriously by Huston.

The film offers a constant reorganization of the three partners in a single frame. (Often one partner appears in the foreground with the activity of the others behind him.) The word "partner" is repeated frequently by each, a condition not so evident in the novel. But sometimes the three-way relationship is seen skeptically. For example, when the three decide to become mining partners at the hotel, Dobbs and Curtin shake hands. Huston shows only their clasped hands in the frame, with Howard's head placed between them, glancing uncertainly from one to the other. (How do we know whether to believe these often self-deceived protagonists? When one of Huston's characters lies down, he generally speaks more honestly than when he is standing—an allusion to couch, dream, confession.)

Denouement: In the novel Curtin says nothing about returning to the United States. It is quite probable that he will accept Howard's offer and join him as an assistant medicine man. (He will remain an emigré in Mexico just as B. Traven had done.) The book ends with Howard getting on his horse. "No sooner was he seated in the saddle than the Indians shouted, whipped their ponies into action, and hurried back home." The last word is "home" and the implication is of resolution and potential peace.

Huston's film ends more ironically. The partnership is dissolved, and Curtin will sell the burros and head for Texas and an uncertain future, although with a visit planned to Cody's ranch and widow. Curtin has gained wisdom and experience and Howard an Indian kingdom. But Huston summarizes the quest for wealth in the last shot of the film: an empty gold bag blowing on the thorns of a desert cactus.

Cinematic Adaptation—A Footnote: Interestingly enough, B. Traven's novel contains a number of specific references to movies, but all such references are deleted in Huston's film version. For example, in the novel Dobbs and Howard discuss taking their money and starting a movie house in Tampico with Howard as business manager and Dobbs as artistic manager. At the end, Curtin and Howard discuss and reject this idea. Perhaps a grocery store would be cheaper.

In the siege by the bandits, one of the miners wishes that he

Howard (Walter Huston), Fred C. Dobbs (Humphrey Bogart), and Curtin (Tim Holt), sifting for gold. *The Treasure of the Sierra Madre* (1948)

were in a movie so he could be rescued. This, indeed, happens. When the bandits suddenly vanish, Howard thinks they have really left, explaining, "They would have to be awfully good movie actors to play a trick like that so perfectly." Finally, there is Dobbs's dread moment of epiphany as the three tramps are about to jump him:

> It flashed through his mind that he had seen many a movie in which the hero was trapped in a situation like this. But he realized at the same time that he could not remember one single picture in which the producer had not done his utmost to help the trapped hero out again to save the girl from the clutches of a bunch of villains. Before he could think of any of the tricks he had seen in the pictures by which the hero finally escaped, he felt, with a strange bitterness in his mouth, that his situation was real. And whatever is real is different. No smart film-producer was on hand to open the trap with a good trick.

Of Mice and Men (1937)
John Steinbeck

Thoughts on a Great Adaptation

BY WILLIAM K. EVERSON

Oddly, short fiction has seldom worked well when transferred to the short film. Damon Runyan and Edgar Allan Poe in particular have fared rather badly when treated in one- and two-reel form, though one might make a case for the several versions of Ambrose Bierce's "The Occurrence at Owl Creek Bridge" as notable exceptions.

But short fiction as the basis for a *feature* picture has often proved extremely felicitous. By its very nature, the short piece often skips details and compresses time; the feature is able to sketch in such material and open up time, deftly and quickly. Richard Connell's superb short melodrama, "The Most Dangerous Game" was justifiably expanded, and emerged as a very taut sixty-eight-minute RKO picture (1932), while Ernest Haycox's "Stage to Lordsburg," little more than a sketch and lacking in real narrative, was enlarged to form John Ford's classic *Stagecoach* (1939). These are only two examples.

In many ways, the 1939 version of *Of Mice and Men,* directed by Lewis Milestone for producer Hal Roach, and scripted by Eugene Solow, represents the "model" transference: totally faithful to text and spirit of John Steinbeck's novella, yet expansive in wholly cinematic terms. *Of Mice and Men* offers a good case for suggesting that occasionally a movie *can* improve on and enhance the values of the original fiction, turning an established work of art into, yes, a *greater* work of art in its new medium. Yet it should be emphasized that the core of its greatness still lies in the original writing, without which the technical expertise and directorial skill would come to nothing.

Lewis Milestone, incidentally, seems an almost inspired choice as the film's director. He was never a *great* director, though he made some outstanding, highly stylized films—*All Quiet on the Western Front* (1930) and *The Front Page* (1931) being especially notable—and he was essentially a *heavy* director. *Of Mice and Men* needed the unrelenting heaviness that he brought to it; a subtler, more emotional director such as Frank Borzage, who made *A Farewell to Arms* from Hemingway (1932) might have lingered too much over the beauty and poignancy in lesser incidents, and thrown the film off balance. Moreover, Milestone's concern for visible cinematic technique—and especially for his unofficial trademark, the sweeping, lateral tracking shot—helps to keep the potentially static nature of the story fluid and moving, through *Of Mice and Men*'s hundred minutes of footage.

Aaron Copland's simple, evocative, unobtrusive, and entirely original music for the film is clearly an additional asset. Not least, the movie was presented in rich sepiatone in its original release form, adding a warmth and lyrical quality to its already strong visuals, as with the brief, beautiful long shots of the grain wagons heading home at the end of day.

Steinbeck's *Of Mice and Men* deals, of course, with the compassionate and ultimately tragic relationship between two migratory farm workers, George and Lennie, and their reasonable but inevitably impossible dream of settling down in a little place of their own. It was the first Steinbeck work to be transferred to the screen, and its debut was prompted at least partially by the opportunity to cash in on all the publicity (and notoriety) surrounding Steinbeck's *The Grapes of Wrath,* which was about to be filmed by John Ford for Twentieth Century-Fox.

Of Mice and Men came to the screen (aesthetically, if not commercially) at exactly the right time. By 1939, the industry was trying hard to escape from the Never-Never-Land of bland, escapist, family-oriented entertainment in which it had been trapped since the enforcement of the Production Code in 1934.

Moreover, the war in Europe was imminent; America would certainly be affected, and audiences could be expected to demand movie fare with more substantial contact with reality. The scenario does contain one or two mild Code-dictated compromises, but they are neatly camouflaged. In total, *Of Mice and Men* emerges as a perfect example of the tasteful and mature film that could be made in pre-World War II Hollywood—by taking discreet advantage of the slight relaxation of the Production Code. (I hate to think how it might fare on today's "liberated" screen. In fact, there was a concrete example in a television version of *Of Mice and Men* made just a few years ago, in which George and Lennie were turned into homosexuals. Not that there is anything amiss or tasteless in that, but it just is *not* what Steinbeck was writing about. More recently, and more filmically, *Midnight Cowboy* [1969] could well be considered a contemporary parallel to *Of Mice and Men;* undeniably powerful, it is also an ugly film, totally lacking the beauty and touching qualities of Steinbeck's story or Milestone's handling of it.)

The transference to film gets under way even before the main titles, with the first (to my knowledge) and still best usage of a pre-credit sequence. By starting *Of Mice and Men* with George and Lennie fleeing from the lynch mob in Weed (incidents referred to in casual dialogue, well into Steinbeck's narrative), Milestone adroitly sketches in their relationship, their characters, their problems, in a minute or so of footage. When the characters reappear, after the credits, we know them so well that the film can jump right into a key dialogue sequence. The scene on a bus is an added locale, but the verbal exchanges and the information it conveys (including the driver's speech, which reinforces and links up with the pre-credit action) are authentic Steinbeck, from later in the novella. Moving this conversation forward, Milestone brings mobility and pace to the narrative, without altering its main structure.

Camera work and editing play an enormously important role in keeping the film fluid. That does not mean that the narrative is made to move faster (in some cases, the very opposite is achieved), but it is made to move *cinematically*. It only takes a line or two for Steinbeck to describe Curley beating up the stable hand who he thought was paying too much attention to his wife. In the film, Milestone stages the scene in extreme long shot, from the back of the barn. Curley (Bob Steele) and the stable hand (Noah Beery, Jr.) confront each other by walking to the center of the frame from opposing ends; the action is concentrated into a central panel of the screen, almost like a cut-down cinemascope image. As they walk, the camera moves in from rear center screen, matching their pace and turning to a powerful medium shot as they meet.

The scene in which Candy (Roman Bohnen) is pathetically talked into letting his old dog be killed and then must wait interminably to hear the tell-tale fatal shot, *has* to be a long scene. (And the impact is recalled when the parallel scene of Lennie's death arrives at the end of the film.) In a dramatic version of *Of Mice and Men*, the stage composition must be such that, despite other activity and dialogue within the scene, the audience is constantly focused on Candy's torment. In the film, however, Milestone is able to cut away to the other characters—their attitude reflected in dialogue is all the reminder of Candy's presence that we need—and when, finally, we hear the crack of the pistol, the accompanying music acts to create a catharsis, and a sudden cut to Candy stiffening on the bunk, turning over in despair to face the wall, makes a far more effective fadeout than an end-of-act curtain.

Although it is unobtrusive, the film's art direction by Nicolai Remisoff is a major achievement. Some of the film was shot on location at a ranch. But the bunk-house interiors were especially built for the film, and the important locale of the clearing in the woods, with its little stream (where George and Lennie spend their last night before going to work on the ranch, and to which they return for the tragic finale) is so real and so unstylized that at first we assume that it is the real thing. It is only later, after lengthy scenes have been played out there, that we realize that such total control of lighting (among other elements) would be quite impossible except on a studio stage. These sequences are magnificently and consistently integrated with the few genuine location scenes. (If this seems a minor matter, we have only to look at *The Grapes of Wrath* [1940] or *The Ox-Bow Incident*

Lennie (Lon Chaney, Jr.) wants a piece of pie from his friend George
(Burgess Meredith). *Of Mice and Men* (1940)

[1943] to realize how jarring and obvious the shifting back and forth from real exteriors to stylized studio sets can be.)

Of Mice and Men is equally inspired in its casting. None of the major leads (Burgess Meredith, Lon Chaney, Jr., Betty Field) were particularly well known and certainly not possessed of "star" images, so that one could instantly accept them as their characters. On the other hand, certain supporting roles were played by well-established character actors who were suitably typecast. Audiences confronting Charles Bickford, Granville Bates, or Oscar O'Shea in a sense "knew" and felt comfortable with these men already, without time being wasted in establishing "bits of business." Thus when Carlson (Granville Bates) first meets Lennie Small and cracks that he "isn't very small," we *know* both that Carlson is a dull, unimaginative person, and that George and Lennie can expect that kind of remark from similar men on every ranch—something that Steinbeck had to tell us in words.

Deliberate *against*-the-type casting works equally well. In placing Bob Steele, up to that point strictly a traditional and likeable cowboy star hero, as the unpleasant and sadistic Curley, Milestone made audiences resent him all the more because subliminally they remembered him as a "nice guy" and perhaps felt betrayed. The director obviously knew what he was doing by this about-face; Steele's fancy mounts and tricks of horsemanship, in his regular Westerns a sign of grace and agility, are here utilized as an illustration of arrogance and petty showing off.

There are mild transformations of Steinbeck's material within the film, but no actual changes or major additions. A fantasy sequence *was* shot showing Lennie with his aunt, and surrounded by outsize rabbits, but wisely it was dropped. (Would that the reading of the letter in *The Ox-Bow Incident, un*read in the novel, had been similarly excised.) The Production Code forbade the use of such phrases as "son of a bitch" and "what the hell" at that time, and the realistically casual application of those phrases in Steinbeck's original (and they were the strongest phrases that he felt the need to use) are of course deleted (and, happily, not replaced with milder and more unlikely phraseology). The film still presents Steinbeck's best lines, dramatic yet naturalistic, much superior to the pseudo-poetry bestowed upon the author's simple farmers in *The Grapes of Wrath* (1940).

The only mildly jarring note—and even it is well controlled—is the handling of the denouement, after George has no option but to shoot Lennie to save him from the horrors of a lynch mob. It clearly did not matter to Steinbeck whether George's "crime" was either known or punished; the mere fact of having to kill his friend and shatter his own dream of happiness was more than enough punishment. But the Code demanded legal as well as moral retribution, and thus George had to stop the sheriff, hand him the gun, and, without explanatory dialogue, leave with this representative of the law. At that, the film shows courage in bending the Code toward such an ambiguous finale: to George, the outcome is still immaterial and his own torment no less; to the audience, the severity of his punishment—or perhaps total lack of it—is not spelled out, and it is deemed sufficient that due process of law will take place.

In any case, a compromise such as this is certainly acceptable in view of the film's refusal to give ground where it really matters. There must have been much heavy thinking given to the commercial advisability of the stark and no-punches-pulled attack on racial intolerance, as spelled out in the subplot sequences involving Crooks (Leigh Whipper), the Negro handyman. But it remains as Steinbeck wrote it, well before Hollywood became involved with such matters. (In the early days of television, these scenes were often the first to be cut to shorten the picture for air time!)

Earlier we spoke of the film being an advance on the novel. But even this supposition cannot be accepted completely; a mere reading of the story and a screening of the film should at least confirm their equality. Both novel and movie, in their climactic passages, evoke an overwhelming sense of grief, compassion, even personal sorrow. How many books and their film adaptations can stand side by side as producing the *same* emotions at the *same* junctures, even if not quite in the same way? *Of Mice and Men* can—and is thus nearly unique in the whole history of literature-into-film.

To Have and Have Not Adapted a Novel

BY WILLIAM ROTHMAN

> Ernest Hemingway and I were very good friends. . . . I said to him, "I can make a picture out of your worst story." He said, "What's my worst story?" I said, "Why that goddamned piece of junk called *To Have and Have Not*. . . ."
>
> —Howard Hawks in *Crawdaddy*

The film as unrelated to the novel: In his *Film Comment* essay (May-June, 1973), "To Have (Written) and Have Not (Directed)," Robin Wood asserts that Howard Hawks cheated in his demonstration that he could make a film of Hemingway's worst story, *To Have and Have Not* (hereafter *THAHN*): "His movie is in no real sense a version of the novel. Only the first ten minutes—the scenes involving Mr. Johnson, the would-be big-game fisherman—have anything much to do with the original." Although this assertion is ultimately an unacceptable oversimplification, it is important to recognize its tenuous plausibility.

1. The Bogart/Bacall relationship at the heart of the film departs drastically from Harry Morgan's relationship with Marie as Hemingway presents it. Physically, Hemingway's hefty, middle-aged ex-prostitute is poles apart from the young world traveler Bogart insists on calling "Slim" (as she insists on calling him, with no explanation, "Steve," although his name is Harry). In the

70

novel, Harry and Marie are married and have children, and the protection of their shared home is essential to Harry's motivation. The film's basically lighthearted courtship (which provocatively mirrors the real courtship of Humphrey Bogart and Lauren Bacall, who fell in love during production) is not really taken from the novel at all. Hawks has suggested that the film tells the story of how the novel's Harry and Marie originally met and fell in love. But this seems, at first glance, a somewhat facetious explanation.

2. The theme of commitment to anti-Fascism—intricately interwoven with the Bogart/Bacall courtship—is, as Robin Wood points out, more influenced by the film's Warner Brothers genre predecessor *Casablanca* (1942) than by the Hemingway novel. M. and Mme. de Bursac, the French patriots whom Bogart ferries to Martinique (and the great Resistance leader they hope to free from Devil's Island) seem primarily derived from *Casablanca*. (Both scripts assume, interestingly enough, that effective resistance to Fascism is dependent on strong, idealistic leaders who can give the necessary direction and inspiration to the otherwise powerless masses.) Nothing in the novel corresponds to the figure of Crickett (Hoagy Carmichael), whose role is clearly derivative of *Casablanca*'s beloved Sam.

(To suggest the obvious: an analysis of any film as an adaptation is, by itself, far from a complete analysis. Warners' 1944 *THAHN* is a product of a particular studio at a certain moment in the evolution of screen genres and at a particular moment in American history. Then, too, the hand of Jules Furthman, one of the credited scriptwriters, is clearly manifest in the film, and the connections between *THAHN* and certain other Furthman-scripted films—*Morocco* [1930] and *Shanghai Express* [1932], as well as Hawks's *Only Angels Have Wings* [1939]—can be analyzed. By contrast, William Faulkner's contribution to this and other Hawks scripts seems relatively impersonal.)

3. Perhaps the most fundamental difference between novel and film, however, is one of emotional intensity and tone. *THAHN* is, after all, the Hemingway novel that led F. Scott Fitzgerald to invoke Dostoevsky in describing the undeflected intensity of the writing. Gerry Brenner argues that it is

Hemingway's single essay in classical tragedy.[1] Hawks's film is anything but tragic. Infused with the purest form of the Bogart/ Bacall screen magnetism, it is one of Hawks's most enjoyable, pleasurable, easygoing films. There could be no greater emotional contrast than that between (a) Bacall's joyous departing hip-wiggle, Walter Brennan's shuffle, and the closing shot of the musicians, and (b) Hemingway's ending on the widowed Marie's chorus of lamentation.

The film as related to the novel: On the other hand, there are many connections at various levels between the novel and the film. Some of these points of connection reveal that, on certain important issues, novel and film occupy significantly different positions.

1. Neutral traces of the process of adaptation. We discover innumerable details derived by the film from its literary source. In many cases, these details seem to have no particular significance beyond serving as artifacts of the process of adaptation. In both versions, Harry's boat is the "Queen Conch" out of Key West. De Bursac is shot in the right arm in the film, just as Harry is wounded in the right arm in the novel. Bits of dialogue from the novel repeatedly pop up in the course of the film (e.g., in the descriptions of Eddie as a "rummy"). M. Renard, the Gestapo chief, is referred to as "Beelips," the name of an important minor character in the novel.

2. Action lifted bodily from novel to film. As Robin Wood implies, the whole opening reel of the film—the scenes involving the rich American businessman Mr. Johnson, who pays Bogart to take him out on his boat so that he can realize his fantasy of himself as a big-game fisherman—is remarkably faithful to the book. In the spirit of his earlier film *Tiger Shark* (1932), Hawks perfectly renders Hemingway's semidocumentary account of the process of deep-sea fishing. The sequence of events and the action correspond, often point for point, to scenes in the novel. And the characterization of the insensitive, mean-spirited, self-centered, crude American businessman is retained intact. (While

[1] *"To Have and Have Not* as Classical Tragedy," in Richard Astro and Jackson Benson, eds., *Hemingway in Our Time* (Oregon State University Press, 1974), pp. 67–87.

this first reel seems lifted bodily from the novel, the scene invites a special, secondary level of reading. It is tempting to read Bogart's contempt for Mr. Johnson as a reflection of Hawks's own feelings for some of the studio bosses for whom he worked, and the extreme bitterness of the film's depiction of Johnson as an expression of Hawks's alienation from certain aspects of the Hollywood system.)

3. The character of Harry Morgan. Hemingway's Harry Morgan and the Bogart character in the film share an essential characteristic: a potential for shocking acts of violence. The moment when Bogart's pent-up tension is released in the gesture of shooting his gun through the desk drawer, killing one of Renard's men, recalls the episode in the novel when Morgan opens fire on the group of revolutionaries he is illegally carrying on board his boat. Bogart's tactic of pistol-whipping Renard and his lieutenant until either weakens and assures him free passage from Marseilles (Bogart points out that one of them will have to suffer a beating for nothing) recalls the strong streak of sadism in Hemingway's Harry Morgan that has caused consternation in the critical literature. The moment at which Bogart slaps his "rummy" friend Eddie (Walter Brennan) is likewise shocking in its violence. (The novel's Morgan seriously contemplates killing Eddie because if Eddie talks, Harry will lose his payday.)

Although the images of violence in novel and film are in a sense equivalent, their significance is different. The images of Bogart's violence confirm his commitment to love and justice, the commitment he comes to acknowledge in the course of the film. Thus he unleashes violence on Nazi bullies, or affects violence so as to protect those he loves (he slaps Eddie hard so as to stop him from endangering himself by staying on board during the perilous mission). But the violence in the novel—which all but dominates the novel emotionally—is much more problematic, particularly in its bearing on the character of Harry Morgan. The critical literature is divided on its implications. Carlos Baker, in *Hemingway: The Writer as Artist* (4th ed., 1972), maintains that Morgan is Hemingway's first true hero, and that his violent acts are morally justified by the necessity to protect his family. Gerry Brenner sees Morgan as a heroic figure tragically flawed by his violent streak. But the prevailing opinion is most pungently expressed by Edmund Wilson in his review of the novel: Morgan is a combination of a wooden-headed Punch and Popeye the Sailor, a buccaneer, a vicious thug, whose terror we may feel but whom we can never pity.

4. The Harry/Marie relationship. While Hawks's suggestion that the Bogart/Bacall relationship is only an earlier stage of the novel's Harry/Marie relationship may be facetious, the two relationships have an affinity as at least limited triumphs of Eros. As Richard Hovey points out in *Hemingway: The Inward Terrain* (1968), "Marie and Harry are the only couple in all the Hemingway novels who find happiness in a marriage that works." *THAHN* is Hawks's most joyous representation of an erotic relationship between a man and a woman.[2] And Eros is represented in the novel with a positiveness unique in Hemingway (although even here Hemingway seems to be suggesting that the love of man and woman is not enough: thus Robert Lewis, Jr.'s pertinent argument in *Hemingway on Love* (1965) that the tragedy of the novel is Harry's failure to merge Eros and *agape*, involvement with one's fellow man).

5. Plot design. As Hemingway was working on *THAHN*, the civil war broke out in Spain. The diverted novelist hastily completed the novel by adding to the two Harry Morgan stories he had already published a third, much longer, story, which follows Harry's career to its tragic end. This finale contrasts the fulfilled erotic relationship of Harry and Marie to the unfulfilled relationships of several other figures, notably the failed author Richard Gordon and his wife. (This subplot in particular has been bemoaned by critics, and it is as much as anything in the book responsible for the low esteem in which the novel is generally held.) M. and Mme. de Bursac, though distinct from Mr. and Mrs. Gordon, serve a comparable function of contrast with Bogart and Bacall, by virtue of Madame's lack of perception and adulterous yearnings and Monsieur's ineptness and weakness. (However, de Bursac's weakness is not, as is Richard Gordon's, absolute. He has the power to perceive a basic truth about Bogart's

[2] Editors' note. Interestingly, Hawks's wife at the time was nicknamed "Slim," and she had been the one to suggest neophyte Bacall for the role.

character, that "betrayal for a price" is something Harry Morgan will never do. He plays an important role in bringing Bogart to self-awareness; and Bogart comes to respect him.)

6. Theme. The rhetorical center of Hemingway's novel is the "message" that Harry Morgan utters dying: that a man alone stands no chance in this world. The film revolves rhetorically around a similar idea. Bogart comes to the realization of the need to break the bounds of isolation, and the film ends with a union of three characters—"Steve," "Slim," and Eddie—who acknowledge this principle, committing themselves to each other and to the fight against Fascism.

The dying words of Hemingway's Harry Morgan, which sum up the consciousness toward which he was striving his whole life, form a nexus of debate in the critical literature. Critics disagree as to whether they reflect a convincing "conversion," and also as to what the precise nature of the conversion is. Does this message demonstrate a new "social conscience" and a recognition of political commitment awakened in Hemingway after years of criticism from the Left? Or does it reflect only a generalized consciousness of the need for love?

In the film, the theme of commitment is clarified. That a man alone stands no chance is very much the premise of both *THAHN*'s political plot and its romance. The film's Harry Morgan is a man who acts self-sufficiently, but who ultimately comes to recognize the "strings" which tie him to Bacall and to a partisan political cause. Frenchy (Marcel Dalio), Bogart's closest friend in the Resistance,[3] constantly interrupts Bogart and Bacall in their flirtation, reminding them of the urgent political situation. Crickett continually directs them back toward erotic union as he works on the song he is composing. It is as if music and the spirit of anti-Fascism are in secret alliance, conspiring to teach Bogart a double lesson about himself.

In the novel, Harry Morgan's "conversion" comes too late for meaningful action. He is completely isolated when he attains

[3] Editors' note. The casting of Dalio, famous for his role as the Jew, Rosenthal, who flees the Germans to freedom in Jean Renoir's 1937 *La Grande Illusion*, added a cinematic resonance to his casting as a Resistance figure in Hawks's film.

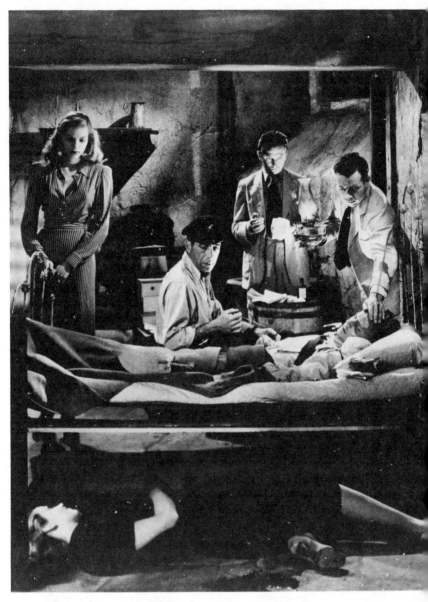

Harry Morgan (Humphrey Bogart), Slim (Lauren Bacall), and Frenchy (Marcel Dalio) tend to the wounded Paul de Bursac (Walter Molnar) as Helene de Bursac (Dolores Moran) faints away. *To Have and Have Not* (1944)

his understanding, and his dying words are mistaken for delirious ravings. Family or no family, Harry *is* a man alone. In the film, however, Bogart only *acts* as if he were alone and "self-sufficient." He does not come to drop this act on his own but is encouraged to do so by the concerted efforts of the Hawksian community, which educates him about himself.

7. Narrative technique. *THAHN* is, more than any other Hemingway novel, an experiment in narrative point of view. Part One is narrated in the first person from Harry Morgan's point of view. Part Two is narrated "objectively," in the third person. In the long Part Three, the narrative point of view undergoes several shifts: first-person narration by a minor character; first-person narration by Harry; "objective"; "objective" mixed with Harry's stream of consciousness; narration by Richard Gordon's wife; "objective"; Marie Morgan's stream of consciousness.

Hawks's film is in its own subtle way as experimental in narrative technique as the novel. The film's departures from conventional Hollywood narrative technique primarily derive from Hawks's attempt to articulate through formal means the process by which Bogart's "self-sufficient" pose is exposed and broken down. This process is the main thrust of the film's narrative.

We will consider one specific strategy in this regard. This is Hawks's repeated gesture of concluding sequence after sequence with a reaction shot of Bogart, in the course of which Bogart, unobserved by anyone within the world of the film, appears to reflect on the scene he has just witnessed, then breaks into a laugh (or at least a smile), as if in self-satisfaction at his superior detachment from the world. For example, when Bacall sidles over to a sailor to fleece him as her evening's work, the sequence ends with just such a final shot of Bogart. He reflects on Bacall's accosting of the sailor and finally laughs to himself at the fade out. (Even Bogart's violent slap at Eddie is part of a sequence which ends with an image of the solitary Bogart laughing.)

It is Bogart *acting for himself* that the camera discloses in these recurring reaction shots. This constitutes a real break with the Hollywood tradition. The conventional reaction shot extracts the character from what might be called the "social space" within which he can be observed by others in the world of the film. Thus isolated, the character exposes his innermost thoughts and feelings in a transparent, expression "reaction." But Hawks's implication throughout *THAHN* is that, even when Bogart is placed within the sanctuary of the private space of a reaction shot, he continues to act theatrically, with himself as audience. His "reactions" do not give us privileged access to his innermost subjectivity. They are cover-ups.

One figure—Bogart—dominates the shot by shot construction of *THAHN*. He is on screen in nearly every shot, and in most of the others, his point of view is projected. Yet the film as a whole declares, formally, that, despite Bogart's omnipresence, he is incomplete and inadequate unto himself.

Hawks's films and Hemingway's writing: The terms in which Hawks's work is usually discussed (cf. Robin Wood's 1968 *Howard Hawks*) relate directly to terms in which Hemingway's writing is often described. Both share a concern for the camaraderie of "men without women," for men in life and death situations; for men facing death in adherence to a noble, unwritten code. The celebrated directness of Hemingway's prose seems analogous to the stripped-down "functional" cinematic style of Hawks, with its eschewal of fancy cutting and elaborate camera movements.

Yet the affinity between Hawks and Hemingway must not be overemphasized. For Hemingway, especially prior to *For Whom the Bell Tolls* (1940), man is ultimately alone—tragically and nobly alone. For Hawks, man is by nature social. Although human society can all too readily be poisoned by those (e.g., Fascists) who are ultimately unwilling or unable to acknowledge their humanity, Hawks continually celebrates the positive values of true human community. Hawks believes in the need for social relations. Hawks believes, specifically, in sexuality, in spontaneous music making, in wit, and in making films which both celebrate and exemplify such positivities.

Hemingway too often accepted the ideal of the "macho" hero and modeled his public (and, increasingly, his literary) persona on that role. If Hemingway in this persona were a figure in a

Hawks film, Hawks might treat him ironically, implicitly criticizing him; perhaps placing him within a community which cares enough about him to "convert" him, educating him about his own act. After all, it is by a similar treatment of Hemingway's hero, Harry Morgan, that Hawks made a film he believes in out of that "goddamned piece of junk."

The Big Sleep (1939)

Raymond Chandler

Who Cares Who Killed Owen Taylor?

BY ROGER SHATZKIN

Raymond Chandler's *The Big Sleep* appears to fit that category of novel critic Edmund Wilson identified as capable of being "poured . . . on to the screen as easily as if it had been written in the studios . . ." ("The Boys in the Back Room" [1940]). In many respects, director Howard Hawks and his collaborators did succeed in pouring the essence of Chandler into their 1946 film. Most notably, they recreated the novel's atmosphere of evanescent corruption and emphasized character at the expense of formal considerations of plot. Nevertheless, the glibness of Wilson's metaphor disguises the "filtering" process operant in any transfer of narrative from one medium to another: Chandler's story of his hero's failed individualistic and Romantic quest became on screen a dark romantic comedy that explores the feasibility of human and sexual commitment between a man and a woman, in this case the film's stars and real-life lovers, Humphrey Bogart and Lauren Bacall. (In practical terms, Hawks was making a sequel to *To Have and Have Not* [1944], which first starred the pair.)

For *The Big Sleep*, there are added problems with Wilson's simple-minded notion of adaptation: Chandler's rather loosely plotted and crowded narrative (synthesized ingeniously out of four pulp magazine stories) became even more complex on screen. The reason for this was a seemingly straightforward

80

filtering mechanism: the Hollywood Production Code's objection to "censorable" aspects of the novel. "Much of the illogic of the film," James Monaco has written, "is simply due to cuts which were made to conform to the Code." [1] But let us take a closer look at some of the misconceptions surrounding the novel and the film, and the apparently intertwined issues of incomprehensibility and censorship.

The first misconception: *The Big Sleep*, both as novel and film, defies comprehension. True, Raymond Chandler confessed to suffering "plot-constipation," wished to possess "one of these facile plotting brains, like Erle [Stanley] Gardner or somebody," and admitted that *The Big Sleep* "happens to be more interested in people than in plot . . ." And granted, director Hawks persisted in glorifying the illogic of his adaptation: in interview after interview he insisted that he "never could figure the story out . . ." that he "can't follow it," and so on. What is more, one of the oft-repeated anecdotes about a film's production links author and *auteur* in mutual confusion: during the filming, Bogart, the picture's Philip Marlowe, apparently asked Hawks just who killed one of the minor characters, a chauffeur named Owen Taylor. (Taylor turns up in his employer's Buick, awash in the Pacific.) Since neither Hawks nor his screenwriters William Faulkner and Leigh Brackett knew, they cabled Chandler. And Chandler wired back: "I don't know." [2]

For the record: with a little effort, novel and film *can* be comprehended, if what is meant by that is that their plots can be linearized, sorted out. (Paul Jensen deserves credit for mentioning this in his article on Chandler in *Film Comment*, November–December, 1974.) But to shift perspective, the popular

[1] "Notes on *The Big Sleep* Thirty Years After," *Sight and Sound*, Winter, 1974–75.

[2] There are numerous variations on this anecdote, regarding who said or wired exactly what to whom. Critic Paul Jensen in "Raymond Chandler: The World You Live In" (*Film Comment*, November-December, 1974), has already pointed out that the film duplicates the novel's loose end in regard to Taylor's fate. Jensen takes this as an indication of the film's faithfulness to the novel.

Michael Winner's 1978 remake of *The Big Sleep* was about to premiere as this piece was being revised. According to pre-release publicity, Winner makes a point to clarify the cause of Taylor's death.

myths about *The Big Sleep* are important. Though their events and characterizations may be ultimately deciphered, novel and film are texts *about* confusion; impenetrability, if not their final result, is at their core. So the question becomes, not "who killed Owen Taylor?" but, more properly (to echo Edmund Wilson's skepticism about detective fiction), "who *cares* who killed Owen Taylor?"

Neither Chandler, nor Marlowe, the novel's detective-narrator, seems to have cared. Hired by the elderly, infirm General Sternwood to investigate some gambling debts his younger daughter, Carmen, has incurred, debts which in turn may become the basis for blackmail, Marlowe plunges into intrigue more complex than circumstances would seem to warrant. For one thing, the General's son-in-law, "Rusty" Regan is missing, and his older daughter, Regan's wife Vivian, suspects that Marlowe has been engaged to find him. As is clear in Chandler: Carmen's ostensible blackmailer, Arthur Geiger, runs a pornographic lending library; Geiger is murdered at his home in the presence of a stupefied Carmen; he has provided drugs and photographed her nude for future extortion schemes. Marlowe rescues Carmen, entering Geiger's place after hearing shots and observing two men leaving in quick succession. The first man turns out to be Taylor, who drives off to his mysterious death.

Marlowe (and Chandler) forget about Taylor. Attention shifts instead to the second man out of the house, Joe Brody, who, like Taylor, is an ex-boyfriend of Carmen's. Brody somehow obtains the negatives of Carmen and proceeds to blackmail her. Marlowe goes to Brody's apartment to recover the negatives and pictures; he first disarms Brody and then Carmen, who has come to retrieve the blackmail materials herself. After Carmen leaves, Carol Lundgren, Geiger's valet and lover shoots Brody, mistakenly thinking that Brody has killed Geiger. As Marlowe later explains, Taylor, chivalrously defending his old flame Carmen, had actually done the deed.[3]

[3] To keep those readers unfamiliar with the rest of the plot apprised, here is a brief summary: Marlowe hands Lundgren over to the police as Brody's murderer. In a cover up, Brody gets blamed posthumously for Geiger's death. The General assumes the case is closed; Marlowe assumes differently. While

Either William Faulkner or Leigh Brackett (Hawks's original screenwriters) was the person concerned about what happened to Taylor. One of them wrote some dialogue for a scene, patterned after one in the novel (but cut from the final film), that sums up, more neatly than Chandler, what happened. In this scene, mid-way through the novel and screenplay, Marlowe is explaining his involvement in the affair to the district attorney. In the novel, Marlowe merely alludes to the events that have transpired and then responds to the D.A.'s queries. In the

---

investigating, he has run into Eddie Mars, an ex-bootlegger and a casino owner-friend of Vivian's. Vivian's husband, Rusty Regan, has reputedly run off with Mar's wife, Mona. Marlowe goes to the Bureau of Missing Persons to inquire about Regan and gets no information other than to learn indirectly that the General *has* been looking for his erstwhile son-in-law. Marlowe meets Vivian Regan inadvertently at Mars's gambling house and ends up taking her home; they warm to each other and begin to get intimate. Marlowe calls matters to a halt, however, when he insists on knowing what Mars "has on" Vivian. Vivian becomes indignant and Marlowe returns her home. Upon entering his own apartment, he finds Carmen Sternwood, naked, in his bed. He ejects her from his apartment with considerable force and revulsion. Marlowe next runs into Harry Jones, a man who has been trailing him for several days hoping to sell him information about the whereabouts of Mona Mars. Before he can peddle his information, Jones is poisoned by Lash Canino, Mars's henchman. Jones obtains directions to Mona's hideout but is captured by Canino once he gets there. Mona Mars's attraction to him saves his life; she frees him and he kills Canino in a gun duel. Marlowe returns to the General who is angered by Marlowe's persistence in staying on the case; but the General now asks him directly to try and find Regan. While at the house, Marlowe returns to Carmen a gun which he had taken from her the night Brody was killed. Carmen wants him to teach her how to shoot. Down in the old oilfield beneath the mansion, Carmen attempts to shoot Marlowe, point blank. He has had the foresight, however, to put blank cartridges in the gun. When she perceives that she has not killed him, Carmen has a seizure. Returning to the house, Marlowe confronts Vivian with what has happened. Apparently, as Marlowe surmised, Carmen had killed Regan for precisely the same reason she tried to kill him: he refused her sexual advances. Vivian had called in Eddie Mars to help her dispose of Regan's body in the sump. Mars had then used Geiger as a "cat's paw" to determine how easy it would be to blackmail the Sternwoods. If the General was not a "soft touch" for paying the hush money, then Mars would have to wait to collect from Vivian. To divert attention from the fact Regan was dead, he placed Mona, his wife, in hiding and spread the rumor that she had run off with Regan. Because he does not want to hurt the General, whom he has come to like, Marlowe makes Vivian promise to have Carmen institutionalized and cured of her seizures, nymphomania, and murderous impulses. Marlowe tells Vivian he will take care of Mars.

screenplay, the D.A., in dialogue never filmed, adds his own summation:

> So Taylor killed Geiger because he was in love with the Sternwood girl. And Brody followed Taylor, sapped him and took the photographs and pushed Taylor into the ocean. And the punk [Lundgren] killed Brody because the punk thought he should have inherited Geiger's business and Brody was throwing him out.[4]

Although no one involved with the production seems to recall this unshot speech, the screenwriters' D.A. would have settled the question of Taylor's demise once and for all, tying up a "loose end" over which Chandler himself apparently never fretted.

Faulkner or Brackett's dialogue here strives for order (despite Hawks's recollection that "there was no sense in making [the story] logical. So we didn't"). And the dialogue, in changing Lundgren's motivation from a lover's revenge also manifests another tendency toward "logic." And this brings us to the second misconception about the film: how it censored the novel.

Throughout the two drafts of the script, the screenwriters anticipated that many sections of the novel might offend the Production Code—matters of sexual conduct, police misconduct, Marlowe's final decision to let a murderer go free—and they took steps to circumvent possible problems. Many of the novel's "objectionable" aspects did have to be cut from the final film. Geiger's pornography racket is nowhere mentioned (we just see some posh clients skulking about his "bookstore"), nor is the homosexual relationship between Geiger and Lundgren. Both of these omissions cause confusions (as does the film's ending to a degree, but for reasons other than censorship). But other changes, such as presenting a clothed Carmen at Geiger's and later at Marlowe's apartment, do not alter the final quality of the

[4] The screenplays are in the United Artists Collection at the Wisconsin Center for Film and Theater Research. There are three versions: a script of September 11, 1944; a Temporary script of September 26 (which has been published); and a Cutter's script of March 16, 1945. Two additional scenes, added to the film in January, 1946, are added to the Cutter's script in the New York Public Library at Lincoln Center.

film. A recent assessment, such as Gavin Lambert's that the movie "seems badly hobbled by censorship" (*The Dangerous Edge*, 1975), hardly seems appropriate.

Prior censorship was the rule in the screenplays. The screen-writers transformed Geiger's business from pornography and extortion to the vaguer endeavor of blackmail alone (late in the second script draft Marlowe actually finds packing cases of "manilla filing envelopes, ledgers, etc."). Lundgren's relation-ship to Geiger becomes all business. Even Carmen Sternwood's nymphomania is de-sexed (though one wonders how Martha Vickers sultry performance in the film could have possibly jibed with the script's conception). Carmen's psychotic and homicidal behavior is brought on by jealousy. She murders Regan and attempts to murder Marlowe, according to Faulkner and Brack-ett, because she has lost the affections of both of them (at least in her mind) to her sister Vivian, and *not* because they are the only two men who refuse to sleep with her. And though Hawks has credited the Production Code office with rejecting the novel's ending and, when prodded, providing their own, Faulk-ner and Brackett had already altered Chandler's denouement in their first script. (In letting Carmen go free to be "cured" in the book, Marlowe violates the Code's provision against un-punished crimes. The film's ending is actually a *third* script re-vision of the novel's ending.) [5]

But Faulkner and Brackett's careful anticipation of the Code

---

[5] The two endings preceding the one now in the film are as follows: In the first draft, to win her father's sympathy in the face of her guilt in killing Regan, Carmen is going to feign suicide. Norris the butler, though, replaces the blanks in her gun (which Marlowe had loaded it with for his protec-tion) with real bullets; Carmen kills herself. For the Code, this ending presented the dual problem of presenting a combined suicide/condoned murder. The ending in the second draft occurs at Geiger's house. After Mar-lowe has extracted a confession from Carmen, she taunts him with the knowledge that it would destroy her father if the information got out. She walks out the door and is killed my Mars's men in a trap set, ironically, for Marlowe, who guns down Mars when he comes to inspect Carmen's body. This version must have been censorable on the grounds of Marlowe's com-plicity in Carmen's death—he knows what awaits her outside—and his killing of Mars is gratuitous if Carmen is the murderer. Curiously, Chandler him-self offered an ending that was rather inappropriate. (See Frank MacShane, *The Life of Raymond Chandler* [1976], p. 125.)

and their finely wrought "logic" were to no avail. Hawks excised a number of scenes from their screenplay as he shot. And the filming, done from the second draft or Temporary script, had run too long. So "Jules Furthman was called in," according to Leigh Brackett, "for a rewrite to cut the remaining or unshot portion [of the script] into a manageable length. . . ." [6] Whatever coherence the original screenwriters had concocted (or preserved from Chandler) was eradicated in shortening an overlong screenplay; it was not the direct evisceration of the novel for the censors, as Monaco and other critics have averred, that cause the movie's notorious incomprehensibility.

But the film, in its final and less "coherent" form, becomes—in the best Hawks tradition—a type of Rorschach test in which the elipses can be filled in by the audience. And, paradoxically, it moves closer to the novel as a result. In the minds of viewers imbued with the requisite imagination, the spirit of the book's censorable content remains, albeit sometimes between the lines. As Charles Gregory has written, despite the fact that the movie had to avoid "explicit references to sex, dope and pornography that are woven into the novel . . . somehow the film reflects all this to the sophisticated viewer without ever drawing the ire of the censors or even the notice of the prudes." [7]

Typical of the cuts made to shorten the script was the removal of a shot in the first scene showing Owen Taylor washing the Sternwood Buick as Marlowe passes from the General's mansion to his hothouse (a direct transposition from the novel intended to identify the chauffeur and foreshadow his complicity in Geiger's murder). In the film, Marlowe simply walks from the mansion's hallway into the greenhouse—the magic of film editing has connected the two edifices. And Taylor gets whisked away to the limbo of legend.

But as Leigh Brackett observed: "Audiences came away feeling that they had seen the hell and all of a film even if they didn't rightly know what it was all about. Again, who cared? It was grand fun, with sex and danger and a lot of laughs. . . ."

[6] "From *The Big Sleep* to *The Long Goodbye*," *Take One*, vol. 10, no. 4, January, 1974.
[7] "Knight Without Meaning?" *Sight and Sound*, Summer, 1973.

Again, who cared? Let us turn to the novel and film in more detail to see if we can decipher what they are all about—and if it matters if they are *about* anything.

For that matter, what *is* Raymond Chandler's *The Big Sleep* about? The novel functions as an entertainment, a sometimes self-satiric, self-contained world of double-cross, moral and political corruption in which our confusion as readers helps engender our involvement and our identification with the hero, Philip Marlowe. The central movement of the novel, though, focuses on its protagonist's quest, not for the solution to a puzzle or a mystery (though that is necessarily accomplished), but primarily for his double, his *doppelganger*. It is this covert quest —which informs the bulk of Chandler's novels but is most prominent in *The Big Sleep* and *The Long Goodbye* (1954)—and its requisite failure that create many of the novel's strong, if fugitive, resonances.

Marlowe's search for Terence "Rusty" Regan is the hidden energizing force of the novel (hidden, in some ways, from Chandler himself). It is also the genesis of the novel's seeming confusion and impenetrability. But the pattern of Marlowe's search for Regan does not emerge readily from the narrative. Throughout roughly the first half of the novel, questions about Regan, Vivian Sternwood's missing husband, keep surfacing, but Marlowe's chief preoccupation lies with keeping Carmen safe and the Sternwood's family name unbesmirched through the three deaths that touch on them (i.e., Geiger's, Taylor's, and Brody's). Marlowe's identification with Regan is established at his initial visit to the General (where he replaces Regan as the old man's sensual surrogate—drinking and smoking for Sternwood's vicarious enjoyment—and is hired for a job that Regan, the General's confidant as well as son-in-law, would probably have undertaken). But Marlowe does not turn his attention to the missing man until the mystery that propels the beginning half of the action, concerning Carmen's blackmail, has ostensibly been resolved. And all along, he denies various allegations that he *is* looking for Regan, even though, ironically, they are true.

At this point, to better understand Regan's place in the novel, it will help to clarify the structure of *The Big Sleep*. Writing on the film, James Monaco has offered a helpful description that applies equally well to the novel. He notes in the movie's construction a "dual structure: a 'surface' mystery (usually the client's) and a 'deep' mystery (the metaphysical or political problem which presents itself to the detective)." Fredric Jameson views Chandler's dual structure slightly differently, noting a tendency for the novels to mislead readers because a Chandler work "passes itself off as a murder mystery." Jameson points out that "In fact Chandler's stories are first and foremost descriptions of searches . . ." Here the "murder mystery" corresponds to Monaco's "surface" enigma, the "search" to the "deep" structure. Jameson later expresses the double nature of the narrative in terms of time:

> The final element in Chandler's characteristic form is that the underlying crime is always old, lying half-forgotten in the pasts of the characters before the book begins. This is the principal reason why the readers attention is diverted from [the underlying crime]; he assumes it to be a part of the dimension of the present. . . .[8]

Relating this to *The Big Sleep* then, this is what happens: the crime in the past that generates the whole novel, yet which is unknown to Marlowe or the reader at the outset of the book, is the murder of Regan by Carmen Sternwood. Regan, like some entombed character in Poe, lies mouldering in a sump in the oilfield below the Sternwood mansion while four more deaths result from the unrecognized cover-up of his demise. And Marlowe spends all his initial energy treating the symptoms of the case, the surface of the present, before turning to their cause in the past.

I do not believe that Chandler was in complete touch with the metaphysical significance of Regan for his protagonist. Chandler, as is most clearly exemplified in his *Atlantic* essay, "The Simple

[8] "On Raymond Chandler," *Southern Review*, July, 1970. For a more theoretical discussion of narrative structures in detective fiction, see Tzvetan Todorov, "The Typology of Detective Fiction," in *The Poetics of Prose*, translated by Richard Howard (Ithaca: Cornell University Press, 1977), pp. 42–52.

Art of Murder," written five years after *The Big Sleep*, tended to conceive of his hero in extremely idealized terms:

> . . . Down these mean streets a man must go who is not himself mean, who is neither tarnished nor afraid. . . . He must be the best man in his world and a good enough man for any world!

Despite Chandler's notion of the hero as knight in a corrupt world (a conception taken up too uncritically by many who have written about him), Marlowe is a far from simplistic character. In the beginning of *The Big Sleep*, he does literally project himself into a tableau on a stained-glass panel in the Sternwood home, depicting "a knight in dark armor rescuing a lady . . . [who] didn't have any clothes on . . ." "I would have to climb up there and help him," Marlowe says to himself. "He didn't seem to be really trying." However, later in the novel, when a naked Carmen invades his bedroom, he looks down at his chessboard and concludes that "Knights had no meaning in this game. It wasn't a game for knights." The thought is reemphasized when he enters the Sternwood house for the last time and observes the knight, who "still wasn't getting anywhere. . . ."

In short, a dialectic exists within the novel: Marlowe begins as knight, but is forced to cope in a sordid world: to do so he must be willing to summon a darker side of himself. Chandler's idealization represses this darker side. This is where Regan as "double" comes in: Chandler fractionalizes his hero into two characters. Regan, missing and dead (ultimately repressed!) throughout the entire novel represents the potentially corruptible side of his protagonist which Chandler cannot brook. Regan has crossed the line. He is beyond the law all the way—a successful gangster-bootlegger. He commits himself sexually to women: he marries Vivian Sternwood; he (probably) has an affair with Mona Mars, before and after she is married. He commits himself to public social causes: he fought for the I.R.A. in 1922. He commits himself to having (if not coveting) money: he carries fifteen thousand dollars in bills at all times. In fact, the D.A. surmises that the real reason Sternwood hired Marlowe in the first place was to find out if Regan had betrayed his trust by being the real force behind the blackmail instigated by Geiger (ironically, he is). In sum, Regan is Marlowe's alter ego, an adult version of the detective's adolescent, solipsistic Romantic, who in "growing up" has taken the fall.

Throughout the novel we are given hints of the Marlowe-Regan bond. Marlowe resembles Regan: the D.A.'s man Bernie Ohls describes Regan as a "big guy as tall as you and a shade heavier." Both men are in their thirties. Their relationships to women intersect completely. Vivian Sternwood and Mona Mars are both attracted to Marlowe as they were to Regan, and Carmen tries to shoot Marlowe, as she did Regan, because he too would not sleep with her. (The link of the two men through the women is possibly covert evidence of Marlowe's repressed homoerotic attraction to Regan.) General Sternwood's butler explicitly compares the two men, and the General takes a paternal (and perhaps homosexual) interest in both. And when Marlowe confronts a photograph of Regan, the detective describes his impressions in terms he might as easily use for himself. It was "Not the face of a tough guy and not the face of a man who could be pushed around much by anybody . . . [It was] a face that looked a little taut, the face of a man who would move fast and play for keeps. . . ." Marlowe concludes portentously, "I would know that face if I saw it."

So Marlowe's search for Regan represents maximally an investigation into his own identity, into his own soul's potential weaknesses and arrested tendencies. In his final soliloquy Marlowe intones the following famous lines in speaking of his entombed "brother" Regan:

> Where did it matter where you lay once you were dead? In a dirty sump or in a marble tower on top of a high hill? You were dead, you were sleeping the big sleep, you were not bothered by things like that. Oil and water were the same as wind and air to you. You just slept the big sleep, not caring about the nastiness of how you died or where you fell. Me, I was part of the nastiness now. Far more a part of it than Rusty Regan was. . . .

Marlowe, who when captive at one point made macabre jokes about his choice of casket and about Eddie Mars's henchman digging *him* a grave, finally comes face to face with his own mortality only through Regan. In so doing, he begins to understand his corruptibility, as well (on the ethical level as "knight" he has let murderess Carmen go unpunished). He is "part of the nastiness now . . ." and that is the full import of his search. For the reader, as Fredric Jameson has put it, the end of the novel "is able to bring us up short, without warning, against the reality of death itself, stale death, reaching out to remind the living of its own mouldering resting place." [9]

Paradoxically, Faulkner, Brackett, and Hawks's screen version immediately makes the Marlowe-Regan connection much more explicit than in the novel. In the Hawksian tradition of professional equals, Marlowe's first dialogue with the General reveals that he and Regan have been respectful opponents during prohibition, each on a different side of the law ("We used to swap shots between drinks, or drinks between shots—whichever you like."). But if anything, Regan (mysteriously now named "Shawn") is invoked quickly only to be exorcised. Though the surface mystery in the film remains the same, still concerning Carmen's blackmail, the deep mystery will ultimately concern, as Monaco has pointed out, what gambler Eddie Mars "has" on Vivian Sternwood Rutledge (Lauren Bacall), here a divorcee. (In the novel, Mars is blackmailing Vivian over Carmen's murder of Regan; he has helped her dispose of Regan's body.) The question of what Mars "has" on Vivian masks the real thrust of Hawks's film, which is to determine with whom Vivian will ultimately side, and as in his best comedies whether or not she and Marlowe will realize their mutual romantic attraction.

To emphasize leading lady Bacall as Vivian, Hawks and his writers placed her in three scenes in which she does not appear in the novel (Marlowe returning Carmen to her home, his visit to Brody's apartment, his incarceration in Realito at the hands

[9] Only one scene in Hawks's movie comes near the evocative power of Marlowe's speech (which strongly recalls Hamlet's oration over Yorick). When Marlowe first enters Geiger's house in the film, he finds Geiger dead and Carmen giddy and intoxicated. He puts Carmen to sleep on a couch, and at one point later in his investigation, glances from the supine dead man to the drugged woman. Only in that fleeting instant, does the mutability of life into death loom as large as in Chandler.

of Mars's man Canino); they lengthened one encounter from the book (Vivian's visit to Marlowe's office), and added one long scene that appears only in the film. This scene, the famous Cafe/Horserace double entendre sequence (mandated by Warners' front office a full year after the rest of the movie was in the can, to give the stars yet more exposure together) is indicative of a pattern of attraction-repulsion between Vivian and Marlowe that firmly establishes as the center of the film the question of their eventual fate together.

In almost every scene in which they appear together, up until the penultimate one, Marlowe and Vivian begin a wary, but cordial verbal sparring. But each encounter ends in witty vitriol ("Kissing is nice, but your father didn't hire me to sleep with you."). The first mode of verbal skirmishing is the substitute for and correlative of a romantic language founded on emotion that Hawks employs throughout his romantic "screwball" comedies. Though Hawks took this convention from his comedies, in *The Big Sleep* he left its significance open ended. The dialogue between Marlowe and Vivian can end in romance or—in keeping with Chandler, the tradition of the *femme fatale* in general and of *film noir* in particular—in betrayal.

Near the end of the film, an obligatory "lay off the case" scene with Bernie Ohls (Regis Toomey) was written into the film; it confirms that Marlowe's vacillating relationship with Vivian has become the film's deep structure and raison d'être. After Ohls has conveyed his message instructing Marlowe to desist, the detective recapitulates the case so far and indicates why he must go on:

> "Bernie, put yourself in my shoes for a minute. A nice old guy has two daughters. One of them is, well, wonderful. And the other is not so wonderful. As a result somebody gets something on her. The father hires me to pay off. Before I can get to the guy, the family chauffeur kills him! But that didn't stop things. It just starts them. And two murders later I find out somebody's got something on wonderful."

So the film comes down to Marlowe's endeavors to "clear" and win "wonderful."

Philip Marlowe (Humphrey Bogart) greets Vivian Sternwood Rutledge (Lauren Bacall) from a doorway in Eddie Mars's casino. *The Big Sleep* (1946)

When the ending does come, it makes little plot sense. Marlowe and Vivian are united after the detective forces Mars, his only serious "rival," out of a door into a hail of machine-gun fire. In Jules Furthman's reworking of the conclusion, the only logical extra-textual explanation for Mars's death is that he, not Carmen, killed Regan, and that he is blackmailing Vivian by making her think Carmen did it.

If the narrative logic is flawed, the emotional logic is not. We care about Marlowe/Bogart and Vivian/Bacall; they have earned our respect through their mutual (and mostly verbal) abilities to cope with a hostile environment. And it is satisfying to see their compatibility, which we have sensed all along, romantically vindicated. Likewise, in the novel, despite his limitations, we care about Marlowe. His voice unifies the quicksilver and chaotic world in which he operates, a world in which almost all events can never be known but only hypothesized about. And that extends to one misplaced chauffeur, at sea in the depths of illogic, about whom one ultimately need not care. Peace to you, Owen Taylor.

The Day of the Locust (1939)

Nathanael West

The Madding Crowd in the Movies

BY SIDNEY GOTTLIEB

When Nathanael West was finishing work on *The Day of the Locust* (1939), he was concerned that it be read as he intended it. Fearing that his novel might be taken too superficially, he urged his publisher to design and promote it in a way that would make clear that "the book isn't another 'Boy Meets Girl,' 'Once in a Lifetime,' or 'Queer People,' but that it has a real and even 'serious' theme." [1] John Schlesinger and Waldo Salt, the director and scriptwriter of the film version of *The Day of the Locust* (1975) are clearly aware that they have sacrificed more than a bit of West's "seriousness" in their work. Schlesinger and Salt have extracted what is essentially a love story with an hysterical climax from a novel that plots out deeper things: the disintegration of American society and the threat of class warfare in the precarious days before World War II.

I was tempted to say "only" a love story, but that would slight the achievement of the film. As a love story, the film focuses much more intently than the novel on characterization, and its greatest success is surely its presentation of the major figures and their odd relationships. The casting—William Atherton as Tod, Karen Black as Faye Greener, Donald Sutherland as Homer Simpson, Burgess Meredith as Harry Greener—is excellent, and

[1] Quoted in Jay Martin's *Nathanael West: The Art of His Life* (1970).

the actors ably bring to light aspects of the characters that are purposefully underdeveloped in the novel.

Tod Hackett is the most important figure in the story, and West barely evades making him too likable. Early on, West makes sure to point out Tod's "large sprawling body, his slow blue eyes and sloppy grin," his "doltish" appearance, and comments that "he was lazy and didn't like to walk." West also takes great pains to show the violent underside of Tod, that his "love" for Faye is largely based on his terrible desire to crush "her egglike self-sufficiency." Tod has recurring rape fantasies and once even attacks Faye, although somewhat half-heartedly. West says of Tod that "he was really a very complicated young man with a whole set of personalities, one inside the other like a nest of Chinese boxes." This can be taken to mean that Tod has a certain "depth" which distinguishes him from the others in the novel; but it also may indicate what he shares with them: multiple cracks in his psychology, a personality ranging from passive and perceptive to suspicious and highly dangerous.

William Atherton's Tod in the movie is normally so amiable and untroubled that, unlike West's enigmatic creation, we are rarely out of sympathy with him. Yet even here, Tod is no stalwart Olympian observer; his unfettered outside betrays a core of irrationality and violence. In the film Tod seriously tries to rape Faye when they visit Miguel's camp in the woods; and although some critics felt this scene uncalled for, it is quite in line with Tod's character and West's message: like everybody else, Tod is teased and cheated and messed over, and his response is sometimes no less pathological.

But in spite of Atherton's sharp characterization, the film runs into problems precisely because Tod's key role as an observer is not exploited as it might be. Ultimately we should sympathize with Tod *not* because of his actions—he is a compromised character involved with, even in love with, the decaying world around him—but because he alone has some perspective on what he sees. We watch as Tod pieces together his most important work of art, "The Burning of Los Angeles," and we are well aware that he is the only character able to register something beyond a personal feeling of frustration and disappointment. But we simply do not get enough of his vision of the world. We see him looking past Faye occasionally, but for the most part he only looks at her, and this limits the scope of the film.

Faye is a fascinating character and Karen Black's performance brings her to life. She is the embodiment of sexuality as dry heat, as friction, as an emptiness which is sometimes entered but never filled. Faye is rarely tender and never fragile, but she is always alluring, and West spends much of his time trying to articulate her appeal:

> Her invitation wasn't to pleasure, but to struggle, hard and sharp, closer to murder than to love. If you threw yourself on her, it would be like throwing yourself from the parapet of a skyscraper. You would do it with a scream. You couldn't expect to rise again. Your teeth would be driven into your skull like nails into a pine board and your back would be broken. You wouldn't even have time to sweat or close your eyes.

Perhaps even more than the novel, the film explores the brutality that is never far from Faye's love. We see not only Tod driven to violence by his feelings for Faye, but Faye's other lovers as well; they become the real victims. When Miguel is attracted to her at the campsite, he is smashed on the head with a stick by Earle. When Earle tries to dance with her at the party, he is rammed in the groin by Abe Kusich, the midget. When Abe goes for her, he is thrown head first across the room onto a table by Miguel. And Homer Simpson, who wants only to love and care for Faye, is her most pathetic victim. His death is a stark enactment of the fate prophesized in the passage quoted above: he is literally broken and torn apart.

Still, we never completely abandon our sympathy for Faye. Just as we must not like Tod too much in West's novel, it is important that we not hate Faye too much. The film of *Day of the Locust* follows West's presentation in carefully placing Faye beyond our reproach. Although incredibly vain, shallow, self-involved, and shrill, she somehow manages to come out looking fresh, newborn, and pure. When Karen Black sits down in front of a makeup mirror reflecting three views of her face and sings

"Jeepers, Creepers, / Where'd ya get those peepers?" to herself, we have a perfect image of Faye's triumphant narcissism.

Perhaps it is this desire to emphasize Faye's absolute purity and self-sufficiency—West's own description of her—that leads Schlesinger and Salt to end the movie by focusing on Faye. In his uncomplimentary review of the film, Stanley Kauffmann questioned the wisdom of this choice:

> Why should it be Faye who comes back one day to look at Tod's now-empty apartment in the building where once they both lived? Surely, if the film is to have a shred of esthetic and psychological consistency, it ought to close with Tod. Why couldn't he have come back to look at *her* empty apartment? [2]

The film could have ended with the riot at the Hollywood movie premiere, but perhaps Schlesinger and Salt are pursuing the implications of this essential passage about Faye from the novel:

> Nothing could hurt her. She was like a cork. No matter how rough the sea got, she would go dancing over the same waves that sank iron ships and tore away piers of reinforced concrete. [Tod] pictured her riding a tremendous sea. Wave after wave reared its ton on ton of solid water and crashed down only to have her spin gaily away.

The film may be perfectly right in deciding that Tod leaves but Faye remains. More than a survivor, she surfaces virtually untouched.

Homer Simpson is the last of the major characters, and he is obviously more troubled and grotesque than Tod or Faye. Tod's first view of Homer in the novel is right to the point: "He didn't mean to be rude but at first glance this man seemed an exact model for the kind of person who comes to California to die, perfect in every detail down to fever eyes and unruly hands." Donald Sutherland follows West's clues closely in creating this man who is a pathetic study in repression. Unlike Faye, who is completely buoyant and untouchable, and Tod, who is able to

[2] *New Republic,* May 17, 1975.

Star-struck Faye Greener (Karen Black) under the famous sign announcing "Hollywood." *The Day of the Locust* (1975)

alternate between involvement and detachment, Homer is a constant prisoner of emotions which can never be expressed or satisfied. According to the ancient definition of the word, he is an idiot, an absolutely private man. Much like the characters in William Gass's story "In the Heart of the Heart of the Country" (1967), Homer "lives alone—how alone it is impossible to fathom."

Sutherland's physical appearance and mannerisms perfectly convey Homer's clumsiness and vulnerability. His stare is vacant and only his hands speak truly for him; they are always rubbing together, wandering, nearly out of control. His belly sticks out, almost inviting a punch, and nearly everyone takes an opportunity to abuse him.

Beyond following Nathanael West's hints in picturing Homer, John Schlesinger decided to add a religious dimension to his characterization, and this is not always successful or appropriate. It is absurd for Homer to be a religious fanatic, to be the one who brings the Greeners to the revivalist church meeting. In the novel he has nothing at all: no illusions and no solace. He simply coils tighter and tighter. In the film, after the cockfight and the party where he is terribly humiliated, Homer is moved to a kind of biblical wrath. In a voice that is uncharacteristically threatening, he says "O Lord, forgive me . . . but sometimes I wish I could tear it all down." This forced glimpse into Homer's psyche undercuts the power of his sudden turn to violence at the end. When Adore Loomis, that hideous little androgyne, hits him in the face with a rock, we should be totally surprised by Homer's murderous response.

More strangely, Schlesinger suddenly sees Homer as an unlikely Christ, enraged at Adore, he who casts the first stone. As Homer is tossed by the mob at the end of the film, his arms are flung outward, as though on a cross. West does not entertain this kind of religious parody except for his title of *The Day of the Locust* (perhaps he had exhausted this vein in his earlier novel, *Miss Lonelyhearts* [1933]). Yet, Schlesinger and Salt use this form of burlesque elsewhere quite effectively, not only to characterize Homer's situation, but also to remind us that the film is set deep in a fallen world.

There are several striking sequences set in Homer's backyard, which is meant as a kind of primordial garden turned to seed. In the first of these scenes, Homer sits alone. Fruit drops around him, but there is no sense of lushness; the garden is overgrown with weeds and there is only a lizard to stare at. Everything is quiet and Homer is, as always, restless. His hands move aimlessly until they seize on a child's game to play; "Here is the church, here is the steeple" is a neurotic ritual for Homer, repeated constantly as in the novel, but the claustrophobic film setting manifests that this is the only kind of church he can build there, in this post-Edenic wasteland. In a later scene in the backyard, Faye joins Homer in a depressing tableau: they stand in this ruined garden as overweight Adam and eternally tempted Eve.

Now, given that the film of *The Day of the Locust* is filled with generally excellent characterization, and given that it is not "merely" a love story, what exactly is the film missing? First of all, the film is lacking the philosophical insights—most often conveyed third person, through Tod's observations—which give meaning to many incidents in the novel. Secondly, characterization is developed in a void. The characters form too exclusive a society, whereas West carefully placed them in a much broader social context. Until the end, the film virtually avoids the most potent force in the novel, the mob of people who are never even named, except in one of West's original titles for this story: *The Cheated.*

There are three major scenes in which Schlesinger and Salt apparently try to go beyond the individual characters to more general and significant points but none succeeds fully. The collapse of the set during the filming of the Battle of Waterloo, the visit to the revivalist church meeting, and, of course, the riot at the Hollywood premiere are all extremely important to the story, and it is worth analyzing how the film and the novel differ in these parts to see why the film falls short.

In the film, while searching for Faye, Tod walks onto the set where the Battle of Waterloo is being reenacted. The director is not at all pleased with the action and, to Tod's amusement, he orders the extras to be killed again and again. While this goes on, though, Tod notices something more serious: the carpenters have not finished building the supports for part of the set and signs warning everyone off are hidden from sight. As the battle continues, the actors advance onto the unfinished hill and it falls apart, injuring many of them. This is visually a spectacular scene, but hardly any real meaning is squeezed out of it. It serves only two limited purposes. First, it brings Tod and Faye together for one tender, loving moment. They embrace outside the set and confess how worried they were about each other when the hill collapsed. (Needless to say, there is no such "tender moment" in the novel.) Secondly, we get a fleeting view of how the Hollywood tycoons respond to the near tragedy: they insist that the signs were properly posted and that in any event the insurance companies will take care of the damages. (Film historians may look back on this as another of the obligatory "cover-up" scenes that dot so many American films of the Watergate 1970s.)

When we inspect this scene in the novel we become aware of how much the film has cut out and how it has trivialized what remains. Here more than in any other place in *The Day of the Locust* West expresses what he feels the Hollywood movie-making enterprise is all about. In his walk across the movie sets in search of Faye, Tod enters into an "Unreal City." West's description comes directly from his own experience of Hollywood studios and it is worthy of Eliot and Baudelaire:

> He pushed his way through a tangle of briars, old flats and iron junk, skirting the skeleton of a Zeppelin, a bamboo stockade, an adobe fort, the wooden horse of Troy, a flight of baroque palace stairs that started in a bed of weeds and ended against the branches of an oak, part of the Fourteenth Street elevated station, a Dutch windmill, the bones of a dinosaur, the upper half of the Merrimac, a corner of a Mayan temple, until he finally reached the road.

The rapid shift from one scene to another to make a striking association is an important part of film art, but the above is not montage: it is madness. As West goes on to show, Hollywood is a "dream dump" where entropy and disorder rule. Yet this walk through the movie sets, so important as a prelude to the chaos to follow on the Waterloo set, is missing from the film.

In the novel, the section in which the set collapses is meant to do considerably more than dramatize the irresponsibility of Hollywood producers. West is trying to work out something much deeper. Whether consciously or not, he is giving dramatic form to two ominous observations on human history. The first is philosopher George Santayana's well-known statement that those who do not learn from the errors of the past are doomed to repeat them. West points out clearly that the mistake on the movie set is the same that Napoleon actually made at Waterloo. The mistake is not quite as devastating here, of course, but it connects well with the second idea of history that may also have been in West's mind: Marx's notion that events occur first as tragedy, then recur as farce. Here is West's description of the battle:

> The French killed General Picton with a ball through the head and he returned to his dressing room. Alten was put to the sword and also retired. The colors of the Lunenberg battalion, borne by a prince of the family of Deux-Ponts, were captured by a famous child star in the uniform of a Parisian drummer boy. The Scotch Grays were destroyed and went to change into another uniform. Ponsonby's heavy dragoons were also cut to ribbons. Mr. Grotenstein would have a large bill to pay at the Western Costume Company.

West seems to suggest that we are in an age of diminution, and that this is an irreversible process. We can never again reach the heights of tragedy; and as we see when the set collapses, the inevitable next stage after farce is chaos.

The scenes in the film of the gigantic revival meeting are further indications that Schlesinger and Salt are quite willing to be satirical and spectacular but that they generally hold back from more serious analyses. Harry Greener (Burgess Meredith) is quite sick and Homer and daughter Faye escort him to a church service where he may be "cured." As we might expect, this service is done Hollywood style: it is an extravaganza. There is quick cutting to help raise the emotional pitch and, for the first time in the film, we see a great mass of people getting worked up about something. The music is loud and insistent, and a neon cross urges everyone "to give" in the most meaningful way—by sending in money. In front of a large broadcast microphone stands a woman who is both preacher and M.C., but her pleas and prayers contain more than a trace of bullying and her "miracles" are most unseemly. It is not enough to make the lame walk; to the roars of the crowd, she insists that an old woman run back and forth across the stage.

Harry Greener is placed in a wheelchair, wheeled to the front, and then, to the astonishment of all, miraculously brought back to his feet. He swoons for a moment, but, once on stage, Harry literally does come to life. The gospel music slowly blends into a ragtime tune until finally we are in the middle of a Hollywood production number. It is all splendidly ludicrous. Harry conspicuously winks at us as he begins his old soft shoe routine to pleasantly usher out the scene. We are meant to smile and shrug our shoulders with Harry. After all, religion is just another kind of show biz, so dance along.

To point out that religion is a racket, and a show business racket at that, is hardly sufficient for West, though, and his description of Tod's wandering among the new churches springing up is anything but charmingly cynical:

> He visited the "Church of Christ, Physical" where holiness was attained through the constant use of chestweights and spring grips; the "Church Invisible" where fortunes were told and the dead made to find lost objects; the "Tabernacle of the Third Coming" where a woman in male clothing preached the "Crusade Against Salt"; and the "Temple Moderne" under whose glass and chromium roof "Brain-Breathing, the Secret of the Aztecs" was taught.

This is certainly ridiculous, but not easily laughed away. And the crowds of worshipers who attend these churches are not at all comical:

> He would not satirize them as Hogarth or Daumier might, nor would he pity them. He would paint their fury with respect, appreciating its awful, anarchic power and aware that they had it in them to destroy civilization.

This section on the weird churches is only one of the many crowd scenes throughout the novel. As noted, the mob is never far from West's mind; and rather than being merely the background for the action, their existence is really the main subject of the book. Like many other writers and political thinkers of the late 1930s, West was preoccupied with the question of whether the lower-middle classes of America would turn toward Fascism as their counterparts in Italy and Germany had already done. Perhaps at another time in history West might have had the luxury to pick out the comedy in the crazy behavior of the crowds, but at this time he was rightly more sensitive to the threatening and brutal side of all instances of irrationality. By 1938, when he was rewriting and completing the novel, West saw only locusts, not comedians, in the mob.

The film seems hardly interested in the masses of people at all; they become a concern only at the very end, in the scenes of the riot at the Hollywood premiere. Where have they been all this time? For a while the crowd is only mildly intimidating, unconscious of its own power and thus able to be held back by the comparatively weak barriers set up by the police. But when Homer Simpson, the most repressed character of all, springs to action, it is a signal for everyone to crash through the barriers. Homer stomps child star Adore Loomis to death and he is almost immediately seized by the crowd and brutally executed. Once begun, the violence can hardly stop here. Cars are overturned, the movie stars are attacked, windows are smashed, and soon everything is in flames. Tod's leg has been crushed somehow and he cannot flee. Instead he is forced to watch and scream in horror as his collage, "The Burning of Los Angeles," comes to life.

One cannot fault John Schlesinger on his presentation of the riot. It is quite lengthy and appropriately overexaggerated. The visual effects are sometimes excruciatingly painful and this is as it should be in a scene that attempts to envision the apocalypse. There are fine touches of nightmare here: the crowd swarms eerily, some frighteningly masked—locusts, glimpsed in full riot regalia. Even the screen we are watching seems to burn through, the film becoming, at least for that brief illumination, a self-consuming artifact, victimized by the disorderly throng it presents and warns against.

Ironically, though, the intensity of the climax reminds us of how superficial and tangential much of the earlier part of the film has been. The riot, though well done, is virtually unsupported by all that precedes it, and its impact is undercut by its abruptness. We are shocked by the sudden violence, but we are never given any real clues as to why these people act as they do. Throughout the novel, on the other hand, West not only keeps the mob before our eyes but also explains why they are so dangerous and how they got that way:

> It was a mistake to think them harmless curiosity seekers. They were savage and bitter, especially the middle-aged and the old, and had been made so by boredom and disappointment. . . . They realize that they've been tricked and burn with resentment. Every day of their lives they read the newspapers and went to the movies. Both fed them on lynchings, murder, sex crimes, explosions, wrecks, love nests, fires, miracles, revolutions, wars. This daily diet made sophisticates of them. The sun is a joke. Oranges can't titillate their jaded palates. Nothing can ever be violent enough to make taut their slack minds and bodies. They have been cheated and betrayed. They have slaved and saved for nothing.

For the film to have been so broadly perceptive as West's analysis, for it to have underscored and understood the role of the crowd, it would have had to have been as continually intense and disquieting as the novel. Although we are often given quite vivid images of a whole landscape and its inhabitants literally coming apart, *The Day of the Locust* remains a shy and uneven film, clear in portraying the disintegrating relationships of its main characters, but unclear about the context within which these breakups and breakdowns occur—or even why they are so frightening.

The Grapes of Wrath (1939)

John Steinbeck

Trampling Out the Vintage: Sour Grapes

BY RUSSELL CAMPBELL

Published in March, 1939, *The Grapes of Wrath* was the culminating social protest novel of the Depression years, an unruly, angry epic which John Steinbeck would never surpass, and which was at once a best seller and American classic.

The fictional tradition it grew out of was that of critical social realism, pioneered in America by Dreiser, Norris, Sinclair, and Crane; developed by Lewis, Farrell, and Dos Passos; and given a push to the Left by writers of proletarian fiction, such as Clara Weatherwax and Jack Conroy, during the 1930s. The realist school had always incorporated sociological material in its fiction, but what is remarkable about *The Grapes of Wrath* is the extreme to which it takes this process. In *Documentary Expression and Thirties America* (1973) William Stott argues that Steinbeck's book is "no doubt the Thirties' novel most closely related to doumentary," and states that the novelist had initially planned to produce, with *Life* photographer Horace Bristol, a book of photojournalism along the lines of Erskine Caldwell and Margaret Bourke-White's acclaimed *You Have Seen Their Faces* (1937), a study of poverty in the South. Other critics have conjectured that the intercalary chapters of thematic and contrapuntal discourse were inspired by the narration in the documentary films *The Plow That Broke the Plains* (1936) and *The*

River (1937) by Pare Lorentz, a friend of Steinbeck's. Whatever the merit of these speculations, it is certainly true that the novel contains a substantial amount of contemporary sociopolitical description, analysis, and argumentation: it is not simply the tragic drama of the Joad family, but an epic narrative of one of the largest mass migrations in American history.

Steinbeck seized on the movement westward to recast journalism into an archetypal mold. With the trek from the dustbowl to the fruitful fields of California he invokes both the American myth of the wagon-train pioneers and the biblical myth of the flight of the homeless and persecuted Israelites from Egypt to Canaan—and both myths he cruelly subverts. The frontier territories are already occupied; the land of milk and honey withholds its offerings from newcomers. And contained in this irony is the political meaning of the novel: the Okies reach California to find ranged against them very familiar antagonists—the banks and corporate landholders that had tractored them off their lands in the Midwest. In the ensuing class conflict lies the dynamic thrust of the narrative.

There is a certain conservative element in Steinbeck's presentation of this conflict, in his heavy emphasis on the family as social unit and his nostalgic harking back to a Jeffersonian agrarianism predating the mechanization of farming. More predominant, however, are the book's left-wing implications, ranging ideologically from New Deal liberalism to revolutionary socialism.

Steinbeck strongly endorses federal government intervention to ease the plight of the migrants in the idyllic Weedpatch camp interlude. But to reverse the present exploitative and repressive power relationships will, he implies, take more than well-meant palliatives. The radical alternative is suggested in the book's repeated and scathing attacks on the ethos of business. ("Them sons-a-bitches at their desks," Muley characteristically remarks apropos the dispossession of the tenant farmers, "they jus' chopped folks in two for their margin a profit.") It is also implicit in the novel's celebration of solidarity and grass-roots democracy (for example, chapter 17), and its dark prophecies of the explosive change to come:

And the great owners, who had become through their holdings both more and less than men, ran to their destruction, and used every means that in the long run would destroy them. Every little means, every violence . . . cemented the inevitability of the day.

Darryl F. Zanuck, production chief at Twentieth Century-Fox, purchased the movie rights to *The Grapes of Wrath* in May, 1939, making it, as it turned out, the most expensive cinematic property that year.[1] Zanuck personally produced the film, assigning Fox scenarist-producer Nunnally Johnson to write the script and John Ford, under contract at Fox, to direct. Despite pressure on the studio and its controlling bank, the Chase National in New York, to kill the production, Zanuck continued unperturbed, declaring that the book was ". . . a stirring indictment of conditions which I think are a disgrace and ought to be remedied." [2]

The screenplay, which was contractually bound to preserve the theme of the novel, was approved by Steinbeck on August 8. Ford pressed for, and was granted, Henry Fonda in the lead role of Tom Joad—over Fox contract players Don Ameche or Tyrone Power; in return he was forced to accept studio regular Jane Darwell as Ma, though he would have preferred Beulah Bondi. Shooting took place over a seven-week period beginning September 28. Principal photography was carried out at the studio, while a second Unit under Otto Brower took location shots along Highway 66, going as far as Texas and Oklahoma.

The film was edited swiftly under the personal supervision of Zanuck (Ford entrusted the editing of all his Fox films to his boss), and was premiered on January 24, 1940, to extraordinarily favorable reviews. The picture ultimately won two Academy Awards: Ford took Best Direction and Darwell was honored as Best Supporting Actress.

At the box office the film did well (though not as well as expected in rural areas) and became Twentieth Century-Fox's most profitable production in a bad year for the studio. In Cali-

[1] For facts about the production of the film I am indebted to research by Rebecca Pulliam published in *The Velvet Light Trap*, No. 2, 1971.

[2] Quoted in J. P. McEvoy's "He's Got Something," *Saturday Evening Post*, July 1, 1939.

fornia, release of *The Grapes of Wrath* spurred at least one mass meeting—at which cast members appeared—to discuss the plight of the migrant agricultural workers.

Unquestionably the driving force behind the production was Zanuck. As executive producer at Warner Brothers earlier in the decade, he had pioneered the "social exposé" genre with films on such subjects as the exploitation of Southern share-croppers (*Cabin in the Cotton* [1932]) and injustice and brutality in the penal system (*I Am a Fugitive from a Chain Gang* [1932]). After *The Grapes of Wrath,* Zanuck would return later in the 1940s to films of social consciousness with *Gentleman's Agreement* (1947), about anti-Semitism, *The Snake Pit* (1949), treatment of mental illness, and *Pinky* (1949), racial prejudice.

A Republican—he campaigned for Wendell Willkie in 1940— Zanuck was nevertheless friendly with Franklin Roosevelt and had a zeal for social activism unusual among Hollywood tycoons. Elia Kazan, who directed *Gentleman's Agreement, Pinky,* and Steinbeck's *Viva Zapata!* (1952) for him, commented in *Kazan on Kazan* (1974):

> Zanuck was always a man of the people. If anything was being felt, he felt it. He was a very good geiger-counter. He lay over the society and when things began to move, he noticed them. He was a man of liberal instincts, more than intellect.

His influence was no doubt felt mostly in the preparation of the screenplay: a writer himself, Zanuck was accustomed to spend several hours a day in script conferences. One can surmise that he was committed to faithfully translating Steinbeck's work to the screen insofar as it was an exposure of a social problem amenable to reformist solution—and that he was not at all sympathetic to those aspects of the novel which hinted at a revolutionary alternative to the American capitalist system. An examination of the screenplay bears out this hypothesis: the effect of Nunnally Johnson's distillation of the novel into a simplified, linear narrative is to preserve Steinbeck's outrage at the miserable fate of the Okies while muting the book's radical implications.

Tom Joad (Henry Fonda), Ma Joad (Jane Darwell), and Rosasharn
(Dorris Bowdon) stopped in their truck. *The Grapes of Wrath* (1940)

The most striking omission, of course, is most of the material in the intercalary chapters, in which Steinbeck generalizes the narrative beyond the particular experience of the Joads and articulates more directly his political concerns. The chapters deal with topics scarcely touched on in the film, such as the cheating of desperate migrants by used-car salesmen, the growth of revolutionary solidarity among the dispossessed, communal living at the roadside camps, the evolution of California agriculture into large-scale industry, and the dumping of food "surpluses."

The Joad story itself is drastically pruned. Characters such as the Wilsons, who join forces with the Joads on the road, are lost; family members like Grampa, Granma, Al, Noah, and Uncle John become caricatures or marginal, shadowy figures (Noah actually disappears halfway through the film without anyone remarking on his absence); and the elements in the novel of bawdy comedy and religious satire are dropped. The effect of this surgery, while only indirectly relevant to the film's political stance, is to focus attention even more narrowly on the personal drama of Ma and Tom, negating Steinbeck's constant reminders that the evicted tenant farmers numbered in the hundreds of thousands, with the potential of building a class-based movement.

Another significant modification is the inversion of the order of the government camp and peach ranch sequences. As George Bluestone has pointed out in *Novels into Film* (1957), this simple expedient serves to temper considerably the impact of the story. Instead of experiencing the relief of a federally-sponsored haven soon after their arrival in California only to be rudely returned to the realities of a cruelly exploitative capitalist economy, the Joads find shelter in the government camp toward the *end* of the film. Basically, then, the California experience traces an optimistic, upward trajectory, while that in the novel moves downward into desperation.

Consistent with this, the screenplay curtails the story so as to omit in its entirety the tragic finale. Gone is the episode in which the Joads go cotton-picking and are flooded out, in which Rosasharn gives birth to a stillborn child, and the family is reduced to total destitution. Omitted, of course, is the notorious final incident of Rosasharn's giving her breast to a starving man.

The unsettling effect of the novel's ending was integral, Steinbeck felt, to his conception: he told his editor, who had suggested changing it, "I am not writing a satisfying story. I've done my damndest to rip a reader's nerves to rags, I don't want him satisfied. . . ."[3] At the end of the film, in quite a different mood, what is left of the family heads north for twenty days' work and Ma Joad affirms her mystic faith in the enduring qualities of "the people":

> Rich fellas come up, an' they die, an' their kids ain't no good, an *they* die out, but we keep a-comin'. We're the people that live. They can't wipe us out, they can't lick us. We'll go on forever Pa, 'cause we're the people.

It is a speech which is extracted almost verbatim from an earlier section of the novel, but there it has a different context and none of the emphasis that its placement in the film lends it.

The script, which the film follows closely, does retain political ingredients most unusual for Hollywood. These include the incident in which Floyd, the Hooverville "agitator," is almost arrested on an obviously phoney charge for explaining the law about labor contracting; the action of a deputy sheriff in firing his gun wildly and injuring a woman bystander; the lengthy discussion between Preacher Casy and Tom about the ranch-owners' tactics in strike-breaking and cutting wages; and the murder of Casy, in his role of labor leader, by vigilantes. Paradoxically, it is these elements which were probably least congenial to director John Ford. An examination of Ford's substantial oeuvre suggests that contemporary social drama was quite foreign to his temperament. In a large proportion of his films there is a *distancing*, whether in space (his movies set in China, the Pacific Islands, Ireland, Africa, Mexico, etc.) or in time (his Westerns and period melodramas). Pervaded by a sense of loss, his work is backward-looking; it is no surprise that his study of New England city politics, *The Last Hurrah* (1958), is an epitaph to an obsolescent style of campaigning, or that his

[3] *Steinbeck: A Life in Letters*, edited by Elaine Steinbeck and Robert Wallsten (1975).

Aunt Jemima-like Negroes for *Pinky* impelled Zanuck to replace him and scrap his footage.

Ideologically, Ford was a conservative populist, and in his movies he gave vivid realization to a vision of a traditional, communal way of life which perhaps never existed at all outside his imagination. He was drawn to stories centered on the family and its tenuous survival in the face of outside forces (war, industrialization) threatening its very existence: his popular silent *Four Sons* (1928) recounts the life of a Bavarian mother who loses three of her boys in the Great War and is eventually reunited with the fourth in America; his *How Green Was My Valley* (1941) deals with the destruction of a Welsh family in a mining village transformed and ultimately ruined by the indiscriminate application of new techniques. His feeling for imperiled communities is evidenced again in *Cheyenne Autumn* (1964) in which a whole people is displaced, forced to trek across the country, harassed continually by the authorities.

It was clearly similar thematic concerns in *The Grapes of Wrath* which attracted Ford to the project. He told Peter Bogdanovich:

> I just liked it, that's all. I'd read the book—it was a good story—and Darryl Zanuck had a good script on it. The whole thing appealed to me—being about simple people—and the story was similar to the famine in Ireland, when they threw the people off the land and left them wandering on the roads to starve.[4]

It is an interesting comment, for it reveals the extent to which Ford viewed the Okies in a metaphorical perspective; in its reference to "simple people" it hints at the source of the "folksy" qualities in the film, and in particular its sentimental idealization of Ma.

Steinbeck's Ma, it must be admitted, looms at times larger than life, she whose "hazel eyes seemed to have experienced all possible tragedy and to have mounted pain and suffering like steps into a high calm and a superhuman understanding." Yet for the most part she is drawn in more prosaic terms, and she

[4] *John Ford* (1968), p. 76.

emerges with an astringency clearly not in keeping with Ford's conception of the character. The script called for a scene, based on an incident in the novel, in which Ma brandishes a jackhandle in a ferocious assertion of her authority over Pa. The scene is missing from the film, and it is hard to imagine Jane Darwell's dignified Okie materfamilias ever acting in so violent a fashion. In ideological terms the metamorphosis is significant—what in the novel is a fierce resistance to the breakup of the family becomes in the film a passive resignation to the vagaries of fate.

Ford certainly tries to evoke pathos in his presentation of Ma, but the limitations of the script undercut his attempts. About three-quarters of the way through the film she delivers a speech to Tom which Ford shoots in a single take, a minute and forty seconds long. "They was a time when we was on the lan'," it begins. "They was a boundary to us then. Ol' folks died off, an' little fellas come. She was always one thing—we was the fambly —kinda whole and clear. . . ." The speech, which goes on to detail what is happening to each member of the family, is drawn almost word for word from the novel, but the emotional charge which Ford seeks to extract from it here is unearned, since we do not *know* the family, we have not *seen* its disintegration. Al's restlessness has, in the film, hardly been hinted at. Uncle John's neurotic obsession with sin and the past has not been documented, nor has his periodic compulsion to go on a bender. He is simply a face. Of Pa we have seen little more. Ruthie and Winfield, whom Ma speaks of as "growin' up wild . . . jus' like animals," are just a couple of lively, healthy kids awed by flush toilets and the thought of manbones in the desert. The tremulous tones of Darwell's delivery, heightened by the unmoving camera, ring hollow with forced rhetoric.

To other scenes with Ma, however, Ford imparts a dramatic intensity that is quite genuine. One example is Ma silently consigning mementoes to the flames prior to setting out for California, and picturing herself with the earrings of her youth; another is Ma handing the scrapings of the stew pot to ragged, hungry kids in the Hooverville camp. Most moving, perhaps, is her dance at the Saturday night hoedown. The scene as conceived by Steinbeck is a celebration of communal living climaxed by a demonstration of strength in solidarity with the efficient thwarting of the vigilante plot. The film faithfully dramatizes the action as written, yet the emotional appeal of the episode rests on a moment which is pure Ford, prefigured in neither the novel nor the screenplay. Ma dances with Tom, her face suffused with a rare joy which gradually turns to sorrow as Tom sings "Red River Valley"—". . . and the boy who has loved you so true"—and the pain of their coming inevitable separation is evoked with immensely understated power. In the tenderness and intimacy of this dance there is expressed a private world view far removed from the epic sociology of Steinbeck and the reformist ardor of Zanuck.

Given this disparity of vision, it is remarkable how accurately in many respects the film does capture the spirit of the novel. This is true particularly of the casting and acting. John Qualen's Muley, John Carradine's Casy, Russell Simpson's Pa are all vivid incarnations of the Steinbeck originals, but it is of course Henry Fonda who is outstanding. Various aspects of the Fonda persona converged in the creation of his Tom Joad: the working-class protagonist (telephone lineman in *Slim*, 1937), the freedom fighter (anti-Fascist combatant in *Blockade* [1938]), the common man in search of justice (Lincoln as trial lawyer in *Young Mr. Lincoln* [1939]). In his controlled belligerence and his brash candor, Fonda projects an intensely felt moral anger that is perfect for the part.

Visually, *The Grapes of Wrath* impressed at the time of its release with its "documentary" look. Steinbeck himself found this the source of the movie's strength; he wrote (in a letter to Elizabeth Otis):

> Zanuck has more than kept his word. He has a hard, straight picture in which the actors are submerged so completely that it looks and feels like a documentary film and certainly it has a hard, truthful ring. No punches were pulled—in fact, with descriptive matter removed, it is a harsher thing than the book, by far. It seems unbelievable but it is true.

Within the context of Hollywood production in the 1930s and early 1940s, the reaction is understandable. At a time when location photography was rare, the film does show us the real Highway 66; and it does have a cast of minor players with only one star. Gregg Toland's lighting is largely naturalistic—in strong contrast, for example, to his romantic mood-painting in *Wuthering Heights* (1939) or his dramatic deep focus in *Citizen Kane* (1941). The sets have the weatherbeaten look and the poky scale of the real tents and shacks the Okies lived in, and the actors wear no make-up. Yet, as the more perceptive contemporary critics noted, this genuflection toward a documentary style is hardly adequate to convey the true sweep of Steinbeck's novel.

Thus Edwin Locke, who was a scriptwriter for Pare Lorentz, commented:

> The opening of the picture is greatly weakened because he has given us no feeling of the country or of the people's background. Where are the vast stretches of the dustbowl and the tiny houses as lonely as ships at sea? Where is the dust? . . . It is baffling to hear that a camera crew was sent into Oklahoma along Route 66; certainly but a few feet of their film was used. It is regrettable that the Joads were snatched across the beautiful and terrifying expanses of the country in a few pans and process shots; we could justly have expected more. We could have expected more of what it is like to be tractored off the land, more than the knocking over of a prop house by a Caterpillar roaming at large, more than a hackneyed montage of clanking monsters in abstract maneuvers.[5]

Deficient in its imagery of the dustbowl, the film also fails to evoke the complementary fertility of California, "the vineyards, the orchards, the great flat valley, green and beautiful, the trees set in rows, and the farm houses. . . . The peach trees and the walnut groves, and the dark green patches of oranges." We are never shown the Joads actually *working* picking fruit or cotton.

To most critics in 1940, though, it was enough of a miracle that *The Grapes of Wrath* had been brought to the screen without being travestied in the process. One can grant the enthusiasm accorded the film in the heat of the historical moment, while noting that today it seems a less than adequate rendition of Steinbeck's sprawling epic. The book, primarily radical in its

[5] *Films*, vol. 1, no. 2, 1940, pp. 49–55.

political analysis, is rich and ambiguous enough to sustain both reformist and conservative readings—but whether a mixture of the two can work is open to question. The distance between Zanuck and Ford, which could be mistaken at the time for a fertile creative tension, now seems a clash of mutually incompatible temperaments. *The Grapes of Wrath* tries to be both exposé and elegy, and doesn't quite come off as either.

Two Planetary Systems

BY ROBERT ALDRIDGE

In an unfortunate metaphor in *The New Yorker*, August 3, 1968, Penelope Gilliatt described the film of *The Heart Is a Lonely Hunter* as a hippopotamus which had swallowed a tiny, shining minnow, Carson McCullers' prized 1940 novel. The minnow is obviously the hero of the metaphor; the hippo is the villain. But the conception is inaccurate about who is ingesting whom. The book contains a far wider and more complex range of theme, plot, and characterization, as well as McCullers' undeniable genius. The motion picture is more modest in range and is devoid of even claim to genius, except perhaps the acting of Alan Arkin. If either has been swallowed up, it is surely this nearly forgotten 1968 film. Yet, as shall be discussed, the movie of *The Heart Is a Lonely Hunter* deserves respect—as a quiet, principled complement to McCullers' vision rather than as the animalist antagonist of Gilliatt's tortured formulation.

Originally called *The Mute*, the novel *The Heart Is a Lonely Hunter* appeared in 1940 to almost universal applause. The critics agreed that here was a sizable talent and that McCullers's insights into human suffering were far beyond her twenty-three years. Klaus Mann (son of Thomas Mann) referred to the book as "the melancholy novel by that strange girl, Carson McCullers. . . . An abysmal sadness yet remarkably devoid of sentimentality. Rather grim and concise. What astounding insight into the ultimate inconsolability and incurability of the human soul." He described Carson McCullers herself as "uncannily versed in the secret of all freaks and pariahs. . . ." [1]

McCullers's book places a series of interrelated stories within the frame tale of deaf-mute John Singer's intense devotion to another deaf-mute, Spiros Antonopalous, who has the mind and temperament of a child. Spiros must be committed to an institution, where eventually he dies. Deprived of his reason for living, Singer commits suicide. Within this frame are the lives of four major characters touched by Singer: Mick Kelly, a lonely adolescent girl; Biff Brannon, a cafe owner who is widowed early in the novel; Jake Blount, a roving revolutionary outraged over the oppression of laborers by capitalist bosses; and Dr. Copeland, a black physician who has struggled bitterly throughout his career to inspire other blacks to rise from their oppression.

The essential tension between the outer and inner stories is that Singer actually has found meaning in his life (Antonopalous) before losing it: the others seek endlessly for the resolution of sweeping social conflicts (Jake and Dr. Copeland) or for self-fulfillment and identity (Mick and Biff). But because they never learn of the Singer-Antonopalous relationship—it is a tale without words—the message of Singer's suicide remains a puzzle to them. Even though Biff Brannon realizes in a flash of revelation that "love" is the hope of man, none of the characters has grasped the secret lesson of the deaf-mute who passed through their lives.

The 1968 filmmakers faced an ominous task in making *The Heart Is a Lonely Hunter*. Screenwriter Thomas C. Ryan, producers Marc Nelson and Joel Freeman, and director Robert Ellis Miller had to consider the twenty-eight year difference in milieu, the large cast of characters (there are at least thirteen developed personages in the novel, in addition to a sizable supporting cast), and McCullers's multitude of orbital themes surrounding her central one (to be discussed later). The result was perhaps the best it could be—a more tightly focused story which omits most of the 1930s topicality (except for the race issue) but

[1] Virginia Spencer Carr, *The Lonely Hunter: A Biography of Carson McCullers* (1975), p. 100.

which retains much of the lyricism and, most important, the central theme of the book: that individual human communication based upon love and compassion is the most powerful of weapons.

Characterization: The young girl Mick is the dominant character in both novel and film. She grows and changes as a character in both, pushing toward maturation and adulthood, and there are unmistakable parallels between her and her creator Carson McCullers (for example, the love of music and the sensitive and yearning nature). But it is John Singer who provides a center of gravity for the orbiting characters in their various quests. He provides the key to the relationship between characters and plot, though in the novel he occupies less narrative space than Mick.

The Singer of the novel is both close to and removed from the other characters. He cares for Mick, Jake, Biff, and Dr. Copeland as people, and he can feel their deep unhappiness. But he cannot understand the full meaning of their lonely quests. In his letter to Antonopalous (who, of course, cannot read), he describes the others: about Jake he says, "The one with the mustache I think is crazy. . . . He thinks he and I have a secret together but I do not know what it is"; about Dr. Copeland he says, "This black man frightens me sometimes. His eyes are hot and bright. . . . He has many books"; about Mick he says, "She is not yet a young lady. . . . She likes music. I wish I knew what it is she hears"; and about Biff, "He watches. . . . Aha, says the owner of the New York Cafe. He is a thoughtful one." (This last statement is prophetic, for after Singer's death, it is Biff who senses the significance of the Singer-Antonopalous relationship without really knowing that it even existed.)

By contrast, the Singer of the film—played by Alan Arkin—has a more personal relationship to the major characters who revolve about him. He shares their loneliness. He is, as in the novel, a listener; but he is also more than that, he is a friend to each: Mick, Dr. Copeland, Jake. And Mick and Dr. Copeland, at least, know more about him than they do in the novel. They realize his isolation (Mick especially) and they offer mutual comfort.

The relationships that Singer has established provide, by their rapport, for the best scenes of the film, all without parallel mo-

John Singer (Alan Arkin) descends from a bus on his way to visit fellow deaf-mute Antonopalous. *The Heart Is a Lonely Hunter* (1968)

ments in the novel. Perhaps the finest sequence in the picture occurs when Mick suddenly realizes that Singer is as lonely as she is. She attempts to share her love of music with him by standing before the phonograph and conducting. She talks to Mr. Singer with her hands, instead of her lips; and though he does not grasp the rhythms of music, he understands her physical expressions of compassion. Another excellent scene is the one in which Dr. Copeland shows Singer the x-ray which conveys to Dr. Copeland news of his own impending death; but it is not because of his x-ray or his words, but because of his poignant facial expressions and physical gestures that Singer understands that the doctor will die.

Other characters are missing from the film. The black characters orbiting Dr. Copeland have been homogenized into a nearly silent mass—all save Portia, his daughter, and Willie, Portia's simple-minded, accepting, gentle husband. The pharmacist Marshall Nicolls (soft-spoken, polite acquaintance of Copeland, neither revolutionary nor Uncle Tom) is gone; perhaps he would have done little for the film, which is, at 124 minutes, a rather long one. But more important, the tragically fated Lancy Davis has been removed. His militancy and bitterness lifted him above the other blacks of the novel, and his meaningless, untimely death added the hardest strokes of pathos. Of all absent characters, he is perhaps the most sorely missed in the film. Unless, that is, one considers Biff Brannon, reduced here to a background role, a "missing character."

Even before the death of his wife Alice in the novel (she is missing from the film), Biff is perhaps the most desolate character of all. His unrequited love for Mick and his sad realization that she has changed and moved away from him are among the most heartfelt elements in the novel. Biff's almost androgynous personality—in contrast to his rough appearance he enjoys pretty things and domestic duties—establishes a parallel with the tomboy Mick, but one that is never carried through in personal terms. But in the film a character named Biff Brannon appears merely as the owner of the New York Cafe (without Alice, his sister-in-law Lucille, and his niece Baby Wilson, all from the novel) and as a "freak fancier" who is kind to Singer. But in a sense

Biff's identity is not missing from the movie: he is merged with his soul-mate Mick. She alone carries the burden of the quest for fulfillment and meaning in the film version. And it is Mick who articulates the theme, although she may not know it, when she utters her epilogue over the grave of Singer.

There are three other important characters who are changed significantly in the film: Dr. Copeland, Portia, and Jake Blount. Benedict Mady Copeland and Jake Blount are restless, bitter, probably doomed characters in the novel. Dr. Copeland, hopelessly tubercular, drives himself relentlessly, despite illness, in his effort to pull the Negroes up out of despair and degradation. Jake cannot avoid violence in his frustrated struggle against capitalist exploitation—he is both outwardly and inwardly destructive. Both remain pitiably isolated in the novel. Because of their single-mindedness and strident zeal, neither can communicate with the other, and neither sees his dreams come to fruition: Dr. Copeland is moved to the country by his own family, probably to die. And Jake, as has apparently been his life pattern, vanishes from the scene, violence on his heels, heading perhaps toward more violence.

In the film, Dr. Copeland's fate is rather definite: he knows he will die soon, and he has time to prepare. He also has the friendship and sympathy of Singer; and through Singer's friendship, this proud black man—tempestuous and driven like Lear and culturally alienated like Shylock—is reunited with his daughter, whom he named Portia. This, it would seem, makes for a much more optimistic ending: some frustrated dreams, yes, and a too early death; but also reconciliation and peace.

Jake is much less realized as a film character. As in McCullers's novel, he is a secretive, bitter, violent man, although we learn less of his past and of the nature of his quest. He vanishes quite early in the film (not until the end of the novel), having provided a touch of humor, some insight into Singer, and a look at the brutal nature of racism, but never seeming to merge with the core idea of the film. He is almost, as he quotes the judge, "irrelevant and immaterial."

And then, Portia. It is tempting to say that the character was changed to suit the talents of Cicely Tyson: it is difficult to imagine Tyson as the religious, stoically accepting Portia of the novel, who says after Willie's mutilation, "Nothing us could do would make no difference. Best thing we can do is keep our mouth shut." And after Mick says she wishes she could kill the men who did it: "that ain't no Christian way to talk. . . . Us can just rest back and know they going to be chopped up with pitchforks and fried everlasting by Satan." Obviously, the Portia of the film is quite different: bitter, strong-minded, capable of intense love and loyalty and also of hatred. The harsh scenes in which she relates Willie's mutilation and in which she promises her father that she will learn to despise him are particularly illustrative of her changed, outspoken screen character. Willie merges the Willie (her brother) and the Highboy (her husband) of the book; but the effect is the same simple, uneducated innocence, working against the worldly, knowledgeable Portias of both versions.

Plot Structure: The important question becomes: what is the major difference in the overall plot structures? In McCullers's novel, the central, solar figure of Singer is orbited by two pairs of planets: each pair is bound in trajectory by parallel characterization; first, there are the two inner planets Mick and Biff, inner because they are representative of the lonely quest for beauty and meaning and therefore closest to the emotional nature of Singer (whose only drive in life is to love); and second, there are the outer planets, Jake and Dr. Copeland, outer because their quest is for social justice, in terms of masses of people and generalized ideologies. Neither pair is successful in altering their paths to achieve the goal, or one might say grail, of their quest. Yet each pair senses some central core of meaning radiating from Singer, something *beyond* the quest—akin to it perhaps, but overwhelmingly simple and more beautiful.

In the film we find another planetary system—Singer again as sun; but instead of paired planets in each orbit, we now have individual planets revolving about him: Mick, Dr. Copeland, Jake. It is not simply the overwhelming performance of Alan Arkin which lends this great importance to the character of Singer (an idea suggested by numerous critics); it is the plot structure itself which makes the character so pivotal.

In Mick he arouses sympathy and a deepened understanding of the suffering of others (again—the scene with the phonograph). In Jake he fosters a sense of confidence and sensitivity to those directly around him (at least a need to notice his own irrelevance). And he lightens the bitterness of Dr. Copeland and brings him together with Portia.

In both versions the episodes are tightly bound together: in the novel by the parallel characterizations and by characters who link more than one line of action (such as Portia, Biff, and Mick, whose lives touch on several quests), and in the film—in addition to the powerful gravital force of Singer—by meaningful joining of episodes through transitional devices, primarily strategic uses of the dissolve to link the various personages. Two examples: (1) the dissolve from the scene of Mick conducting the record for Singer to a deaf-mute black boy on the porch, with Singer acting as sign-language interpreter (hence, the connection made by linking two scenes of nonverbal communication), and (2) the dissolve from the stunning brightness of the blank x-ray screen in Copeland's office to the hot summer sky above the creek bank where Mick has her first sexual encounter (two scenes depicting the transition from illusion to reality).

Milieu: The novel bristles with the major issues of the late Depression in the United States and the growing possibility of war in Europe. Poverty, bigotry, Marxism, anti-Semitism, Fascism— these were the issues when the book appeared, and should they be less significant twenty-eight years later in 1968? Of these themes, racial bigotry *was* considered by the filmmakers to be of paramount importance, hence Dr. Copeland remains a key ideological figure in the film, just as he had been in the novel. The year 1968 was marked by the assassination of Dr. Martin Luther King, and some of this movie was filmed in the town he made famous, Selma, Alabama.

But the other topics were considered passé or irrelevant by Hollywood in 1968, at least when compared with the urgency with which Carson McCullers had treated them. So Harry Minnowitz becomes, in the screen version, a handsome Southern white, instead of the restless Southern Jew of the novel who is eager to be off to the new war and kill Hitler. His chief function in the film is to introduce Mick to the world of dating and then, with almost contradictory innocence, to that favorite topic of fiction and film: the first sexual experience.

Labor reform, too, had no real place in this 1968 film. It was *the* central injustice of Jake Blount's world view in the book; Jake's near-religious zeal for a revolution among the proletariat could not radiate as much power in a film made during the period of the greatest prosperity workers in America had (or have) ever enjoyed. His words from the novel would connote something very different in 1968: "The only solution is for the people to *know*," he tells Dr. Copeland, "Once they know the truth they can be oppressed no longer." He means one kind of truth, obviously, in 1940; but there would be a different kind of truth in the era of George Meany, James Hoffa, Lyndon Johnson, and the Great Society.

And what about the South? Jake Blount's "strangled . . . wasted . . . slavish South" of the late Depression, the South that Carson McCullers knew firsthand, has become in the film a scenic background, a shallow movie set. Southern accents are amusing, and the stereotypes predictable, timid, and unserious. Even the cynical, insensate sheriff of the novel has lost any pretense to other than verbal cruelty in the film. (Dr. Copeland is beaten and jailed in the novel when he insists upon seeing the judge. In the film he is only ridiculed and tricked.) Of race prejudice there remains the racially motivated mutilation of Willie, though reduced from the loss of both feet to the loss of one leg. Through the vehicle of Cicely Tyson's compelling portrayal of Portia, in which she exhibits a rare gift for combining a steely dignity with bitter indignation, all the dread and repulsion of this act of unspeakable brutality are preserved intact from the novel. This is "reported violence" of the finest kind, reminiscent of speeches of harrowing off-stage deaths in Greek tragedy. The bigotry, then, is the only truly Southern theme in the film; and so Dr. Copeland and Portia and Willie and the sheriff are the only truly Southern characters. Except for those funny accents and passing stereotypes, the other characters are universals: a change in speech patterns could place them in Iowa, Colorado, California, or New England.

And what of the anti-Semitism and Fascism? Neither had vanished from the land or the world in 1968, but the treatment of both in the novel had been so closely tied to Hitler, Mussolini, and the war that reintegration in the film would have been clumsy and inappropriate. The same is true of repeating the deeply felt anti-Fascist sentiment of the 1940 novel.

Poverty was one key issue in the milieu of the novel which was transferred almost *per se* to the film, but the transition is a shaky one. Mick does not seem to be the daughter in a desperately poor family. For one thing, in McCullers's book there are other boarders in the house and their presence is mandatory for the survival of the Kelly family. And there is the Baby Wilson episode—when Mick's brother Bubber has shot Baby in the head with his pellet gun and the family must deplete whatever small financial security they have to pay the medical costs. There is also the general novelistic framework of the Depression, which lends instant credibility to financial deprivation. But the Kelly family in the film enjoys sway over their rather spacious domain (a house which most Americans of 1968 might welcome for personal living space). In addition, Mick's position in the society of the little town is misleading—she mingles with the elite as though there were no other difference than a little money. In short, it seems unconvincing that Mick must drop out of school to help the family to continue on.

The book's Marxist motif (which originates with Dr. Copeland and his attempts to educate the poor blacks about Marx's ideas) predictably is missing from the film. There is no mention of the fact that Dr. Copeland has a child named Karl Marx, and the image of him as teacher is absent. So too is the marvelous Christmas scene from the novel and Dr. Copeland's Christmas lecture: "It is natural for us to share with each other. We have long realized that it is more blessed to give than to receive. The words of Karl Marx have always been known in our hearts: 'From each according to his ability, to each according to his needs.'" This speech in the film might have established one interesting and pungent parallel between two decades, a parallel to Dr. King's social concerns perhaps; but Dr. King's message was democratic reform, not Marxist class warfare. And to change

Dr. Copeland to suit the parallel would have required bold liberties.

But what is the effect of all this rearrangement of topicality? The proposition here is that the filmmakers were, in the main, right in their decision to emphasize the race issue above all and to concentrate most heavily upon Mick's quest for beauty and meaning in a puzzling, lonely universe and Singer's silent answer to that quest—love.

Revelation of Theme: There is a sense of rushing at the end of both the novel and the film, with theme coalescing rapidly. In the novel all flies asunder at the suicide of Singer; the center of gravity is released with awesome suddenness and simplicity by McCullers (reminiscent of E. A. Robinson's "Richard Cory"): "Then when he had washed the ash tray and the glass he brought out a pistol from his pocket and put a bullet in his chest." In the film the rising tempo begins earlier, with the departure of Jake Blount, and continues through Dr. Copeland's revelation to Portia of his approaching death, the financial collapse of Mick's family, her loss of innocence, the death of Antonapalous, and the suicide of Singer, which is portrayed with much the same suddenness and deliberateness as in the novel.

Both use epilogues to drive home their points: in the book McCullers carries us through the full course of a single day a month after Singer's funeral (in August, 1939—significantly, the month before Hitler's invasion of Poland and the beginning of World War II). In a section called "Morning," we see the departure of Dr. Copeland for the country and for eventual death. In "Afternoon," we witness the flight of Jake Blount from the violence which has cost the life of Lancy Davis. And in "Evening," we behold the terrible epiphany of Biff Brannon, alone in his New York Cafe, listening to the radio from which he hears only mystifying and ominous foreign voices:

Then suddenly he felt a quickening in him. . . . For in a swift radiance of illumination he saw a glimpse of human struggle and of valor. Of the endless fluid passage of humanity through endless time. And of those who labor and of those who—one word—love. His soul expanded. But for a moment only. . . . For in him he felt a warning, a shaft of terror. And he was suspended between radiance and darkness. Between bitter irony and faith. Sharply he turned away.

The epilogue of the film takes place in the cemetery beside Singer's grave. Dr. Copeland (who is still practicing in the town) and Mick meet and ponder the mystery of Singer's death. Then Mick is left alone at the grave. She, too, is suspended between two worlds: she does not understand the enigmatic sadness of life as it has been revealed to her during the course of this one summer. But she seems to realize the secret power of Singer, the one word which Biff saw in his flash of revelation in the novel. And it is she now who articulates the central theme of both book and film when she says, "I loved you, Mr. Singer. I loved you."

The theme of love—individual love—is preserved, then, realized by Biff Brannon in the novel, Mick Kelly in the film. It is this singular love between people which can transcend the misery of living, which can supply meaning and purpose in the midst of the chaos of war, oppression, and violence. But even this love is transitory, and the misery is still there. For McCullers *and* her adaptors, the heart remains a lonely hunter.

Native Son (1940)

Richard Wright

Two Wrights, One Wrong

BY PETER BRUNETTE

When Richard Wright's brilliant and angry *Native Son* appeared in March, 1940, it created a phenomenal stir. The trade edition alone sold two hundred thousand copies within three weeks of publication, confirming the Book-of-the-Month Club's wisdom in choosing the novel as its first main selection by a black writer.

The story must also have seemed a natural for the movies. It concerns an ignorant, frustrated Chicago black, Bigger Thomas, who accidentally smothers the beautiful daughter of his rich white employer because he is afraid of being discovered in her bedroom. Trying desperately to cover his tracks, he burns her body in the furnace, and—after a feeble attempt to extort ransom money—he flees, only to be captured after a relentless manhunt. The final section of the book consists of his trial (always a favorite film scene), the humanitarian arguments of his white Communist lawyer, and his ultimate conviction. All the raw elements for good cinema were there—and it was serious fiction to boot!

Richard Wright was himself an avid filmgoer, who often saw two or three movies a day, and conceived of his novel largely in cinematic terms. In "How Bigger Was Born," a 1941 essay for the *Saturday Review* he noted:

For the most part the novel is rendered in the present; I wanted the reader to feel that Bigger's story was happening *now*, like a

play upon the stage or a movie. . . . Action follows action. . . .
Wherever possible, I told of Bigger's life in close-up, slow-motion,
giving the feel of the grain in the passing of time . . . this was the
best way to "enclose" the reader's mind in a new world, to blot
out all reality except that which I was giving him.

Wright's goal was to put his literate and liberal audience
(white and black) so thoroughly into Bigger's shoes as to force
them to transcend mere humanist intellectualizing about the
"Negro problem." Aiming to "blot out all reality" except Bigger's
immediate experience, Wright adopted *filmic* strategies—uti-
lizing cinema's ability to focus the viewer's attention, to exclude
the extraneous, to serve up a never-ending stream of new narrative information which prevents immediate rumination. What
Wright wanted was heightened feeling, preintellectual understanding that would *change* the reader by forcing him to perceive unpleasant reality in strange new ways.

By keeping his focus fastened uncompromisingly on his in-
articulate, criminal hero, Wright pulled off a major tour de force.
The literary audience, which sees nothing of the world of *Native
Son* except what is filtered through the consciousness of Bigger
Thomas, becomes emotionally entwined in the fate of this young
man, who is, objectively, a brutal, sadistic (and black) killer.
The murder of the rich white girl—for whose family he works as a
chauffeur—is accidental, but her death is the only logical outcome of Bigger's hatred of his white oppressor. Even more disturbing for the reader is the realization that the greatest crimes
against morality result, in a life as cruelly warped as Bigger's,
in an undeniable blossoming of freedom and selfhood.

Wright also wanted to head off the liberal reaction of pity for
the "poor little ghetto kid" not responsible for his antisocial acts.
To circumvent such facile sympathy, he has Bigger chop off
Mary Dalton's head with an axe, cremate her in the family furnace, try to extort money from the worried family, and later
smash in the head of his black girlfriend with a brick. This last
atrocity comes about because she is infringing on Bigger's newly
discovered "freedom" with her great need to be loved.

It is precisely this ultimate ambiguity, the creative tension of attraction/repulsion we feel toward the protagonist, which makes *Native Son* such a powerful novel. While Wright wanted us, through a profound identification with Bigger, to experience in some small way the torment of being black in a racist society, he refused to make his hero pleasing and acceptable, certainly nothing like a Sidney Poitier with straight A's at Harvard Medical School.

For nearly ten years, Wright spurned Hollywood's eager approach to *Native Son*, for he imagined all too vividly what certain schlock merchants could do to his book. Typical was a 1947 offer from producer Harold Hecht, who outlined a tentative screenplay in a letter: "The plans are to change the leading Negro character to an oppressed minority white man, but rest assured that we have every desire to preserve the integrity of the original work. . . . It will have a relationship to life as it is lived in this country and not be a glamorized, fictional Hollywood report." According to biographer Constance Webb, Wright laughed "until tears streamed down his cheeks. . . ."

Wright was much more favorably disposed to the offer of director Pierre Chenal to shoot the film in France, Wright's adopted home after the war. But in February, 1949, the Centre National de la Cinématographie Française advised the producer to postpone filming indefinitely "for reasons dictated by international policy." Wright had thus to look elsewhere, for, as he told the *New York Times* in 1950, "no nation receiving substantial aid from the United States would risk offending that country by making a movie which deals with the Negroes' dilemma in a pretty uncompromising way." Eventually the Uruguayan producer, Jaime Prades, who had joined with Wright and Chenal, interested Attilio Mentasti, head of Sono-Films, in making the film in Argentina.[1]

Some searing, realistic exteriors were photographed in the south Chicago ghetto where Wright had lived. Unfortunately, these shots constitute only select moments in a film produced in a not very Chicago-like Buenos Aires. But Wright and Chenal

[1] I am indebted additionally to Michel Fabre's biography *The Unfinished Quest of Richard Wright* (New York: William Morrow, 1973) for many production details of the film.

made the best of the situation. The sets—painstakingly assembled to satisfy Wright's passion for realism—were mostly effective; and the Argentine blacks hired as extras to play the teeming masses of Chicago proved unobtrusive and even convincing. A few of the major roles were filled by competent character actors imported from Hollywood, including Willa Pearl Curtiss, Nicholas Joy, and Charles Kane. Jean Wallace, future star of Joseph H. Lewis's cult classic, *The Big Combo* (1955), agreed to portray Mary Dalton, the white murder victim, after several other Hollywood actresses had balked at being held by a black man on screen.

Unfortunately, the middle-level roles were cast quite haphazardly. Bigger's sister and brother were played respectively by a sixteen-year-old Brazilian girl learning English and an itinerant mechanic from New Guinea. Mary Dalton's boyfriend, Jan Erlone was acted by an American tourist. The more important roles were not spared either, and Bigger's girlfriend Bessie Mears, a pitiful, low-life alcoholic in the novel, was strangely transformed into a sort of very proper graduate of a white-gloves Southern black girl's academy. She was played by Gloria Madison, an archeology major at the University of Chicago.

Most ill-advised was the incredible choice for the protagonist. Canada Lee—who had been so successful as Bigger in the Broadway dramatization on which Wright collaborated with Paul Green [2]—was hospitalized at the time of the shooting. With understandable misgivings, Wright, just turned fifty and without acting experience, cast himself as the twenty-year-old Bigger Thomas. Strict diet and grueling exercise brought him down from a middle-aged 180 pounds to a more youthful 145, and in the

[2] The white playwright Paul Green was the author of *In Abraham's Bosom* (1927), a Pulitzer Prize play about Negro life, and *Hymn to the Rising Sun* (1936), a realistic portrayal of a black chain gang. Only the most salient dramatic features of the novel were retained in the ten scenes of the play, and the characters and plot were simplified. Orson Welles (fresh from *Citizen Kane*) and John Houseman directed for the Mercury Theater Company, and the play opened at the St. James Theatre in New York on March 25, 1941. After a successful run of 115 performances, it played to appreciative white and (especially) black audiences in Harlem, the Bronx, New Jersey, and other parts of the country. (See Michel Fabre's biography [note 1] for an excellent analysis of the play and its relation to the novel.)

Bessie Mears (Gloria Madison) is confronted by Bigger Thomas (Richard Wright). *Native Son* (1951)

film his relatively advanced age is only occasionally a problem. But his nearly complete lack of acting skill frustrates his screen debut and dooms his attempt to translate into dramatic terms his obviously complex feelings about the character.

Native Son was shot, then handed over, with hope, to an independent American distributor, the tiny Walter Gould Agency. Hope was the wrong emotion. By the time of its release, the film was mutilated almost beyond recognition. The New York State Board of Censors demanded that over a half hour (twenty-five hundred feet) be cut prior to the opening. Even then, the states of Pennsylvania, Wisconsin, and Ohio refused to allow the film to be shown.

Wright wrote bitterly to his agent in August, 1951:

> People everywhere know that the film was cut, that the killing of the rat was cut, that making of the homegun was cut, that the real heart of the boys' attempt at robbery was cut, that most of dialogue between the newspaper men was cut. . . .
>
> But the cut that did the greatest damage was the cutting of the trial. . . . the trial is shown with arms waving and mouths moving but nothing is heard.[3]

Another probable cut occurs when Bigger kisses the white girl just before suffocating her. In the novel, the scene is heavily sexual, as Bigger, alone with the forbidden fruit for the first time, amuses himself by holding the drunken girl's breast. Fabre's biography reproduces a production still showing Bigger kissing Mary Dalton. However, this moment is missing from the extant film copy on file at the Library of Congress. Presumably, somewhere along the distribution path, this impious moment was severed.

What is ironic and sad in all this is that Wright and Chenal, in filming, had anticipated trouble and had already made extensive changes from the novel to accommodate the conservatism of the 1950s. But Wright knew that to make Bigger an asexual eunuch—of the type so favored by white audiences—would be to destroy him. While it is obviously "normal" for him to desire

[3] Michel Fabre, *The Unfinished Quest of Richard Wright*, 1973.

the beautiful Mary, the combination of racial hysteria and sexual puritanism of the times made it difficult to translate any of this to the American screen. Therefore, the film audience for *Native Son* is forced to rely on alertness and imagination to sense the subtly present sexuality. Lightly hinting at the taboo area, for example, Bessie kids Bigger about "that white girl [he's] gonna drive around tonight." But that is all.

In the novel (and the Wright-Green drama as well), much of Bigger's animosity is directed explicitly toward whites. As he carries Mary up the stairs, he thinks, "she was beautiful, slender, with an air that made him feel that she did not hate him with the hate of other white people. But, for all that, she was white and he hated her." In the film, Bigger's blind antiwhite racism is muted (as is the rabid, sexually-obsessed racism of the white journalists). Only once or twice does he mention whites as a specific class at all. Even the social worker, conceived in the novel and the play as the front-line representative of white oppression, becomes vaguely mulatto in the film.

The more brutal aspects of Bigger's deeds are downplayed, since their pure surface horror, unredeemed by the filter Bigger's consciousness provided in the novel, would alienate, maybe frighten the audience. In the movie, for example, a half-hearted attempt is made to keep the audience sentiment with Bigger as long as possible by withholding until the end information that he has killed Bessie. When he does confess, a flashback reveals that he mistakenly thought she had informed the police of his whereabouts; he kills her, off camera, by throwing her down an elevator shaft, sparing her (and those watching) the brick. Thus, as the brutality of the murder is softened, the motivation behind it becomes a bit more "human."

The dialogue is cleaned up as well, tending to highlight the artificiality of the film even further. The appropriate black dialect of the novel and play ("He say a lot he hadn't ought to," "there he go," "He the boss") is sanitized in the movie to the point that actors hardly let drop the final consonant, let alone whole verbs.

In the book, Mary's boyfriend, Jan Erlone, is a somewhat bumbling but ultimately sympathetic 1940s Communist militant.

By the time of the movie, however, America's always dim view of radicals had grown substantially dimmer. Jan is now associated by the film's establishment characters with "that outfit" and demoted to "labor leader" of a vague but dangerous "labor gang." (One wonders if HUAC was baffled by this camouflage.)

The religious ambience implicit in the novel also undergoes fairly major alterations and, almost predictably, is stressed and defined in the film. In all three versions, Bigger's mother offers evangelical Christianity as the socially acceptable antidote to the wrongs of white society. Bigger rejects her pietism at the beginning of each version, but each ending manifests a substantially different final viewpoint. (Wright's own view seems ambivalent and confused.)

Near the end of the book, Bigger is visited in jail by the Reverend Hammond, pastor of his mother's church. Bigger's first response is hostile, but, as the preacher's words begin to lull him, he feels the power of the "familiar images in which his mother had given him a reason for living, had explained the world." The preacher dramatically holds out the cross to him, and, to make his mother happy, Bigger wearily pretends to give in. Later, after the torment of the inquest, he spots a burning Ku Klux Klan cross on a rooftop, which he suddenly equates with the preacher's gift. When he gets back to his cell, he tears off the cross and threatens to kill the preacher. Out of this passionate denial of Christianity comes a stronger sense of self: "whatever he thought or did from now on would have to come from him and him alone, or not at all. He wanted no more crosses that might turn to fire while still on his chest."

The play version casts the religious theme in a single image: a "large colored lithograph of Jesus Christ hanging on the Cross, with the motto—'I am the Resurrection and the Life.'" Bigger's hatred crystallizes around this icon of white society, and he rails at it several times during the play, the final scene of which suggests that Bigger's final forgiveness and vindication are to be achieved in the next world.

In the film, Wright gives in even further. If Bigger himself remains neutral and passive, Wright seems now to view religion as the final value which transcends Bigger's personal acceptance or nonacceptance. The film even adds a scene which shows Hannah in church fervently praying for her son. She later pleads with Bigger in his jail cell to accept the Lord, and in the last shot, Bigger is seen lying passively on his bed, stripes of light and shadow extending through the cell and across his body. The camera shoots downward at the supine Bigger; the lighting suggests a kind of spirituality which overtakes the film, if not Bigger himself. The mood is capped by the rich tones of a Negro spiritual which promises that a "higher judge will look past his skin into his heart," and wash his sins away. We are perhaps at the furthest point from the forthright anti-Christianity and the primitive existentialism of Wright's novel.

The movie is by no means all concession and watering down. An addition of which Wright was proud is a dream sequence recounted in flashback near the end. Bigger is frantically trying to hide what seems to be Mary's head in a pile of very black coal. Behind him the surrealistic set and the roaring furnace maintain the hell-hole symbolism so important in the book. Bessie appears and tells him to take his bundle "over there where it's all white." He stumbles over to a massive field of bright white cotton and spies his father (killed in a race riot) beckoning from the path. The dead man is dressed in a straw hat and coveralls, and a big white beard covers his black face. Bigger rushes to him joyously and falls to his knees, hugging his father's legs. Suddenly, harsh, derisive laughter comes from the old man, and the camera tilts up with Bigger's gaping eyes to reveal the cruel Britten, the Daltons' private investigator, who has been Bigger's chief nemesis and the film's most virulent racist. The idea is a provocative one, but the little cabin and the jolly black man amid the lake of cotton are just too much like the happy darkies of *Uncle Tom's Cabin* to be taken very seriously.

Several other visualizations distinguish the film and effectively extend the book. Bigger and his friends, milling about at night, debate whether to hold up Blum's store. The streets and buildings are blocked and crisscrossed by the superstructure of a rumbling el train above, giving the scene the claustrophobic appearance of a prison yard. The film then cuts sharply to another exterior shot: daytime, a spacious, well-groomed boulevard, tall trees and freshly-painted parallel traffic lines which plunge back toward the vanishing point. Bigger, the center of focus, walks forward between them. The camera, panning right to follow Bigger, reveals a huge mansion instantly recognizable as the Dalton's. The startling contrast of life styles between poor black and rich white is made without comment or superfluous elaboration.

Another excellent added sequence occurs when Bigger takes Bessie for an illicit spin in Mr. Dalton's limousine. They go to an amusement park, and much of the tension exists because we know that he is pushing his luck. Bigger says significantly that he wants "to see everything." Then, in one of the most effective additions to the film, they go for a ride on the roller coaster. For once, Chenal's generally lackluster direction is perfect: the confusion and pressure that are about to invade Bigger's life (that night, in fact) are here wonderfully presaged. The lovers roar down the steep tracks, shouting, laughing, frightened —out of control of events. Bigger hollers to Bessie over the noise, "They say sometimes you're up and sometimes you're down. It's just like life." "And you never know when you're gonna be up or down," Bessie shouts back. The noise, the strain, and the thrill all work together to indicate that something dreadful is about to break in their lives. This scene is appropriately followed by a short sequence on a beach, where Chenal's admirable mise-en-scene, isolating Bigger in a long shot against empty sand and sky, forms a sharp contrast to the hurly-burly of the previous scene and highlights his essential aloneness.

Another successful visual moment is the very chilling, Gestapo-like round up when the police are looking for Bigger. Chenal wisely plants his camera in front of a wide brick building and pans slowly and gracefully from window to window. Inside, brutal white policemen herd frightened and passive blacks from their apartments. It is during the all too infrequent scenes like this one that the film takes on a resonance and truth which transcend the crime thriller it often seems intent to remain.

Without question, the most effective part of the whole film is the night chase, actually filmed on the rooftops of Chicago.

Here, Chenal was able to improve on the book's often ama-
teurish symbolism by translating Bigger's mental state into brilliant visual imagery. Bigger and Bessie are in flight. The scene
opens with a momentary shot of the bare, black sky. Then, suddenly, filling the screen, a giant "Sunkist" sun of hundreds of
lights blinks off and on; the alternating total dark of the sky and
total light of the huge outdoor advertisement underline magnificently the white/black dialectic so severely and prudently muted
in the rest of the film.

The camera remains fixed on the blinking sun a few moments,
then pulls back to Bessie staring out the window. She moans
dolefully, "Sun won't shine for us anymore." They are merely rats
being hunted down, just as Bigger had trapped and destroyed a
rat in the opening (cut from the film by its distributor). This is
probably the moment of greatest empathy with Bigger (and undoubtedly why Wright decided to hold off revealing Bessie's
murder, which occurs at this point in the novel, until near the
end).

Bigger runs off alone, and is finally chased to the rooftops of
the south side tenements. He jumps in front of another huge,
blinking sunlike sign, but this time it is not the sun, but an
immense hourglass with the words *Williams Funeral Garden—
24 Hour Service*. In the context of the chase, the image is not at
all as ponderous as it might seem. In its cold determinism, the
film insists naturally upon the passive fate which a hostile society has forced on Bigger Thomas, black man.

Here is Bigger's real tragedy, and, to Wright's mind, the essential tragedy of racism. Since white society continually represses
the socially acceptable aspects of aggression, i.e., ambition and
the desire "to get ahead," Bigger can only assert his being and
achieve identity through acts of cruel, wanton violence. This is
what the book relentlessly insists on, even on the last page:

> "What I killed for must've been good!" Bigger's voice was full of
> frenzied anguish. "It must've been good! When a man kills, it's for
> something. . . . I didn't know I was really alive in this world until
> I felt things hard enough to kill for 'em. . . ."

It is the articulation of this disturbing truth that makes *Native Son* a profound novel despite its faults. It is also this truth that creates, finally, the insurmountable barriers that keep *Native Son* on film from playing the theaters, even in this tamed and emasculated version.

Independent Woman, Doomed Sister

BY SERAFINA KENT BATHRICK

With Ellen Glasgow, we can trace the struggle of a creator who
intimately experienced the clash between instinct and reason,
and who believed she recognized in history itself the same
conflict, the same biological determinism. *In This Our Life* told
of "the rise of the middle class as the dominant force in Southern
democracy," [1] an account of Glasgow's own class and own generation. Recalling the anxious "modern South" of the pre-World
War II years, Glasgow explained the task of her last novel:

> The problem I had set myself was an analysis in fiction of the
> modern temper; and the modern temper as it pressed round me, in
> a single community, appeared confused, vacillating, and distracted
> from permanent values. [2]

Let us briefly outline the rather complex story of *In This Our
Time.*

Asa Timberlake at sixty is the father of three children in their
twenties, husband of a tyrannical hypochondriac, Lavinia, and
office worker in a tobacco factory in Queenborough, Virginia.
The factory had belonged to his family at one time, but was taken
over by his wife's ambitious Uncle William after the suicide of

[1] Ellen Glasgow, *A Certain Measure* (New York, 1938), p. 4.
[2] *A Certain Measure,* p. 249.

Asa's father. The tired Asa laments his family ties throughout the novel, "For it seemed to him that family feelings had stood in the way of everything he had ever wanted to do." [3] Asa looks forward to Sundays, his only pleasurable days, which he spends with a local widow. He hopes to live with her, that is, if William should die and leave Lavinia with enough money to free Asa of his marital responsibility.

At the outset, in the Spring of 1938, Asa's youngest daughter, Stanley, beloved by her mother and spoiled by her uncle, is about to marry a liberal young lawyer, Craig Fleming. Just before the wedding, however, she runs off with Peter Kingsman, her sister Roy's surgeon husband. But Peter and Stanley's subsequent marriage soon collapses under the pleasure-seeking demands of the latter. Peter commits suicide; Stanley returns home. In a bored and angry mood, she kills a child in her speeding car and conveniently blames the would-be lawyer son of the family's black cook. Her sister and father refuse to defend her, and in a single moment of assertiveness, Asa forces his child to tell the truth. Perry, the young black, is thus freed, but has been humiliated and destroyed by his brief imprisonment.

Meanwhile Asa has watched his other daughter, Roy, harden with determination after granting her husband a divorce and continuing her work as an interior decorator. "She's as square as a man," he notes with a mixture of admiration and anxiety for Roy and her generation. But Roy and Stanley's status as "modern women" must be seen within a narrow perspective, bound by their biological and institutional inheritance. The two women's masculine names signal both their patriarchal lineage and their entrenchment in Southern customs. Thus family laws continue to dictate behavior and to obstruct love or communication. When Roy's love for Craig, her sister's bereft fiancé, becomes momentarily a way by which these two can help each other, the social and familial pressure to protect and harbor Stanley has dire consequences. Stanley, through her tantrums and coyness, is able to lure Craig away from Roy, who leaves home desolate but free.

In order to articulate the conflict played out in the family,

[3] Ellen Glasgow, *In This Our Life* (New York, 1941), p. 16.

Glasgow chose a style and organizational principles which could follow and characterize her "wandering flow of thought and emotion." [4] The shifting point of view is perhaps the novel's most important structural component. The work is divided into three major sections, in each of which different characters are given short chapters permitting glimpses into their individual psyches. But the basic rhythm of the novel results from a kind of dialogue that exists between the two "civilized" characters, Asa and Roy. Asa's capacity to view his family's generational changes is typified by his recollections about his own mother. Glasgow gently probes Asa's Oedipal attachments, which partially explain his sensitivity: the awareness that he himself is "encrusted with the outworn shape of the past," at the same time that he gains strength from these memories. In a remarkably filmic passage, Glasgow describes Asa's "flashback":

> While he stood there, frowning moodily at William, two memories drifted into his mind and rippled out again, as frail and fugitive images in running water. He saw his mother bending over his crib. . . .

At many moments in the novel, Asa turns suddenly inward while enduring the routines that frustrate and fragment life within his family. Asa's continued commentary under torment provides the novel with its real (moral?) center, for we come to believe that both Asa's and Roy's refusals to surrender to the confused values of the times reflect Glasgow's own credo. Basic to her narrative is the notion that individual character, not an individual's politics, provides the hope for society. "Every decision, right or wrong, must be reached alone, and enacted in complete loneliness," Glasgow says in *In This Our Life*.

Why does Roy survive? Her persistence is more a feature of her inheritance—she is the loving daughter of a good and honorable man—than of her being a liberated "modern woman." As for the other characters, not lucky enough to have Timberlake "roots," they have no armor against the destructive powers of society embodied in a spoiled woman. Craig's liberal convic-

[4] *A Certain Measure*, p. 251.

tions crumble when he is confronted by his old desires to protect Stanley. Peter is similarly destroyed by her passion; and when Stanley humiliates Perry, the scapegoat, for her own monstrous crime, he too is left dazed. Asa concludes that as a black, a "natural-born fatalist," Perry must be devastated by his mere twenty-four hours in jail. And so it goes with the characters touched by Stanley. It is interesting to note Ellen Glasgow's willingness to accept and reaffirm the idea of woman as principal vassal and victim of the most irrational and threatening forces to civilized society.

In May, 1942, *In This Our Life* was chosen for the Pulitzer Prize. And in that same month it became known to a new public when Warner Brothers released a film version: a star vehicle for recent Academy Award nominees Bette Davis (Stanley) and Olivia de Havilland (Roy), and a tight melodrama in which two sisters competed for the same man. It was directed by John Huston, fresh from his acclaimed debut with *The Maltese Falcon* (1941), and adapted for the screen by Howard Koch.

Among the women's pictures at Warners in the late 1930s and 1940s, the frequency of films that focused on the relationship of sisters is remarkable: *Four Daughters* (1938), *Four Wives* (1939), *Four Mothers* (1941), the Lane Sisters' trilogy; *The Gay Sisters* (1942), *The Hard Way* (1943), and *Devotion* (1946), the last the story of the Bronte sisters. The genre's apotheosis was *A Stolen Life* (1946), in which Bette Davis played twin sisters, one good, the other a viper. In most of these films, the conflict between the good-natured sister who could reaffirm the family by being the perfect woman, wife, or mother was threatened by her evil-natured counterpart, a sister whose destructive impulses, sometimes childlike and sometimes sinister, threatened the very foundation of American life: the sanctity of the home. Significantly, the sister story became an effective way to reinforce the "naturalness" of the family through the inevitable purging of the "bad" seed and the final regrouping of the family-whole.

Ellen Glasgow's novel was hardly intended as an exposé of sister rivalry, and Warners' melodramatic promotional campaign sent the author into a turmoil. At the gala movie premiere in

Richmond, Virginia, the prize-winning novelist chose not to be present. She wrote a friend a few months later, explaining why she had not even seen the film:

> The advertisements were enough to make me understand that Hollywood had filmed a different book, not mine at all, and had entirely missed the point of my novel. I hated the whole thing, but there were practical reasons why I had to let it be done. The sister conflict was, of course, a minor theme, and the character of Stanley a minor figure, who was treated objectively, from the first page to the last. The major theme, as I meant it, and you must have understood, was the conflict of human beings with human nature. In Asa and in Roy, I probed into this, but how brutally obvious one has to be in print to be comprehended. And how I dislike the obvious in any and in every form! Yet was the question too subtle? [5]

Ellen Glasgow's book has its strong subversive streak. Glasgow recognized as obsolete the familial law that governed the Timberlakes, and she believed that Southern family tradition was a serious obstruction to those who looked to social reform and class equality as prerequisites for individual happiness. Yet, ironically, it was Glasgow's unwillingness to explore in depth the social bases for behavior that must be responsible in part for the personalizing and naturalizing of the female animosity which dominates the Warners' film. Glasgow's method in *In This Our Life* was to emphasize inner monologue and individual torment at the expense of class or historical analysis. Thus the novelist's fascination with the rudiments of both Freud and Darwin left her vulnerable to the heavy hands of Hollywood.

Howard Koch might have agreed with Ellen Glasgow's acid apprehensions about the film. Prior to composing the brilliant script for *Casablanca* (1942), Koch was assigned, quite unhappily, to adapt *In This Our Life* to the screen. He felt that Glasgow's novel should not be made into a movie because the story was too "diffuse." An adaptation would require compression, which would force the sisters "in too sharp a contrast." [6]

[5] *Letters of Ellen Glasgow*, ed. Blair Rouse (New York, 1958), Letter to Bessie Zaban Jones, July, 1942, p. 302.

[6] Howard Koch, "Reflections on a Golden Boy," *Film Comment*, vol. 9, no. 3 (May–June, 1973), p. 14.

Koch's fears proved true. A close reading of his four versions of the screenplay shows that the theme of sister rivalry becomes more and more central to the narrative, and the script focuses increasingly on the irrational actions of Stanley.[7] Howard Koch's ideological intentions were eclipsed by the "naturally" determined behavior of the two women.

Already in Koch's earliest screen version, dated April, 1941, the character of Asa is virtually ignored. He is a frail, hen-pecked old man who quietly disapproves of his younger daughter and seems more puzzled than contemplative. But Stanley is more vacillating and temperamental than evil, spoiled, yet capable of rapport with Roy. Similarly, Roy is a headstrong character, determined and prideful. Thus in this first proposal Koch finds a neat compromise between Glasgow and Hollywood by ending with Stanley's admission of guilt and with the two sisters reaching a full understanding—Roy realizes that *all* the family is guilty for having overprotected the younger sibling.

In the second version the two sisters have a terrific fight, when Roy realizes Stanley's guilt in the murder. "You're not human. You're a fiend," she shouts, and Koch's directions describe Roy's firm actions. "She springs on Stanley, takes her by the neck. Roy gets her down, shakes her like a cat shaking a rat." Yet this physical intimacy leads also to reconciliation; as Stanley enters her sister's prison cell, they kiss and ask forgiveness of each other.

By the third version this testy comradeship is gone. In its place is the conflict between two alien and unlike sisters. Ironically the fight is eliminated from the movie because the *good* sister perpetrated it. The quiescence of Roy now becomes a central structural component of the drama. The split between aggressiveness and passivity continues into the final screenplay and onto the screen itself. In casting Davis and de Havilland in the opposing roles, Warners exploited the Scarlett-Melanie conflict of 1939's *Gone With the Wind* (which certainly put Olivia de

[7] Scripts used for this comparison are from the United Artist's Collection of the Wisconsin Center of Film and Theater Research, located at the State Historical Society in Madison, Wisconsin.

Havilland forever in the Passivity Hall of Fame, from *The Heiress* [1949] to *Hush . . . Hush, Sweet Charlotte* [1964]).

But what did Howard Koch mean to make of this story? What is constant in his Hollywood career was genuine adherence to his stated principle that the screenwriter should play a socially conscious role in relation to the industry, being "half its ghost and half its conscience." [8] His hand in the authorship of the Popular Front movies *Sergeant York* (1941), *Casablanca* (1942), and *Mission to Moscow* (1943) is more than a coincidence of Warners' assignments. For *In This Our Life,* Koch's intentions were to pick up on some of Ellen Glasgow's scattered themes— those which suggested the operation of racial, economic, and even sexual oppression, and to give them substantial consideration in the film.

Through the second screenplay, Koch conveys his ideological purpose by making Roy the mouthpiece for social concerns. As an assertive modern woman she voices a real hatred for her ever-sickly mother and her materialistic uncle. After Peter abandons her, she has the sign on her shop door altered, reclaiming her own name after the divorce. Also, Roy's love for Craig is heavily influenced by his commitment to social reform and his strong civil rights position as a lawyer. And because she feels that with Craig she stands on "rock," not on "sand" as with Peter, she expresses real disgust and outrage when Craig is tempted to defend the guilty Stanley. Roy lectures him in a twenty-seven-line verbal assault which begins on a note compatible with Glasgow's picture of her: "I don't believe anything any more. . . ." She speaks out against racism in defense of Perry, her sister's scapegoat: "He's only a Negro and this is a white man's world. A fine world we've made of it."

Earlier in this second screen adaptation, Craig had demonstrated his political integrity by refusing an offer from Uncle William that would bring him more clients and prestige. He had educated the whole family as to why he rejected patronage from this "captain of industry," even teaching them a thing or two

[8] Howard Koch, "A Playwright Looks at the 'Filmwright,'" *Sight and Sound*, vol. 19, no. 5 (July, 1950), p. 214.

about the subtleties of political philosophy: "You say that our views are often the result of circumstances—I think you mean our interests." At the end of version two, Craig regains his ideological purity—as Howard Koch integrates the love relationship of Craig and Roy with their political ideals. Craig tells his beloved that he has found the true meaning of justice after looking into the eyes of the now freed black man. Roy stares adoringly at her man and says she too sees justice—in his eyes. A final directive conveys the scriptwriter's reconciliation of politics and love: "They smile at each other with faith renewed and exalted."

When producer Hal Wallis read over the third treatment of the script, he marked the inside cover of his copy with a handwritten critical comment: "Too many scenes and situations are underwritten—show some of the action—auto accident—Peter's suicide—all the melodrama that can be photographed." [9] But this July, 1941, script had already dropped most of the earlier wordiness of scripts one and two, which emphasized Craig's politics and the didactic exchanges between Craig and Roy. Her assertiveness is softened, so Roy now listens passively to Craig's abbreviated confrontation with her uncle. She merely comments on how "proud" she feels, assuring him that, in some vague way, "you're doing things that matter." Craig and Roy's unique relationship is reduced to a standard formula. She adores him and waits patiently while her idealist man separates his immature longings for Stanley from his sense of good works. The contrast of temperament between the two sisters emerges at the film's center.

By this third script Howard Koch must have been cognizant of the casting of Bette Davis as Stanley, for his characterization seems to play to Davis's shifting moods as an actress, her velocity and protean energy. Stanley's need "to move" is depicted by her demands for a fast car, dance music, and many changes of clothing. At this stage in Koch's revisions, Stanley gets her best line. After refusing to sit through a movie with Craig and Roy who invite her out, she snaps, "I'd rather do anything than keep still."

[9] UA Collection.

Craig Fleming (George Brent) and Stanley Timberlake (Bette Davis) talk to the jailed Parry Clay (Ernest Anderson). *In This Our Life* (1942)

Her incessant motions thus provide the tempo which propels her, and those around her, into an even more dangerous collision course—literally culminating in a *second* car crash which, veering from Ellen Glasgow's novel, kills Stanley off.

By the final version of the screenplay Koch has abandoned almost entirely the issues which permitted him to politicize the narrative. Jettisoning the static dialogue and stagnant visuals that bothered producer Wallis, Koch lets biological determinism prevail. Roy is characterized mainly by comparison with Asa's mother (in the film itself, Roy appears in the frame with the older woman's imposing portrait). For Stanley, this script offers an expanded exploration of her incestuous flirtations with her uncle. The lecherous old man panders to his nubile niece, and gone is the suggestion made in earlier scripts which links his capitalist ideology to systematic racism. While William flirts with Stanley, as they drink and giggle together, he takes special pleasure in confiding how he swindled her father out of the family business. He "saw the depression coming," persuaded Asa to "sink every cent into new machinery," and when tobacco prices fell, he bought out his honest relative at the receivership sale. This tiny speech, a leftover from Howard Koch's scripts of social concerns, is also a 1940s remainder of a constant political theme in Warner Brothers pictures of the 1930s: that the "little people" required the New Deal to save them from shysters like William.

In the filmed version the scene remains, but the impact is more cynical than political. Director John Huston emphasizes the physical nearness of the two destructive people who huddle together, enveloped by a fat flowered couch. The pleasure of financial success is linked to perverse sexuality, more sensationalist Freud than sensible Marx.

Bosley Crowther (the *New York Times*, May 9, 1942)—a critic characteristically in search of a liberal "message"—was impressed by the film's willingness to "define the Negro as an educated and comprehending character," and it is perhaps to John Huston's credit that he cast a young black (Ernest Anderson) who had not been trained to caricature his race. Still, Crowther's comments may be more indicative of his easily soothed social conscience than of the fact that the film conveyed Koch's wishes to spare some of the melodrama and explore the issues. The movie successfully avoids any analysis of institutionalized racism (the blacks in prison with Perry are humming spirituals and shooting craps); and Perry is as benign as Craig is benevolent, for Glasgow's own pessimism is coated by a construct in which all the characters are defined in relation to the evil personality of Stanley in their midst. But Hollywood's tendency to polarize and thus exploit "inborn" human traits facilitates the ways in which melodrama ignores social forces and personalizes struggle through naturalization of individual behavior. Gone is Glasgow's understanding of family conflict as the basis for both inherited and learned values; gone is Koch's attempt to proselytize through the words of a liberal lawyer.

Huston chooses not to employ flashbacks or long soliloquies which might give the character analysis a detailed psycho-analytic or historical dimension. Rather he opts for a style which brings to the fore, through cinematic shorthand, the singular evil of the younger sister. Huston establishes Stanley's willful deter-mination to disrupt and destroy those around her by the standard devices of melodrama—showy music, flamboyant editing, flashy camera movements—propelling the audience along the bad sis-ter's collision course.

Time is ahistoric, having nothing to do with Glasgow's attempt to characterize the years before World War II, everything to do with one woman's capacity for destruction. Time is bridged and elided by surges of the powerful music, which accentuate Stan-ley's potently aberrant personality. The melody rises and falls as Stanley's rhythms affect the lives of others, and the matching of image and sound (Stanley's car is always assigned an ominous-ness by the accompanying orchestral gushes) provides that kind of redundancy which both satisfies and stuns an audience. The idea of Stanley the monster is conveyed also by her predisposi-tion to move to the beat of the rhumba—as prurient and sugges-tive a musical interest to the 1940s audience as rock and roll would be to the mid-1950s.

Finally, Stanley is associated with one key symbolic prop, her most prized object, her get-away-from-the-family escape and weapon: the shiny convertible. A gift from William, it also signifies her sexuality and the destruction it will bring. Producer Hal Wallis's request to increase the melodrama is met by John Huston's speedily moving camera, which tracks and cranes along with Stanley's racing automobile. The final chase scene, almost a parody of the gangster genre, pictures Stanley in medium close-up, staring ahead in terror and turning occasionally to glance at the police cars in hot pursuit. The camera lurks outside her front windshield as we cut to see the car crash (from Stanley's point of view) through a guard rail and then go spinning through the air, Stanley's screams merging with the sirens. Huston gives us a long shot of the car in flames, fully satisfying our need to know that the wicked witch is dead.

The first and last shots of Stanley in *In This Our Life* show her in that precious car, both shots are at night, and both are reinforced by their juxtaposition to shots of the home-bound sister Roy. Huston's editing underlines the central opposition in the film: the stability of the family woman versus the driven independence of the other, an economy of technique and ideology which reinforces the fearsome potential of the active woman.

Ellen Glasgow had questioned the "modern temper," showing how those trapped in *family* patterns are obliged to accept defeat—never to win or to be happy. The novelist dismissed the younger generation of men, idealists all: Perry, Craig, and Peter. The film ultimately affirms the family, its regenerative capacities made more emphatic by its ability to reknit and rediscover its center. Perry and Craig will survive as future husbands and lawyers, moral leaders in their private and public lives. The complementary roles of Craig and Perry, the lawyer and his cause, further reinforce the male hegemony which is needed to reestablish the correct relationship between the future man and wife. In the final scene Craig receives word via telephone of Stanley's fiery death and, as they stand in the Timberlake hallway, blessed by that family space, he looks down on Roy with a gesture that reeks of paternalism. "It's out of our hands," he says piously to his childlike bride.

As we have seen, Ellen Glasgow attempted to portray in Roy a female who survives precisely because she accepts her own autonomy and finally leaves home. But Hollywood heroines are rewarded for exactly opposite qualities. Since sister Stanley's destructive rampage had formed the very matrix and movement of the film, we are coerced—as part of that childish public which Koch so wished to educate—into believing, at the least, that family is both natural and enduring, capable of survival when good women such as Roy stay home.

Mr. Saroyan's Thoroughly American Movie

BY PATRICK MC GILLIGAN

There is a prologue. In December, 1941, the Japanese bombed
Pearl Harbor, and William Saroyan announced his association
with Metro-Goldwyn-Mayer in Hollywood, two not *entirely* unrelated events. Saroyan, "whose talent has been described as the
most undisciplined in the theatre," in the piquant words of the
New York Times, did not immediately sign a contract with
MGM, "the cinema's most conservative citadel." Instead he shook
hands with studio head Louis B. Mayer. Having won the Pulitzer
Prize for Drama in 1940 with *The Time of Your Life,* Saroyan
said he now intended to direct his own "thoroughly American
movie," which he modestly called "Saroyan's picture." Mayer was
naturally swollen with prestige at the arrangement and the
details were left graciously unsaid. Uneasy in the lavish, air-
conditioned Irving Thalberg Memorial Building, the sweet-
natured Armenian author moved his typewriter into an abandoned still-picture gallery in a loft above Metro's Stage Four. "I
like dumps," he explained succinctly. Of the picture to be, he
predicted, "It will neither offend intellectuals nor confuse anyone
else."

Two months passed while Saroyan tinkered freely with ideas.
In mid-February, 1942, Saroyan went on the MGM payroll at
one thousand dollars weekly. Mayer had tactfully suggested that
Saroyan cut his teeth on a short subject, and thus Saroyan swiftly

wrote an eighteen-minute short subject he entitled *Jive*, adapted from his story, "A Number of the Poor." *Jive* eventually became a two-reeler called *The Good Job*, written, produced, and directed by Saroyan; Louis B. Mayer shelved it, and the little item is today one of the more intriguing lost nuggets in the dustbin of cinema history. Saroyan, meanwhile, conceived a screenplay called *The Human Comedy*. He explained, "Many people think it's the simplest, most wonderful thing I've got." Legend, which is about as reliable as anything in these matters, holds that Mayer wept openly three times when Saroyan first told him the story—Louis B. often recoiled at actually reading any of his proposed screenplays, and what got made sometimes depended on how dynamic the writer was as a story-teller; Saroyan was quite good. The story, Mayer announced, would be a vehicle for Mickey Rooney. Saroyan then sold *The Human Comedy* to MGM for sixty thousand dollars, with verbal assurances from Mayer that he, Saroyan, would direct. Two more months passed. Rooney was assigned to *A Yank at Eton* (1942) and announced for Rudyard Kipling's *Kim* (ultimately made in 1950, *without* Rooney). Saroyan grew suspicious. Then he became nervous, restless, and cantankerous. Finally, he mentioned his misgivings to Louis B., who politely dropped a bombshell: Saroyan was simply not "experienced enough" to direct an MGM motion picture.

May, 1942. The "mutual trust" arrangement between MGM and William Saroyan concluded with a bitter walkout, and an allegorical Saroyanesque tirade in *Daily Variety* entitled "Why I Am No Longer at Metro-Goldwyn-Mayer, or The California Shore-Bird in Its Native Habitat, or Brahms' Double Concerto in A Minor." Saroyan, out of pique, offered to purchase the screen rights of *The Human Comedy* for eighty thousand dollars, but MGM did not budge. "I was naive," Saroyan complained to the press, "I am curious about one thing, and that is whether Mr. Mayer believes I am *experienced enough* to have written the *story?*" In *Daily Variety*, Saroyan expounded murkily, cloaking his bitterness in an ornithological tribute to the shore-bird and its simple life, concluding, "I left the joint also because, sooner or later, a man gets bored with bores, finaglers and jitney politicians. A man just naturally gets fed up with the baloney. He gets tired of witnessing the continuous and disgraceful crying, trembling, and shaking. . . ."

MGM reacted with typical corporate effrontery, pretending that nothing out of the ordinary had occurred. Howard Dietz, MGM's erstwhile vice president and a sometime lyricist, said, "It has always been a little difficult to know exactly what Saroyan means, but his essay on leaving Metro gives an aroma which suggests he feels the studio treated him kind of messily." Citing Saroyan's "handsome salary while he experimented," Dietz described *The Good Job* as "the most expensive short produced in two years" at the studio. He continued, "At any rate, the esteemed dramatist got a chance to write that farewell-to-Hollywood piece which has almost gone out of fashion with authors who flop." Undaunted, MGM went ahead with its plans for the production of *The Human Comedy*. Clarence Brown, Louis B. Mayer's personal friend, well known for Gable and Garbo vehicles, was quietly signed to direct.

But Saroyan had, literally, the last word. He announced his own plans—to write a novel based on his screenplay, also called *The Human Comedy*, and to coincide publication with release of MGM's picture. What happened next depends on accounts. Either Saroyan retired to his beloved San Francisco to fester and muse, or he bought a large Cadillac with his Hollywood earnings and drove east for a vacation to visit Cincinnati, a town with a name so musical that it always enchanted him. True to his vow, Saroyan published *The Human Comedy* in 1943, the year in which Louis B. Mayer released his prestige feature of the very same name.

Neither book nor movie, though remarkably alike, is a latent masterpiece waiting to be hailed afresh today; both are timeworn bits of Americana, contrived, somewhat dated, albeit effusive in good will and idiosyncratic humor. Nineteen forty-two, the year in which Saroyan began to write *The Human Comedy*, was precarious for the nation, indeed the world. Abroad, Hitler and the Axis looked indomitable. At home, the social psychosis of wartime—spiraling juvenile delinquency, venereal

disease, and white-collar crime—began to afflict the land; politically convenient wartime measures—rationing (which hit poor
people the hardest), the no-strike pledge (which retarded worker's victories of the 1930s), and the internment of Japanese-
Americans—stirred a deep, justifiable resentment among sectors
of the population. Hollywood, exemplified by Warner Brothers'
Sergeant York (1941) and *Yankee Doodle Dandy* (1942)—both,
like *The Human Comedy*, domestic war-rallying parables—
coalesced behind FDR and the war effort in one monolithic
"united front." Saroyan and normally-Republican-leaning MGM,
"to both of whom life tends to be a chocolate soda made out of
words," in Manny Farber's droll phrase, came together on this
common nation-reassuring ground: to extoll the family, virtue,
patriotism, and the republic. To accomplish this, Saroyan focused
on one exemplary family—the Macauleys of Ithaca, California,
and their inspiring contributions to the war campaign. In the
movie, this story is credited to Saroyan; the screenplay itself is
claimed by Howard Estabrook. But the aborted gentleman's
agreement between MGM and William Saroyan did not entirely
suffocate the author; much of what survives on the screen is
distinctly Saroyanesque, coated with MGM gloss. Few authors
would be more difficult to rewrite.

William Saroyan is a rambling, vernacular, wistful, hyperbolic,
garrulous sort of writer, who excels with mood and theme, and
soars buoyantly with character sketches. Plot does not interest
him greatly. (Perhaps this is why a modern director like Robert
Altman, whose style is very improvisatory and free flowing, cites
Saroyan as a key influence.) Saroyan is more fascinated by the
road than the route. The characters of *The Human Comedy*
(book and film) are introduced in quintessential Saroyan fashion, without fanfare or to-do, as they are encountered in turn on
their daily errands in Ithaca: Ulysses Macauley, the boy; Homer
Macauley, his brother, the fastest-moving telegraph messenger
in the San Joaquin Valley; brother Marcus, away in the Army;
Mrs. Macauley, the mother; Bess, the sister, and Mary, the girl-
next-door, betrothed to Marcus; Thomas Spangler, the manager
of the telegraph office; and Mr. Willie Grogan, weary, worn-out,
and, at 67, the aged Homer incarnate, himself once the fastest-

moving messenger in the whole wide world. The Ithaca citizenry includes the usual batch of Saroyan eccentrics, such as the spoiled Hubert Ackley III, ancient history teacher Miss Hicks, three soldiers (one, in the movie, played by a youthful Robert Mitchum) on an evening sally, and even a giddy holdup artist who is debated out of his intended crime. Of course, this is not *only* Ithaca, California; this is Saroyan's microcosm, the nation, the globe, life. Further, the metaphor (Homer, Ithaca, etc.) translates simply: this is ancient Greece, eternally renewed, in the ceaseless quest for a civilized world.

Saroyan was lucky with his conception; things could have turned out worse in the MGM factory. The director, as it happened, was a genuine craftsman, best known for directing seven pictures with Greta Garbo, beginning in the silent era with *Flesh and the Devil* (1926), and in the twilight of his career, for directing sincere literary adaptations (*Ah, Wilderness!* [1935], *Anna Karenina* [1948], *Intruder in the Dust* [1949]) [1] and children's classics (*National Velvet* [1945], *The Yearling* [1946]). Probably the subtlest, most lyric, most intelligent contract director on the MGM lot, Clarence Brown had an acknowledged touch with delicate performers (such as Garbo or children), and a trademark of visual excellence. His silent-era mentor, Maurice Tourneur (they collaborated in 1920 on *The Last of the Mohicans*), took the chiaroscuro paintings of Rembrandt as his pictorial inspiration, and Brown self-consciously imitated the lighting of the Old Masters. (Note the scenes filmed in the telegraph office: the foreground muted, window-shade light patterns dancing on the wall, brilliant sunlight streaming through the transom—utterly pictorial and utterly natural.) And, most importantly, Brown was himself raised in the rural South; he had a heartfelt feeling for the dignity of small-town existence (much of *The Human Comedy* was photographed in authentic small-town locales) and the ironies of growing up there. His sensibility was kindred to Saroyan's. *The Human Comedy* is not his best film, certainly, but it shows his care.

The cast is no less perfectly suited, especially Mickey Rooney,

1 Editors' note. See E. Pauline Degenfelder's essay on *Intruder in the Dust* elsewhere in this volume.

Homer Macauley (Mickey Rooney) on the job at the telegraph office.
The Human Comedy (1943)

for whom the yarn was ostensibly written. Rooney is an actor-personality who has been swallowed by time, neglected, underrated, certainly no longer fashionable among the cognoscenti (James Agee loved him). He occasionally resorted to *shtick*, true, but his genius never disappointed under the eye of a decent director like Clarence Brown. At the peak of his talents and popularity, then in his early twenties, manchild Rooney played sixteen-year-old Homer Macauley with breathless precocity. Sensitive, eloquent, effortlessly beguiling, he performed with wonderful restraint and savvy, underplaying some of the most shameless scenes ever written for the screen. (A messenger of death, he must ultimately deliver a Department of War telegram to his own family.) Equaling this powerful performance is Frank Morgan, MGM's versatile character veteran (famous today as the Wizard of Oz), who plays the philosophical telegrapher, Willie Grogan, with a tragic, chilling flourish, drinking himself merrily into an early grave. ("In the event of drunkenness— mine, not yours," he informs the tousle-haired Rooney, with a wry smile, "I shall ask from you a depth of understanding that only comes from children.") The rest of the cast, seen briefly and less successfully, include Fay Bainter (Mrs. Macauley), Donna Reed (Bess Macauley), James Craig (Tom Spangler), and Van Johnson (Marcus Macauley). But the real gem is five-year-old Jack Jenkins, a very wistful Ulysses, who cannot make sense of anything in the universe; in one exquisite scene, Ulysses and his best friend Lionel (the young Darryl Hickman), a bookworm excluded from local sandlot games, wander amidst the aisles of the town library, gazing with awe at the thousands of mysterious volumes overhead.

But, given the excesses of both works, the movie is inferior to, less persuasively moving than, the book—despite the skilled director and mostly plausible cast. Between screenplay (part Saroyan) and novel (whole Saroyan) lies the difference, a fragile little moral that all of Saroyan is better than some. MGM fared best when it stuck close to what must have been, originally, a very novelistic Saroyan screenplay. Whole passages that appear in the novel occur almost verbatim in the movie, presumably intact from Saroyan's original screen draft, and these passages, significantly, comprise the most consistent, credible, engrossing moments in the film. The opening, for example, is virtually a literal visual transcription of Saroyan's beginning novel chapter. First, a shot of Ulysses Macauley as he stands "over the new gopher hole in the backyard of his house"; then, a shot of "the gopher of this hole [who] pushed up fresh moist dirt and peeked out at the boy." Saroyan's working script must have been very precise; the first two sentences of the novel match the first two narrative shots of the movie. Director Brown filmed the sequence —said to be Louis B. Mayer's favorite opening in an MGM picture—as a kind of innocent reverie. Cut to Ulysses running down an alleyway. Cut to a bucolic field of tall, wind-blown grass. Cut to a "negro" waving hello to Ulysses from a train speeding by: "Goin' home boy! Goin' home where I belong!" Evocative, sentimental, hugely appealing—straight Saroyan—the scene conjures a sweet, pastoral, (ultimately) disingenuous image of America, one as much in the tradition of Metro-Goldwyn-Mayer as of its putative author.

The movie essentially blunders when it strays from what must have been the Saroyan screenplay; the mistakes are of two species, letter or spirit, or sometimes a combination of the two. The novel, for example, is brimming with old-fashioned morals and beatitudes and civic aureoles, but Saroyan wisely balances the sweetness with a keen edge of irony—aging, defeat, death, bitterness, and sorrow pervade the novel. World War II, for example, hovers over Ithaca like a great and tragic mist, yet Saroyan treats it almost casually, incidentally, except for those constant telegrams, announcing distant soldierly deaths. Feared, inexplicable, omnipresent, war is the manifest symbol of all humankind's failure. Saroyan needed to say little more to the war-conscious audiences of 1942. But in the movie, the opening reel scarcely ticks by before the first jarring reminder about World War II occurs as Homer Macauley is pedaling his bicycle carelessly down a country lane. The film cuts dramatically to fighter planes zooming overhead, then to soldiers carousing along in a combat jeep. Preparedness is thus pounded home. Saroyan goes for the heart while MGM goes for the jugular. Author is elliptical—the telegrams suffice—while studio is repeatedly too blunt.

This violation (albeit minor) of spirit corresponds to Howard Estabrook's awkward script, a violation of letter. Two characters of no concern to Saroyan, for example, drift in and out of the movie with disastrous consequences. The deceased Mr. Macauley (Ray Collins), who actually does not figure at all in the book, appears in the filmed *The Human Comedy* with annoying regularity, as an omniscient specter. The movie opens with a preface: luminous, billowing clouds part, and the voice of the late Macauley patriarch booms, "I am Matt Macauley; I have been dead for two years. But so much of me is still living that I know the end is really the beginning . . . my beliefs still live on in the lives of my loved ones." Having thus spelled out a no-nonsense theme, the camera cuts to gopher, Ulysses, Homer, etc., while a disembodied voice from the heavens introduces the characters ("my second son, Homer . . ."). (This venerable-old-man-as-storyteller device flourished in Hollywood in the 1940s—vide Anatole Litvak's *City for Conquest* [1940]—perhaps originating with the Stage Manager in Thornton Wilder's 1938 *Our Town.*) Spectral Macauley senior returns to earth several times during the filmed *The Human Comedy*, and each instance is ludicrous, jarring, and theatrical. Materializing during an especially disheartening moment, phantom Macauley senior comforts Mrs. Macauley in her rocker. He kisses her lightly on the forehead and whispers, "I'll always be with you." She pauses, looks up from reading her Bible (naturally), brightens, and pats her hair self-consciously where the ghostly lips alighted. Exit the wraith of MGM's fertile imagination.

Meanwhile, the character of Marcus Macauley (the soldier, World War II personified) also flits in and out of the movie with ruinous results. Saroyan, in his novel, had the good sense to limit this character's intrusive "existence"; other Ithacacians talk about Marcus incessantly but he himself appears only once, three-quarters of the way through the novel. MGM (undoubtedly padding Van Johnson's role) created several painfully similar scenes for Marcus, in which the simple soul is caught customarily mid-speech intoning the splendors of life in home-town Ithaca, listened to intently by lunkheaded Tobey George (John Craven). Then, characteristically, Marcus and Tobey lead a roomful of homesick soldiers in a few verses of "Leaning on the Everlasting Arms," Marcus pumping the accordion. One dose of this John Fordian hokum is enough in Saroyan's novel; Tobey, Marcus, and faithful accordion recur like a nightmare in the filmed *The Human Comedy*. When Marcus is finally killed in battle (off-camera), the stage is set for an extraordinary finale. "Ma, Bess and Mary!" shouts Homer, choking back the tears, "The soldier has come home!" The soldier is *not* Marcus, but Tobey George, an orphan who arrives limping "home" to Ithaca. Suddenly, not one ghost but *two* materialize arm in arm—eldest son Marcus and Macauley senior—and they mount the porch and step through the open screen door, home: the circle is unbroken, the ending is only the beginning.

These cinematic lapses into extreme unctuousness exceed even Saroyan's normal bounds. When a Mexican-American *madre* is informed of the death of her soldier son, the camera instantly dissolves to a heavy-handed visual metaphor: mother rocking the baby, the image used conspicuously as far back as D. W. Griffith's *Intolerance* in 1916. When daughter Bess Macauley attends the local cinema with three off-duty soldiers, a photograph of FDR flashes pointedly across the screen during a newsreel. "I get a lump in my throat everytime I see the flag," Bess confesses with a gulp, "it reminds me of my brother, Marcus." (What better evidence of a united-in-war Hollywood than FDR in an MGM movie? Saroyan at least had the discretion to avoid a *specific* homage to FDR in his novel.) But the most excruciating moment of the filmed *The Human Comedy* occurs when Mr. Spangler and his high-society sweetheart Diana Steed (Marsha Hunt) cruise leisurely by an Ithaca town picnic in their open-air convertible. The camera pans slowly along, eye level with the car, for one of the lengthiest tracking shots in memory, as Mr. Spangler and beloved gaze fondly upon the picnic, the lagoon, the revelry, the feast. In one of the most absurdly stylized visions of a liberal Hollywood, Greeks, Poles, Spaniards, Mexicans, Russians, Swedes, and Armenians ("you can always tell the Armenians by the priests and kids; that's what they believe in, God and children") are witnessed in turn, enacting their native customs, dancing their native dances, and garbed in native regalia, as Mr. Spangler gushes deliriously about the virtues of melting-pot (nay, united-front) America. Saroyan dusts off this little episode with less than five hundred words in his novel, very coolly and prudently. Only a director such as Frank Capra could have transformed this fragile patriotic sentiment into credible cinema and he, alas (or fortunately), was not employed by Metro-Goldwyn-Mayer.

The overall result is a not very organic movie that careens crazily between cheap, maudlin melodrama and natural, poignant experience, seeming honestly undecided between emotional extremes. But it is this imprecision in tone and outlook that mars what is otherwise coherent Saroyan whimsy. Best among the movie's scenes are those which are least pontifical and those with a genuine colloquial flavor (Saroyan's characters have an enormous passion for bursting into American folk songs at the tiniest opportunity.) These are scenes notably dominated either by Mickey Rooney's Homer or Jack Jenkins's Ulysses who, still being youths, are less prone to reflect upon universal truths. There is an excellent vignette in an apricot orchard, for example, when Ulysses and a gang of young boys (among them, Carl "Alfalfa" Switzer) are frightened away by a senile gigglepuss named Old Man Henderson (Clem Bevans). And there is another lovely scene, which takes place in the early morning between Ulysses and Homer, as the younger boy dreamily asks a captivating series of childishly curious questions ("What's that?" "Exercises." "What for?" "Muscle."). Mickey Rooney even gets away with an unashamedly tear-coaxing scene (again, identical to the novel) in which he reads a letter from his brother in uniform, who stolidly bequeathes his fishing tackle, etc., to the new "man in the family." "You are what we are fighting for, you my brother," Homer reads aloud, eyes widening, "When we meet, I will let you wrestle me down in the parlor in front of Ma and Bessie. . . ." Rooney's face tightens, darkens, as the tears begin to well. "I'll spit at the world if my brother is killed!" he shouts, whirling to vanish wet-cheeked. It is prime Saroyan, prime MGM, and one of the moments that make *The Human Comedy,* flaws notwithstanding, an intriguing and sometimes seductive movie.

There is a postscript. *The Human Comedy* (novel) became a best seller, one of Saroyan's most critically acclaimed works. The movie became one of the most popular films of 1943, and also one of the most talked about. "Sentimental showmanship," sniffed Bosley Crowther of the *New York Times,* who wrote, "In an almost formless tribute to the goodness and sweetness of man's soul, are spliced some quick, penetrating glimpses with long stretches of sheer banality." "Most of my friends detest it," said James Agee, writing in the *Nation,* adding "in its rare successes, it interests me more than any other film I have seen for a good while." History does not record William Saroyan's response to his own unceremoniously usurped movie. But the screen became an obsessive subject of many essays, and he authored a stage play about his experiences in the film colony, called *Get Away Old Man* (the characters included a sweet-mannered, youthful scenarist and a viciously caricatured studio mogul who wants to produce a picture about "Mother") that flopped miserably. Needless to say, Saroyan never again ventured to Hollywood. And when, three years later, MGM offered the astonishing sum of 225,000 dollars for the rights to *The Time of Your Life,* the author had his belated revenge. Instead, he leased the rights to James Cagney and his independent Cagney Productions on a seven-year, 150,000-dollar contract, thinking Cagney just right as Joe, philosopher of the waterfront saloon. The resulting movie is little seen today (only two known copies exist, one in the Cagney vaults and the other in the Library of Congress) but it is widely assumed that Saroyan, on principle if not quality, always preferred the second movie to its Hollywood predecessor.

All the King's Men (1946)
Robert Penn Warren

In Which Humpty Dumpty Becomes King

BY WILLIAM WALLING

One of the dominant themes of twentieth-century literature has been its insistence on our social and psychological fragmentation. William Butler Yeats's "Second Coming" (1919) perhaps gives the best-known expression to this idea: "Things fall apart," Yeats writes; "the center cannot hold; / Mere anarchy is loosed upon the world." Robert Penn Warren's Pulitzer-prize winning novel of 1946, *All the King's Men*, surely participates, if only by its title's allusion to Humpty Dumpty's great fall, in this same vision of incoherence.

But there is more to Warren's novel than merely its title to suggest his participation in such a theme. Loosely basing his narrative on the career of Huey Long, the man who dominated Louisiana politics with near-dictatorial power during the years 1928–35, Warren has written a kind of lengthy parable on "the terrible division of [the] age." [1] And in his parable Warren makes clear his own belief that modern political movements are, probably, absolutely futile as remedies for the fragmentation of our times. Indeed, as if to underscore how little importance politics holds in his own view of experience, Warren has declared that the novel "was never intended to be a book about politics. Politics merely provided the framework story in which

[1] The phrase occurs near the end of the novel and is meant to suggest what Warren's narrator, Jack Burden, has learned from Willie Stark's career.

the deeper concerns, whatever their final significance, might work themselves out." [2]

Nevertheless, since Warren has also conceded that his original idea for *All the King's Men* (first embodied in a play entitled *Proud Flesh*) [3] was "the career of Long and the atmosphere of Louisiana," [4] it will probably be useful to say a few words about Huey Long himself. Born in 1893, Long became governor of Louisiana in 1928. Two years later, in 1930, he was elected to the U.S. Senate. By 1932, he had assumed a prominent place in national politics, gaining widespread attention with a radical platform of income redistribution (including a guaranteed annual income for every family in the United States). Simultaneous with his senatorial position, however, Long maintained an iron grip over Louisiana politics, often returning to the state capitol at Baton Rouge, and it was there, on September 8, 1935, that he was assassinated by a rather obscure physician named Carl Austin Weiss, Jr., the son-in-law of one of Long's bitterest enemies.

Clearly enough, Warren (and Robert Rossen, for that matter) departs most significantly from Long's actual career by suppressing all references to the U.S. Senate. So prominent was Long on the national scene, in fact, that there was every indication that he would be a third-party presidential candidate either in 1936 or 1940 (to be sure, a faint hint of this historical reality is given by Rossen in the sequence where most of the main characters view a *March of Time*-like newsreel based on Willie Stark's career). Yet there are so many other departures in the novel from Long's actual life—although admittedly of a less obvious sort—that it seems only just to accept Warren's own insistence that "Long was but one of the figures that stood in the shadows of imagination behind Willie Stark." [5] At the same time, it may be worth mentioning one small suggestive point: in 1933

[2] Warren's "Introduction" to the Modern Library edition of *All the King's Men* (New York: Random House), p. vi.

[3] *Proud Flesh*, a drama written in verse and colloquial prose, is quite different from the novel. Willie Talos is the central character throughout, and Jack Burden has only a minor part.

[4] "Introduction," Modern Library edition, p. vi.

[5] Ibid.

Long published his autobiography, with a title intended to make unmistakable the social implications of his economic platform; and that title in turn almost surely must have contributed, in Warren's imagination, to the ironic implications of the nursery rhyme about Humpty Dumpty, for Long called his autobiography *Every Man a King*.

Of much greater importance for the reader of *All the King's Men,* however, is an awareness of Warren's fundamental technique in transforming his narrative into something other than the mere rise and fall of a political figure named Willie Stark. For by casting his novel in the first person, and by making his narrator the kind of man Jack Burden is, Warren has shifted dramatic focus away from Stark's actions to Burden's perception of them (and, of course, to Burden's perception of the actions of everyone else in the novel as well, including his own). In short, the real drama of *All the King's Men* is meant to reside in how, and what, Jack Burden learns from Willie Stark's career.

We can sum up that learning process briefly enough. For most of the novel Burden is a distinctly rootless man. He has broken away from his own privileged class (represented by the community at Burden's Landing), has attached himself to Willie Stark (as if Stark and the populist ideas he represents will heal Burden's own class rootlessness), and has persisted in a sentimental, essentially adolescent attachment to Anne Stanton (who herself belongs to Burden's Landing and who represents the great love of his young manhood). Under the pressure of Stark's relentless drive for power, however, Burden ultimately learns of the mysterious spiritual unity of all men, despite "the terrible division of [the] age" which class consciousness seems to intensify.

"Each of us is the son of a million fathers," Burden declares near the end of the novel. And by claiming this he indicates that he has begun "to understand" Cass Mastern, a great-uncle of his who had been the subject years ago of Burden's unfinished doctoral dissertation. For in the course of his research Burden had discovered his great-uncle's faith "that the world is like an enormous spider web. . . . Your happy foot or your gay wing may have brushed it ever so lightly, but what happens always happens and there is the spider, bearded black and with his great faceted eyes glittering like mirrors in the sun, or like God's eye, and the fangs dripping."

The imagery of interrelationship conveyed by the spider's web is unmistakable. Individual human beings may feel fragmented; in their fragmentation they may turn to other, seemingly stronger human beings in the hope of losing their sense of isolation; but every human is bound together in a mysterious network of vulnerability created by "the spider." And the spider's eyes, as the quoted passage indicates, just happen to be "like God's eye." By the close of the novel, then, Warren's narrator has won through to a vision of human existence which is very close to a religious faith.

But more than that. Since *All the King's Men* becomes, through Warren's technique, Jack Burden's story rather than Willie Stark's, we can also see that "the king" of the book's title must be the same as "the spider" of Cass Mastern's faith.[6] And if this is so, then Willie Stark has to be perceived as a character no less significantly vulnerable and fragmented than anyone else in the novel. (Indeed, in the drama Warren wrote before revising it into the novel we now have, the female character who is to become Anne Stanton asks desperately of the figure who becomes Willie Stark, "If you are fragmentary, what of us others?"[7]) In other words, the implicit parable of *All the King's Men* is to cast Willie Stark as no higher than Humpty Dumpty; above him, and above every other character too (hence the "all" of the title), an unknowable vision watches over man's destiny, "like God's eye," binding humanity together.

Robert Rossen's film version, which appeared three years later, makes a much different impact from the novel. As Warren himself was to remark long after he had first seen the film (and

[6] Cf. James Ruoff, "Humpty Dumpty and *All the King's Men*," in *The Modern American Novel*, ed. Max Westbrook (New York: Random House, 1966), pp. 196–208.

[7] *Proud Flesh*; lines cited by William M. Schutte, "The Dramatic Versions of the Willie Stark Story," in *All the King's Men: A Symposium* (Pittsburgh: Carnegie Press, 1957), p. 81.

his comments are particularly instructive to anyone interested in the relationship between literature and film), "I think that [*All the King's Men*] is an extraordinarily good movie, with [Rossen's] very special touch. I can praise it, because it seems to me that when a movie is made from a novel the novel is merely raw material, the movie is a new creation, and the novelist can properly attract neither praise nor blame for it. The movie, as a matter of fact, does not 'mean' what I think my book meant. It is Bob's [Rossen's] movie." [8]

A specific comparison between the beginning and end of the two versions should make Warren's point clear. In the novel the narrative opens in 1936, with Willie Stark already governor and Jack Burden riding along with him (and some of the other central characters) in a limousine speeding across one of the new highways Stark's administration has built throughout the state. In the film the story opens somewhere in the 1920s, in a newspaper office, with Jack Burden (John Ireland) soon receiving an assignment from his editor to cover an obscure rural candidate named Willie Stark (Broderick Crawford).

Based on these two different openings, a number of points seem worth making. For one thing, the novel breaks up ordinary chronological sequence by first showing us Stark near the height of his power; the film, on the other hand, presents us with a relatively straightforward account in time of Willie's rise from obscure beginnings. And from this difference we can see how the novel's freer handling of time contributes importantly to its shape as Burden's story, for from the start the emphasis falls on *his* awareness of events (if Burden does not remember things they do not exist) rather than on Willie's active involvement with them. Conversely, Rossen's film, with its chronologically direct account of Willie's rise and fall, has much more of a tendency to cast Burden into the role of a secondary participant (from the opening scene onward, of course, he is usually someone taking orders, either from his editor or from Willie). Indeed, it may be that Rossen's handling of the "raw material" of the

[8] A letter of Warren's published by Alan Casty, "The Films of Robert Rossen," *Film Quarterly*, XX, No. 2 (1966–67), p. 9.

Warren novel, with the dramatic focus now largely shifted to Willie's grand rise and his violent downfall, makes more evident than any other film Rossen ever directed how genuine was his declared admiration for Macbeth.[9]

Moreover, the two different endings Warren and Rossen provide surely reinforce the alternate emphases of the openings. For in the novel there are forty pages which follow Willie's assassination, pages which center upon Burden's changing attitude toward life, not to mention his eventual marriage to Anne Stanton. In the film, however, after a brief exchange between Burden and Anne, we close with a final image of Willie Stark slumping into death, as if to make unmistakable Rossen's shift in intention. "It could have been the whole world," Stark mutters with his dying breath. "The whole world." In brief, then, Rossen's version brings Willie Stark to the center of the viewer's concern.

Nor is this all. For by bringing Willie Stark forward, Rossen's film becomes susceptible to a political interpretation rather different from the quasi-religious implications of Warren's novel. On the most obvious level, of course, this is simply because Rossen's film presents us with a wholly secular universe, where human actions are the sole determining force (in the novel, on the other hand, the outcome seems ultimately to depend on some unknowable design). But we might go even further and describe the political impact of Rossen's film as a powerful reflection of his regret for the failure of the potential of American democracy to realize itself. Certainly his own biographical situation at the time of making the film would seem to support such a viewing of it. In the spring of 1947, in response to the increasing tensions of the Cold War, the Committee on Un-American Activities began hearings on the alleged Communist infiltration of Hollywood. Rossen was one of the first people named by a so-called friendly witness as having had a history of Communist affiliations. In 1948, as a means of preserving his career, Rossen sent a confidential letter to the president of Columbia Pictures

[9] See Alan Casty, *The Films of Robert Rossen* (New York: The Museum of Modern Art, 1969), p. 3.

Willie Stark (Broderick Crawford) with Pa Stark (H. C. Miller), Tom Stark (John Derek), Sadie Burke (Mercedes McCambridge), and newspaperman Jack Burden (John Ireland) envisioning Willie's political future. *All the King's Men* (1949)

attesting to his present nonmembership in the Communist Party.[10] We know that at the same time he was busily working on *All the King's Men,* revising Warren's novel for the screen. Thus, a particularly ironic moment in the film, the brief close-up of the motto engraved on the wall of the state capitol during the mob action of a gullible electorate to protect Stark, *The Will of the People Is the Will of the State,* may be Rossen's quiet de-murral from what he perceived as the Committee's perversion of democratic principles. After all, the earlier political activity of Rossen—through the middle 1940s—suggests a faith in the best ideals of democracy. Only later, in the early 1950s, did Rossen capitulate to the pressures of the Committee on Un-American Activities by becoming a cooperative witness.

Much less debatable, however, is the way the motto functions within the context of the film itself. For Willie really does begin as a man of the people. Naive, idealistic, honestly caring for others, Willie first emerges into effective prominence when he publicly recognizes his shared roots with an entire class of the dispossessed. "Listen to me, you hicks!" he roars, in the fair-grounds speech that makes him a vital statewide candidate. "This is the truth. You're a hick. And nobody ever helped a hick but the hick himself!" Indeed, in one of Rossen's most brilliant additions to the raw material of the novel, the film shows us the badly hung-over Willie slumping into a child's swing shortly before his speech, as if in instinctive return to the impoverished origins he shares with so many others at the fair. Yet, of course, this is the same Willie Stark whom we later see perverting justice so often in order to advance his own ends. Hence Rossen's close-up of the motto on the wall of the state capitol, *The Will of the People Is the Will of the State,* at the same time that busloads of "hicks" are being brought into the city to assure Willie's autocratic rule, suggests both the terrible power and the capacity for perversion of the democratic process.

And this indication of uncertainty about the processes of democracy is surely reinforced by the symbolic use Rossen makes of Burden's repeated visits back to his own supposed roots at

---

[10] Casty, *Film Quarterly,* p. 6.

Burden's Landing. Admittedly, this portion of the film is weaker than the scenes which concentrate on Willie's public life. Moreover, it was here that Rossen did a good deal of his cutting when he was compelled to shorten the playing time for the film by almost an hour.[11] But Burden's several visits "home" serve at least two important functions in Rossen's overall treatment. First, they convey visually most of what Rossen has been able to transmit of the theme of fragmentation which plays so large a part in Warren's novel (each trip to Burden's Landing, with its crossing of the water that separates the Landing from the mainland, reminds us not only of the class divisions of society but also of the existence of a privileged minority thoroughly divorced from the initial source of Willie's strength). And second, the trips to Burden's Landing present us with the historical reality that usually confronts the candidate who has been swept into office by a democratic tide (eventually Willie must deal as best he can with the people who have held power in the past by virtue of their birth and wealth).

We can see, then, that Willie's decline in the film is associated with his inability to remain wholly inside the class that brought him to power. (Surely it is no accident that both his last mistress and his assassin belong to Burden's Landing.) At the same time Rossen presents us with a vision of political ambition much less implicitly futile than Warren's. For although Willie of course meets with a violent downfall in both versions, in Rossen's film we also experience far more directly the sheer energy of his rise. And where one man can rise from the dispossessed—and fall— another may rise and somehow handle both the historical problem of dealing with a privileged minority and the psychological temptations inherent in the privilege of power itself. Rossen himself might deny so relatively optimistic a reading of his film; nevertheless, the secularity of the world the film presents, coupled with the images of energetic change it presents, surely does suggest the possibility of further hope. Accordingly, it may be most useful to conclude with a brief reconsideration of Warren's title. In the novel, as I have already suggested, Willie seems to

11 Ibid.

be cast as Humpty Dumpty, while "the king" of *All the King's Men* appears to be meant as something analogous to God. In Rossen's film, however, Willie himself strikes us as "the king"— at least in his potential. And both the tragedy and the promise of the film version bring us clearly into touch with an order of experience quite different from Warren's, one in which we may even find the implication that America is still capable of reordering its social and political destiny, in a fashion wholly secular and humanistic.

Intruder in the Dust (1948)

William Faulkner

Rites of Passage: Novel to Film

BY E. PAULINE DEGENFELDER

Intruder in the Dust is one of the few outstanding Hollywood adaptations of Faulkner's fiction, the more remarkable considering that it appeared in 1949, when the House Un-American Activities Committee investigations were creating fear in the film industry. While others in 1949 produced "message" films dealing with racial tension (*Home of the Brave, Lost Boundaries,* and *Pinky*), *Intruder in the Dust* is the most forthright. The credit is due to MGM producer-director, Clarence Brown, a Southerner who chose to film the novel out of a clear ethical commitment. Ben Maddow, author of the script, explained (in a letter to this writer) what the novel and its adaptation meant to Brown:

> He had witnessed when he was a young man . . . a so-called "race riot" in which blacks were shot down on the streets and piled onto a flatcar at the railway station, and then dumped in the woods miles away from the scene of slaughter. To him, the film was a kind of payment of his conscience, and the fact that Faulkner, too, was a disturbed Southerner was not irrelevant to his choice.

Having adapted *Anna Christie* (1930), *Anna Karenina* (1935), *Ah, Wilderness!* (1935), and *The Human Comedy* (1943),

This is a revised and abridged version of an article that originally appeared as "The Film Adaptation of Faulkner's *Intruder in the Dust*," in *Literature/Film Quarterly,* Vol. I, No. 2, April, 1973. Reprinted by permission of the editor and author.

178

Brown was well versed in the problems of transposition from a literary to a visual medium. He was also able to take advantage of favorable conditions within the studio at MGM. Production control was passing to Dore Schary, a liberal who wholly approved the project. Consequently, when Brown insisted that Faulkner's locale was absolutely essential to verisimilitude, MGM allowed ninety percent of the film to be shot in Oxford, Mississippi, where a nonprofessional cast of townspeople was hired for dramatic crowd scenes.

Ben Maddow, whose previous film work was in documentary, was an appropriate philosophical choice for screenwriter.[1] Elizabeth Patterson, a native of Savannah, Tennessee, with a long career as a filmic incarnation of the genteel Southern lady behind her (including a role as Aunt Jenny in *The Story of Temple Drake,* a 1933 adaptation of *Sanctuary*), was cast as the indomitable and heroic Miss Habersham. Claude Jarman, Jr., another Southerner, was selected for the leading role of young Chick Mallison. Brown had directed Jarman as the boy in *The Yearling* (1946) and was capitalizing on Jarman's newly acquired gangling adolescence for his role in *Intruder in the Dust.*

The adolescent rite of passage—Chick's growth toward adulthood—underlies both novel and film, though it receives very different treatments. In his book, Faulkner presents initiation as the accepting of the preestablished concepts of the community one wishes to enter. In contrast, the film stresses the notion that passage requires the repudiation of traditional values (and thus perhaps foreshadows the open break between parent and child in later films such as *Rebel Without a Cause* [1955]). Nowhere is this novel/film opposition clearer than in the ideas about Chick's proper relation to the community before and after the nearly tragic lynching of the proud black man, Lucas.

The film opens with Lucas Beauchamp, a black, being taken to jail, accused of killing a white man, Vinson, a son of the vindictive Gowrie clan. As repayment for rescuing Chick from drowning some years earlier, Lucas bids Chick summon his

[1] Editors' note. Since this article was written, Joseph Blotner has reported that Faulkner did some uncredited work on the screenplay (*Faulkner: A Biography,* New York: Random House, 1974, p. 1278).

Chick Mallison (Claude Jarman, Jr.)—extreme left—and townspeople look on as Lucas Beauchamp (Juano Hernandez) makes a purchase. *Intruder in the Dust* (1949)

lawyer-uncle John Stevens (Gavin Stevens in the novel) to help. Stevens is only lukewarm in his commitment to Lucas, so Chick promises Lucas that he himself will exhume Vinson's body to prove Lucas innocent by showing that the bullet could not have come from his gun. Chick, his black companion, Alec, and Miss Habersham open the coffin, only to find it empty; the next day the sheriff's search party finds the body in quicksand. While Miss Habersham guards the jail to prevent Lucas from being lynched, Stevens and the sheriff apprehend the killer, Crawford "Nub" Gowrie, Vinson's brother. Lucas is freed, the community returns to normality, but the experience spells out for Chick and his uncle the need for constant vigilance to protect justice.

In Faulkner's novel, Chick is stunned by "the face of the crowd" demanding Lucas's death. The mob is "insensate, vacant of thought or even passion [with] an Expression significantless . . . without dignity and not even evocative of horror: just neckless slack-muscled and asleep. . . ." But following the exhausting night, there is hope. Lucas lives, and Faulkner argues the South's ability to solve its own racial problems, the inherited birthright of a Southern aristocracy of virtue. The Past furnishes wisdom and moral strength to the Present.

Miss Habersham is descended from one of the three founders of the town of Jefferson. Her involvement in Lucas's case stems from her near-sisterhood with Lucas's wife, Molly, for Miss Habersham and Molly were both reared by Molly's mother. Likewise, Chick senses an identity between Lucas and his own grandfather. In the end, Chick articulates his own noble ties with the past—a psychic fugue inherited from, and identical in thought to, his uncle's reflections:

> It's all *now* you see. Yesterday won't be over until tomorrow and tomorrow began ten thousand years ago. For every Southern boy fourteen years old, not once but whenever he wants it, there is the instant when it's not yet two o'clock on that July afternoon in 1863, the brigades are in position behind the rail fence.

At the end of Faulkner's *Intruder*, Chick not only regards himself as belonging to an organic community, but his interior monologues recapitulate the dogma of Gavin Stevens, the most ideological defender of that community.

The film is never so assuring. In attempting to save Lucas, Chick is motivated by one man's moral obligation to another—outside of the historical frame. Miss Habersham's involvement, likewise, springs solely from a personal sense of justice and has nothing to do with her rich Southern heritage. Therefore when Chick states at the conclusion that Lucas is "the keeper of our conscience," the reference is apparently only to himself and his uncle and Miss Habersham, but certainly not to the community.

To reinforce this theme of separation visually in the film, Chick is associated only once with the crowd. At the beginning, Chick appears in the gathering which awaits Lucas's arrival. However, after Lucas designates him as emissary ("You, young man, tell your uncle I want to see him.") he never again joins the white townspeople—as they evolve into a porcine, pusillanimous mass, a repulsive mob. To further justify Chick's aversion to his community, Clarence Brown invents a scene of the mob waiting outside the jail for Lucas's burning. The vignette is enacted matter-of-factly and in full daylight. The gathering is a festive occasion. The loudspeaker blares, men arrive by the busload, and a woman holding a baby asks when the fire will start. The sequence is doubly terrifying because Chick is not there to intervene between the audience and the events. (He *is* present in the novel.)

Brown conveys Chick's tenuous connection to his community in still other ways. When seen with white adults, Chick occupies either a subservient or marginal position, signifying visually his "threshold" situation. Brown photographs Chick in doorways: of the jail cell, Uncle John's office, Sheriff Hampton's kitchen. At the Mallison home, Chick is scolded by his father for being late to the meal and warned to remain uninvolved in the Lucas case. Seated at dinner with a napkin tucked under his chin—at his father's insistence—Chick positively exudes childishness. But his subsequent flight from the dining room indicates his deepening disassociation from family and his growing realization that Lucas deserves justice.

This scene is juxtaposed by Brown with a second of Faulkner's dinner scenes, recounted by Chick in flashback in the movie. He tells Uncle John of going hunting with Alec and falling into the creek. Alec tries to extend a pole to Chick, but a bodiless voice then orders Alec to withdraw. Chick is forced to climb out of the creek without assistance. From a low-angle shot, the figure of Lucas towers above miraculously—a visual metaphor for Lucas's almost biblical role as judge as well as a show of his psychic domination over Chick.

Soon, stripped of his own garments and wrapped in Lucas's blanket, Chick sits eating a meal which Lucas's wife Molly has prepared—Negro food. The meal is simple, wholesome, and acceptable to Chick. Lucas stands in the next room watching him, but Chick is allowed to eat unharassed. This immersion sequence—critic Andrew Lytle has characterized it as Chick's baptismal [2]—combined with the subsequent dinner, establish an unmistakable ritual pattern in both novel and film. (In neither, however, can Chick grow exclusively in Lucas's world. He must assert his position in the white world as well.)

In the film, both Lucas and Uncle John are guides in Chick's initiation ritual. Lucas's role as judge, reinforced visually by his stature, his frock coat, and his chain, is a counterpart and contrast to John Stevens's legal position. Stevens articulates precepts for Chick; Lucas assists Chick in transforming precepts into deeds.

The novel is filled with Stevens's lengthy disquisitions, which Faulkner respects. By contrast, Clarence Brown regards Stevens somewhat critically, as more a talker than a doer, a man enervated by words and surrounded by his law books. (Ironically, even to make this point, Brown still had to pare down Stevens's speeches from the novel to functional dimensions. He excluded also Stevens's obnoxious polemic in the novel about the white aristocracy's ability to help "Sambo.")

The film diminishes John (Gavin) Stevens and magnifies Lucas, the man who fuses words and deeds in his multifaceted identity as patriarch, judge, teacher, and—in Stevens's words at the end—keeper of conscience. (Actually, according to Ben

[2] "Regeneration for the Man," *Faulkner: A Collection of Critical Essays* (Englewood Cliffs, N.J.: Prentice-Hall, 1966), p. 236.

Maddow, these were producer Dore Schary's words: "There goes our conscience." Maddow comments, "Mr. Schary . . . insisted that the moral of the film be placed where the moral in a cautionary tale would be, at the end. This displacement, in my opinion, gives the film a falsely sentimental turn." [3]) This outright moralizing, one of the few flaws in the movie, is absent in the final scene of the novel, although Quentin Compson makes similar comments on the functions of blacks in *The Sound and the Fury* (1929)—("They come into white people's lives . . . in sudden sharp black trickles that isolate white facts for an instant in unarguable truth like under a microscope").

While Lucas's personality is strengthened in the film, Alec, Chick's companion, is weakened. In the novel Alec is defiantly black. He resists Lucas's individualism by claiming that "It's the ones like Lucas makes trouble for everybody," but by his very defiance he often echoes Lucas. Alec of the film, much less articulate than his novelistic counterpart, frequently performs a comic function. In the graveyard scene, his fear causes his eyes to bulge. This is unfortunate indulgence on Clarence Brown's part, for it seriously distorts Faulkner's concept of the Negro, which by this point in his career had advanced beyond the minstrel types found in *Sartoris* (1929). Maddow writes that the convention was one which Brown, who had been directing since 1920, inherited from the silent film:

> It was a fixed tradition in early American films that ghosts and graveyards would make any black's eyes enlarge to the point of monstrosity. I think Clarence Brown felt that this treatment of Alec was perfectly natural and funny. It is not written in the screenplay, of course, and I must admit to being somewhat shocked at seeing it in the film itself.

This is the only occasion where Clarence Brown's experience from the silent era results in a disservice to Faulkner. In many other spots in his film, Brown finds an appropriate visual equivalent for a key Faulkner passage. To show the rapport between Chick and Uncle John, Brown has them toss a baseball. To show

[3] Letter from Maddow to the author.

Mr. Gowrie's grief at finding the body of his son Vinson in the quicksand, Brown focuses on Gowrie's tear-filled eyes and his dignified attempt to remove the mud from his son's face. The silence is broken only by the baying hounds and the sighing pines, objective correlatives to the father's unverbalized sorrow.

A final sequence which substitutes for dialogue occurs during Chick's ride toward Caledonia Chapel. In the novel Chick notes that since Lucas's apprehension, other Negroes have retreated from sight: "They were acting exactly as Negroes and whites both would have expected Negroes to act at such a time, they were still there, they had not fled, you just didn't see them. . . ." In the film it is Chick's actions which break this silence: as his horse's hoofbeats resound along the road, Brown shows the retreat of the blacks—a mother covering her children, a man peering from behind a door, other Negroes indoors playing cards.

The visual emphasis on hands—black and white—in the film of *Intruder* develops into a sophisticated motif. In the opening, the camera records only a set of manacled black hands—a fitting symbol of the black's history of enforced subservience—and only when the car stops before a jail is there a shot of Lucas's entire body. Later, in a scene where the elder Mr. Gowrie sits in Lucas's cabin, there is a shot first of a pair of gnarled hands pointing a revolver and then a full view of Gowrie. Hunter and hunted are paralleled. Not only does Gowrie look like Lucas as he sits in Lucas's chair, but after he stares at a portrait of Lucas and his deceased wife Molly, he comments on his own wife's death.

The motif is clarified during Chick's interview with Lucas at the jail. While they talk through the barred entrance, the camera angles in on the white and black hands gripping the latticed door and creates a deliberate ambiguity: it is impossible to tell who is imprisoned. Brown implies a mutual obligation between Chick and Lucas to free each other.

Earlier, in the flashback at Lucas's cabin, Chick attempts to pay Molly for the meal and the camera shows a near meeting of the white and black hands. But Lucas refuses the sum and Chick flings the coins on the floor, ordering Lucas to pick them up. Again Lucas refuses, and this time it is Alec whose hands are photographed retrieving the money. In the final scene of the movie, Lucas counts out his token payment for John Stevens's services. Significantly, Chick does not receive payment for helping to save Lucas's life. Money does not count in this authentic relationship which is both obligatory and, paradoxically, liberating. By committing himself to Lucas, Chick has completed the rite of passage into adulthood.

For most critics, Faulkner had presented the South in an unobjectionable light in *Intruder in the Dust*. But Clarence Brown, beyond his insistence on creating an authentic Southern milieu in his movie version, had deleted most of those passages vindicating the South. At the end of the novel, as Cleanth Brooks points out in his *William Faulkner: The Yoknapatawpha County* (1963), Faulkner's mouthpiece Stevens "evidently finds the unanimity of the community something of hope rather than menace." But Clarence Brown's protagonist Chick remains, by choice, an outsider. In the concluding scene of the movie, Chick is seated on his uncle's balcony, detached from the crowd, with a superior vision, both figuratively and literally, of his relationship to the community.

Through Chick, Brown implies that moral obligations can be satisfied, not by recourse to community, but rather by recourse to the human values of discrete—and elite—individuals.

The Naked and the Dead (1948)

Norman Mailer

Naked Before the Camera

BY NORMAN MAILER

[F. Anthony Macklin, editor of *Film Heritage,* once embarked on a feature for the magazine entitled "The Writer and Hollywood." The purpose was to "ask writers the following two questions in an attempt to clarify the writer's relationship to Hollywood: (1) Has Hollywood treated your work justly? (2) Can the serious writer's work survive in Hollywood?" Here are Norman Mailer's responses.]

1. *The Naked and the Dead* [1958] was one of the worst movies ever made. If it had been just a little worse than that it would have come out the other end and been extraordinarily funny, a sort of pioneer classic of pop art, and film critics might have decided that it had a profound influence on the James Bonds. But the picture was finally not bad enough. Here and there the vestige of a serious attempt manifested itself, and so the picture never got through the tunnel at all, it just expired in its own glop. Of course they can always use it as an orientation film for Viet Nam, since that after all is a good comic strip war, or will be if Robert McNamara will consent to play Daddy Warbucks.

2. I think as a working rule of thumb, a novelist or playwright

Editors' note. This originally appeared as "The Writer and Hollywood: Norman Mailer," in *Film Heritage,* vol. 2, no. 1, Fall, 1966, p. 23. Reprinted by permission.

The armed forces hypnotized by the fanciful striptease of Lily (Lili St. Cyr). *The Naked and the Dead* (1958)

cannot hope for his work to survive in Hollywood. It can only be adulterated or improved, and since filming a good novel makes everyone concerned quite tense, and justifiably so, since no one wishes particularly to adulterate good art—there are few rewards in heaven for that—I think if I were a director I would look for the sort of modest novel which can make a fine movie. I think the best example is *The Asphalt Jungle*.[1] But generally speaking, there is something tiresome about question 2. A novelist or playwright sells his work to Hollywood not in order that the work shall survive the translation, but to purchase time for himself, so all belly-aching, including my own, smacks too much of sniffing the armpit and wrestler's moans.

[1] Editors' note. The 1950 film directed by John Huston and based on the novel by W. R. Burnett (1949).

The Man with the Golden Arm (1949)

Nelson Algren

Anatomy of a Junkie Movie

BY ROBERT C. ROSEN

While I don't like to measure success in terms of money, still the real success of a picture lies in how many people come, enjoy it, and tell their friends to come.

—Otto Preminger

The role of the writer is always to stand against the culture he is in.
—Nelson Algren

If the "problem" films of producer-director Otto Preminger testify to the power of our culture to absorb what opposes it, the fiction of Nelson Algren demonstrates both the virtue and the difficulty of sustaining an effective opposition. Algren's independence and rebelliousness led him first to work with the Communist Party in the early 1930s, and then to reject its orthodoxy later in the decade, "although," he adds twenty years after, "I still hate the profit motive." [1] Preminger, on the other hand, seems at peace with the profit motive, despite his self-appointed role as freedom fighter. His pathbreaking independence from the big studios; his well-publicized fight against restrictive production codes and the Hollywood blacklists; his eager tackling of "controversial" issues like racism, virginity, addiction, rape, abortion, and LSD—

[1] Quoted in Kenneth Allsop, "A Talk on the Wild Side," *The Spectator* (Oct. 16, 1959).

these have only proved that his artistic and pecuniary goals are easily synthesized.

In 1931, Nelson Algren graduated into the Depression with a B.A. in journalism but no newspaper job. He hitchhiked and rode freights around the country, picked up odd jobs, and spent time in jail. Though he eventually made a name for himself as a writer, and his *The Man with the Golden Arm* won the 1950 National Book Award, he continued to support left-wing causes, and his sympathies remained with the disinherited. Committed to never selling out, he has lived, perhaps a bit self-consciously, in the "worst" neighborhoods, often in a room.[2] These neighborhoods and their people are not only his material as a writer but also his first love: "My concern is the same as Whitman saying, 'I feel I am of them, I belong to those convicts and prostitutes myself, therefore I cannot deny them, for how can I deny myself?' "[3] The difficulty of this identification creates some of the problems in Algren's work.

Frankie Majcinek, hero of *The Man with the Golden Arm*, is one of the many "luckless living soon to become the luckless dead" trapped in Chicago's run-down West Division Street Polish neighborhood. He returns from an army evacuation hospital with a piece of shrapnel in his liver and a dependence on morphine. Still a famously smooth and honest card dealer (hence the nickname "Machine"), Frankie picks up his old job again. Guilt rather than love binds him to his wife Sophie: she has been crippled, psychosomatically, since a car accident in which Frankie was the drunken driver. Frankie often seeks refuge from her with the selfless Molly Novotny.

In an argument, Frankie accidentally kills Nifty Louie Fomorowski, the local pusher. The unsolved crime becomes an election issue, and police captain Bednar pressures Frankie's best friend Sparrow into naming the killer. Frankie is discovered hiding with Molly, but he escapes, lightly wounded and desperate for a fix. The police find him in a flophouse, where he

---

[2] At this writing, Algren had moved from Chicago to Paterson, New Jersey, initially to write on Rubin "Hurricane" Carter and John Artis.

[3] Quoted in David Ray, "A Talk on the Wild Side: A Bowl of Coffee with Nelson Algren," *The Reporter* (June 11, 1959).

has hanged himself from the chicken-wire top of his cubicle. Without Frankie, Sophie's sanity has deteriorated, and she is institutionalized, locked up.

Much of the symbolism in *The Arm* (as Algren often calls it) is naturalistic and bleak—a roach drowning in a bucket of water, a kite caught in telephone wires, and so on—for their environment clearly propels these characters toward their gloomy ends. Nonetheless, as Malcolm Cowley points out in *The Literary Situation* (1955), the novel begins where pessimistic naturalism leaves off. A veritable police lineup of minor characters peoples the book, some comic, some grotesque, some both, but all with a vitality and an indomitable humanity that prove them better than their world and fates. A prisoner awaiting the electric chair cracks, "This is certainly going to be a good lesson to me." The clash between the realistically depicted environment and the humor and energy with which these characters resist its ravages gives the novel its peculiarly disturbing quality. The comedy, even when bawdy, does not relieve, but intensifies the book's harshness. As Alfred Kazin says, it "hurt[s] like a blow."

Although Algren comes out of the 1930s tradition of "proletarian literature," *The Man with the Golden Arm* is neither a novel of ideas nor one of social analysis. We never really understand where skid row comes from or who benefits from its existence. Algren does take a few pot shots at business: Louie the pusher stands out from the rest as the perfect capitalist selling the perfect commodity ("anything that pays ain't nothin' to be ashamed of," he explains); and Sparrow, a not too competent petty thief, asks only to be backed up with "five grand tonight," and "tomorrow mornin' I get a invitation to join the Chamber of Commerce 'n no questions asked." However, the novel's radicalism comes not from an analysis of capitalism, but simply through partisan support for its more obvious victims. Their entrapment, so intensely depicted, gives the lie to prevailing myths of progress and upward mobility for all.

But *The Arm*'s reach occasionally exceeds its political grasp. Though the novel's characters are sometimes grotesque in their degradation, Algren's omniscient narration and poetic flights awkwardly ask us to identify with them, to share their experience. Algren demands our anger at the oppression of these people with nowhere to go, but at the same time he verges on romanticizing them and their defeat. This contradiction nearly undermines the tough-minded realism and the social criticism of the book as a whole.

Still, as Algren puts it, perhaps too modestly, "*The Arm* was a solid job which humanized and personalized an American street corner lying in the path of an expanding national traffic in drugs." [4] Algren frankly likes the people in his book and finds their values as sound as those of "the business classes," and "a lot truer in a way." But his goal is more to *épater le bourgeoisie* than to overthrow them. He finds "a certain over-all satisfaction in kind of scooping up a shovelful of these people and dumping them in somebody's parlor." [5]

Nelson Algren was soon to find himself in Otto Preminger's parlor. Hired to write a screenplay for *The Arm*, Algren knew immediately that it was not going to work out, that Preminger "wouldn't touch Frankie Machine . . . wouldn't say hello to him." The producer asked Algren, "How come you know such terrible people you write about?"

Algren had originally sold his novel to John Garfield. Convinced the actor genuinely liked and understood Frankie Machine, he was hopeful and collaborated on a script. But Garfield died. Preminger bought the property, rejected the original script, and sent for Algren. The two fought first about money and then about writing. Finally, Algren wrote an insulting mock treatment, and Preminger fired him.

Walter Newman proved a more congenial and accommodating screenwriter.[6] According to Newman, Preminger first envisioned the film as "a murder mystery about a jazz trumpeter, maybe William Holden," but Newman insisted it was "too good a book to muck with." Nonetheless, he soon began to muck, chang-

[4] Ibid.
[5] In *Writers at Work: The Paris Review Interviews,* edited by Malcolm Cowley (1959).
[6] The credits also list Lewis Meltzer as screenwriter. But Newman explains that Meltzer worked only on the earlier screenplay for John Garfield's company, never for Preminger.

ing Frankie, as he put it, from "a salmon going downstream with the current" to "a salmon going upstream." This created the drama necessary to make it "workable as a film," Newman felt, for "a movie-maker's first responsibility is to the people who put up the money . . . no backers, no movies." [7]

While it makes no sense to set up any novel as an ideal to which a film adaptation ought to be faithful, the changes deserve explanation. They can be revealing. In the movie—released in 1955—Preminger and Newman have transformed Algren's emotionally unsettling and subversive story into a voyeuristic slumming adventure with a glib 1950s resolution.

Newman certainly succeeded in making his script dramatic. Sophie's confinement to a wheelchair is no longer psychosomatic but *faked* in the film, and only the audience knows this. When Louie, the pusher, catches her standing and threatens to expose her, she lunges at him and he falls down a stairwell to his death. Frankie, suspected of murdering Louie, hides with Molly and goes "cold turkey" in a big scene. Cured, he comes to tell Sophie he is leaving her. Just as she frantically stands up to stop him from going, police captain Bednar shows up. Now everybody knows who killed Louie! Sophie panics, runs to escape, and plunges three stories to the street. Dying, she tells Frankie how much she loves him, and as the ambulance carries her away, Molly takes Frankie's arm and, sadly, they walk off into the future together. We feel a twinge of pain as Sparrow, Frankie's loyal friend and representative of his old life, is left behind. But we know that Frankie (Frank Sinatra) and Molly (Kim Novak) will make it.

Preminger has taken a novel about the sham of the American Dream and turned it into a success story. Algren's Frankie dreams briefly of changing his name to Jack Duval and becoming a famous drummer, but within seconds the fantasy has "collapsed of its own weight," and become just another bitterly ironic comment on the trap Frankie is in. Preminger makes this dream believable and important, the central thrust of the film. Sophie hides

[7] Quoted in interview by Rui Nogueira, "Writing for the Movies—Walter Newman," *Focus on Film* (U.K.), Autumn, 1972.

Frankie's drumsticks, yells at him when he practices, and tells him he will never succeed. She fears success will release her grip on him. But Molly encourages him. She lets Frankie practice in her place, insists he pursue an audition offer, and helps him get off dope.

The parable of success then is tied to a struggle between the "good woman" and the "bad woman" for Frankie. Sophie, sympathetic and clearly a victim in the novel, is flattened into a sometimes pathetic, but mainly "hysterical," manipulative, destructive figure in the film. Her exposure as a faker, and her death, come as a relief. In the novel, Molly's "big heart" only gets her hurt. But in the film, once she rejects the wrong man (Drunky Johnnie) for the right man (Frankie), this same heart makes her potentially the perfect 1950s wife, supportive and self-denying. With her help, Frankie can work hard and win his fight against addiction and for a new life. Love—impossible in the brutalizing world of the novel—here conquers all (provided the wife dies).[8]

What awaits the new couple is displayed in a very skillful scene about halfway through the film, emblematic of Preminger's conformist vision. Molly meets Frankie downtown, where he has just picked up the musicians' union card he needs for an audition. The day is bright. Strolling along the busy sidewalk, they stop at a very large store window containing a modern kitchen (stove, refrigerator, the works) and two well-dressed mannequins, an apron-clad woman at the stove, and a comfortably seated man reading the newspaper. In profile, in front of the window, Frankie and Molly playfully act out a similar scene and talk about the dummy couple. They kiss. Visually they are absorbed into this immaculately clean, glass-enclosed dream of consumer happiness, which contrasts so strikingly with the dirty stove and sink in a corner of Frankie's cramped, dreary apartment, where crippled Sophie screams instead of cooking quietly.

Algren's skid row characters, Frankie and Molly included, will never achieve this promised happiness. Further, they are pun-

---

[8] Algren found this miraculous rehabilitation of Frankie "ridiculous." "But then," he added, "I wrote the book before I saw Kim Novak. Who knows?"

ished by its very promise. For they are burdened, Algren writes, with

> the great, secret and special American guilt of owning nothing, nothing at all, in the one land where ownership and virtue are one. Guilt that lay crouched behind every billboard which gave each man his commandments, for each man here had failed the billboards all down the line.

Preminger's American Dream is the possibility of achieving what is on those billboards.

The question of a social system's success or failure has been stood on its head, transformed into that of individuals' successes or failures. The novel's people are unjustly trapped; the film implicitly blames the victims for their own abysmal fates. Preminger's Molly shouts sarcastically at a despairing Frankie, "You had a dog's life, sure. Don't face it like other people." Frankie does face it and kicks his habit. He and Molly will succeed. The others, presumably weaker, will not. At the start of the film, Frankie returns from a federal institution which has cured his addiction and taught him to play the drums (none of this is in the novel). Later, in a plush office at the top of a tall building, Mr. Lane, a booking agent, promises to arrange an audition for him, because he likes to help out guys like Frankie. Big business and the government, the film implies, benevolently give the individual every chance, and his success or failure after that is his own.[9]

This sense of the film as a morality play about upward mobility owes more to Otto Preminger's direction than to his strong hand in the writing. Preminger's approach seems deliberately overstated. His outdoor sets (streets, alleys) are theatrical, almost expressionistic, a lurid, weirdly glowing scene of low life and vice. He uses Elmer Bernstein's jazz score loudly and in-

[9] Even Preminger's famous hiring of blacklisted writers demonstrated this perverse form of patriotic optimism. In defense of hiring Dalton Trumbo to work on *Exodus*, Preminger explained, "In our free democratic way of life, we do not keep on punishing a man once he has paid for violating the law."

Frankie Machine (Frank Sinatra) in a confrontation at the card table, backed by Sparrow (Arnold Stang) and confronted by Schwiefka the gambler (Robert Strauss). *The Man with the Golden Arm* (1955)

sistently to foreshadow and accentuate dramatic moments. The music sensationally announces each fix. Preminger even synchronizes a big jazz beat with each prohibited item—needle, spoon, rubber tubing—that Louie takes from the drawer.

In the novel, morphine is part of the whole environment that destroys Frankie. But the film abstracts the question of addiction from its social context, and transforms Frankie from a veteran whose habit began with his war wound, to a fool who first took this unnamed drug "for kicks." Shadows across Frankie's face replace the novel's complex depiction of forces that actually trap him. Social statement gives way to picture-frame melodrama.

This symbolically dramatic quality is reinforced by the director's mise-en-scene. "Every cut," Preminger has explained, "interrupts the flow of story-telling," and so he creates his meanings through stylized composition rather than editing. When Frankie is torn between his need for a fix and his desire for Molly's help in resisting it, he stands physically between Louie looming in the foreground and Molly waiting in the back. When Frankie visits Molly at the Safari Club where she works, close-ups and medium shots show them talking, as strippers on stage in the background dramatize Frankie's desire for Molly. Preminger frames such scenes with consistent care to visual meaning. Equally carefully he establishes the moral geography of Frankie's world, tying different physical locations to different choices. Good things happen in Molly's room, bad things in Louie's and Sophie's. The round table by the window in Antek's tavern is a place of friendship and hope; but at the actual bar, Schwiefka the gambler strongarms Frankie, and Louie tempts him. When Frankie makes the right moves on this cinematic gameboard, he progresses toward victory.

Perhaps the most crucial thing Frankie wins by the end of the film is his heterosexual "manhood." Preminger depicts his enslavement to Louie in sexual terms. More a seducer than a businessman, Louie repeatedly and knowingly invites Frankie to "come over my place." He pulls down the shade and personally injects him, rendering Frankie totally passive. Close-ups of Frankie's face and of his extended arm relaxing foreshadow later Hollywood clichés for a woman's orgasm. His sexless marriage to Sophie unmans Frankie as well, and only her death finally frees him to become a "real man" with Molly.

In leaving Sparrow behind in the last scene, Frankie leaves behind another impediment to his manhood. Sparrow is sexually adult in the novel, but in the film he is played by Arnold Stang. His baseball hat and his whiny nasal voice make clear that Frankie's friendship with him is an adolescent one and must be shed. But this friendship is also part of a whole network of friendships around Antek's bar. When, at the end, Frankie walks off alone with Molly (and into the camera), his rite of passage implies a severing of all lumpen, ethnic community ties. Renamed Jack Duval—who knows?—he may even buy a house in the suburbs.

The Man with the Golden Arm—early on the growing list of Preminger's films on important social issues, and famous for breaking the Production Code's ban on drugs—testifies persuasively to Dwight McDonald's assertion about Preminger that "no one is more skilled at giving the appearance of dealing with large 'controversial' themes in a 'bold' way without making the tactical error of doing so." [10]

Whether Preminger works, as two different critics have suggested, with "both eyes" or only "an eye and a half" on the box office, he has clearly gutted Algren's novel and made it conform to commercial 1950s notions of sexual roles, advancement through individual initiative, and the imminent solvability of social problems. As Algren tells it, Preminger gave the following impossible reason for not filming on location in Chicago, "Oh, that neighborhood's all built up now; there are no slums left." Algren worked hard to make real these invisible people on the wrong side of the billboard. To the 1950s audiences of Preminger's *Man with the Golden Arm* they remained invisible and unreal.

[10] Dwight McDonald, "The Preminger Problem," in *Dwight McDonald on Movies* (1969).

The Old Man and the Sea (1952)

Ernest Hemingway

Film and Mythic Heroism: Sturges's Old Man

BY ROBERT L. NADEAU

Director John Sturges must surely have been excited, as any director would be, about the prospect of making a film based on Hemingway's *The Old Man and the Sea:* Picture long shots on the wide screen of a small roughly-hewn fishing boat containing the slouched but indomitable figure of the old man, set against the heaving immensity of ocean and cloudless expanse of intense blue sky. Imagine shots of the marlin, huge beyond the wildest expectations, leaping majestically into view, and both boat and man dwarfed in the sudden visual contrast. Think of underwater shots of swift sharks ripping flesh from the body of the once magnificent fish, then close shots of the old man as he endures unspeakable torment to preserve the lifeless form of the creature he loves. And so on. All of these are contained in the 1958 Warners film, and could be the stuff from which great films are made. And yet the movie fails miserably, unable to catch for the screen the essential image of Hemingway's Santiago.

Interestingly enough, this novel's range of subjective experience is well suited to the film form. The internal life of Hemingway's Santiago is never elaborately constructed and much of what we do learn about it is verbalized in the novel: the old man has developed the habit of talking to himself. Santiago muses aloud

199

about his sense of communion with the sea, the nature of human suffering, the impossibility of man accepting final defeat, and his own hubris in venturing out too far in his battle with the great marlin. Spencer Tracy, who plays Santiago in the film, talks to himself at sea about each of these matters in precisely the same language used by Hemingway. The problem that remains unresolved, however, is that the complexity of Santiago as character cannot finally be divorced from the process through which a reader constructs his conception of that character in the act of reading.

Santiago was obviously intended by Hemingway to function as a mythic hero and, like all such heroes in literature, he is not entirely individuated. In a 1954 *Time* magazine interview, Hemingway explained that in *The Old Man and the Sea* he tried to "make a real old man, a real boy, a real sea and a real fish and real sharks. But if I made them good enough they would mean many things." Although there is, as this statements suggests, a pronounced element of realism in the narrative, the story on another level does "mean many things" outside of the strict conventions of realist fiction. Santiago also functions as a collage of attitudes and behaviors designed to conjure up associations with figures in the collective experience, which seem most fully to embody the characterological ideals of the culture. To put it differently: the mythic dimensions of Santiago render him a good deal *larger* than life.

Santiago achieves this status in Hemingway primarily through the omniscient narrator, who suggests the function of the character:

> The old man was thin and gaunt with deep wrinkles in the back of his neck. The brown blotches of the benevolent skin cancer the sun brings from its reflection on the tropic sea were on his cheeks. The blotches ran well down the side of his face and his hands had the deep crusted scars from handling heavy fish on the cords. But none of these scars were fresh. They were as old as erosions in a fishless desert.
>
> Everything about him was old except his eyes and they were the same color as the sea and were cheerful and undefeated.

Santiago (Spencer Tracy) readies his harpoon. *The Old Man and the Sea* (1958)

It is not the physical appearance of Santiago which is the primary concern in this passage but rather the relationship of character to the scene of his epoch battles, the sea. The relative open-endedness of a written text allows the reader to make incongruous associations, such as that between skin cancer and the sun's reflection on the tropic sea. The reader is guided to arrive at an absurdly "positive" view of this gruesome ailment because of Hemingway's inspired juxtaposition.

The literalness of a photographed image cannot possibly suggest that skin cancer is "benevolent," as Hemingway puts it. Deep scars on aging hands might evoke pity, pathos, or horror on film, but "deep creased scars" as "old as erosions in a fishless desert," envisioned in organic relation to Santiago's immortal confrontation with the elements, can never be explained on film. Skillful use of color stock can suggest that the old man's eyes are "similar" to the color of the sea but never can convey the profound idea that the color is "like" that of the sea. Altogether, no image can equal Hemingway's, especially if it is as concrete as that of Spencer Tracy, whose familiar presence anchors the viewers' perceptions and imparts a circumscribed specificity upon the consciousness.

The filmmakers obviously grasped the impossibility of capturing the mythic dimension of Santiago (as indicated in the Hemingway passage above) purely through the photographic image. Director John Sturges and screenwriter Peter Viertel decided to utilize a voice-over reading of the entire description from Hemingway as the old man returned from his eighty-fourth day at sea without a catch. It proves ludicrous—as if, on some city street, a disembodied extraterrestrial being hovered above, claiming that a kindly old wino up the alley is Hector of Troy reincarnate. The fact that Spencer Tracy, without the contrived Spanish accent he uses for Santiago, recites these lines does nothing to alleviate the problem. (Rather, it raises cosmological questions: just who *is* the voice-over? What relationship does this voice-over have to Tracy as Santiago? Is the audience supposed to know that Tracy is the voice-over?)

The narration continues throughout the film as an intrusive and ineffectual presence. When the old man struggles with the marlin, the voice-over feeds off Hemingway's descriptive material, and describes in earnest yet soporific tones Santiago's great love for and identification with the fish, his Christ-like humility and yet fierce pagan pride in the face of certain defeat, his guilt in feeling compelled to take life from one of nature's noblest creations, and the resolution of that guilt in the realization that "everything kills something in some way." Unfortunately, the viewer can only perceive this supposedly larger-than-life representative of heroic virtue in terms of what is seen on the screen —the image of an impoverished old Cuban fisherman, lacking in common sense but possessed of more than the usual amount of courage, and acted, rather indifferently and incongruously, by Hollywood star Spencer Tracy.

I do not mean to suggest that the film is entirely without merit. The shots I mentioned in the opening paragraph are, for example, technically well executed with occasionally breathtaking results. The old man's reverie about the lions seen playing on the beach in his youth is not only visually pleasing but also consistent with Santiago's belief that beauty, innocence, and aggression are inextricably linked in the life of nature. The relationship between the old man and the boy is tender without being saccharine. The fishing village is a real fishing village and not some curious pastoral landscape that many Hollywood directors would doubtless have turned it into. Every detail in the film suggests that it is an honest effort to make a really good movie, which was not finally made.

All of which leads one to conclude that director John Sturges and company should have left Ernest Hemingway's *The Old Man and the Sea* where it functions best—in the hands of a reader. It is simply one of those works of American literature, like Thoreau's *Walden* or Faulkner's *The Bear,* in which the mode of narration or of characterization eludes the conventional filmic image.

Charles Laughton on Grubb Street

BY ROBIN WOOD

The Night of the Hunter was directed by Charles Laughton
from James Agee's screenplay from a novel by Davis Grubb. The
screenplay follows the novel very closely, and Laughton, in his
turn, makes few and small modifications to a script which lays
down much of the *mise-en-scene*. When one calls the film a work
of genius, to whose genius is one referring?

For all the apparent fidelity to events (little is added, little
omitted), the film strikes one as quite distinct from and decidedly superior to Grubb's novel. The difference is primarily of
style and tone. That of the book is highly suspect, characterized
by that gooey, pseudo-poetic self-indulgence that too often passes
for "lyricism." The concept of nature plays a vital role in both
book and film, but in the book this role is vitiated by Grubb's
presentation. In his nature, frogs don't croak, they "chant their
unending litany of love." And here is Grubb's rendering of the
coming of spring:

> It had come overnight:
> a burgeoning and stirring in the land
> that was tired and musty-smelling
> like the flesh of old folks

Editors' title. This article appeared originally as "Night of the Hunter/Novel
into Film," in *On Film*, 1, No. Zero (n.d.), pp. 68–71. Reprinted by permission of Robin Wood.

after the death of winter;
now the land was alive and the air was ripe
and musky with the spring river smell
like the ripe, passionate sweat
of a country waitress.

Agee manages to trim away the fat of pretentious verbosity
and the lush, sticky imagery of the novel. What he retains is the
strongly planned structure of the fable which Grubb's language
tends to obscure rather than illuminate. Where the book is self-
indulgent and corrupt, the film is rigorous and pure. Here it is
difficult to distinguish clearly Laughton's contribution from
Agee's. In a sense "it's all in the script"—nearly. Laughton sets
himself to realize Agee's intentions (the script abounds in striking cinematic ideas) with a humility surprising to those who
know him only through his screen persona.

Groupings and compositions, camera movements, even the
difficult helicopter shots, are for the most part as demanded by
Agee. Laughton's respect for Agee's intentions shows itself especially in his leaving stark and bare what almost any other director
would have filled out and decorated. For instance in the short sequence of the Revivalist meeting at which Willa ecstatically
proclaims her sins, there are no establishing shots to lead into it,
decor is reduced to a flaming torch, and the presence of the
congregation is given in a couple of shots of a few faces and
some "noises off." All we need to know here is what has happened
to Willa under Preacher's domination, so that is all we are given.

It may seem wilful to describe as simple and direct the style
of a film that employs all manner of apparently "arty" devices.
It is true the film is extremely stylized and nonnaturalistic; yet
this stylization takes the form of a highly conscious *use* of simplicity and naiveté. Because of the decision to express everything
in the simplest and most direct way, there is no bar on any device that will serve that end.

It is in the use of cinematic devices that Laughton occasionally
improves on Agee. Where Agee stipulates a complicated travel-
ing-cum-tilting shot to reveal the children at the cellar window
as Preacher walks past, Laughton simply narrows the lens,

darkening the whole screen except for the small circle in which we suddenly become aware of the two faces.

The extraordinary and disturbing wipe from right to left that closes the scene of Willa's murder, replacing what we expect to see—the sweep of Preacher's arm as he cuts her throat—is also an inspiration of Laughton's (Agee asks for a dissolve), and one of the few completely justifiable uses of this dubious device.

This deliberate use of "primitive" cinematic effects and of apparently naive imagery—it calls to mind at times "Primitive" painting—is justified by the subject matter of a film which depends for part of its effect on our imaginatively sharing the experiences of children, and in which various forms of Revivalist religion play an essential role. From the interaction of these two aspects arises the use of biblical quotations at the start; the lullabies; the stylized faces of children against a background of stars at the picture's opening; Preacher's song; Mrs. Cooper's simplified bible stories that can be adapted to fit the occasion; the "sentimental" image of the canary in the lighted window when the children are seeking shelter for the night; the allusion to science fiction and "monster" movies in the sound-track noises of Preacher's breaking out of the cellar and in his Frankenstein stride, with arms outstretched, up the cellar stairs.

The strange, intense poetry of the children's river journey—a journey into Nature—derives from this same directness and simplicity of stylization. Any temptation to a facile and spurious "lyricism," all arty camera movements and fuss, à la *Loneliness of the Long Distance Runner* (1962), has been rigorously rejected. Instead we get a sequence of strong simple compositions suggesting illustrations from a child's picture book, with animals in close-up as the boat drifts past in the background: trembling defenseless rabbit, sinister bullfrog, cobweb to evoke the greedy spider. We get nature stylized but not sentimentalized.

On another level, Mr. Grubb's style is notably overheated at incidents involving any overt sexual references, and in a book whose essential theme is a progress toward a natural acceptance of sex this is fatal. In one incident, understandably omitted from the film, Preacher accompanies a drunken whore to her

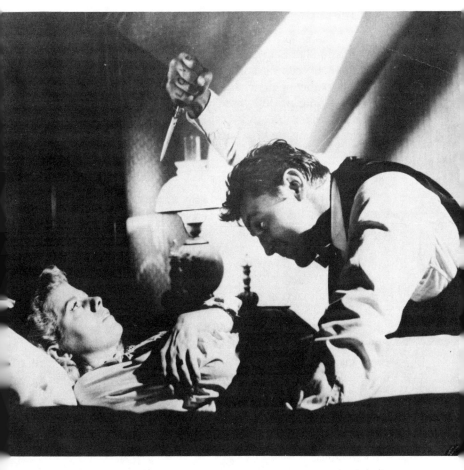

Preacher (Robert Mitchum) perched to murder his wife Willa (Shelley Winters) in a (publicity?) shot missing from the movie. *Night of the Hunter* (1955)

bedroom. She strips, then passes out on the bed, and Preacher cuts a cross on her belly with his switchblade.

The incident seems gratuitous in itself, adding nothing to what we already know of the character. It is narrated in a single sentence containing no less than twelve "ands"; the excited relish seems as much Grubb's as Preacher's.

In the wedding night scene, Preacher makes Willa strip and look at herself in the mirror naked: "He pointed to her shivering loins and the dark feathers of her quivering, convulsed belly."

The sexual feeling here is certainly strong, but somewhat perverted. That of the film is pure and beautiful. The shot in which Willa looks at herself in the mirror *before* Preacher's denunciation (not in the book) shows a tender and pure feeling for female sexuality. Against this is placed a second mirror shot, where she is forced by Preacher to deny the validity of her sexual feelings. In this way, all taint of perverse relish is removed.

Given the style of his prose, Mr. Grubb could never have dared attempt the film's astonishing transitions to farce at moments of climactic tension. These are peculiarly Laughton's contributions: Mitchum's expression when the shelf falls on his head in the cellar; his headlong fall into the mud as the children escape (it's in the book, but not made funny); and the magnificently comic shot (all Laughton's idea) of Mrs. Cooper's shotgun pointing first at Preacher's arse as he grovels after John under the porch with his switchblade, and then into his appalled face as he emerges.

In terms of audience reaction these are strokes of genius, and very daring. They occur at moments when the tension is so great that we would be tempted to relieve it by laughing anyway, and they give us the necessary release without at all mitigating our fears. Since they come across as clearly intentional, they keep us *with* the film when we might have begun building up a defense against it by telling ourselves it was all rather absurd.

These spillings-over into overt slapstick (it amounts to that) are only made possible by Laughton's decision to pitch the whole film on the borderline of absurdity: an audacious undertaking indeed. His perfect command of tone is exhibited at all points in the film where a momentary loss of control on his part would result in a disastrous loss of confidence on ours.

These moments of farce, and our constant awareness of *potential* absurdity, also serve to detach us from the consciousness of the children: obviously, Preacher is never funny to *them*. For, although part of our fear comes from our imaginatively sharing the children's experiences, we are primarily to be afraid *for* them rather than *with* them, and our total response is more complex than one of mere terror. The omnipresent stylization has a similar detaching function.

Despite these comic innovations, Laughton, we recall, remains true to the sequence of events in Grubb's novel. This has curious effects on the film. For, in the transition to the screen, certain incidents take on a broader significance than they are given in the book, suggesting possible lines of inquiry into the basic differences between literature and the cinema too general to be more than touched on here.

For example, the scene in which Uncle Birdie catches the fish and batters it to death in the bottom of the boat is taken intact from the novel, but there, it has only one purpose: to draw a labored, explicit parallel with Preacher. The fish is a gar, useless for food but lurking in the shadows greedily preying on other fish and repeatedly stealing Birdie's bait (the money) before vanishing again into the darkness. Preacher is several times referred to thereafter as the "dark gar" of John's mind. The fact that this parallel would not, I think, spontaneously occur to a spectator of the film effectively demonstrates its artificiality; and it is finally destroyed in the film by having Preacher driven off for a fair trial. In the book the implication is that he was lynched; we leave him with the crowd surging up the prison steps, and later hear of his "last, terrible night on earth"—in other words, his fate is that of the gar, battered to death by Birdie's oar.

Why, one might ask, since its meaning is quite lost, keep the incident in the film at all? In fact, simply by depriving it of its "symbolic" meaning, Agee and Laughton have made it mean much more. In a film whose purpose is to extol the "natural" we need to be reminded, if sentimentality is to be avoided, of the uglier aspects of nature—that creatures live on one another; that the most sympathetic among us has moments when he rejoices in destruction. But this perhaps hardly covers the *violence* of the killing of the fish, which Laughton insists on. This violence becomes, I think, a further expression of the results of that repression of natural instincts demanded by that society the film depicts. Birdie's pathetic relationship to his dead wife is relevant here; and given the central if largely implicit role played by sexuality in the film's meaning, it is not going too far to point out the Freudian significance of fish.

Another incident that changes meaning by being deprived of explicit literary comment is John's refusal to identify Preacher in the courtroom. In the book, a motivation for this is given, but quite unconvincingly, in the context of the boy's forthright and self-assured behavior elsewhere. Grubb implies that John doesn't even understand the question put to him, that he develops a traumatic block: it is not that he refuses to identify Preacher, but that he refuses to *look* at him, because he can't bear to do so.

Deprived of this information from the novel, the audience accepts John's refusal in the film as quite conscious; in fact it takes on a great moral force. The scene is a dramatic embodiment of the teaching "judge not, lest ye be judged," one of the texts quoted at the start of the film (which is found neither in the novel nor in James Agee's script).

The prominence Laughton gives to this text clearly ties up with the decision to save Preacher from the lynch mob, and the resulting unequivocal condemnation of the lynchers (which is decidedly equivocal in the book). The cinema's great limitation —the relative inability to analyze the motivation behind appearances and offer comment on what is shown—can be also a great strength; simply through being restricted to appearances, film can be at once more precise and suggestive than literature.

There are dozens of obviously "cinematic" things in the film for which literature has no equivalent: the uses of the wipe and lens narrowing; the electrifying cut from the close-up of Walt Spoon as he tells Icey that gypsies have knifed a farmer and stolen his horse to the helicopter shot of Preacher *on* the horse pursuing the children; the oppressive low-angle shots of the

train that is bringing Preacher nearer (a Laughton inspiration
—Agee has a long shot of a "toylike" train drawing out of the
station) intercut with the dialogue in which Icey tries to persuade Willa to remarry; the combining of Preacher's song on the
sound track with the shot of Willa dead in the submerged car.

Wipes, shock cuts, surprising juxtapositions of sound and
image are the trappings of cinema rather than its essentials, but
they are clearly related to that which finally distinguishes it from
literature: the fact that, like music, film acts directly upon our
senses and has a fixed duration in time.

Laughton's use of music, in the form of Preacher's song, "Leaning on the Everlasting Arms," seems such a purely cinematic inspiration that one is surprised to find that the song occurs in the
book at precisely the same points in the narrative (except that
it is not related there to any reference to Willa's corpse). While
in the book one is aware of music only as a leitmotif running
through, in the film it is raised to a major structural key.

Translated into film time, the four repeats of the song occur
at roughly equally spaced points in the film. They mark its essential progress by linking in our minds the images with
which they are juxtaposed. The first time we hear the song its
effect is entirely ironic: the moment of extreme unease and
menace when the children, lying in bed, see Preacher's shadow
on the wall. The second time, when it accompanies the image
of Willa's body with the words "Safe and secure from all alarms,"
the irony is still there, but its tone has changed, softened somewhat. Willa, dead in the river, is, in a sense, safe and secure.

The third time, the song disrupts the quiet of the children's
night in the barn during their journey down the river. The irony
is now muted, for although they are still not "safe and secure,"
we have been given clear intimations of coming safety by the
film's gradual progress towards the natural: the sheep seen in the
calm and reassuring tracking shot along behind the udders of
the cows as they walk through a barn, and the last time we
hear the song it is taken up by Mrs. Cooper as she sits, an
image of strength and stability, guarding all the children with
her shotgun, and the irony is abruptly and finally dispersed.

But the major unifying image of the film is that of apples.

Apples occur in the book, too, but (unless one has had one's expectations roused by seeing the film first) one is not very conscious of them—they get lost in the verbiage. The film gives greater emphasis to the crucial instance: John's gift of an apple to Mrs. Cooper and her acceptance of it (the book puts much more stress on the watch). And it adds some instances of its own, notably the pressing of John's head into a barrelful of apples in the cellar (which is not in the script either), and Mrs. Cooper's girls carrying apples to market (in the book they are eggs; in the script, tomatoes).

Like all valid symbols, this one can't be pinned down to one precise meaning. A symbol that simply means something else is useless: if A means B, why not say B and be done with it? One clue is given us at the outset. The last of the opening biblical texts (which have no precedent in Grubb's book) is "By their fruits ye shall know them." It is given greater emphasis than the others, and we move from it straight to the discovery by children of a woman's body in a fruit cellar (also not in the book). Preacher murders women—rich widows—for their money, but we are left in no doubt that the killings also have their roots in perverted sexual feelings. Those traditional associations of apples as representing the sin of Eve are inseparable in the film from those of fertility and harvest. Sex is presented not as an evil in itself, but as one of the great sources of evil.

Apple trees abound in the landscapes: especially, they provide a background for Willa's first appearance and the arrest of her husband, Ben Harper. Preacher and the townswomen sing over a table laden with apples at the Harvest Festival.

Mrs. Cooper and her girls take the apple harvest to town. Those collected by Ruby, the mentally defective who lies with boys for ice cream sodas, are in Mrs. Cooper's words, "scarcely fit to take to market." To Mrs. Cooper, John and Pearl are "a new crop." Soon after this remark, we see the words "John loves Pearl" scrawled on a wall. They obviously have no direct reference to the two children, but remind us that the children will themselves grow up, and are human beings whom sex will involve.

John fetches two apples for himself and for Mrs. Cooper, and holds one in his hand until she agrees that there were "two kings" (for the boy, they stand for himself and Pearl) found in the bushes. Only then does he begin to munch the apple. Finally, his Christmas present to Mrs. Cooper is an apple, presented timidly and half-ashamedly, which she accepts as a precious gift.

Apple imagery runs through the film as blood imagery runs through *Macbeth;* what is important is not precise interpretation of isolated incidents, but the resonance which the associations of the apple build up in the mind, a resonance which reaches its peak with Mrs. Cooper's acceptance of John's present.

The gift of the apple is the climactic moment of a film whose progress is from repression of the natural to acceptance of it, from the hell-fire Revivalism of Preacher to the protective, positive, accepting faith of Mrs. Cooper. Throughout, religious attitudes are related to attitudes to sex. Preacher is a perverted dehumanized monster; yet his attitude to sex is significantly related to that of Icey Spoon, the "kindly" old soul who declares at the harvest thanksgiving (among the symbols of fertility, in public and in her husband's presence):

> When you're married forty years, you know all that don't amount to a hill o' beans. I been married to my Walt that long, and I'll swear in all that time I'd just lie there thinking about my canning . . . The good Lord never meant for a decent woman to want that— not really want it!

Preacher wants to stamp out sin by a rejection of sex altogether, and the society that is so ready to respond to him—the society of which Icey is a characteristic representative—endorses that attitude. It is only with Mrs. Cooper's acceptance of the apple that John—and the spectator—at last finds peace. She accepts it in its dual significance of "sin of Eve" and "richness of life": the incident occurs soon after her other acceptance, of Ruby's need for love and the form in which that need has been finding expression.

Finally Laughton most clearly justifies the high claims one makes for him in his handling of the actors. Agee would perhaps have raised an eyebrow at the casting of Robert Mitchum. In the film, Preacher is not quite the figure whose "sincerity is be-

yond doubt" as called for by the script. The casting constitutes
an alienation effect in itself, since we are always aware that
Mitchum is *acting*. But *Night of the Hunter* is a moral fable, not a
psychological novel, and Mitchum's technically brilliant two-
dimensional performance is exactly what is required—a detailed
psychological portrait would surely have burdened the film un-
necessarily.

Shelley Winters, among the most shamefully misused of Hollywood actresses, is here, at last, done justice. One has only to
compare her performance here with her dreadful hamming
for Stanley Kubrick in *Lolita* (1962). Her warm, womanly, sensuous quality (intensified by the shapeless sack she is dressed in
for the Thanksgiving harvest sequence) illuminates the entire
first part of the film.

Lillian Gish's performance makes of Mrs. Cooper a figure who
can at last convincingly stand up against Preacher—see through
him at a glance, reject him, and eventually destroy him. She
has the moral awareness which Willa fatally lacks, an awareness which is based on faith in her own natural instincts—the
instinct that tells her at once that Preacher is evil. Willa's faith
in her instincts—as we see in the honeymoon sequence—is easily
shaken. In Lillian Gish's performance we have embodied, in all
their strength, the simple, gentle, and wise virtues that make the
triumph of good over evil here for once neither equivocal nor
perfunctory.

In the final analysis, however, Laughton's *Night of the Hunter*
is too *peculiar*, too much outside the main Hollywood tradition,
too much a "sport" (in the botanical sense) for one to be sure
that he would have succeeded with further films—there are
too many devices which, in almost any other context one would
object to vehemently. Nevertheless, one must credit him with the
realization of one masterpiece.

John Ford's Boston

BY ROBERT TAYLOR

"The best political novel I have ever read," Pandit Nehru said of Edwin O'Connor's *The Last Hurrah*. Presumably Nehru was unfamiliar with the gregarious tribal rites and bitter internecine combats of Boston's Irish-American neighborhoods. Given the book by John Kenneth Galbraith, then ambassador to India, he responded to the novel on a political level just as John Ford, born Sean Aloysius O'Fearna, the thirteenth child of an Irish-born saloon keeper in Portland, Maine, responded to its ethnic appeal.

Edwin O'Connor himself, however, was primarily concerned with *The Last Hurrah* as literature, a work of the imagination. He had the opportunity to collaborate upon the screenplay; he declined the opportunity, partly because he was aware of the painful experiences of American novelists in Hollywood, but mostly because he was immersed in writing his third novel, *The Edge of Sadness* (1961). To be sure, he was pleased and greatly excited that John Ford, whose films he admired, planned to direct *The Last Hurrah*. O'Connor was a screen fan. One of the enchanted experiences of his childhood had been a trip to Hollywood. With his father, the nine-year-old boy was visiting his maternal uncle, James Greene, who was then a technical director for Hal Roach, and Edwin had his photo taken with the cast of the *Our Gang* comedies. While it is perhaps exaggerating to call this experience highly significant, O'Connor kept the snapshot, which he was fond of displaying, until his death in 1968, and his novels exhibit an unusually generous percentage of actors and show business denizens such as the old vaudeville star in *I Was Dancing* (1964).

Between *The Last Hurrah*'s publication in 1956 and the film's release in 1958, the press hummed with tantalizing reports about casting and production: Spencer Tracy as Frank Skeffington, the rogue mayor of a city not unlike Boston, making his final bid for office. The Irish wing of the Ford stock company in full cry, with Pat O'Brien for good measure. Jane Darwell, Basil Rathbone, Frank McHugh—undeniably a first-rate supporting cast. The film was eagerly awaited, but when Ford's version appeared it was a disappointment, not least to O'Connor, who, at the Boston preview screening, groaned audibly at various scenes—notably when Tracy takes a young newsman, played by Jeffrey Hunter, to a slum courtyard and indicates the buildings where a cardinal, a mayor, and other dignitaries were born within speaking range of each other—and departed the screening early lest, when the lights came up, he might be identified as the author.

O'Connor considered the slum courtyard scene an outrageous violation of dramatic logic. "Since every character in the film seems to have been born in the same courtyard," he later commented, "I'm surprised Ford left out Casmir Kowalski and 'Nutsy' McGrath" (briefly-mentioned City Hall types).

What else went wrong? Though pallid by comparison with its source, Ford's *Hurrah* was not as awful as O'Connor thought. The film follows the narrative faithfully, perhaps too faithfully, since O'Connor's digressive techniques, which contribute so much to the texture of a novel, are cinematic drawbacks. In Ford's virtuoso handling of a large cast the minor roles are distinguishable; and author and director are not too far apart in regard to politics considered as metaphor. All the same, despite such triumphs as the performance of Basil Rathbone playing a spiteful Yankee banker named Norman Cass—one of his best performances since his Murdstone in *David Copperfield* (1935)—the film belongs in the forgettable category of Ford's *oeuvre*, and the reasons why it failed are interesting.

First, between Ford and O'Connor were two generations of

ethnic change. The Irishness that attracted John Ford, *The Last Hurrah*'s superb comic dialogue, exuberant invention, and closely-observed social rituals, was probably viewed by the director in terms of his own art, the "last hurrah" of the community of actors with whom he had worked for more than forty years. O'Connor's story contained the elements of Ford's fundamental theme, "honorable defeat" as Andrew Sarris puts it, the theme of a generation passing away. The most memorable shot in the movie is elegaic: Spencer Tracy walking in one direction while his rival's victorious supporters move in another, singing "Hail, Hail, the Gang's All Here." At its best *The Last Hurrah* conveys the lonely pride of the undefeated loser.

Ford identified himself with Skeffington; O'Connor did not. O'Connor's attitude to the character and milieu of the old ward boss was sympathetic but critical, and his approach to his material radically different—as different from Ford's as John F. Kennedy's concept of politics, say, was different from Al Smith's. The Irish-Americanism of Sean O'Fearna who joined his director-brother Francis in 1913 and rode as a Klansman in *The Birth of a Nation* (1915), and the Irish-Americanism of Edwin O'Connor, who expected to be denounced (he was not) from parish pulpits for fouling the nest, belonged to separate sensibilities.

The novelist's father was a prominent doctor in Woonsocket, Rhode Island. For a while, upon graduation, he was a broadcaster in Palm Beach, Hartford, Providence, and Boston, but when he sold his first article to the *Atlantic* in 1946, he thenceforth followed the precarious trade of the full-time unaffiliated professional writer. The *Atlantic* became his base. His favorite authors were English: Graham Greene, Evelyn Waugh, Aldous Huxley, Anthony Powell. Although he recognized the merits of the Russian novel and, early on, of Saul Bellow and Norman Mailer, he had a tendency toward the satiric, the socially oriented and the urbane. His personal choice for the role of Frank Skeffington was not Spencer Tracy. O'Connor liked Tracy, but deemed him insufficiently suave. "If I were doing it instead of Ford, and mind you this is just a hunch," he declared to a friend, "I would have cast Claude Rains."

Second, rather than writing a book about politics, O'Connor

set out to dissect the character of a man who happened to be a politician. Of course Nehru's response validated the universality of *The Last Hurrah's* political descriptions. Moreover, O'Connor was amused by the reactions of Boston ward-heelers, for almost invariably they considered the work a *roman à clef* which could only have been done by an intimate of flamboyant mayor James Michael Curley. The author, however, was not recycling data which had been diligently sifted by political scientists. "All I wanted to do," he told an interviewer," was to write a novel about human beings in politics." During the second World War O'Connor had been stationed as a coast guardsman in Boston. The officer commanding his detachment was Louis Brehms, an erstwhile vaudeville performer who served as city greeter for several municipal administrations, and through Brehms, O'Connor made the acquaintance of old-line Irish politicians, including Clement A. Norton, a character not unlike the novel's Charlie Hennessy. But, treated obliquely in *The Last Hurrah*, political process never became a dominant theme. "Ed was not greatly interested in politics *per se*," declared Arthur Schlesinger, Jr., a close friend. "He had never worked in an election, had never been a political reporter, and did not make any systematic effort to interview or hang about with politicians." Soon after *The Last Hurrah* he moved to an apartment on Beacon Street, close by the State House, and one day, passing the State House, he casually observed that, having written the novel, he ought to go inside. It would be his first visit.

Third, the narrative is totally ambiguous about the ethics of Skeffington. The early reviews noted this and reproached O'Connor for not adopting a strong moral stance. In the *New Yorker*, Anthony West interpreted the sympathetic treatment of Skeffington as a defense of municipal corruption. "[*The Last Hurrah*] persuasively pretends that mean vices are virtues, and it is that rare thing, a genuinely subversive book." West and similar critics overlooked the novel's paradoxes. The old-time politician, whose downfall was in the public interest, also exemplified qualities of personal magnetism and humane feeling. Frank Skeffington in the book cannot understand why he lost the election or that he is an anachronism. Defeat is the pause before

John Ford's stalwart, smoke-filled-backroom cast. Left to right, John Gorman (Pat O'Brien), Sam Weinberg (Ricardo Cortez), Cuke Gillen (James Gleason), Ditto (Edward Brophy), and His Honor Frank Skeffington (Spencer Tracy). *The Last Hurrah* (1958)

another political campaign. Skeffington is unaware that the situation has unalterably changed; that his constituents have either died or moved to the suburbs; that television has created the image of a new and plastic candidate; and that his role as dispenser of patronage has been usurped by the federal government. He is prevented by his history and values from realizing what has happened to him. Sometimes he dimly comprehends; but he is denied true self-awareness. Admirably controlled irony pervades *The Last Hurrah* and supplies its characteristic "black" tone, which is not the tone of slapstick or farce or buffoonery. The irony was perceived by Julian Moynihan in the *New York Review of Books:* "If *The Last Hurrah*—any of it—is 'hilarious' then the defenestration of the Earl of Gloucester in *King Lear* is a laff-riot."

On three levels, ethnicity, politics and irony, John Ford misinterpreted the novel. Hugh Rank's *Edwin O'Connor* asserts that O'Connor was "the first major novelist to reflect the influence of the emergence of liberal Catholicism and the disintegration of the old ghetto mentality," but the film version is a throwback to the ghetto mentality. It opens with the superscription "A New England City" over a classic studio back lot, the home of Frank Skeffington, where we are introduced to the Mayor and his cronies. Merely seeing the cast, Ricardo Cortez, J. Edward Brophy, James Gleason, will arouse pleasure in the connoisseur of bygone character acting. There are too many of them, however, for any to emerge from the blur of one-dimensionality. Missing from the prelude, which accomplishes the scene setting and introductions of characters with Ford's customary naturalness, are the tensions of politics. Who is to be master? True, an election will occur, an election involving Skeffington; nevertheless, the campaign is regarded almost as an abstraction. The reward of battle will not be the ego-gratifying exercise of political power, but a victory without spoils.

Tracy's performance is a good one, rugged, virile, understated; still one can understand why O'Connor mentioned Rains. Skeffington's temperament is that of the conscious actor; he appreciated the virtuoso effects of his performance. If one has had the opportunity to hear the recording (CMS Records, New York,

CMS #574, 1969) in which O'Connor reads excerpts from *The Last Hurrah*, the distance between the Tracy-Ford conception and that of the novelist is apparent. O'Connor reads Skeffington's dialogue with a rolling fustian relish. His Skeffington is intelligent enough to know that political success depends on a certain amount of blarney; he is not a charlatan, but he displays both the true Irish enthusiasm for rhetoric and a healthy skepticism about his public role. Tracy's humor is mainstream "American"— dry, self-deprecatory, given to the spare wisecrack rather than the expansive anecdote. Katherine Hepburn brought out those qualities in him during their fine collaborations; *The Last Hurrah*, however, required other characteristics. The novel's Skeffington, seeing himself as a tribal chieftain and something of a public performer, enjoys the bombast of public life in a manner that Tracy finds foreign. The public men he played in the last phase of his career, judges, lawyers, dispensers of even-handed justice, are by no means stuffed shirts; nevertheless, common to each of them is the integrity that guards a private self. This is wrong for Skeffington, whose private self, by the time the story opens, has become indistinguishable from his public persona.

If Tracy was miscast, what is one to say about Jeffrey Hunter, who plays the novel's point-of-view character, Adam Caulfield? With his pork-pie hat, raincoat, and pipe, he represents a mid-1950s version of the leading-man-as-journalist. Of course, part of the character's problem lies in the difference between the techniques of fiction and the techniques of film. Adam's function in the novel is highly important. The story is told by an omniscient narrator, but the election campaign, Skeffington's last hurrah, is seen through the eyes of Adam, a neutral insider invited as a kind of surrogate son to witness the scene. In the novel, Adam, the nephew of Skeffington, is a cartoonist, a job which gives him freedom of movement and time; in the movie he is curiously transmuted into a sports columnist. Since we never find him attending a sports event or making a reference to sports —the obvious analogy between athletic competition and political campaigning suggests itself—and since the visual possibilities of the cartoonist are so much greater than those of a writer, the reasons behind the change are obscure. More significant is the loss of an individual sensibility, a filter through which the drama may be perceived. The loss accounts for the lack of resonance in those scenes in which Hunter appears. No worse (and no better) than the ordinary 1950s leading man, he can only *react* to events; he cannot comment upon them or even indicate that he is a participant.

The better portions of the film concern Yankee-Irish animosities, a subject with which Ford is conversant: the scheme by which Skeffington outwits Rathbone's flinty banker through benevolent blackmail, the appointment of the banker's fatuous son as fire commissioner, the rasping conversations between Rathbone and John Carradine, who plays a reactionary newspaper publisher. Ford's direction misses the novel's dual vision, both affectionate and scathing, of American life. One of the vivid set pieces in O'Connor's novel is chapter eight, Knocko Minihan's wake. Like the Eddie McLaughlin testimonial banquet later, the scene permits Adam to reflect upon Irish-American custom. O'Connor's explanation of the political maneuvering at the wake is thoroughly persuasive against a background which entwines shrewd remarks about death and patronage. Showing up at the wake, Charles Hennessy harangues the crowd about Skeffington, against whom he is also campaigning. "Remember that while he may be a bum administrator, we have to admit two things about him . . . A terrible mayor but a great entertainer." No one listens to this diatribe with more pleasure than Skeffington. The subtlety of O'Connor's dialogue, the responses of his characters, are elided from John Ford's film, which avoids the discomforts of complexity. Instead of the cutting ironies of the novel, the film presents celestial Irish harps on its sound track and a toora-loora-loora deathbed scene that may be the most protracted in screen history; it is assuredly the most sentimental.

Why then does John Ford's *The Last Hurrah* possess a claim to our attention? Simply because the source material still merits what Nehru said about it. Enough survives to suggest the Film That Might Have Been. The novel's diversity of voices clamor with Dickensian vitality. Although the movie echoes them faintly, they now and then break through, comic, angry, jubilant, vindictive, tough, cheerful, a chorus conveying the textures and ambiguities of life itself. While Ford helped fabricate the myth of the American West, he left open the political myth of his own ancestry. The film of Edwin O'Connor's *The Last Hurrah* is yet to be made.[1]

[1] Editors' note. Since this article was written there has been a made-for-television adaptation of *The Last Hurrah*. However, Mr. Taylor's final sentence still stands.

Lolita (1955)
Vladimir Nabokov

The Celluloid Lolita: A Not-So-Crazy Quilt

BY BRANDON FRENCH

> My first reaction to the picture was a mixture of aggravation, re-
> gret, and reluctant pleasure.
>
> —Vladimir Nabokov

Vladimir Nabokov's novel begins with memories of the French
Riviera, the origin of the narrator Humbert Humbert's obsession
with nymphets. "In point of fact, there might have been no
Lolita at all had I not loved, one summer, a certain initial girl
child." Only a little boy himself, Humbert loses his Annabel Leigh
before their love is consummated, to interfering parents and a
fatal case of typhus. As a young adult, he marries Valeria because
of "the imitation she gave of a little girl," but divorces her four
years later when his "large, puffy, short-legged and brainless
baba" runs off with another man.

Humbert emigrates to the United States and, between bouts of
insanity, establishes himself as a French literary scholar. Freshly
out of a sanitarium, he settles for the summer in the New England
town of Ramsdale. Here, as the lodger of a plump, culturally
ambitious widow named Charlotte Haze, he meets Lolita, Charlotte's elfin eleven-year-old daughter, "my Riviera love peering at
me over dark glasses . . . the same child."

He marries Charlotte to obtain control over Lolita and is soon
conveniently widowed only to lose his nymphet to the mysteri-

ous playwright, Clare Quilty—author of *The Nymphet*—whom he pursues across the country in a three-year chase.

One key to Nabokov's effect in the novel is his playful revelation that we as readers are in the hands of an unreliable (to say the least) narrator. We are informed almost immediately that Humbert Humbert is off balance. A fictitious John Ray, Jr., Ph.D., of Widworth, Massachusetts, who introduces the novel, describes Humbert as a "paradoxical prude"; "our demented diarist"; "horrible . . . a shining example of moral leprosy . . . ponderously capricious, [many of whose] casual opinions are ludicrous; [in short] a panting maniac." And Humbert does little to assure us otherwise when he interrupts an impassioned description of Lolita, "light of my life, fire of my loins," to remark parenthetically that "you can always count on a murderer for a fancy prose style," and when he structures his recollection of Annabel Leigh with heavy-handed allusions to Poe's "Annabel Lee," demonstrating his awareness of himself as a player with words, a *writer*. Nor is our trust bolstered by Humbert's admission that he has "a sensational but incomplete and unorthodox memory"; nor by Humbert's account of bouts of insanity coupled with his growing awareness as the novel progresses that he may *still* be insane. We are forced to make a paradoxical distinction between the "true" fictions and the "false" ones as we read the novel, just as Humbert struggles to distinguish between reality, on the one hand, and hallucination, paranoia, psychopathic jealousy, guilt, and despair, on the other, within the novel itself.

Nabokov guides us through this maze by manipulating our responses to his narrator, so that we may sometimes be totally aligned with Humbert, as we are in our shared attitude of amused contempt for Lolita's mother, and at other times lifted, for purposes of cosmic laughter, far above our narrator's paranoid and romantically blundering head. But Humbert has the last laugh, since we are ultimately trapped by his subjective perspective—although Humbert fails to spot Quilty, while we see him everywhere.

Humbert tells us that "only an artist and a madman . . . with a bubble of hot poison in [his] loins" can detect a nymphet, that her attraction is in fact invisible to "normal" eyes "like the cheapest of cheap cuties. For that is what nymphets imitate—while we moan and die." This elitist conception of invisible excellence which only the aesthete can perceive is really the essence of romantic love, in which one discovers an object onto which to project romantic fantasies and then mistakes the projection for a revelation of the object's true nature. The alleged theme of Clare Quilty's play *The Enchanted Hunters* is that "mirage and reality merge in love." In effect, the novel *Lolita* requires us to see what is not there ("real love" of the sort we are accustomed to encounter in conventional romantic literature), what may or may not be there (Quilty), and what is at best only partially there (Lolita's demoniac charm).

A conventional notion of cinema as a recorder of what is preeminently *there* seems problematic for a novel which concerns itself with intangibles, uncertainties, and invisibilities, partial or total. But, theoretical considerations aside, there are a number of films which have dealt with these elements successfully, for example Resnais's *Last Year at Marienbad* (1961), Jack Clayton's *The Innocents* (1962), Antonioni's *Blow-Up* (1966), Robert Altman's *Images* (1972), and Francis Ford Coppola's *The Conversation* (1974). In addition, fantasy projections and distortions have been well handled in Fellini's *8½* (1963), Roman Polanski's *Repulsion* (1965), and Ingmar Bergman's *Cries and Whispers* (1972), and as far back as Robert Wiene's 1919 film *The Cabinet of Dr. Caligari*. The device of unreliable narration is employed simply in John Schlesinger's *Darling* (1965), and very complexly in Alain Robbe-Grillet's *The Man Who Tells Lies* (1967). The filmmaker's capacity to play with images as a writer can play with words has been evident since Georges Méliès began to make films at the turn of the century. But the most convincing evidence that the film medium might have accommodated even Nabokov's peculiar literary complexity exists in the film *Lolita* itself, in the first sequence (the last one in the novel), when Humbert confronts and kills Quilty.

As the movie opens, we see Humbert's white station wagon traveling down a deserted, misty road at dawn. He (James Mason) approaches what appears to be a small fairy-tale castle, shrouded in mist. We hear music of a tinkling, eerie sort, fore-shadowing not danger but the fantastic, the dreamlike, the sur-real. The interior of the "castle" looks like a poor man's version of *Citizen Kane*'s Xanadu, filled with statues, sheeted furniture, a harp, and a multitude of other irrelevant treasures. Humbert stumbles on bottles and glasses left from a recent party. He calls out to Quilty (Peter Sellers), who emerges from beneath a sheeted chair (upon which his glasses were resting, as if he were a nearsighted ghost). When Humbert asks if he is Quilty, Quilty replies, "No, I'm Spartacus." (This is one of several self-reflexive jokes from Stanley Kubrick, who directed *Spartacus* in 1960, two years before he directed *Lolita*. Kubrick's *film* jok-ing and movie allusions are in keeping with Nabokov's literary allusions and personal jokes throughout his novel: for example, the fact that Vivian Darkbloom, Quilty's sometime companion, is an anagram of Vladimir Nabokov, just as his Clare Quilty is a corruption of "clearly guilty".)

Quilty transforms his sheet into a Roman toga and invites Humbert to play a game of "Roman" ping pong "like two civilized senators." Humbert resists momentarily, but then begins to play, badly. Quilty appears to have an endless supply of ping pong balls (a hollow emblem of his impotence) which he draws from his dressing gown like a magician. ("My motto is 'Be prepared.'") Humbert loses the game and draws his gun (his symbol of out-raged virility). He produces a list of accusations against Quilty, which Quilty reads back in a Gabby Hayes impersonation: "What's this? a deed to the ranch?" Quilty is incapable of taking anything, even his own death, seriously. He refuses to enter into a dignified *European* romantic duel with Humbert. Instead, he draws on boxing gloves in order to die American movie style "like a champ" and Humbert shoots him in the glove. Quilty then resorts to music (to soothe the savage beast, perhaps), playing Chopin's "military" polonaise "which I just wrote last week." Nervously, he tries to supply lyrics for it, subconsciously betraying his competition with Humbert for Lolita (Sue Lyon): "The moon is blue and so are you. . . . And I tonight . . . she's mine toni—*yours*, she's *yours* tonight. . . ." Suddenly he bolts, making a dash for cover. Humbert shoots him in the leg. Quilty drags himself slowly toward an eighteenth-century portrait of a young girl who vaguely resembles Lolita and tries to hide behind it. Humbert shoots through the painting at the now invisible Quilty, making five lethal black holes.

One significant effect of this scene is that, though these odd events are not denied their actuality, we perceive them as preposterous. Our minds wobble gently between credulity and denial. A microcosm of the complex working of Nabokov's original story is, in this one instance, complexly rendered: the unreal reality of the setting; the obsessive game playing,[1] which is both stylistic and a concrete part of the action; Quilty's rumpled androgyny (his first name is Clare and he lisps); his decadence against which Humbert's perverse passion appears absurdly innocent; his phantom existence, his protean shift from identity to identity (ghost, Roman, ping pong champion, boxer, Old Western coot, composer, and corpse); the symbolic nature of the conflict (Quilty's ping pong balls versus Humbert's pistol, Humbert's European romanticism versus Quilty's Roman/American barbarity, Quilty's appropriation of everything from Lolita to the Boy Scout motto to Chopin's music); finally, his destruction through a work of art (literally), a painting of a girl which suggests the intimate connection between Quilty and Lolita in Humbert's mind and hints at Lolita's elusive immortality as an artifact (in Humbert's book, in Quilty's plays)—all these elements reflect the original novel's complex thematic network. And although the film which follows does not maintain this extreme aesthetic density, it is certainly not bereft of it.

To begin with, Kubrick uses music effectively to convey certain collisions of worlds which Nabokov conveys verbally. Humbert's theme, an imitation Tchaikovsky piano concerto, dissolves into

[1] In the novel, Humbert says, "I suppose I am especially susceptible to the magic of games." But in the film Humbert tells Lolita, "I am no good at games or guessing," signifying a measure of the difference between the tormented but dynamic Humbert of the novel and the weaker, befuddled professor in the film. This character shift, in addition to guaranteeing greater sympathy for the movie Humbert, may be Kubrick's allusion to the love-wrecked Professor Unrath and his demoniac Lola Lola in von Sternberg's *The Blue Angel*, Kubrick once again replacing a literary allusion, such as Nabokov's to the *Carmen* triangle, with a cinematic one.

Lolita's theme, an imitation radio-flat rendition of late 1950s rock, which substitutes "yah-yah" for "sha-na-na-na," "bip-bip-bip-bip," "sh-boom," and "wah-wah." And both the saturated passion of Humbert's theme and the gum-popping banality of Lolita's are juxtaposed with the eerie, nearly nonmusic of Quilty's theme, which introduces or accompanies each of his appearances.

The old *Gaslight* (1943) trick of causing a person to doubt his own sensuous perceptions, an inherent part of the novel's technique of unreliability, is played by almost everyone on everyone else in Kubrick's film.[2] When Charlotte discovers Humbert's diary, he says, "You're having a hallucination, Charlotte. You're crazy." When Humbert accuses Lolita of conspiring with their pursuer, she says, "You're sick—you need help. You're imagining things." And Quilty makes a concerted attempt to drive Humbert mad. Disguised as a state police conventioneer, he tells Humbert, who is on the verge of devirginizing his stepdaughter (or so he thinks), "When I saw you, I said, 'There's a guy with the most normal looking face I ever saw in my life.'" Quilty's insistence on Humbert's normality when he is about to perform an abnormal act, together with Quilty's chummy policeman's disguise, unnerve Humbert—as they are intended to do.

The idea of "normal" is satirized throughout the film. When Humbert tells Lolita that Charlotte (Shelley Winters) is dead, only a scene after Lolita has made love to him, Lolita wails, "Everything has changed all of a sudden. Everything was so, I don't know, normal." When Lolita reveals to Humbert near the end of the film her abiding love for Quilty ("I guess he was the only guy I was ever really crazy about"), she explains with maddening matter-of-factness, "He wasn't like you and me. He wasn't a normal person. He was a genius." This satire is remini-

[2] Even the viewer is given pause when the film cuts from Humbert's first lustful perusal of Lolita to a horror film in mid-scream, only to reveal a moment later that Humbert, Lolita, and Charlotte are watching a drive-in movie. This is, by the way, the second element reminiscent of *Citizen Kane*, which cuts abruptly from the somber, gothic, expressionist scene of Kane's death to an up-tempo newsreel, and from the departure of Kane's second wife to a screaming cockatoo. The references to this film are appropriate, since Kane too is a romantic obsessed with transforming things into the image of his desire, first a newspaper, then his second wife, and finally Xanadu.

Lolita (Sue Lyon) plants a not-so-innocent kiss on the cheek of Humbert Humbert (James Mason), while mother Charlotte Haze (Shelley Winters) plays chess obliviously. *Lolita* (1962)

scent of one of the novel's most startlingly funny lines, "I, on my part, was as naive as only a pervert can be," since naiveté and perversion seem almost as strange bedfellows as incest and normality.

Another element which survives from the novel, an isolated but marvelous fragment of Nabokov's "invention of America," is the bathroom motif. To induce Humbert to rent a room in her house, Charlotte leads him to the bathroom, points out the quaint "European" plumbing, and flushes the toilet for emphasis. The bathroom door later facilitates Humbert and Charlotte's first postmarital separation, Humbert locked inside the john scribbling in his diary, Charlotte outside in the hall, whining for reassurance. And after Charlotte's death, Humbert receives a procession of mourners while lying benignly in the bathtub like a drunken Marat.[3]

Many of the correspondences that blur the distinctions between characters in the novel are maintained in the film adaptation. Charlotte whispers in Quilty's ear to remind him of their sexual adventure; later, Lolita whispers in Humbert's ear about the "little game" she learned from Charlie, the only boy at Camp Climax. When Lolita shrieks at Humbert after her debut in Quilty's play, she sounds like her mother, and her later banal domesticity as Mrs. Richard Schiller demonstrates the continuity of generations. Humbert, in turn, begins to sound increasingly like Charlotte the frustrated parent as he threatens, interrogates, and cajoles Lolita for her infractions of his rules. Humbert Humbert and Harold Haze (Charlotte's first husband and Lolita's real father) have the same initials. And all the women Humbert encounters in the film make sly sexual advances toward him, mistaking Humbert's adult disguise—"a great big handsome hunk of movieland manhood"—for the real item.

---

[3] "Quite a few of the extraneous inventions (such as the macabre ping-pong scene or that rapturous swig of Scotch in the bathtub) struck me as appropriate and delightful." Vladimir Nabokov, *Lolita: A Screenplay* (New York: McGraw-Hill, 1974), p. xiii. For the most part, however, Nabokov found the film a disappointment. Despite his credit as the screenwriter of Kubrick's movie, very little of Nabokov's screenplay survived in the finished film. But in fairness to Kubrick, it should be said that Nabokov's screenplay was not particularly good.

The film retains various other random elements from the novel. The connection between Humbert and the nymphet-loving Edgar Allan Poe is established when Humbert alludes to "the divine Edgar" and reads to Lolita from Poe's "Ulalume." Sunglasses, employed in the novel as a lust-guilt symbol, are used in the film to link Lolita to Quilty (she wears heart-shaped sunglasses in her first scene in the movie, and Quilty leaves his dark glasses behind in her hospital room for Humbert to discover). In addition, Humbert's disease of the heart (how appropriate for a victim of love to die of a coronary!) and Lolita's husband's Alaska scheme (Alaska, the last American success frontier) are mentioned in the movie, although nothing much is made of either. And Quilty says, "I know all about this tragedy and comedy and fantasy sort of thing," explicitly referring to the mixing of genre tonalities in the story both as it was written and filmed.

However, these elements do not coalesce into a film experience sufficiently rich to compare with the original novel. For the film lacks an analogue for the Nabokovian prose invention of a world which both contains and transcends real life.

In 1961, Stanley Kubrick wrote:

> People have asked me how it is possible to make a film out of *Lolita* when so much of the quality of the book depends on Nabokov's prose style. But to take the prose style as any more than just a part of a great book is simply misunderstanding just what a great book is.[4]

That "simple misunderstanding" which Kubrick blithely dismisses, supplying his own theory of what makes great art great ("the writer's obsession with his subject, with a theme and a concept and a view of life and an understanding of character") is the fundamental downfall of almost every adaptive endeavor which seeks to reduce the unyieldingly mysterious phenomenon of art to a practical formulation. It does not matter if, according to Norman Kagan in *The Cinema of Stanley Kubrick* (1972), "Nabokov agreed at the time that the main narrative tension was in Humbert's pursuit of the nymphet [and that after Humbert]

4 "Words and Movies," *Sight and Sound*, Winter, 1961.

got Lolita into bed halfway through the book, interest sagged." It does not matter if Kubrick's decision to, in his words, "invent action which will be an objective correlative of the book's psychological content, will accurately dramatize this in an implicit, off-the-nose way . . ." is theoretically sound. The fact remains that the dominant narrative energy of *Lolita* the novel derives from actions of the mind expressed through Nabokov's prose style, only a small portion of which can be adequately accommodated by the essentially realistic manner Kubrick adopted for the film.

Kubrick photographed *Lolita* predominantly in medium shots, the least intrusive choice a director can make. There are virtually no distortions of lens or angle, no flourishes of movement, no extreme close-ups or long shots or zooms. The lighting is consistently naturalistic. And there is no appreciable audio manipulation. Kubrick's decision to film in this manner may have been based on his assumption that the bizarre nature of the material required directorial detachment for balance. That assumption works in the opening scene between Humbert and Quilty described earlier, in which the events are genuinely bizarre, and later when a "phantom" car (most likely Quilty's) stops mysteriously behind Humbert's station wagon somewhere in the deserted Southwest. But the majority of *Lolita*'s content is banal until it is worked upon by Humbert's distorted romantic perspective. To accommodate that content appropriately, Kubrick needed a stylistic equivalent for Nabokov's prose.

There are a number of directors whose obtrusive, highly visible styles might have provided such an equivalent: Orson Welles, Bernardo Bertolucci, Luchino Visconti, Roman Polanski, all of whom combine romanticism, irony, expressive excess, and a sense of decadence in calculated technical variations. But the best directorial equivalent for Nabokov, in my opinion, is Josef von Sternberg, with his affinity for the material, his delirious romantic distortions of his heroines, his delight in grotesque comic and melodramatic excess, his European eye for decadence, his graceful camera movements, his cluttered, dreamlike sets, and his ethereal lighting.

Consider, for example, how von Sternberg might have treated Nabokov's transformation of "dead time"—time in which essentially nothing happens—into a tense metaphor of Humbert's predatory explorations of Lolita:

> My white pajamas have a lilac design on the back. I am like one of those inflated pale spiders you see in old gardens. Sitting in the middle of a luminous web and giving little jerks to this or that strand. *My* web is spread all over the house as I listen from my chair where I sit like a wily wizard. Is Lo in her room? Gently I tug on the silk. She is not. . . . Let us have a strand of silk descend the stairs. I satisfy myself by this means that she is not in the kitchen. . . . Raylike, I glide in thought to the parlor and find the radio silent. . . . So my nymphet is not in the house at all! Gone! What I thought was a prismatic weave turns out to be but an old gray cobweb, the house is empty, is dead. And then comes Lolita's soft sweet chuckle through my half open door.

What we get as viewers of the film, however, seems flat, matter of fact, at best titillating, tawdry, satirical, but never ecstatic and rarely an imaginative transport into the world of Humbert's lyrical fever. As the critic Andrew Sarris wrote, "We are never shown the inspired gestures and movements, which transform even the most emotionally impoverished nymphet into a creature of fantasy and desire." [5]

In addition to Kubrick's stylistic reserve, Sue Lyon, the actress who plays Lolita, although sexy, never approaches the intoxicating apricot innocence of Humbert's ultimate nymphet. The little girl in the 1962 French film *Sundays and Cybele*, another story of an erotic attachment between a girl child and an adult male, is a much closer approximation, perhaps because she really is a little girl, instead of a fifteen-year-old "sex kitten" who happens to be attracted to weird older men. But the buried prototype of Lolita, the true "creature of fantasy and desire" for the American culture, is Shirley Temple, who throughout her prepubescent movie career was paired off with adult males who loved her to distraction. Imagine the impact (barring censorship) of an American movie which brought Humbert and Shirley together. In comparison to that explosive fantasy, Kubrick's *Lolita* seems merely naughty.

[5] "Movie Journal," *The Village Voice*, July 5, 1962.

Stanley Kubrick, with what Arlene Croce appropriately calls his "cry, calculated, and neutrally sinister . . . deadpan" directorial style,[6] provides us with a version of Nabokov's banal Lolita, "a combination," according to Humbert, "of naiveté and deception, of charm and vulgarity, of blue sulks and rosy mirth. . . ." But the other Lolita—"the little deadly demon" with "the elusive, shifty, soul-shattering insidious charm" who can be evoked only "with shut eyes, on the dark innerside of your eyelids . . ." and whom we *must* experience to appreciate adequately both the agony and the hilarity of Humbert's dilemma—eludes both Kubrick and us. Only once, in the title sequence, during which we watch a man's arm tenderly apply toenail polish to a young girl's foot, do we have the space to fantasize on the dark innersides of our own eyelids a slavish devotion to an impossible object worthy of *our* desire. But once is not enough.

> O me, what eyes hath Love put in my head
> Which have no correspondence with true sight.
> Shakespeare, Sonnet 148

[6] "Lolita," *Sight and Sound,* Autumn, 1962.

Brunch on Moon River

BY LESLIE CLARK

In the midst of Holly Golightly's cocktail party in Truman Capote's *Breakfast at Tiffany's,* a Hollywood producer named O. J. Berman offers the unnamed young writer-narrator a curious description of their outlandish hostess. "She isn't a phoney because she's a *real* phoney," Berman asserts, pleased to think he understands her.

The more we know of Holly the more Berman's self-contradictory observation comes to make deep sense. Holly lives conspicuously in a world of amoral, high-priced hustling, and she looks and acts like a girl on the make. But she never pretends to be much else. She may practice phoniness (her role as a society playgirl is a euphemism for a kind of informal prostitution), yet she *is* genuine. Her refusal to serve as a state's witness against someone she thinks has been good to her ("Testify against a friend I will not.") demonstrates her integrity even as this act precipitates her downfall. She may be, as she says, rotten to the core, but at the core she has a sense of honor.

O. J. Berman makes the identical pronouncement about Holly in the Blake Edwards film version of *Breakfast at Tiffany's* (1961); she is a *"real* phoney." And this time also we can take his meaning to stand as the thematic centerpiece of the work. However, Edwards is not in the least interested in Holly's convictions about decency and fair play. She qualifies as a *real*

Holly Golightly (Audrey Hepburn) peeks in the famous jeweler's window. *Breakfast at Tiffany's* (1961)

phoney because she believes wholeheartedly that glamor can fulfill dreams, just as she is susceptible to fairy tales and making wishes on a star.

Edwards gallantly rewards Holly's fantasizing with a happy fairy-tale ending, even though love and matrimony-ever-after are assuredly not what Capote's Holly had in mind.

New York Times film critic A. H. Weiler aptly described Capote's 1958 novella as a "wistful memoir." Set in New York during the wartime 1940s, it is a bittersweet, ironic study of how a nineteen-year-old girl is forced into womanhood before her time. She wants to play the society game like a gambler after high stakes, not for the money but for a chance at getting what she never had, which is, paradoxically, what only money can buy. Capote's writer-narrator calls her a "glittery voyager," committed to her makeshift headful of dreams. The difference between Holly and virtually everyone else we encounter is that, in O. J.'s words, "she believes all this crap she believes." Who beside Holly would seek after an elusive vision of peace in New York City and would latch on to the tolerant benevolence of Tiffany's, because "nothing very bad can happen to you there"?

Despite her romantic idealism, Capote's Holly is resilient, self-aware, and knows how to take care of herself; her beliefs give her the tenacity to survive. Most of the episodes missing from the film are those in the novella in which Holly displays her own strength and ability to manage (or manipulate) a situation. She nurses Mag Wildwood back to health after the famous cocktail party and moves Mag into her apartment; then she has no qualms about seducing her friend's rich South American "prospect" José. She saves the writer-narrator's life after a runaway horse nearly kills him; as a consequence, her illegitimate child miscarries (a development not in the film). Most of all, she *does* take the plane to Brazil, "travelling light," looking for whatever it is in the world that feels as nice as Tiffany's.

For Blake Edwards the fantasy of Tiffany's as a sanctuary from the pain of reality is the kind of dreaming that renders Holly fragile and soon despoiled. His Holly is deemed appealing precisely because she *cannot* take care of herself. She is just so vulnerable, so waiflike. Instead of the boyish elegance of Capote's heroine, her particular attraction is the fragility of Audrey Hepburn's acting. Accordingly, there is considerably more discretion about exactly how she collects her nightly fifty-dollar "powder room" tips in posh restaurants. (Edwards sugarcoats it for us, more, I suspect, from personal design than from concession to the moral standards of Hollywood, 1962.) For Blake Edwards, Holly is hooked, just as she started hooking, for the sake of dreaming and her own romantic impulses. And it is her dreaming which has sold her down (Moon) river.

It is a long distance from the Libertyphones and V-letters of the novella's world to the affluent, glossy, magazine-cover ambience of the film, and from Capote's admiring study of a character with spunk to a situation piece close to a gently sudsy, rather than soap, opera. The effect has been to lighten the substance. There are no pink panthers in the lush afterglow of a New York summer in the film version of *Breakfast at Tiffany's*, but it is a place as clean and sparkling as a brimming champagne glass, and just as giddy with promise. Well, almost.

Beneath the high-class swank of plush brownstone addresses, of fashion models and designer dresses, of handsome "kept" young authors, it is all just a big fake. From beginning to end, Holly Golightly leads a confetti existence, at best a charming but precarious masquerade. And no scene demonstrates this as does the cocktail party, the film's showcase for imposture. Blake Edwards looks on with the eye of a person long practiced at the art of appearances, and his camera takes a witty, malicious pleasure at betraying it. But what the removal of "masks," comic and otherwise, reveals is a sad, rather frightened humanity.

As it happens, even while his caustic attitude exposes the whole "scene" as sham, Edwards makes its enticements strong and compelling. Full of visual gags, wisecracks, bandbox color, slapstick, corny stunts, and a bouncing Henry Mancini score, the party is also the movie's one fully *auteurist* sequence, nicely anticipating Edwards's 1968 film with Peter Sellers called *The Party:* that whole movie is the party and almost nothing else. As for *Breakfast at Tiffany's*, Blake Edwards has explained:

> The thing I do take credit for was the party. . . . It was indicated
> in the screenplay; there were certain things written down such as
> a couple of speeches. But the general party was only indicated
> and I had to improvise it on the set. . . .[1]

In *Breakfast,* the party is how deception "looks." The scene begins with a tracking shot of O. J. Berman trying to talk to a
stuffed green parrot in a cage, the bird looking larger than life
(ironically, it is a movie producer who walks the border between
the real and the phoney). Berman's next move is to a curvaceous
blonde who says her name is "Irving." And so it goes; a succession
of masks. It looks glib and silly, but the editing imposes a cutting edge that gives this strange roomful of dissemblances an
unexpected, rather startling poignancy.

We see Holly in conversation with a young man wearing a
picturesque black eye patch; later the camera cuts back to him
having an argument so heated that he slides off the patch and
exposes a perfectly normal eye beneath. A tipsy woman is laughing to herself in a large mirror; the camera pans away to watch
the party, then pans back to her, now sobbing at her wretched
reflection, black mascara running down her face. Two women are
exchanging small talk; one glances away briefly, while the other
suddenly elevates out of the frame, seated on the shoulders of
a man who then stands nonchalantly sipping a drink. The other
woman looks back, and we are left with her bewildered reaction.
The trouble with subterfuge, with putting others on or "faking
them out," Edwards seems to indicate, is how isolated people can
become behind their exteriors, and how treacherously those exteriors can fail them.

Even Holly herself, with her preposterously long cigarette
holder, is transparently acting the golddigger. But it is Mag
Wildwood, a walking punchline from Arkansas, who passes out
on the zebra-skin rug and puts the exclamation point to Edwards's proceedings. The party shows itself for what it is: a dizzy
and more than somewhat devastating debacle. Mag typifies the
vacuity around her, part of the big swindle Edwards sees foisted
like angelfood cake on people who are hungry. (It is not all so

[1] Interview in *Cahiers du Cinema in English,* No. 3, 1966.

self-righteous, of course, but it is intended to create something of a moral hangover.)

The party Capote describes is also the big scene of the novella, although it does not compare with Edwards's elaborately staged production, so disproportionate in length to the rest of the film. Capote's fête, more or less a stag affair, is memorably described: "It was as if the hostess had distributed her invitations while zigzagging through various bars; which was probably the case." As for Mag, Capote is more amused than disheartened by the charade of a Southern Cracker in the guise of a New York fashion sophisticate. In all, Mag Wildwood is a fuller presence in the novella. Her "career" and temperament—the materialism, the big city bitchery—contrast with Holly's throughout. The movie Mag is a caricature, a wild side show who never reappears after the party.

But the masks and facades *do* reappear in other guises in Edwards's film. Paul Varjak's wealthy mistress is introduced as his "interior decorator," and she calls him "Lucille" on the telephone when her husband unexpectedly walks into her end of the conversation. Holly's former husband, Doc Barnes, is mistaken for a detective, and he in turn offers the startling revelation of Holly's hidden married past. But perhaps the most facetious example of imposture is the Japanese photographer played by Mickey Rooney. And fraudulence directly affects the growing liaison between Holly and Paul (the film's version of Capote's unnamed writer-narrator).

Paul pretends that his being expensively "supported" will give him a chance to write. Holly pretends that her hustling will some day fulfill her dream of owning a horse ranch in Mexico with her brother Fred. To facilitate her goal, Holly keeps a mirror, lipstick, and perfume in the mailbox so that she can put on her "face" before confronting the world of her late-night escorts. The only way for Holly to evade facades is by way of the apartment fire escape. There she takes refuge from too-adamant callers, and there she asks Paul to help her take Doc to the bus depot, because she "can't play the scene alone." (Holly's immersion in a world of deception is reaffirmed by Edwards's mise-en-scene in the sequence where Doc meets Paul in Central Park to talk about

Holly. Their discussion takes place in front of a deserted band shell—a correlative to Holly's "empty performance" of which these two people are privileged spectators.)

Basically, what Truman Capote admires as a style, an éclat, which Holly and her entourage fully recognize for its artifice, Edwards regards more severely as he commiserates with Holly's misguided spirit. Capote has respect for Holly and a sense of camaraderie with her. But Edwards demands that Holly come to terms on screen with the deceit of her fantasies. When she receives news of the death of her adored brother, Fred, Holly finds her dream of a home for the two of them shattered like glass. Edwards's camera cuts to a high, omniscient overhead shot and holds on Holly lying on her bed. She is a broken carnival doll amidst the wrecked junk of her bedroom. It is only after this expression of grief, the acknowledgment of dreams destroyed, that Edwards allows his own brand of happy ending for his heroine: the Right Man comes along. The conclusion hinges on perhaps the most essential change in the movie, the transformation of Paul Varjak, Capote's nameless narrator, into a respectable, and most importantly, *heterosexual* hero. In translation: Audrey Hepburn wins George Peppard.

The attachment between Holly and Capote's narrator is possibly of the heart but not of the body. Despite the feelings of kinship (they are both Southerners living in the same New York building) and the deep sympathy between them, there are never any moments of boy-girl interest. When he describes her physically, he praises only her qualities which are the most ambiguously feminine: he likes the tawny streaks of color in her "boy's hair," her slim and straight-hipped figure, and the "hoarse, breaking tones of a boy's adolescent voice" when she plays her guitar and sings. But usually his concern is platonic, surrogate brotherly. He is a spectator and a confidante. And when he does admit jealousy about Holly's other men, it is a carefully qualified declaration: "For I *was* in love with her. Just as I'd once been in love with my mother's elderly colored cook and a postman who let me follow him in his rounds and a whole family named McKendrick. That category of love generates jealousy too."

The movie adaptation, by Edwards and screenwriter George

Axelrod, eliminates the many innuendos and implications of homosexuality in the novella. The changeover to a "straight" character is essential to analyzing the contours of the film and helps to interpret the new ending, a possibly irksome one for viewers demanding a "faithful" screen version. A. H. Weiler in the *New York Times* (Oct. 6, 1961), for one, expressed his dissatisfaction about Blake Edwards's remade male protagonist:

> In transforming him from a dispassionate admirer, as amoral as Holly, into a gent being subsidized for purely romantic purposes, by a rich, comely woman, the character loses conviction. . . . *Breakfast at Tiffany's* loses momentum as it heads toward that happy ending. . . .

In conceiving his film, Blake Edwards knew exactly how forbidden the intimations of Capote's original might be. He later recalled:

> Today, you could do it a lot closer. In those days, it frightened many people. It was too cynical; you touched on subjects that I believe people would be afraid to dramatize—the homosexual influence of the leading man, the sexual relationships of Holly that were so amoral—she lived with lesbians because they're good housekeepers—and things like that that have a great wonderful sardonic humor to them. You couldn't say things like that on the screen. . . .[2]

However, what Edwards *was* able to "say" in the film lies within the realm of possibilities which the story's lack of explicitness makes available. More to the point, the suppression of homosexuality in the writer-narrator is more consonant with Edwards's heterosexual romanticism: in the fairy-tale setting, Paul Varjak belongs as a lover not a friend. Simply, Edwards does give the story an ending, while Capote leaves it unresolved. Interestingly, Holly complains to Capote's hero, after listening to him read some of his stories, that they sounded as though he had "written them without knowing the ending." The novella's Holly disappears in

[2] *Cahiers du Cinéma in English,* No. 3, 1966.

the African bush, apparently, and Capote begins his story as a recollection of the time a few years ago when the narrator had known her.

Capote's Holly has as tough a spirit as she has imagination; she would rather wander, a vagabond, than disown her soul: "Be anything but a coward, a pretender, an emotional crook, a whore: I'd rather have cancer than a dishonest heart." Holly's noncomformity is her most vivid trait; her destination is unknown, but somehow, her fate is secure: she is not lost, she has just gone looking.

For Blake Edwards, Holly reaches her Moon River (it virtually pours down on her in the rainstorm at the film's end) when she quits yearning after gold-plated counterfeits of happiness and accepts the limitations of her own human self. It is a relinquishment of sorts, having her use her common sense and forget all that phoney nonsense in her head, but it is such a comfortable solution. Thus the fancy-free, arrogant, gutsy child-woman Capote's writer knew succumbs to tears and a tender embrace in Edwards's film and never even comes close to an airport. The rain-drenched kiss in the alleyway, creating a family tableau of Holly, Paul, and her no-name cat, in effect persuades by its very insubstantiality; the undeniable delight of the scene comes out of its unbelievable magic, especially in contrast to a garbage-strewn alley (psychologically an astute location since it undercuts sentimentality).

Holly and Paul hire a yellow cab to carry them off to their happy ending. The connection between going and coming in cabs is, thinking back, a special one. Even before the title credits rolled, in a long shot of an early summer's morning at sunrise, a yellow taxi glides rapidly down Fifth Avenue and pulls up in front of Tiffany's. Holly gets out. Nothing else happens, except the sound of the lyrics of "Moon River" on the sound track, but the materialization and movement of the cab down the empty street suggests such a consummate sense of a wondrous and privileged excursion out of the everyday, that it is exactly reminiscent of coming down the yellow brick road with another country girl named Dorothy. The absolute quiet of the street, the "breakfast" of the solitary Holly indulging in private make-believe, sets up a dreamy unreality that is always latent in the rest of the film. The completion, not of the dreams but of the dreaminess, comes in the other cab ride at the end of the film, where, after she refuses to listen to Paul's pleading with her not to run away any more, Holly "learns" about how people belong to each other and, presumably, finds another place like Tiffany's right there in Paul's arms. She can settle down at last, and cat will have a name.

Holly and Paul are thus transformed into the prototype of the ideal American couple of their era; their stroll around New York during the day they spend together has a well-fed, suburban satisfaction to it. Their tribulations are exotic, but the success they seem promised to achieve is an affluent, middle-class ever-after. The pasts are risqué but forgivable, and their social acceptability is never at stake. And such upbeat people, glad and hopeful of an upbeat fate, bear faint resemblance to the idiosyncratic, exceptional, and offbeat characters of Truman Capote's novella.

But the conformist ending does not do much to conceal Blake Edwards's deep streak of cynicism, inextricable from an even more deeply felt romanticism. Robert Haller, in writing on Edwards's famous private eye, Peter Gunn, noticed the same quality of disenchantment: "Through most of Edwards's films, the comedies, mysteries, and dramas, there runs an undercurrent of bitterness. . . . This bitterness transforms comedy into an anagram for anguish. . . ." [3] It is more of a prose than a poetic sensibility, and it shows little comprehension of the subtler idea of romance Truman Capote described, but neither can Edwards's sensibility be understood completely by such an explicit comparison to that of the novella; he is, in the film, true to the spirit of what he sees.

It is as someone with a sour stomach for reality, and a temperament for romantic, highly-colored love stories, that Blake Edwards imagined *Breakfast at Tiffany's*. He is, in fact, quite similar in style and approach to the character of Joe Bell, the

[3] *Film Heritage,* Summer, 1968.

dyspeptic bartender in Capote's novel (and not in the film), who customarily arranges fresh cut flowers in his bar, who sucks Tums to placate his indigestion, and who, from a great distance —say, as far as Moon River is wide—loves Holly Golightly very much.

Rabbit, Run (1960)

John Updike

Rabbit Runs Down

BY GARY SIEGEL

Gary Arnold of the *Washington Post* called the film of John Updike's *Rabbit, Run,* "the worst massacre of an interesting American novel since John Barth's *End of the Road.*" With few exceptions, the film's other reviews were equally hostile. Reacting to the severe notices and the ensuing negative publicity (actress Carrie Snodgrass, one of the stars, denounced *Rabbit, Run* on television talk shows [1]), Warner Brothers ordered its Los Angeles release in November, 1970, in a "dump-it-and-scram" multiple distribution. Warners did not even exhibit the film in the East until four years later. Most persons who have seen it have only done so thanks to CBS "Monday Night at the Movies" on television.

Let it be said immediately that the critics' response was almost completely justified. Still, the intense attack was somewhat unfortunate, since *Rabbit, Run* began not as a celluloid excuse to exploit a novel's title, but as a very caring and personal attempt at adaptation by director Jack Smight. That Smight's version of Updike flopped so badly might be ascribable to the studio's unfeeling editing of the final print. (Six months before the film's release, Smight wrote frantically to Joseph Youngerman, executive secretary of the Directors Guild, demanding that his name

[1] Charles Champlin, "Rabbit, Run," *Los Angeles Times,* "Calendar," December 6, 1969, p. 36.

be struck from the credits: "The cut . . . by Warner Brothers is so different from my interpretation that I cannot have my name connected with the picture as its director."[2]) Yet judging from the film that exists, Smight must have intuited that problems ran deeper than editing. He was not discrediting just any project, but a film he had devoted nine years to bringing to the screen.

Smight had bought the rights to Updike's first novel shortly after it was published in 1960. Much later, unable to get studios interested in a production, he borrowed fifteen thousand dollars from Warners as a personal loan to renew rights to the book (he was directing *Harper* for Warners at the time). Smight even scouted locations long before the project was optioned by a studio. All through the 1960s, while he was employed on such middlebrow, mildly unusual pictures as *Harper* (1966), *Kaleidoscope* (1966), *No Way to Treat a Lady* (1968), and *The Illustrated Man* (1969), Smight kept up the pressure. Finally, in 1969, Warners succumbed; they agreed to finance *Rabbit, Run.*

In the meantime, Jack Smight had written a preliminary screenplay himself; yet insisting on only the best for *Rabbit, Run*, he filed away his script as unsuitable for the film. Smight told *Variety:*

> It twisted things around to make them more cinematic and in so doing missed the essence of Updike. Everything was in movie terms. Voice-over narrative and things like that. Then when I was making *The Illustrated Man* for Warners, I mentioned my problem to the screenwriter Howard Kreitsek. He took the book and came back with a new script in eight days—not because he's that fast a writer, but because he simply cut the novel down to two hours of screen time and didn't add anything of his own.[3]

Apparently Kreitsek was affected by Jack Smight's reverential attitude toward John Updike's novel. He was determined to be meticulous in reproducing *Rabbit, Run*, even to the extent of calling his script a "transcription" rather than a screenplay. He attempted to duplicate the book almost scene by scene, for he

[2] *Hollywood Reporter,* June 5, 1970, p. 1.
[3] Stuart Byron, "W7 'Faithful' to *Rabbit, Run*," *Variety,* August 20, 1969, p. 26.

well realized that the story—of Harry "Rabbit" Angstrom, age twenty-six, caught in a trap chiefly of his own making—is the very stuff of cinema: Rabbit playing golf with Minister Jack Eccles, Rabbit on the basketball court, Rabbit's sudden drive south to West Virginia, his incessant running up and down the streets of his hometown, Brewer, Pennsylvania. John Updike, in fact, had conceived of the novel in consciously filmic terms:

> I originally wrote *Rabbit, Run* in the present tense in a sort of cinematic way. I thought of it as *Rabbit, Run: A Movie*. Novels are descended from chronicles of what has long ago happened, but movies happen to you in the present as you sit there.[4]

Whenever his novel tells of events that occurred in the distant past, Updike uses stream of consciousness to blend all into the present. And Rabbit's rapid responses to these events are also mixed into the stream of consciousness, as the narrator constantly jumps about, montage-like, to assume Rabbit's diverse perspectives. The result of Updike's borrowing from the movies is that the reader must have quick reflexes to keep a guard on the changing, twisting, and shifting protagonist. Character judgment cannot be rendered with any surety: Rabbit is not always self-centered lover or self-righteous saint, strong and sympathetic protagonist or sorry ex-basketball star turned goat. John Updike offers a myriad of perspectives.

Despite the attempt at slavish fidelity, the Smight-Kreitsek version of events offers no such challenge; Updike's authorial complexity is broken down and blunted; Rabbit is spoon-fed to the viewer in prepackaged morsels of minimalist stereotyped behavior. Rabbit is made one-dimensionally unreliable, irresponsible, and irrational.

The problems begin with Kreitsek's method of transcription. He isolates passages of dialogue, selects key moments of the novel by lifting them out of context. Consequently, events lose their dramatic tension; actions seem unmotivated; transcription falls short of adequate translation.

---

[4] Jane Howard, "Can a Nice Novelist Finish First?" *Life*, November 4, 1966, p. 88.

Harry "Rabbit" Angstrom (James Caan) has breakfast with Lucy Eccles (Melodie Johnson), the swinging wife of a soul-saving minister. *Rabbit, Run* (1970)

For example: in the novel Rabbit tells his wife Janice about a basketball game he played with some kids down the block. Janice fails to be impressed and relates how tired she is. "You're supposed to look tired," Rabbit says. "You're a housewife." Janice replies, "And meanwhile you're off playing like a twelve-year-old?" The discussion continues on for a few heated minutes, ending in Rabbit's blurted, "Screw you. Just screw you," as he makes ready to flee the house.

In the book, Rabbit's reasons for leaving are expressed exquisitely through the omniscient vantage of John Updike. The author describes Rabbit's growing revulsion at

> the clutter behind him in the room—the old-fashioned glass with its corrupt dregs, the choked ashtray balanced on the easy-chair arm, the rumpled rug, the floppy stacks of slippery newspapers, the kid's toys here and there broken and stuck and jammed, a leg off a doll and a piece of bent cardboard that went with some breakfast-box cutout, the rolls of fuzz under the radiators, the continual crisscrossing mess—cling[ing] to his back like a tightening net.

In this passage Rabbit's anger mounts under the increasing weight of the house's confusion, until he reaches a terrible epiphany—Rabbit "senses he is in a trap. It seems certain." As he exits, his wife's request for cigarettes, "in a normal voice that says everything is forgiven, everything is the same," reinforces his desperate alienation.

Updike seems to admire the energy behind Rabbit's thought processes at the same time that he demonstrates the suicidal consequences of Rabbit's choice of imperatives. In the film of *Rabbit, Run*, there is no attempt to translate Rabbit's elaborate network of imaginative responses or to explain the defense system of rationalizations that Rabbit concocts for himself. Likewise, the emotions are absent: he spouts obscenities at Janice and immediately leaves. Rabbit's behavior appears sudden and erratic, and the viewer is ill prepared to accept or understand it.

Examples of this missing thread between Rabbit's thoughts and his peculiar actions abound in the film. The dialogue at the baby's funeral scene is much the same as in the novel. Rabbit turns to his relatives and says maniacally, "I didn't do it. . . . She killed him, not me." The film viewer knows he is right. He did not really kill the baby—it drowned accidentally in the bathtub because of Janice's negligence. But the reader knows how, by running out on Janice to rejoin his lover Ruth, he has indeed shared complicity in the baby's death. John Updike spells out the chain of events leading to the tragedy and makes understandable, in context, the unhappy rationalization—that Rabbit would put the blame on others for all his misfortunes. The film of *Rabbit, Run* can only keep harping on the one overdone character trait of its protagonist: his inability to cope and comprehend. Rabbit of the Movies is a Type—he who constantly retreats and runs, escapes and hides.

Beyond the simpleminded characterization of Rabbit (played fairly capably by James Caan), the film has other supporting characters who are unsatisfactorily realized. Ruth (Anjanette Comer) is depicted in the novel as an occasional prostitute, yet she is not unsympathetically drawn. In the movie, there is no question that her vocation is considered unsavory. In the scene where Ruth takes Rabbit home, the camera pulls back for an extended view of Ruth walking up a long stairway, dressed in a very short miniskirt, glancing down the steps and signaling for Rabbit to follow. She is a professional streetwalker on the job. Just as with Rabbit, where the novel humanizes character, warts and all, the film brutalizes character into a one-dimensioned portrait.

Rabbit's wife Janice (Carrie Snodgrass, in the film's best performance) is equally lacking in dimension. Although she is granted a tour-de-force scene when, in a drunken stupor, she tries to fix her elder son a sandwich, desperately struggling for composure as she performs the task, the viewer never truly gets to know her. Ironically, in the scene where she bathes the baby and lets it drown, the shallowness of her characterization becomes an artistic virtue. Jack Smight treats the sequence with a harsh naturalism that is heightened by Janice's nondefinition. She is caught by forces out of control: the sleeves of her bathrobe get wet; she cannot lift her arms from the water. The image of Janice's reflection in the bathwater as she attempts to pull the deceased child out of the tub is eerie and frightening—a form both insubstantial and powerless, an image of an image.

Few moments in the film sustain the intensity of this scene. Despite the admirable attempt to reproduce details of the novel (the film was shot in Reading, Pennsylvania, the model for the town of Brewer; reportedly five thousand dollars was spent on fake rhododendrums for scenes between Rabbit and Mrs. Smith), Kreitsek and Smight never tracked down Updike's metaphoric locale. And even though the filmmakers superimposed the closing sentence from the book over the film's end ("He runs. Ah: runs. Runs.") they missed John Updike's even more subtle sense of affirmation, the "sweet panic" that characterizes Rabbit's escape.

The ensuing panic at the box office was not the sweet kind either. Even an ad campaign in the trade papers, headlined "John Updike took a look at Hollywood's version of John Updike and liked what he saw," was no aid for business. Potential bookers remained wary despite a seemingly sincere letter of praise from Updike to Howard Kreitsek, quoted in part in the Warners publicity:

> . . . I want to thank you, again, for your evident respect for the book—you followed it closely indeed, and I was touched to see my name so conspicuously displayed. The ending worked just fine for me, just fine. . . . It is a brave picture that does attempt to take us into a real middle America and not a caricature, that does try to cope with how much of our lives happens below the belt, and which has many scenes that will be permanently imprinted on my brain. . . . It will be hard to shake some of your imagery, in my imagining.[5]

Nor did a second ad campaign succeed when it linked *Rabbit, Run* to other "explosive" films of the late 1960s. This time, audiences were melodramatically warned of the consequences of seeing "a film not afraid to cope with how much of our lives happens below the belt. It will leave a permanent imprint on your brain." [6] This vulgarization of John Updike's comments

[5] *Variety*, October 22, 1970, p. 6.
[6] *Box Office*, November 16, 1970, p. 11.

shows the box-office strategy that Warners instantly invented in 1969–70, upon the unexpected financial success elsewhere of the two youth-oriented films, *Easy Rider* and *Midnight Cowboy*.

In fact the film version of *Rabbit, Run* updates the novel ten years, so that the story takes place in the 1960s. Jack Smight explained in *Variety*, August 20, 1969, exactly contemporary with *Easy Rider*'s stupendous original theatrical run, that he felt Updike's story was even more relevent to the 1960s than to the time in which the novel was written, the late 1950s. Updike was, in Smight's opinion, "something of a prophet [who] foresaw the great dissatisfaction of the young which is taking place today."

Rabbit *is* dissatisfied and alienated, yet he seems more a victim of the complacent 1950s than the turbulent 1960s; he is not out to "seek a place to be free"; he escapes Brewer only to retreat there again, remain in a dreamy past searching aimlessly for people who will remember his twenty-eight points in the big game with Altoona Central. In Updike's sequel, *Rabbit Redux* (1971), set in the 1960s, Updike makes appropriate changes: Rabbit becomes less self-centered and more politically conscious; he listens not to the sugar-coated philosophy of Reverend Eccles, but to the angry political rhetoric of a black revolutionary spouting Marxist doctrine; and Rabbit lives not with an ex-prostitute but with a flower child, who has left her home and rebelled against her parent's upper-middle-class values.

As for the film, the characters and action of *Rabbit, Run*, originally set in Eisenhower's becalmed America, are displaced— and misplaced—in their new movie time slot. The film version— which barely revamps the story by using modern dress and a rock musical score with a title song, "Hey, Man"—curiously portrays the 1960s from a 1950s perspective, and in a much disjointed manner. Thus the movie of *Rabbit, Run* fails on one more level.

Since the debacle of *Rabbit, Run*, director Jack Smight and screenwriter Howard Kreitsek (who together adapted *The Illustrated Man* [1969] from Ray Bradbury's short stories) have separately turned their energies from adaptations of classics back to more formulaic assignments. Jack Smight has proved several more times a middling talent who can direct popular hits: with *Airport '75* and *Midway* (1976). Howard Kreitsek coscripted

Breakout (1975) and then wrote the screenplays for *Walking Tall, Part Two* (1975) and *Walking Tall: The Final Chapter* (1977). To everyone's satisfaction, this artistic ex-team is leaving one sequel alone. There is no word reported of Jack Smight scouting locations for *Rabbit Redux.*

Catch-22 (1961)

Joseph Heller

Did the Author Catch the Movie?

A DISCUSSION WITH JOSEPH HELLER

[After giving a somewhat "off-the-cuff" lecture on his experiences as an author whose novel has been turned into "a very grim and very powerful and very engrossing and disturbing movie," Joseph Heller opened the floor to questions at the Poetry Center, Young Men's Hebrew Association, New York City, December, 1970.]

Q. You mentioned Jon Voight [as Milo Minderbender] and Orson Welles [as General Dreedle].

Heller: In saying that I couldn't get used to Voight, it doesn't mean that I disapprove of Nichols' conception. Nichols' conception of Milo was different from mine. To say it's different is not saying that in a pejorative sense. I think, for example, that the way Milo goes out of the book, which is kind of vanishing, he just disappears to go smuggle tobacco, would not be as effective on the screen. I think Voight's last moment on the screen is tremendously effective, if you recall it. It's just to say the Voight characterization was different. I had no objection to Welles in the movie. I think that it could have been just as well played by

Editors' title. This discussion appeared originally as the "Questions and Answers" portion of "On Translating *Catch-22* into a Movie," by Joseph Heller in *A Catch-22 Casebook*, Frederick Kiley and Walter McDonald, eds. (New York: Thomas Y. Crowell, 1973), pp. 357–362. Reprinted by permission of the Dun-Donnelley Publishing Corporation.

Yossarian (Alan Arkin) gets a mess-hall mental inspiration while
Nately (Art Garfunkel) waits, pen in hand. *Catch-22* (1970)

Martin Balsam or somebody else, that Welles was wasted in the sense that he is a huge personality and should have had more.

Q. Would you name some of the things you really liked and some of the things you didn't?

A. I wasn't as reactive to the comedy in the movie as audiences were. I think there were moments on the screen where more could have been made out of the minute or two or three when the characters were talking and there was a kind of nonsense dialogue going on, which added nothing; it was just time filling. If you want a specific example, there is a scene when Alan Arkin is trying to make love to Paula Prentiss on the beach, and she is saying something, just talking nonsense: "I'm the only girl on the base and it's so difficult." In that moment, minute or minute and a half, I think that it would have been better to have gotten in what is in the book, that she herself is breaking off a love affair of some duration with him so that she too was rejecting him and it wasn't simply a kind of rape scene on the beach but an indication that he was losing something he wanted. And that would have given a little more meaning to a later scene, which I don't understand, where Arkin is swimming in the water toward the raft and she is on the raft naked. I think there were about two or three places where they tried to create a dialogue like *Catch-22* dialogue which didn't work, for me anyway; there was no need to have any dialogue at all in those places.

I missed one thing only from the book. I wished that they had put in the movie at least one of what I consider the interrogation scenes or inquisition scenes or trial scenes. There are three in the book. I know three fairly full ones. There were none in the movie. And yet I can't think of anything in the movie I would take out that would allow the five or six minutes that would be necessary to provide for that scene. To me one of the most, I guess *the* most effective, scene is the one of the Italian woman in the whorehouse with Yossarian when he comes back to the whorehouse and it's empty and she's sitting there smoking a cigarette, and she just answers, almost doesn't react. There's a kind of weary age-old resignation in her remarks. He is reacting to what she's saying with horror and surprise; then she says, "Catch-a-22." It's as though she realizes, as the old man did, that in the long view of history this is the way life is. And you know she's not happy about it, but why all the surprise? That remains I think for me the most powerful of the scenes. The gory scenes are gory, and they make an impact, but I don't think they're as meaningful as that particular scene.

Q. How realistic are the details in Catch-22?

A. I would say all the physical details, and almost all of what might be called the realistic details do come out of my own experiences as a bombardier in World War II. The organization of a mission, the targets—most of the missions that are in the book were missions that I did fly on. The structure of a B-25, the fact that there are no fighters in *Catch*-22 (there were no German fighters when I was overseas), the organization of a squadron, the fact that there is an intelligence tent, there is a mess hall, there are enlisted men, there was a squadron commander, the flight surgeon—all of these as details come out of my experience. In many cases, actual people I know were starting points for the characters. The mission to Avignon, for example—and that's the one on which Snowden gets killed—corresponds perhaps ninety percent to what I did experience. I did have a copilot go beserk and grab the controls. The earphones did pull out. I did think I was dying for what seemed thirty minutes but was actually three-hundredths of a second. When I did plug my earphones in, there was a guy sobbing on the intercom, "Help the bombardier," but the gunner was only shot in the leg. The other part is something I did add to it.

I want to stress it's just the physical details. Yossarian's emotions, Yossarian's reaction to the war in the squadron were not those I experienced when I was overseas. *Catch*-22 is not really about World War II. It was written during the Korean War and during the period when Senator Joe McCarthy was riding high in the Senate and when John Foster Dulles was bringing us to the brink of war with Russia about every other week. There are many other [laughter]. . . . Well, he was and he did boast about it. That's his phrase that he used in an interview in *Life* magazine. Now I think my tensions, my antagonisms, my concerns are those which are in *Catch*-22, along with, I suppose, an age-old preoccupation with mortality which runs all through the book. I very carefully set the moment of decision for Yossarian, his approach to the point of crisis, to coincide with the collapse of Germany as a military threat. Now none of that's in the movie, but in the novel I trace the course of the European war and Germany's collapse as a threat is all over at the time that Yossarian has to make his decision, and Yossarian is able to say near the end, "The country's not in danger anymore, but I am," and be speaking truthfully. And *Catch-22*'s pretty much about a quarrel, a conflict, a predicament I think we in this country have had ever since the end of World War II. That is, a conflict, a danger, not so much from foreign military force but from our own authorities and our own superiors. I felt that at the time that I wrote *Catch-22*. Nothing is said of Hitler in *Catch-22* although here and there is an opposition to Fascism, and I think that's almost self-evident. Nothing is said of Japan, but the conflicts and dangers do come from the superior officers who were either corrupt, indifferent, or stupid, or unconcerned with the human factors.

Q. Do you know why the pictures on the wall in Major Major's office change?

A. Concerning the movie, do I know why the pictures on the wall of Major Major's office would change? Usually you have to see the picture two or three times to realize that each time Major Major crosses in front of a photograph, the photograph changes. First it was Roosevelt, then it's Stalin (I forget), then it's Churchill. I would say that was an attempt at humor, whimsical humor, on the part of the people who made the movie. It's nothing I would have recommended doing, and if I were consulted I would say, "Don't do it." There's another place in the movie that Nichols told me his friends advised him to delete. I didn't see *2001* [1968], but apparently it has a Richard Strauss theme in it—and when Yossarian's eyes fall on Luciana, that theme is played and the audiences, when I've seen it, do laugh. Now he was told by certain friends, "Don't do it—it's inside humor, and it's self-indulgence," and he told me this, that he weighed it and wrestled with it, and figured that he's allowed a certain amount of self-indulgence; so he left it in there. I laughed just because the music seemed to lend something to the moment;

I didn't know it was in *2001*. I had a feeling that the thing with the photograph was of that nature as well—a kind of whim— that's it. There is a framework to the movie which doesn't exist in the book, and if somebody wants to go very deeply into literary criticism and interpretation, they would have to deal with this difference. In the movie, anything is permissible because it all can be explained in terms of an hallucination, a nightmare, by Yossarian, who is nearly dead and is reliving all this in terms of how events of the past cross his imagination, so none of it has to be literally true. That's in the movie and that can be explained, I suppose, in terms of Yossarian's consciousness, awareness of people like Churchill and Roosevelt, and the other one, Stalin. In the novel, everything that happens *really does happen*. Almost everything, except for a few things described as dreams. Now if one wanted to go into the method of interpretation, one can actually come up with two different meanings because of that fundamental difference, but I don't think anybody is going to go into it that deeply.

Q. What do you think of people who say you must read the book, see the film, then read the book again in order to get it?

A. People who have not read the book and seen the film tend to react more favorably to the film than people who had read the book first. And even mixed in with their reaction is a large degree of puzzlement. There are many loose ends in the film, but somehow those loose ends in themselves form a pattern of the inexplicable. If there were just one loose end in the film, one thing that was not tied up, then you might say it's an oversight, but there are five, six, or seven. Now the question was asked of me while I was waiting to come out here tonight, and it's been asked of me before, about how people can know who stabs Yossarian, if it's Nately's whore. Most people miss it who don't know the book. I bumped into Buck Henry a few weeks ago on Second Avenue, and we talked for an hour or two about it, and it was not the intention to leave that vague. Certain things just don't show up in certain scenes as planned, but by that time I had come around to the opinion that even if you thought that it was a GI, a strange GI who you never saw before, who took this big knife and sunk it into his side, it would not be inconsistent with what is happening in the movie with everything else that is attacking him or endangering him.

Q. How do you think the film presents "Snowden's secret"?

A. Well, the film doesn't work out Snowden's secret as Snowden's secret because that question isn't raised in the film. I think the film does work out the very slow death and the discovery of death in a most effective and dramatic way. The novel is literary; the film doesn't try to be literary. Most films that are adaptations of novels and plays don't succeed as films, and one reason they don't succeed is because they try to do little more than to photograph, in the case of a novel, to photograph a work that is mainly literary, to put literary values into visual terms. *Catch-22* as a movie doesn't do that; it's non-literary. So the phrase "Snowden's secret" is never evoked. Other things that are of a verbal nature are never introduced. People have asked me this question: "Was Henry Fonda ever thought of for Major Major?" Since nothing is said in the film about the resemblance of Major Major to Henry Fonda, there would be no point in putting Henry Fonda into the part. I think Nichols did what I would have advised him to do; that is, he took the novel and ceased considering it as a novel; kind of flattened it out into material and out of that material tried to arrange a motion picture which said partly what the novel said, mostly what the novel said; and mostly what he himself feels. Now I think, it's been intimated to me, that Nichols did want an Aryan for Milo Minderbinder. In terms of Nichols' own experiences with the Nazis, he wanted a Nazi, not an American middle-class executive, and that's why Voight was chosen and that's why he was developed that way. It is really Nichols' conception of a film taken from material in *Catch-22*, and I think it would have been an atrocious film if he'd tried any other thing.

Q. How would you describe the structure of Catch-22?

A. The structure of the book, and it's not entirely an original structure because I think William Faulkner does it in many of his works, is to tell a large narrative largely in terms of fragments and slow feeding of interrupted episodes. Things do happen twice in *Catch-22* or more than twice; things do repeat themselves. The time structure, chronological time, becomes immaterial. For example, Snowden has been wounded and dies before the time of the first chapter. The mission to Bologna has been flown before the first chapter. Milo has bombed his squadron before the time of the first chapter. Most of the events with which the book deals have already taken place. Chronological time is kind of meaningless in the novel itself; what seems to be operating is psychological time. Now I know *why* I wanted things to recur. There are two reasons. I'll tell you quite frankly that one of those reasons is that I felt intuitively the story could better be told that way rather than any other way. (I could have been wrong in that or right.) The second one is a theme that I wanted to give, a feeling of timelessness, that the same things will happen again unless something is done, and do happen again. The chaplain's sense of *déjà vu* which he has is not inaccurate because almost all the things he thinks he has experienced before have happened before, if not to him then we know they've happened. And when Yossarian makes that trip through Rome, called "The Eternal City," it's really a surrealistic scene told in realistic details. As he goes from one scene of cruelty and crime and brutality to another, a sense of guilt begins developing in himself—a feeling of responsibility—and he comes to understand why (I may have even used this sentence): although he has done nothing to cause Nately's death, he's done nothing to prevent it. When he's on that street and watching that man beat the little boy, and there's a crowd around him (this I know is in there), he wonders why nobody intervenes and then realizes he is there also and he is not intervening. What he does is that he doesn't stop the man but he runs away from that scene to the next one. And after the last one (I think it's an old woman who is being defrauded in some way by a younger woman), he turns away again into the darkness, but I have him do it with a growing sense of guilt—afraid that the woman would now start following him. I forgot your question, but things do happen recurringly. . . .

Q. Do you like the ending of the film?

A. The first time I saw it in the film I thought it was fine. It was kind of comical and humorous and with feeling. You saw the way the camera pulled back and you realized how far he had to go. Then I had a discussion with a very bright writer for a Los Angeles paper who saw it here and was very familiar with the book and he raised a point, and the point was that he found the ending a little ludicrous because it seemed impossible that Yossarian could get to Sweden in the boat. Then I remembered that in the novel Yossarian doesn't say that he's going to get to Sweden. In fact, two or three times Major Danby says, "You're never going to get there," and he says, "I know, but I can get to Rome if you keep your mouth shut." Then I mentioned to this guy that it would have been a good idea in the film if Yossarian had said, "Well, I think I can get to the mainland if you just keep quiet when I leave here." I think if you saw him in that boat, the tiny yellow raft, and you knew he had to get from this island to the Italian mainland, and make his way from there, you would believe that he had a good chance of making it. The way it ends with Sweden, I think you have a feeling that maybe there's no chance at all. But anyway, at least he's trying. I like the ending—I think it would have been a little more effective if you knew a little more convincingly that the struggle would continue to go on. The novel ends with the fact, I think it's implied or stated, that he'll get to Rome and from then on he's a fugitive. It would have been a good idea to have Nately's whore after him with a knife again, just to indicate that he was not getting out of danger too easily. A surprising number of reviewers and people who wrote letters just take it for granted that Yossarian escapes to Sweden in a boat. They got that impression from the movie. It's not the impression Nichols wanted to create, which is why he organized that scene with a close-up of Arkin paddling that raft and then the camera pulls back and shows him only about ten yards off shore with miles and miles and miles to go. So it was not Nichols' intention to indicate he's getting to Sweden.

Q. Do you like the sense of humor in the film?

A. I think there is a much smaller quantity of humor, a lower proportion of humor in the film than there is in the book. But I think underlying the book from the very first chapter—and I know this because I wrote it—there is an undercurrent of the morbid danger of war.

Q. How would you rate the film adaptation of the novel?

A. Look, *I* think it's a better book than a movie, if you're going to ask me that question. I would like to have seen this done (but it couldn't be done), that if this film were an Italian film by Fellini or Antonioni (and it came to this country with titles and we didn't have to use dialogue—all dialogue is bad in a film) I think every American critic who saw this film by Ingmar Bergman (or whoever else) would have hailed it as an unprecedented film masterpiece. Everybody would. It's because so many of the people, the reviewers, know the book so well that comparisons, I suppose, are inevitable, but I don't think they're valid. I judge it as a film. I can't think of any film I've seen in years, any American film, that I would put on the same level. I can think of a few European films, but that has to do with my taste, and I know what I like in films and I know what I like in novels. But if it's going to be compared with the book, then it suffers in just this inevitable way: I can't think of any film ever adapted from any work of literature that I or other people feel has any quality to it that even approaches the original work of literature that was its source.

One Flew Over the Cuckoo's Nest (1962)

Ken Kesey

Kesey Cured: Forman's Sweet Insanity

BY MOLLY HASKELL

Dare I admit it: It wasn't until after I had seen Milos Forman's movie of *One Flew Over the Cuckoo's Nest* that I finally read Ken Kesey's 1962 novel all the way through. And having read it, I must say I'm not sorry to have Jack Nicholson's features imprinted upon, and modifying forever in my mind, the image of R. P. McMurphy, the "Irish rowdy from a work farm" who is the subversive soul of Kesey's novel. McMurphy is the charismatic bounder who, before the story begins, has faked insanity in order to get himself transferred from the prison where he has been working off a charge of statutory rape. He lands in the institution of the title, in the bin where less critical loonies are kept. Gambling with his own sanity, he tried to liberate them from the creeping catatonia to which they are fast succumbing with a little help from shock therapy.

In the book, he is one of those lusty, brawling, larger-than-life figures of Northwest folklore, the kind of hard-drinking, hard-living, whoring, swearing, scarred ubermensch that one associates with California Redwoods, Sterling Hayden, Paul Bunyan, loggers (e.g., Kesey's own *Sometimes a Great Notion* [1964]),

Editors' title. Molly Haskell's review originally appeared as "Nicholson Kneads a Fine Madness" in the *Village Voice*, December 1, 1975. Reprinted by permission of the Village Voice. Copyright © The Village Voice, Inc., 1975.

or the poetry of Robinson Jeffers. He's the real machismo, not some city-bred affectation (see Paul Newman in *Cool Hand Luke* [1967]), but machismo nonetheless, in a book that is virtually a paean to virility. Yes, it's a tale of eccentric humanity pitted against institutional tyranny, and yes, it's a dramatization of that definitively 1960s Laingian paradox of "so-called sanity" versus "so-called insanity" (the sane response to an insane society is schizophrenia). But it is also a battle to death between Dad and Mom for the spirits of their sons, blubbering eunuchs who must be initiated into manhood (rebellion, freedom) and released from the emasculating influence of smothering, mothering Mom. McMurphy is the free spirit of a father who returns to the roost to find his sons feminized. McMurphy's nemesis, the gorgon of femininity, is of course the Big Nurse, Nurse Ratched. As conceived by Kesey, she is a dragon lady, breathing fire behind a plastic smile, a monster as pure and sadistic as any character in recent fiction. McMurphy, on the other hand, as her opposite, is a thinly disguised saint. Beneath the scars and swagger beats the heart of a missionary, reclaiming lost souls to manhood. Even the gambling victories in which he robs his buddies and briefly incurs their distrust are ploys to toughen them up for flight. In the end, he succeeds in salvaging only one soul, the half-Creole Chief Bromden. Appropriately, he pays for it with his life.

The mere presence of Nicholson in the role of McMurphy, and Louise Fletcher—memorable as the homespun maternal presence in Robert Altman's *Thieves Like Us* (1975)—as Nurse Ratched, are an indication of the degree to which Forman has softened Kesey's archetypes into life-sized characters. Fletcher's Nurse Ratched, squinty-eyed but handsome, a small voice belying a steel will, is younger than her literary prototype, and more realistically disturbing. With her 1940s hairstyle and her frozen femininity there is a hint (and Forman, in an interview-conversation we had in his hotel room after the film, confirmed this as deliberate) of an earlier trauma, an arrested emotional development. (I am not sure that even this is adequate. Ironically, in making her three-dimensional, Forman has made us want to know, and understand, more.) As for Nicholson, he is nothing short of miraculous in the role of McMurphy.

In the stage play, a thoroughly conventional, "Mr. Roberts"-against-the-institution type of comedy (which was, I believe, repudiated by Kesey), the role was taken by Kirk Douglas. And it was Douglas actually who acquired the movie rights and originally sought Forman to direct. But due to some missed connections on the closely-watched Czech frontier, the two never made contact, and by the time Forman was brought in on the project Douglas felt he was too old to play the part, and Nicholson had been signed on. Even though Nicholson preceded Forman as a condition of the film, he seems to sum up Forman's angle of vision and modified approach to the material.

The difference between Douglas's strutting, chin-jutting, smile-curling bravura and Nicholson's less physical, self-mocking style is the difference between a rooster and a bantam, between straight and ironic braggadocio. Nicholson is no "woman's man"; he can take them or leave them, which has made him less than a favorite with many women viewers I know. But he is not quite a man's man either. There is too much ironic self-awareness, too much distance and doubt between him and the jock ritual of male camaraderie.

Only Nicholson could make palatable, in these sensitive times, the account McMurphy must give of his rape experience. "She was fifteen, said she was seventeen," he says, or words to this effect, "and she was so willin' I took to sewing my pants shut." The words occur during a private interview—not in the book or play—between McMurphy and the head of the institution, a gentle, ineffectual cavalier, beautifully played by Dean R. Brooks, the actual director of the insane asylum where the film was shot. More from incomprehension than disapproval, he deflects Nicholson's nudging but playful locker-room confidences, and a deeper bond of sympathy is established between them.

The sweetness of this scene is characteristic of the whole movie. Forman has eliminated the cruder details, and softened the boisterous, hallucinatory quality of Kesey's "trip" into a choreographed fantasy, with the lunatics, the disenfranchised, banding together for a few brief moments of shared joy. Occasionally, Forman's projection of a Vigoesque romantic lyricism onto adult men seems *too* soft. There are moments of Hollywood senti-

McMurphy (Jack Nicholson) versus Nurse Ratched (Louise Fletcher).
One Flew Over the Cuckoo's Nest (1975)

mentality when these "holy fools" coalesce with an esprit de corps that would seem unlikely in a far more "adjusted" or homogeneous group. But as individuals, they are remarkable: William Redfield as Harding, the "intellectual" of the group, Brad Dourif as the heartbreakingly vulnerable Billy Bibbit, Will Sampson as the stolid, totemlike Chief Bromden. As might have been expected from the director of *The Firemen's Ball* (1967) and *Taking Off* (1971), they have been cast and assembled and directed with an eye for the visually expressive, the wayward, the comic, the pathetic.

The film has the unexpectedly buoyant feeling of a comic ballet, of beautifully balanced mixed moods. It is only when we are forced to confront the message that it becomes ordinary, for it all boils down to yet another tug-of-war between the "ins" (the hip, the fun people) and the "outs" (the ogres, the squares): a child's view of the universe.

But Forman, coming from Czechoslovakia and having seen more than he would like to of institutional tyranny, is coming at *Cuckoo's Nest* from a cultural angle that entitles him to a more dialectical view of society.

"Why shouldn't insane people seem more appealing," he said in answer to my question, "Aren't we more interesting and more appealing than our government officials? Everybody who involves himself with oppressive machinery is paying for it with a loss of humor, with grayness.

"And don't forget," he added, "this is a ward of only moderately crazy people. The hopeless ones are upstairs." (They are enacted by real patients, and we see them whenever one of the characters goes up for shock treatment.)

We talked about the incredible faces, sad and wistful, of the actors who play the main characters. "You know, I never saw a handsome person institutionalized," Forman said. "The loss of self-respect is what causes mental disturbance. Somebody who can't find any way to build self-respect is very vulnerable to mental disease."

Forman said the shooting of the film at the Oregon State Hospital had had a therapeutic effect on the patients. "They're always trying to give patients the feeling that they're accomplishing something . . . but how can you feel this if you're mopping the floor from morning to night? With this film, they got very excited, they all said 'Oh, boy, we're making a Hollywood film.' It sounds like a cliché, but one man who hadn't opened his mouth for years left the institution two weeks after the film was made, talking.

"Sometimes we forget," Forman continued, "what a change has taken place in our view of mental illness. Institutions used to be created to protect the community from Evil! This one was built in 1883, at which time it was five miles from the nearest house. Today it's in the middle of the city. We have to live with the insane, so we had better accept them as human beings."

I asked him about his decision, implemented in the screenplay of Lawrence Hauben and Bo Goldman, to treat the story objectively rather than through the eyes of the Indian, Kesey's point-of-view character.

"'I didn't want that for my movie," he said. "I hate that voice-over, I hate that whole psychedelic 1960s drug free-association thing, going with the camera through somebody's head. That's fine in the book, or on a stage, which is stylized. But in film the sky is real, the grass is real, the tree is real; the people had better be real too.

"You know, I'm glad I didn't know the reputation of the book when I read it, so I didn't have this artificial reverence for the 'cult classic.' And I think it's much better that it was made now than in the 1960s. After a certain time, all the distracting elements fall away, all the transitory psychedelic stuff. And we can follow what it is really about. My film is very simple."

I told him I had certain reservations about the ending, particularly the diabolical revenge of the nurse which takes an even more extreme form than in the novel.

"She is dangerous," said Forman, "because she really believes what she is doing. I have seen this situation, and I know that authority in trouble will sacrifice anything and anyone to prove its point."

Little Big Man (1964)

Thomas Berger

Berger and Penn's West: Visions and Revisions

BY MARK BEZANSON

In a voice coming from the large screen that sounds—true to Thomas Berger's description—like a plucked guitar filled with cinders, Jack Crabb, sole survivor of Custer's Last Stand at Little Bighorn, tells his academic interviewer (who has just accused him of mixing up adventure stories with the Indian way of life) to shut up, turn on the tape recorder, and listen. The one-hundred-and-twenty-year-old ex-Indian (and ex-Indian fighter) stares at us blankly, his head battered by too much experience, his eyes rheumy from too much truth: "I knew Custer for what he was, and the Indians for what they was."

The film cuts from the buzzardlike survivor to the wide, cinemascopic plains of the West. Smoke rises from burned wagons. Flies buzz loudly. Bodies lie draped over wagon wheels and broken Victorian furniture in a static ballet of death. The prairie winds flap at a torn wagon canvas where Jack Crabb and his sister, young survivors from an Indian raid, huddle in fear. A Cheyenne brave rides his pinto in from the desolate, prairie landscape, dismounts, pulls back the canvas. Will he break their heads open with his tomahawk? A blues harmonica vibrates over the wind, titles come on the screen. The brave puts the two orphans on the back of his pony and rides off.

Moments later we are in the Cheyenne camp. The clothes look soiled and used, the women grind corn and stitch hides, the animals graze among the tribe. Cheyenne stroke the air with expressive sign language. The film moves ahead swiftly to scenes of Indian life and of Jack's education as a Cheyenne brave. Old Crabb cackles in his narrative voice-over, "I wasn't just playing Indian, I was livin' Indian."

And vicariously, we are "livin' Indian" too. Director Arthur Penn's detailed canvas looks genuine; colors are toned down so that the teepees seem part of a campground instead of a circus; the Indians are played by Indians, not, as the novel's Old Crabb complains of television, by "Italians, Russians, and the like, with five o'clock shadows and lumpy arms." The film thrusts us into the present-tense heart of the narrative with Penn's typically admirable physical immediacy. As Robin Wood states in his book on Arthur Penn, discussing a career which includes *The Miracle Worker* (1962) and *Bonnie and Clyde* (1967): "Physical sensation . . . is perhaps more consistently vivid in his films than in those of any other director. Again and again he finds an action—often in itself an unusual, hence striking action—likely to communicate a physical 'feel' to the spectator. . . ."

Penn, through Calder Willingham's screenplay, follows Berger's lead in reshaping and reinventing the history, legends, and myths of the Old West. But where Penn resorts to the feel of documentary to satirize and *de*mythologize the Western genre (and finally, as we shall see, to create a metaphoric indictment of American involvement in the Vietnam war), Berger appears to have set out to *re*mythologize, if you will, the popular image of the West. Berger's Crabb comes to us from the oral tradition of the campfire stories, of the tall tales of the Pecos Bills, the Crocketts, and the Boones. And this not-so-moribund centenarian, through the enthusiasms of his eyewitness accounts and the precision of his observations, makes us feel we are meeting and experiencing the familiar heroes and events of the West for the first time. He reinvents the West. Thomas Berger seems to imply, then, that the myth of the West, so entrenched in our culture, can only be changed—or made more truly historical, perhaps—by acts of the fictive imagination.

In short, both Berger and Penn take aim at the standard legends of the West; but while Penn is the idealistic debunker, taking sides with the Indians against the white invaders of the frontier, Berger is the cynical revisionist, whose earthy skepticism spares no one, Indian or white, from full participation in the corruption and vulgarity of the cutthroat times.

Befitting the tall tale as history, the structure of Berger's novel is centrifugal and expansive. We meet more characters than in the film, span more time, witness more events, hear more anecdotes about the motley tatters of humanity, both white and Indian, that wander the American landscape of the last quarter of the last century. This potentially haphazard narrative is held in check by Crabb's omnipresent musings and meditations. As narrator and protagonist, Crabb gives us a popular historian's broad perspective at one moment, and at some other moment narrows our attention to the subject of his sore feet; the shifting focus provides a journal-like sense of historical verisimilitude—a circumstance not duplicated by the random pieces of voice-over narration in the film.

Arthur Penn's film moves with an almost brutal economy; it takes aim at a select group of targets. All the historical characters save Custer and Wild Bill Hickock are eliminated—gone are Wyatt Earp, Kit Carson, Calamity Jane, Buffalo Bill, from Berger's novel. In some cases two characters are combined into one (e.g., Mrs. Pendrake, the preacher's wife, returns a second time in the film, as a prostitute, thus replacing Amelia, Crabb's lost niece in the novel). Like John Ford's classic epic *The Searchers* (1956), which also brought in Custer's Seventh Cavalry, the film's characters move cyclically, recross one another's paths like wound-up toys. But eventually they turn in on themselves—and wind down. Mrs. Pendrake has become a "fallen flower" by the time Crabb meets her on the second go round, Merriweather, the snake-oil swindler, has whittled himself down to fewer limbs, and Wild Bill Hickock, once hero of the West, has become paranoid and guilty, ripe to be shot dead. This cyclical development functions in two ways: it is how the film medium economizes in adapting the sprawling plots of the novel, and it serves as a dynamic vortex, winding tight the film's tensions to the point of blowout around its showpieces—the massacre scenes.

Little Big Man was the perfect political film event to introduce

Jack Crabb (Dustin Hoffman) practices his gun-slinging, as the Soda-Pop Kid, with Wild Bill Hickock (Richard Mulligan). *Little Big Man* (1970)

the 1970s. Youthful audiences, who had grown up from Davy Crockett coonskin caps and killing "Injuns and wetbacks," confronted in Arthur Penn's movie an adult white world no less uncivilized than their own turned out to be. Youth culture could identify strongly with the native Americans, who cherished the earth, sex, handcrafts, the free spirit, communal living, and perhaps less comfortably with the Jack Crabb of Dustin Hoffman, who brought Benjamin's passivity from *The Graduate* (1967) into the grand terrain of *Little Big Man*.

The film tosses an impotent Jack Crabb from one experience to another. Compared by critic Pauline Kael to a modern Candide (*New Yorker*, December 26, 1970), Crabb is rolled about in a random, violent, and amoral world. In a typical Western, as critics Marsha Kinder and Beverle Houston have noted, "the sophisticated audience enjoys the fantasy of the individual being tested by a primitive environment that heightens his strengths and his weaknesses and in which he discovers his identity and is forced to develop his powers of decisive action" (*Close-Up*, 1972). But in Penn's anti-Western, Jack Crabb is overwhelmed by a dog-eat-dog world clearly meant to reflect the Nixonian America of 1970. Crabb is caught between warring races and he is alternately hated and misunderstood by both. Curiously, his position closely resembles that of Howard Campbell, Jr., the protagonist in Kurt Vonnegut, Jr.'s popular novel *Mother Night* (1966), who doesn't know if he is a Nazi war criminal or an American hero. Penn's Crabb takes no decisive action, has no fixed identity, and puts much of his energy into saving his own skin. Crabb is a sorely antiheroic witness to man's inhumanity to man. He is total victim: both with the Indians at the Washita River Massacre, and later with the whites on Custer's fateful foray into Little Big Horn.

As Arthur Penn commented critically about his protagonist in an article by Robin Wood, "Little Big Man is (the) non-active character to a fault. I don't . . . personally subscribe to that as a way of living. . . . I think one must protest at it—resist it—and one struggles against it constantly and violently" (*Movie*, No. 18, Winter, 1970–71). Wood noted further that Penn's protagonist "affects the outcome of events only in a confused and ironic way."

Berger's Crabb is far different. As a fictional/historical figure, he rubs skin and bones with such legendary heroes as Wyatt Earp, Billy the Kid, Wild Bill Hickock, Buffalo Bill, and General Custer. He even takes on legendary, superhuman roles himself during the devious course of his life's experience, as Indian brave, Indian-fighter and cavalry scout, trader, prospector, railroader, cavalry soldier, muleskinner, gunfighter, storekeeper, gambler, buffalo hunter, and vagabond. He gets hit on the head by Earp's buntline, cheats Hickock at cards, escapes getting done in by Billy the Kid, meets someone who traveled with Lewis and Clark, and becomes a Cheyenne chief's "favorite son." Shuttling between the Indian and white worlds, Berger's Crabb is always self-possessed and recalcitrant. Berger depicts a character with substance and will of his own, not a hero who changes events but a hard-nosed citizen who adapts to the tumult without going underground. His Jack is an entrenched white, a near-racist at times, a hustler, and an ambitious business man. Most important to understanding his identity, Crabb prefers the cleanliness and order of the white world to the filth of the Indian camp. He wants a wife, offspring to carry on his name, a good trade, and some land; all to buttress himself from the social chaos and the "threatening" values of the Cheyenne world.

Finally, the Crabb of the novel is far more willing to accept the world's corruption and injustice than the Crabb of the film. He is organically fixed in the vulgarity and filth and violence of his milieu, he is not an alienated outsider. As he ironically comments, "If you want to really relax sometime, just fall to rock bottom and you'll be a happy man. Most all troubles come from having standards." Arthur Penn has standards, so he does not attack with equal relish all of his characters. He saves his vitriol for the hypocrisy and greed of the whites. As Crabb lies dry-heaving in alcoholic stupor in the mud, Merriweather taps by with a new peg leg; his diminishing limbs keep pace with his capitalist schemes. He mutters something about buffalo, and in the background we see Buffalo Bill overseeing the stacking of hundreds of hides. We are told later that Crabb's preacher step-father choked to death in a moment of gluttony.

Further, the white characters in the movie are antisexual and antilife. The minister whips Jack for playing in the hay; Mrs. Pendrake must turn her thwarted sexual needs to prostitution; and Custer, who gargles to get the poison out of his gonads from sitting in the saddle too long, shoots down defenseless Indian women (who "breed like rats") and their children. (At this point, Penn even has Jack Crabb overcome his lethargy to wail to Chief Lodgeskins, "Do you hate the white men now, Grandfather? Do you *hate* them?" and he breaks down weeping at the injustice.)

In contrast, Arthur Penn's Indians seem unabashedly romanticized and humanized, and the conventional stereotypes are, one by one, methodically dispelled. The "crazy Indian" happens to be a Contrary who, ritually, does everything backwards and who spares (the reverse of killing!) Jack Crabb at Little Big Horn. Little Horse is a "gay" Indian who flirts openly with Little Big Man. But he is not mocked by his "straight" peers, for an Indian can do what he wants. The Indians of *Little Big Man* are variable in their behavior and incredibly broadminded.

Old Lodgeskins, the Cheyenne chief (played by Chief Dan George), Penn's most prominent native American, is the most sympathetic character in the film. He mocks himself and muses about issues ranging from the existential (the meaning of his tribe's destruction) to the mundane (how he mounts his squaws). Late in the film, blinded and old, he lies down on a mountain top to die in ritual style ("It's a good day to die, my son"). He awakes to find himself alive: "Am I still in this world? Jeesh! Sometimes the magic works and sometimes it doesn't." Lodgeskins is the sage with the twinkle in his eye, the wise man who shows no unhelpful anger toward the white man's destruction of his people. With stoic resignation and forgiveness, he declares of white men (both in the novel and the film):

> Now I understand them. I no longer believe they are crazy. They want to do these things, and they succeed in doing them. They are a powerful people. The Human Beings (as the Cheyenne call themselves) believe that everything is alive: not only men and animals but also water and earth and stones. . . . But white men believe that everything is dead: stones, earth, animals, and people, even their own people. And if in spite of that, things persist in trying to live, white men will rub them out!

Lodgeskins plays the guru to Hoffman's initiate; to the children of the age of technology, this humane, mystical, and romantic shaman is immensely appealing in a manner similar to such as Carlos Casteneda's "Don Juan" and the various yogis and Eastern spiritual leaders who burst on the scene in the late 1960s.

Berger too treats Chief Lodgeskins as his most important character/spirit. Crabb describes him as an almost legendary piece of landscape, a bottomless vital source:

> Them ravines in his face was so deep that a fly would think twice about treading the bluffs above them. Indeed his visage was a sort of minerature of the ground . . . his mouth being like a river system with tributaries above and below.

And like the novelist and Jack Crabb, his narrator, the Chief has a profound gift for storytelling: "Among the Cheyenne he was a sort of genius," Crabb explains. "It was him who taught me everything I learned that wasn't physical like riding or shooting. The way he done this was by means of stories." Lodgeskins weaves the old legends into the daily fabrics of his people's lives (much as Berger is attempting to do with his novel). He extends the oral tradition of his people's past through their myths, tales, and personal histories.

But as central as Lodgeskins is to his narrative, Berger never idealizes him into a counter-culture hero. Indeed, Berger's novel shows Lodgeskins and the Indians to be as fallible and as ridiculous as the whites. As Robin Wood has commented, it is "greatly to Berger's credit that he gains our sympathy for the Indians without sparing us any of the aspects of their behavior that are likely to appall the white sensibility" (*Movie*, No. 18, Winter, 1970–71). Crabb gets his first taste of Indian life when a Cheyenne brave tears a heart from a dying antelope and pushes the still-beating offering into Jack's mouth. When Crabb returns to the white world, he regains his "proper" white sensibility and hates Indians because of their savagery and stink. Later in the novel, when he returns to the Cheyenne, he notes the smell: "it isn't precisely a stench as white people know one, but a number of stinks melding together into a sort of invisible fog that replaces the air, so that with every breath you draw in all the facts of life concerning mankind and the four-footed animals."

Thomas Berger himself is more a neutralist than a racist like his hero. His Indians are neither worse nor better than the whites. The difference is that they are rubbed out.

Obviously Arthur Penn substituted a more partisan, less Darwinian view of the destruction of the West, insisting on the tragic genocide of its native people by alien invaders. It is therefore appropriate that the infamous Washita River Massacre, with its senseless killing of women, children, babies, the old and infirm by the marauding vanguard of the white race, becomes the dark climax of the movie.

Before the attack we find ourselves living on the reservation among the gentle Indians. Snow is falling on the campground, women are cooking food. The panorama has an eternal stillness and natural beauty. At dawn the strangely cheery sound of fifes filters through the tents. The ponies begin to whinny and stir in alarm. Custer's soldiers advance on the reservation, emerging like phantoms out of the snow-blue mists. Naked women, still warm from the pleasures of the night, clutch their children in their teepees. Custer pulls up to the front of the screen: "the women breed like rats but shouldn't be shot . . . unless . . . they refuse to surrender."

The massacre grows quickly to a symphonic crescendo strained with the wails of dying ponies, screaming children, war cries, and the cacophony of gunfire. The half-naked women flee from the funeral pyres of their blazing tents. Some toss off their flaming robes and fall crisply mutilated to the ground. Crabb, at a safe spot near the river, suddenly spots his wife Sunshine and her newly-born child running from the tents through the soldiers and horses toward the river. He screams at her to run. A soldier shoots her baby's head off and seconds later a volley of gunfire hurls her dead to the ground.

The bottom of the sound track falls out. The colors bleach in the snowy mist. Everything is paralyzed in silence and the Little Big Man, the young Jack Crabb, lies in the snow, frozen immobile, his eyes fixed in a stare toward the still body of his Indian wife only yards away. The haughty jubilance of the fifes rises again as the bluecoats drift back into the early morning fog from which they came.

When the retaliatory massacre of Custer and his forces at Little Big Horn arrives at last, late in the film, it is a futile charade. We cannot cheer the short-lived victory of the Indians, for we know the face of future White History.

We conjure up dreadful images of napalmed villages in a land across the Pacific in 1970, the year of the U.S. invasion of Cambodia. And we can only respect Arthur Penn's personal attempt to challenge Jack Crabb's stance of political powerlessness: the movie of *Little Big Man* turns Thomas Berger's amoral saga of the West into a vehicle of moral protest against the United States's imperial adventure on the Far Eastern frontier.

Slaughterhouse-Five, or The Children's Crusade (1969)
Kurt Vonnegut, Jr.

Novel into Film: So It Goes

At the turn of the century, naturalist Stephen Crane published
the following poem:

> A man said to the universe:
> "Sir, I exist!"
> "However," replied the universe,
> "The fact has not created in me
> A sense of obligation."

That dialogue could as easily have transpired between any of
Kurt Vonnegut, Jr.'s, frustrated rebels. From scientist Paul Pro-
teus in his first novel *Player Piano* (1951) to the wealthy Pontiac
dealer Dwayne Hoover or Vonnegut himself in *Breakfast of
Champions* (1973), all realize their place as chemically-fueled
robots in a clockwork world running down.

If that is no less true for Billy Pilgrim, *Slaughterhouse-Five*
(1969) stands out largely because it leads its main character
not merely to that revelation, but also to a reconciliation with
such a cynically conceived, indifferent universe. And despite

Editors' title. This is a revised version of an article that appeared under the
title, "Reconciliation: Slaughterhouse-Five—the Film and the Novel," in
Film Heritage, 8, No. 2 (Winter 1972–73), pp. 1–12. By permission of *Film
Heritage* and the author.

Billy Pilgrim (Michael Sacks) becomes "unstuck in time" in Dresden, 1945. *Slaughterhouse-Five* (1972)

differences in the media, director George Roy Hill and screen-writer Stephen Geller have effected a reconciliation between their film version and the original in a way that enhances that central theme.

A strength of Vonnegut's book lies in its innovative style which notes in terse, sardonic prose fragmentary, nonsequential episodes out of Billy Pilgrim's life, following him from the time he becomes "unstuck in time" when taken captive by the Germans in 1945, through the abduction by flying saucer to the idyllic planet Tralfamadore on his daughter's wedding night in 1967, to his senseless assassination by a doggedly vindictive "war buddy," Paul Lazzaro, at a lecture on "time" that Billy gives in Chicago on February 13, 1976, exactly thirty-one years after the fire-bombing of Dresden. Told "somewhat in the telegraphic schizo-phrenic manner of tales of the planet Tralfamadore," as the title page explains, the nonchronological style not only echoes Billy's mental instability but also accentuates his relationship to time, so essential in understanding the change he undergoes.

In the novel Billy twice notices that popular Prayer of Serenity, "God grant me the serenity to accept the things I cannot change, courage to change the things I can, and wisdom always to tell the difference." Vonnegut, in typical deadpan fashion, undercuts the tentative wisdom of the saying when he follows Billy's ob-servation the first time with, "Among the things Billy Pilgrim could not change were the past, the present, and the future." But after his sojourn on Tralfamadore, he accepts his powerlessness and comes to understand the seemingly meaningless, unpredict-able moments of life and death and their overall deterministic pattern. It is significant that on the night he is killed, he is speak-ing to an audience about what he learned from the Tralfama-dorians: that time is invariably continuous and death is ultimately negligible. As Billy writes in his second letter to the Ilium *News Leader*,

> The most important thing I learned on Tralfamadore was that when a person dies he only *appears* to die. He is still very much alive in the past, so it is very silly for people to cry at his funeral. All moments, past, present, and future, always have existed, always will exist.

Tralfamadorian books—and not coincidentally Vonnegut's—illus-
trate formally that same philosophy in that they consist of a
series of unconnected scenes "that, when seen all at once, . . .
produce an image of life that is beautiful and surprising and
deep. There is no beginning, no middle, no end, no suspense, no
moral, no causes, no effects." Making a joke at traditional structure, Vonnegut frames the novel by telling us with what words
it will begin and end. But his framework ends there.

While attempting to preserve Vonnegut's vision, scriptwriter
Stephen Geller prepares for the probable confusion of the movie
audience by making his screenplay more "normal." First, he di-
vides Billy's life into three recognizable segments. Second, he
injects a more conventional structure of suspense. Beginning with
Billy (Michael Sacks) typing his first letter to the newspaper
about his becoming "unstuck in time," the film then breaks into
three flashbacks: the prisoner-of-war episode that takes Billy to
the firebombing of Dresden; Billy's family life and career in
optometry; and his abduction and romantic interlude with movie
star Montana Wildhack (Valerie Perrine) in the human zoo on
Tralfamadore. Intricately edited by Dede Allen, the movie traces
each stage chronologically (though scenes from the sections interrupt each other), and it progresses to recognizable climaxes—
the execution of Billy's idealistic schoolteacher friend, Edgar
Derby (Eugene Roche), in the ruins of Dresden; Billy's death;
and the birth of Billy and Montana's baby.

There is occasionally some sense to the transitions from one
scene to another in Vonnegut's novel, which the film appropri-
ates. In a drunken stupor at a New Year's Eve party in 1961,
when Billy tries to locate the steering wheel of his car before
he realizes he's in the back seat, he lapses (almost protocine-
matically in the book) into another kind of stupor from the
freezing cold just before he becomes a prisoner during the war.
And when the saucer that kidnaps him accelerates, he shifts
gears himself to a scene on the boxcar heading for Dresden.
Geller and director George Roy Mill (abetted by editor Dede
Allen?) add some transitions of their own that at least smooth
the movement from one stage to another. For instance, just as a
shock is administered to Billy as treatment for the nervous

breakdown he has during his senior year at optometry school in 1948 (the time is unclear in the movie), the soundtrack blares out a train whistle in a voice-over and the camera cuts back to the POW train. And the flashes of light from the bombs exploding over Dresden blink on and off, trading alternate cuts with the more mundane changing of a streetlight when Billy is driving with his obese but wealthy wife Valencia (Sharon Gans).

These transitions are more neat than thematic, but on occasion they achieve additional narrative impact when Geller juxtaposes scenes for ironic contrast. The half-hearted election of Derby as the leader of the American POWs, for example, seesaws with the uproarious applause that greets Billy's election as president of the Lion's Club in 1957. And when Derby says that he is proud of his son, Billy jumps forward to the time his own son has just been caught toppling gravestones. These contrasts are not Vonnegut's, but they retain his impish tone.

While in the novel Vonnegut scatters references to a number of episodes without regard to time or build-up (we know from the outset, for instance, that Billy is kidnapped by a flying saucer and that Derby dies), Geller withholds the full nature of the episodes to develop a more conventional building up of suspense. Early in the movie Billy sees a strange light descend to Earth, then disappear in the night sky. The moviegoer does not know until the scene is repeated and Billy finally vanishes off the Earth that the light was a spaceship from Tralfamadore. Similarly, we are kept in the dark about Derby's execution for "looting" a piece of Dresden china to replace the broken one he and his wife once had. Neither do we learn of Billy's assassination by the crazed Paul Lazzaro (Ron Liebman) until the end of the film.

While Geller, then, has imposed a greater degree of order in the screenplay to simplify the visual adaptation, director George Roy Hill has wisely chosen to eschew special-effects sensationalism. In the film a fluttering circle of white light grows out of the sky and pauses outside Billy's bedroom window just as he is pixilated off the screen. In the book Vonnegut has the abduction involve a saucer one hundred feet in diameter, complete with zap gun and an imprisoning cone of purple light. The Tralfamadorians in the movie are conveniently invisible because they exist in the fourth dimension. In the book they are ridiculously visible as two-foot-high green plungers with an eye in a hand at the top of the shaft. Hill's avoidance of science-fiction trickery, like the spectacle of saucers and little green sticks, keeps our attention focused on Billy Pilgrim and the more important story of his pilgrimage in character.

It is Billy's passivity that Hill chooses to emphasize in directing novice Michael Sacks, and while the characterization verges on imbecilic simplicity compared to Vonnegut's fuller treatment, Sacks's childlike appearance easily complements Billy's naivete. He clearly appears the type who would accept the "gift" of a blue toga and silver boots from the Germans and who would continue wearing them even after he knows that he is only the butt of a practical joke. Moreover, Sacks's underplaying does underscore Billy's puppetlike helplessness. His passivity almost descends to mere stupidity in sequences like Billy's conversation with Derby where they both repeat the word "nice" so often that their exchange of mindless amenities becomes Beckett-like in its absurdity.

Billy borders on such inanity in the book too—except that he has the intelligence to ask the question "Why?". A Tralfamadorian, sounding like an otherworldly John Steinbeck, repudiates any teleology and entertains only "is-thinking." To Billy's "Why," he retorts,

> That is a very *Earthling* question to ask, Mr. Pilgrim. Why *you?* Why *us* for that matter? Why *anything?* Because this moment simply *is.* Have you ever seen bugs trapped in amber? . . . Well, here we are, Mr. Pilgrim, trapped in the amber of this moment. There is no *why.*

As if to emphasize that he is in fact on a mental pilgrimage of self-discovery, Billy also asks himself in the prison camp, "Where had he come from, and where should he go now?" In addition, Vonnegut's protagonist is a sensitive character who laughs incongruously at his capture, cries compassionately without reason long after the war, and bursts into tears at such things as the tortured horses pulling his wagon through the ruins. Billy in the novel more obviously longs for the beautiful as well, whether he is dreaming of ice skating skillfully in sweatsocks or of female giraffes kissing him in a garden—or simply appreciating on Tralfamadore the nudity of his "real" movie starlet Montana (whose bodily perfection recalls to him the "fantastic architecture in Dresden, before it is bombed," making her a manifestation of his desire to know beauty unviolated by the vicissitudes of time). The movie attempts to convey Billy's sensitivity through his silence, but it is consequently possible to underestimate his depth. Although he would hardly qualify as an intellectual even in the book, Billy Pilgrim is still meant to be more bemused than amusing in his absurd agony.

The movie also tends to oversimplify and distort the reason Billy is abducted to Tralfamadore late in 1967. The saucer comes for the second time, after his wife dies from inhaling the exhaust of her Cadillac when she hurries in melodramatic mawkishness to the hospital where Billy is recovering from a plane accident. The chronological placement of his abduction in the film suggests that his need for a consoling life with Montana on another planet stems from his wife's death. But it is rather doubtful he could be grieving so much for a spouse, when the "quality" he misses her for most is her pancakes. The grief has a much broader base. Although his daughter thinks that the plane accident has damaged his brain (it is only afterward that he brings up his extraterrestrial experience and starts writing letters to the newspaper about it), the real reason for the sudden disorientation in his life probably has more to do with "metapause," or male middle-aged involutional melancholia. Significantly, when Billy is asked if he is happy on Tralfamadore, Vonnegut records, " 'About as happy as I was on Earth,' said Billy Pilgrim, which was true." Nevertheless, the Tralfamadorians and his strange family life with Montana give him the wherewithal to accept life in its entirety. His mother's question in the old people's home, asked only in the novel—"How did I get so old?"— compares in a way with Billy's own remark later in the book, "Where have all the years gone?" Standard questions that trouble everyone at one time or another, but the difference here is that Billy has been able to put time in a new perspective, whether the episode on Tralfamadore is interpreted as dream, symbol, or reality. In another piece of advice translated verbatim to the screen, the Tralfamadorian tells Billy, " 'That's one thing Earthlings might learn to do, if they tried hard enough: Ignore the awful times, and concentrate on the good ones.' " Billy does not really embrace such therapeutic pollyannaism in the book, of course, but his preoccupation with the bad times proves itself a kind of exorcism without which his sexual Eden with Montana would be impossible.

This hopefulness in seeing not only the end but also the beginning of things simultaneously seems the message behind the novel's concluding with a scene set in springtime—and in the film's climactic adaptation. The war now over for some time, Billy again sees the same coffin-shaped wagon drawn by two horses he remembers seeing in Dresden. But it is green this time, the color of growth and continuation, and the last thing Billy hears is a bird asking him, "Poo-tee-weet?" That deliberately recalls a similar moment in *Cat's Cradle* when the narrator, Jonah, looking out over the existential (what else?) Abyss of Nothingness just as the world is about to turn to ice, concludes of the bird, "It seemed to be asking me what had happened." But Billy has more of an answer than Jonah did. These images intertwined with death imply cyclical rebirth. Without resorting to the literary symbolism of Vonnegut's conclusion, the movie effectively communicates that sense when it leaves us watching Montana nursing their baby in the cell with the aged Billy, while the invisible Tralfamadorians rejoice outside in an obvious celebration of life's renewal.

As is often the case, the movie has to omit rather than simply adapt aspects of the novel and in so doing shows up not necessarily its weaknesses but certainly makes us recall the missing strengths of the original. As much as possible the film tries to imitate Vonnegut's dry wit. Because it is a different medium, though, it can never quite duplicate such stylistic touches as Vonnegut's refrain, "So it goes," which follows any report of a death, from that of Billy's friend Derby to the flattening of sparkling champagne. It is that kind of comprehensiveness, incidentally, which reduces so many elements in the book to the absurd. When Billy indicates Tralfamadorians are more interested in Charles Darwin than Jesus Christ, Vonnegut recounts a similar detail from a novel by his fictional science-fiction writer Kilgore Trout by offering us a mocking juxtaposition: "The flying saucer creatures who capture Trout's hero ask him about Darwin. They also ask him about golf." By relying, then, on such incongruity and understatement, and always in a consciously primer-sounding prose, Vonnegut even reduces human suffering to that level. This is the way, for example, he describes Billy's diarrhea at the POW camp:

> Billy coughed when the door was opened, and when he coughed he shit thin gruel. This was in accordance with the Third Law of Motion according to Sir Isaac Newton. This law tells us that for every action there is a reaction which is equal and opposite in direction.
>
> This can be useful in rocketry.

And when Vonnegut describes the POWs taking their places in the showers, he writes, "Their penises were shriveled and their balls were retracted. Reproduction was not the main business of the evening." As one would expect, a black humorist like Vonnegut also depends heavily on irony. For instance, upon finding out that Billy appropriated the diamond for Valencia's engagement ring in the war, Eliot Rosewater remarks. " 'That's the attractive thing about war. . . . Absolutely everybody gets a little something.' " Of course by that point we know that the "little something" Billy really gained from the war was the bitter disillusionment that brought about the mental breakdown that sent him to the hospital in the first place. In a similar vein, a hobo on the POW train always says, "You think this is bad? This ain't bad." —words that are the very ones he utters just before he dies.

While none of these situations appears in the screen version, an ironic vantage is often attempted, although it is never quite as grotesque or as consistently sustained as Vonnegut's. When death is made laughable, as in Valencia's frantically fatal race to the hospital, the humor is patently slapstick. The same is true when, after training his dog as successfully as he has controlled his own life, Billy watches Spot mistake his trunk-sized wife for a tree. And rather than attempt to treat the actual firebombing of Dresden with caustic satire, Hill lapses momentarily into the pseudodocumentary affectation of time titles superimposed on shots of the innocent about to be killed, thus making the film seem at this stage another straightforward antiwar polemic, while Vonnegut's original can never be so plainly categorized.

Probably the most glaring omission, outside of Vonnegut's own autobiographical voice, is the character of Kilgore Trout. Since Trout is here significant only in that his ridiculous science-fiction novels have had a great influence on Billy, especially after they meet in 1964, it is easy to see why he had to be excluded from the film. Just as it would have been awkward to interrupt Billy's cinematic journey with a Vonnegut-like narrator, so too would it have been disruptive to insert references or brief dramatizations of Trout's plots, which Vonnegut can summarize far more effectively at random within the looser structure of his book. But the novels are hardly irrelevant. Trout's *Maniacs in the Fourth Dimension*, a story about people whose mental problems exist only in the fourth dimension and therefore cannot be treated by three-dimensional doctors, becomes relevant since the unbalanced Billy is obsessed with the uncertainties of time, which is the fourth dimension. The alien being in *The Gospel from Outer Space* looks like a Tralfamadorian. In *The Big Board* extraterrestrials abduct a male and female and cage them in a zoo on Zircon-212, a plot more than a little reminiscent of Billy's own experiences on Tralfamadore. It is, of course, no mere coincidence. As Vonnegut writes of Rosewater and Billy,

> They had both found life meaningless, partly because of what they had seen in war. Rosewater, for instance, had shot a fourteen-year-old fireman, mistaking him for a German soldier. So it goes. And Billy had seen the greatest massacre in European history, which was the fire-bombing of Dresden. So it goes.
>
> So they were trying to re-invent themselves and their universe. Science fiction was a big help.

Which is all pretty good evidence that Billy uses Trout as a launching platform for flights of fancy that can do just that— make himself (and the destructive, all-powerful, ultimately indifferent universe) over again.

None of this is to say, of course, that the movie is unsuccessful because it cannot draw on all the resources available to Vonnegut. For in its more conventional structure and execution Hill's *Slaughterhouse-Five* not only clarifies the more experimental novel but also manages to lift itself above jaded tales of war and spacemen that tell us aliens alienate, be they human or not. It may tend to oversimplify the handling of time and character, and it may vacillate somewhat in tone, trying sometimes too hard for humor at the cost of depth or for depth at the cost of humor. But the movie nonetheless shares the novel's thematic consciousness and at least some of its effective irony in following Billy Pilgrim's erratic odyssey through the vacuums of space and the world of man.

Dickey Down the River

BY JAMES F. BEATON

The James Dickey/John Boorman collaboration on *Deliverance* continues to prove itself an enormously popular enterprise, holding down forty-fourth place on *Variety*'s list of "All-Time Rental Champs" (January 5, 1977). It is therefore one of the most lucrative motion pictures ever to be made from an American novel, even though it remains a relatively poor cousin to the long-revered *Gone With the Wind* (1939), and also to such recent supernatural successes as *The Godfather* (1972), *The Exorcist* (1974), and *Jaws* (1975). *Deliverance* is like these other book-films, however, to the extent that it secured its commercial standing with a screenplay and a cinematic style that amplified those elements of its source most conducive to melodramatic and spectacular effects. No one would deny that Dickey's novel yields a dozen opportunities to produce cinematic shock and edge-of-the-seat suspense, even before it undertakes to induce the extraordinary discomforts of the famous rape-sodomy scene. But for all the appropriateness and visceral excitement of these effects, one nevertheless misses in the film the essential subject of Dickey's novel. That subject, controlling and occasionally transcending its melodrama, is the effort of a solitary and ennervated imagination to gain a vital connection with what might be called the elemental sources of experience. More specifically, Ed Gentry's story, and the novel's central theme, is that of a

293

modern mind in search of a body, and the neglect of this theme in the film has meant the surrender of the concrete material of the fiction to a cinematic presentation whose impressive display of visual rhetoric merely disguises a lack of substance and a confusion of meaning.

Deliverance is not a great novel, but it is well made. With thorough understanding and unembarrassed approval, it draws upon that familiar American romance of the wilderness as a world elsewhere, the hypothetical locus of experience where strangers become brothers, and where social and cultural oppositions give way to unexpected natural affinities. Upon this material, Dickey imposes a taut, impactful narrative structure, shaped conspicuously into five acts. What gives the narrative its measure of originality and imaginative range, however, is the character of the narrator, through whose trained eye—he is a graphic artist—and troubled consciousness we "see" the events of the fiction. On the most functional level, Ed Gentry provides the novel with that fairly dense and particularized sense of everyday reality needed to flesh out the archetypal skeleton of the adventure. In his perspective, and only there, realistic contingency and romantic fatality cohere.

The most important thing we learn about Gentry at the outset is that his mind is in distress. Psychologically, morally, even artistically, he is smothering, he says, under "an enormous weight of lassitude," associated with his total immersion in conventional living—"normalcy," as he calls it. At the same time, despite this pressure, he remains skeptical about, even threatened by, ideas or attractions that could alter or disrupt his life's well-balanced, frictionless regularity. He works to convince himself that the middle way is necessary as a sort of breakwater of order and elegance, as Stephen Dedalus put it, against the sordid tide of life within and around him. Yet he too, like James Joyce's hero, finds life eluding his restraints.

One sign of this is his boyish fascination with Lewis Medlock. Medlock has none of Gentry's ambivalence (the names are certainly significant); he is arrogant, single-minded, and aggressively competent; he seems, in fact, to embody an idea of masculine sufficiency as a last resort against chaos—against the day, that is, when "the machines are going to fail, the political systems are going to fail, and a few men are going to take to the hills and start over." All of this challenges the socialized Gentry, and at the same time it engages his restless, alienated spirit. Though he clearly recognizes the flaws in Medlock's personality—his reductiveness, rigidity, and pride—Gentry nevertheless sees them from what he takes to be a position of relative weakness, at best of moral certainty, rather than from any ground of lived and tested experience. Thus Medlock gets the upper hand whenever matters of moral or social value revert to questions of the physical, and implicitly sexual, adequacy needed to sustain such values.

Much of this emerges from the very first paragraph of the novel, which is a figurative exordium anticipating the dramatic action of the whole work. Gentry and his friends are looking over a topographical map of the region they are about to explore:

> It unrolled slowly, forced to show its colors, curling and snapping back whenever one of us turned loose. The whole land was very tense until we put our four steins on its corners and laid the river out to run for us through the mountains 150 miles north. Lewis' hand took a pencil and marked out a small strong X in a place where some of the green bled away and the paper changed with the high ground, and began to work downstream, northeast to southwest through the printed woods. I watched the hand rather than the location, for it seemed to have power over the terrain, and when it stopped for Lewis' voice to explain something, it was as though all the streams everywhere quit running, hanging silently where they were to let the point be made. The pencil turned over and pretended to sketch in with the eraser an area that must have been around fifty miles long, through which the river hooked and cramped.

The map, reluctantly pinned down by the steins, is certainly a figure for the undisclosed psychological landscape the novel is about to reveal; so is the river itself, apparently blocked and subdued by Medlock's ominous inscription, a figure for the natural strength and imaginative fluency that Gentry must free from the depths of his psyche. The association is further confirmed by the character of his dreams: "Something in the world," he says of his anxiety on the eve of the expedition, "had to pull me back, for every night I went down deep, and if I had any sensation during sleep, it was of going deeper and deeper, trying to reach a point or line or border." His waking life, all points and lines and borders, is fathoms away in his dreams, and that distance is a measure of Gentry's self-division.

One cannot explain the particular metaphors of this paragraph, however, without noticing the equally important fact that the narrative here, and throughout, is continuously figurative, and in a manner that reminds us at every point of Gentry's psychological plight. The story is therefore consistently *expressive* of Gentry's interior life, and all its details, even Medlock's deadly hand, take life with the touch of his pliant, intimate, almost erotic attention. Those carefully wrought participles are not just stylizations; they are dramatic registers of his feelings. Without this specific connection, the novel is little more than a sort of Southern Western.

One can readily see how such a narrative presents difficult choices for a filmmaker. Since the action is co-extensive with the narrator's perception, the immediate task, if one is to avoid a narrating voice-over, is to develop a cinematic technique that will register by its own means the same approach to experience, the same "feel" for it, that a reader may discover in the novelist's prose. The exchange takes place, it seems to me, at that level where style may be described in terms of its tone, its rhythm, its density—where, in other words, we may usefully speak of the rhetoric of a film in the same way that a novelist may speak, as Dickey in fact does speak in *Self-Interviews,* of a characteristic way of noticing the world "through a lens of words and by means of the altering perspective of language." [1] To a considerable extent, the film *Deliverance* fails, as I suggested at the outset, because Boorman's cinematic rhetoric, aggressive where Dickey is probing, so alters the novel's aesthetic emphases that we experience the fiction from an awkwardly chosen vantage—less like Gentry's narration and more like the perceptions of

[1] Edited by Barbara and James Reiss (Garden City, N.Y.: Doubleday, 1970), p. 73.

Medlock, who sees the journey down the Cahulawassee as a hand-to-hand combat with nature.[2]

The evidence of this aggressiveness appears in the film's initial sequence of images. The early episodes of the novel have been compressed into a montage of wide-angle, quick-cut shots of a landscape being blasted and stripped in the process of building the dam. Dynamite explodes volcanically, fat-bodied Euclids crawl over the defoliated surface, and in an accompanying voice-over we hear a high-spirited conversation about a canoe trip on the river, the last chance before there's nothing left of it but a few ripples against the fronts of lake-side developments. The voices are then subdued by another thundering explosion that segues into an image of a basin up river, made to seem primordial by the abrasive yet desolate call of a crow.

Without doubt, it is a portentous and unsettling prologue, announcing themes of violation and catastrophe. And it would seem that by mixing together the voices of the men, the mechanical/explosive rumble, and the solitary bird call, along with the transfer of visual associations, there is an attempt being made to suggest a kind of ahistorical dramatic setting where the dam-builders' intention to control the river, and the adventurers' intention to "conquer" it with their canoes, are both expressions of a state of mind as primitive and predatory as any to be found in the actual wilderness beyond. Now this *is* one of the novel's ideas; but it has no meaning of any substance outside the context of Gentry's personal conflicts. In Boorman's presentiment, the tentativeness and critical self-awareness, which keep Gentry apart from the scene as an explorer not a conqueror, are obliterated by the sudden and volatile shift of the images themselves; the rhythm, that is, not only creates a sense of imminent violence but, by preferring spectacle to exposition, participates in that violence as well. What we experience, in other words, is not the visualization of an interior life but a series of shocks that

[2] No published report on the specific roles played by Dickey and Boorman in the creation of this film seems to exist. I have therefore proceeded on the assumption that while Dickey obviously collaborated in the bastardization of his novel, Boorman's direction was responsible for most of what I have found to be objectionable about the film.

are meant to evoke associations in an abstract, and, in the pejorative sense, rhetorical way.

The preoccupation of the film hereafter is to shock the unwitting characters, especially its version of Gentry (Jon Voight), into an awareness of the prologue's implicit idea: that savagery is closer than commuting distance to civilization. Their arrival at Oree, for instance, achieves its effects principally by overstating the contrast between the intruders and the hillbillies, who appear to be impoverished, inscrutable, and literally degenerate. Drew Ballinger's (Ronny Cox) friendliness, and his innocent belief in the good feelings stirred up by the guitar-banjo "duel" (from which the film's score is drawn), are both thwarted a moment later by the banjo boy's sudden unresponsiveness. That antipastoral message, amplified here from only a hint in the novel, is just one of the many schematizations in the film that disregard the novel's attention to human probability and complexity. Another is Boorman's interpolation, presumably approved by Dickey, of the moment when Ed, now cast as the observant one of the group, stares into the Griner brothers' house: what he sees inside—the malformed children, the sick old woman, the squalor surrounding them—is made more disturbing, given its tight, clear focus, than it actually could have been, for Ed looks into the shadows through a screen door. Such schemes prepare him, and us, according to the rhetoric of romance, for the sudden reversal to come. Acute differences become unsuspected likenesses, and Ed, the passive observer, is forced to become the crucial participant.

The novel, as I have suggested, does not trade in such melodramatic devices, at least not in such a crude way. We know before the men ever arrive in Oree that the primitive, the brutal, and the deviant exist latently in each of them, continually and uneasily balanced with the orders of civilization. Both Lewis and Ed, for example, display remarkably animal-like features, the one in his jagged, hawk- or owl-like profile, the other in his abundant, ape-like hairiness. Then too Gentry has often been reminded, he tells us, of "the horrors of biology" by the sight of Drew's son, deformed since birth by a horn-like blood blister on his forehead. In the evening, after their arrival in Oree, Ed reports that while hunting for firewood he tried to avoid shining the light into the chests of the others because "the upcast light gave Bobby's face a greased, Mongoloid cast; Drew's looked sandblasted, with pins of deep shadow stuck all through it in the places where he's had acne."

There are even more dramatically consequential indications of the potential release and "anarchy" of nature in Ed's personality. One of these is recorded in his response to a model he meets while working on a demure underwear ad for the Kitt'n Britches company. Though he is sexually excited by the model's eyes and gestures, he nevertheless expresses humane reservations about the pornographic potential of photography, its ability to "rape the secrecy" of its subject. A few nights later, however, he re-enacts the session in a dream, this time imagining a sadistic version of the famous Coppertone ad, in which the girl's legs and buttocks are repeatedly scratched and bloodied by a frightened cat. Such subconscious lust, as Dickey portrays it, is also a corollary of his latently homosexual attraction to Lewis Medlock. Though he takes pleasure in the familiar movements of his wife's body while they are making love, it seems clear that the tightly controlled muscularity of Lewis interests him more.

When the film attempts to establish this more-than-typical connection between the two men, the effort is flawed by the abstractness of the style. In the fishing scene, Lewis (Burt Reynolds) bewilders Ed by asking him why he, an upholder of urban values, always chooses to go along on such trips; Ed's answer is evasive and, for the viewer, inconclusive. A more ambitious cinematic attempt to suggest the secret-sharer relationship occurs just at the moment when the two men first come upon the river. Boorman here closes in on the figures as they look out on the sunlit water, their heads literally framed by the surrounding leaves, while the river's shadows ripple across their faces in a way that is meant to suggest their collective intimacy. This is an almost exact rendering of a moment in the novel, underscored now, however, by another of Lewis's sententious texts: "Sometimes you have to lose yourself before you can find anything." For all its articulation, the image does not explain itself. We know too little about their motives and values to come up with anything more than hints and guesses about their deeper affinities. And, if anything, Ed comes across as a man of superficial "attitudes" in contrast to Lewis, the voice of unassailable truths.

Such a feeble externalization of Ed and Lewis's friendship is again consistent with the general dilution, and bowdlerization, of Ed's perspective in favor of Boorman's streamlined text on man in nature. Thus we see nothing of Ed's dream-like experience with the talismanic owl that perches upon, and whose claws penetrate, the roof of his tent during the first night of the trip. By the end of the scene it is clear that the owl stands in sexually for Lewis, or at least for the kind of instinctual composure that Lewis embodies. Without this episode, Ed's failure in the film to kill a deer at dawn the next day looks more like the act of a chicken than a fledgling owl; isolated from the preceding night's experience, the scene merely shows that Ed is unprepared to deal with the sort of thing Lewis characterizes as "a gut-survival situation." Any particular connection with Ed's psychological life, any suggestion of his desire to share in the self-possessed power of hunters like Lewis and the owl, is absorbed into the general scheme of a conflict between sentimentality and necessity.

The same sense of insubstantiality pertains to the film's depiction of the river. There is some attempt at symbolic development, but only to the point where the river becomes a metaphor for nature's ambiguity. On the first day, for example, as the men pass under a footbridge, the banjo boy stands above them idly swinging his instrument like a pendulum, a gesture contrived in the film to evoke, presumably, the old theme of time and the river. Again, past and present are fated to run together; human history is blurred. As they continue on the river, they also notice that its idyllic surface hides snakes just below it; and though the power of the rapids can be exhilarating, they soon learn that it can also be deadly. Such easy paradoxes, evasions of a surer but more difficult grasp of the experience, abound in this film. Whereas Dickey had rendered Ed's complex perception of the river in some of the most particularized, finely-detailed, and expressive language in the novel, Boorman's images, for all the visceral excitement and "presence" of those water-level, canoe-side shots of the rapids, remain ironically detached from any consciously perceived, and thus meaningful, reality.

Nowhere is this lack of substance more conspicuous, or more aggressively disguised, than in the notorious rape/sodomy scene. Boorman composes that crucial sequence as a melodrama of disembodied eyes, mouths, and faces, a grotesque abstraction of the event. The film substitutes appalling spectacle (Bobby Trippe [Ned Beatty] being wrestled around in muddy leaves by his attacker, and made to squeal like a pig) for the novel's dramatization of Ed's painful recognition of his own dreams and desires as they are shamefully played out and, in a manner, exorcised, in that ritual of violation and death. The owl-eyed Lewis arrives just in time to save Gentry, but his murder of the sodomite, aptly and fatally piercing him with a broad-head arrow, conveys only shock and horror to the audience because of Boorman's prolonged and enforced camera concentration upon the death throes of the attacker. There *are* hints of ritual in this —the mountain man's last fall is protracted upon an altar-like sapling—but these must seem like only literal (and well-deserved) sufferings to an audience so assaulted by cinematic violence. Further, what I have argued of the film's prologue may similarly be argued here: though an attempt is being made to establish an equation between environmental rape and sexual rape, between public and personal brutality, the connection depends too much upon an echo, a merely verbal association, and a tenuous one at that. It is much more to the point, and truer to the experience of the film, to attest that it makes the most of the extreme discomforts of an ugly and perverse assault, precisely in the same way that Westerns used to revel in the taking of scalps by Indians.

One feels as certain, and as confused, about the subsequent cliff-climbing episode. With the injury of Medlock, Gentry is forced into the role of protector of the weak (Bobby Trippe) and infirm; gradually, hesitantly, he rises to the occasion. What makes the scene confusing is the variety of cinematic "techniques and mystiques" (Gentry had used the phrase to mock Lewis) adduced in the presentation of the climb. As the single,

Bobby Trippe (Ned Beatty) and Ed Gentry (Jon Voight) after the
rape by the mountain men. *Deliverance* (1972)

unaccommodated Gentry inches his way up the sheer gray face of rock, he is virtually pelted by a hail of dissolving images that are full of threat. Is nature angry? Will the gods strike him down for hiding the body of the dead hillbilly? It is probably more likely that the surreal discolorations of these images masterfully achieved by cinematographer Vilmos Zgismond, are meant to suggest something dream-like, or the power of internal turmoil expressing itself in a distortion of the surroundings. But whose dream is this? The film has made no substantial connection between the natural world and Gentry's soul up to this point, so there is no reason why this sequence should be seen as anything more than melodramatic intensification.

Instead of encircling Gentry with these skillful cinematic illusions, Boorman might have been training our vision upon the very texture of that rock, discovering the dream-like by means of a mortal concentration upon its felt reality. The reason for this is that in the novel his ascent of the rock is a descent into himself; here, as Heraclitus put it (in a fragment that is close to the spirit of Dickey's work in general), "the way up and the way down are the same." During that climb, in other words, when Ed survives by the power of his clawing hands and pressing body, he finds in himself the animal tenacity and sexual vitality (improbable as it may seem to readers) he had surrendered to civility and convention.

What happens in the film is that Gentry simply accomplishes the top, prepared to take life and death into his own hands. Having resolved to kill the stalking mountain man, whom he believes to be waiting up there, he gives up his last hold on normal moral reservations. Boorman suggested this by having him remove his wallet at one stalled moment of the climb to look at a photo of his wife and son, and then having him drop it into the river when he almost loses his grip. The poignance and artificiality of such a moment is wholly out of keeping with the novel's enthusiasm; there, one senses Gentry's pride in having at last become a calculating, determined hunter, one who methodically clears away an unobstructed firing position in a pine tree (completing the identification of Lewis as owl-predator), and anticipates carefully the suspected attacking rifleman's strategy. Boorman's Gentry, on the other hand, is frantic rather than assured; placed awkwardly and haplessly on the ground, behind a rock, he awaits his enemy in a suspenseful, beautifully photographed, but essentially empty silence.

That a mountain man should appear, who may *not* be the second, escaped rapist, would be a large coincidence in any novel. Dickey camouflages this with long stretches of meditation, keeping us in Gentry's mind. Boorman, however, executes the ambush in a manner that creates more confusion than controlled uncertainty. The man appears, that is, and Gentry seems to shoot him with an unsteady arrow; but once shot, the rifleman does not fall. Instead, in a version of the old showdown deception, it is Gentry himself who appears fatally wounded, and who then remains so even after the other has collapsed. We do not know why. The novel, that is, simply made it clear that Gentry stabbed himself with his arrow while falling from his perch in the tree; that wound, moreover, alludes to the other sexual penetrations in the narrative, and upon cutting the arrow out of his flesh, he symbolically frees himself from homosexual fascinations. All that is certain in the film is the contrived plot detail that *this* hillbilly has teeth—but they are also false teeth, so he could very well be the wrong man. When Boorman later entangles the two men under water, after the descending rope snaps and they plummet into the river, the nearly fatal embrace of the dead man does succeed, for the reader of the novel that is, in suggesting the ironic intimacy Ed had created for them in his meditations. But it is difficult to see how an unassisted viewer might perceive anything more than the same sort of macabre revenge threatened later by the closing image of the dead hand. Once again, Boorman cannot transcend the film's limitations, though he appears to try with such dream techniques. He can give us Ed caught in a dynamic and dramatic situation, and he can even give evidence of Ed's "conversion" back to nature, but, having from the outset discarded the essentials of Ed's perspective, he cannot free his special effects from the generalized world of melodrama.

After this, the film returns to its theme in a more explicit way, compounding ironies that have surfaced with the dramatic role-reversal I have described. Once the men have acceded to expediency and what they see as necessity, the river becomes calm and carries them back to safety; it even conceals all traces of their own violence. It is also ironic that the first fruit of Ed's profound change of heart on the river is a successful, though probably unnecessary, lie about that experience, almost intuitively abetted by the hospitalized Lewis. The lie seems unnecessary, that is, because the sheriff at Aintry (ponderously played by Dickey himself) proves to be both more civil and more judicious than Ed, or the other survivors, would believe, despite the protestations of Drew. The sheriff's civility is further reflected by the kindness of the rooming house patrons who quietly respect Gentry's momentary breakdown at the dinner table. When Gentry later learns that the man he murdered may have been the deputy's innocent relative, whose wife has been troubled by his absence, the extension of a knowable social world into the "gut-survival situation" up river gives the lie to Lewis's argument that they had no choice but to avoid the law. We too must be disturbed by such discoveries since the film, with its violent self-absorption, allowed us no alternative.

In addition to these circumstantial ironies, the idea of civilized destructiveness is recalled from the beginning when Boorman brings the canoers to shore at a point used for dumping wrecked cars into the river, and then later too when he devises the removal of a small chapel at Aintry to make way for the dam and points out a work crew in the process of digging up graves in the distance as Gentry drives home. Gentry himself is left to bear the burden of all this, as the final image of the film suggests: announced by droning and eerie music. the dead man's hand rises out of the swollen, dammed-up river as a figure for Gentry's guilty dreams; it is an indelible connection with anguished past from which Gentry may never be delivered.

Many reviewers of the film proceeded from this to recite with gravity certain Darwinian truths about how uncivilized we remain despite (or is it because of?) our progress, and about how effectively the film documents our deep and abiding involvement with the brutal and primitive. Stephen Farber, taking a slightly different tack in a *New York Times* article (August 20, 1972), praises what he calls the film's "serious and meaningful challenge to the belief in the rites of manhood." My contention is that, whatever the merits of the film's presentation, and they are technical merits at best, *Deliverance* perjures itself by falsifying the story material on which it is based. What, for example, is the film to make of Gentry's conviction, at the end of the novel, that with all its deadly ironies, the journey down the Cahulawassee River was a providential experience, bringing him back to life?

> The river and everything I remember about it became a possession to me, a personal, private possession, as nothing else in my life ever had. Now it ran nowhere but in my head, but there it ran as though immortally. I could feel it—I can feel it—on different places in my body. It pleases me that the river does not exist, and that I have it. In me it still is, and will be until I die, green, rocky, deep, fast, slow, and beautiful beyond reality.

This beatific vision is of course the novel's resolution of Gentry's self-estrangement: those elements of himself which had been repressed by his socialized will, only released in his dreams, are now "possessed" by his waking consciousness in a fertile and naturally complex way. By neglecting this substantial dimension of the novel, the film neglects what is far more interesting, and more "serious and meaningful" as well, than any glib attacks upon manhood, progress, or, for that matter, river dams.

Appendix: The Politics of Adaptation

It has long been commonplace to regard Hollywood and the American film establishment as unfriendly to "Art" but downright hostile to "Ideas." Remember Louis B. Mayer's motto: "If you want to send a message, use Western Union." One function of this book is to confront this commonplace, as it is exemplified in the transfer from one medium to another, from novel to cinema. To further this end, we have included this special section to investigate the purest kind of ideological struggles behind the barricades of the Hollywood studio system.

Much can be learned from what happens to such "Idea" novels as Upton Sinclair's The Wet Parade, *and Ayn Rand's* The Fountainhead. *Though these works are often excluded from the higher echelons of the literary canon—possibly because they are so transparently ideological—they offer the clearest sort of documentation on how the studios operated. Interestingly, the Hollywood assembly-line did not automatically run to the right (though it did more often than not), as the case of Ayn Rand's own numerous revisions to the screenplay of her novel demonstrate.*

We have also included here an article on Hemingway's Spanish Civil War novel, For Whom the Bell Tolls. *Though decidedly not a "minor" work, the circumstances surrounding the production of the film version—reaching into international intrigue—prove most lucidly that the Hollywood Dream Factory was often wide awake to its role in American cultural and political life.*

The Wet Parade (1931)
Upton Sinclair

Que Viva Prohibition?

BY JOSEPH MANSFIELD

Upton Sinclair's relationship with film is almost always remembered in terms of his disastrous sponsorship of Sergei Eisenstein's uncompleted Mexican film, *Que Viva Mexico*. But in that same year, 1931, Sinclair and his wife visited MGM for the planning and shooting of the film version of his antialcohol novel, *The Wet Parade*, under the direction of Victor Fleming and starring Dorothy Jordan, Robert Young, and Jimmy Durante.

Sinclair was satisfied with the shooting he witnessed and reported that it would result in a "very good picture."[1] Mary Craig Sinclair recalls in her autobiography, *Southern Belle*, a conversation in which Irving Thalberg indicated to Sinclair that "he could not make a Prohibition picture, but he [would give] his word that he would hold the balance fair and give both sides."[2] Rather than attempt a "fair and balanced" picture, however, MGM returned the treatment Sinclair allegedly bestowed upon Eisenstein's doomed project. The film of *The Wet Parade* not only undercuts at every turn the author's argument for prohibition, but rebuts Sinclair's key polemic points: (1) that socialist political action is necessary to stop the flow of alcohol in America, and

[1] Upton Sinclair, *The Autobiography of Upton Sinclair* (New York: Harcourt Brace & World, 1962), p. 248.

[2] Mary Craig Sinclair, *Southern Belle* (New York: Crown Publishers, 1957), p. 327.

(2) that women must be the central force in propelling this radical movement. Instead the film cynically celebrates the American people's passivity in the face of political processes, reducing Sinclair's fervent populism to a parody of its aims.

The Wet Parade is not one of Upton Sinclair's artistic successes, but it is a novel he listed, largely because of its crucial message, along with *The Jungle* (1906) as among his proudest accomplishments. Here Sinclair took to the pulpit, and preached that alcohol is an addictive and lethal drug, literally destructive of all who drink it.

Sinclair's reasons for opposing drink derived from harsh personal experiences. In his autobiography, he states that he became prohibitionist when his father drank himself to death.[3] Later he found further evidence of the inevitably ruinous nature of alcohol among his literary friends. Finally, he came to believe that alcoholism was hereditary and that the children of alcoholics must never drink; their first experience with alcohol would result in certain addiction.

The novel articulates this last idiosyncratic theme by presenting the lives of two parallel families headed by alcoholic fathers and by tracing the intertwining lives of their children. Both of the fathers, Roger Chillicote, Sr., and Pow Tarleton, are given to binges; they are hospitalized for detoxification and are ultimately destroyed. The sons, set in temperamental contrast to one another, still share an alcohol-related fate because of their tainted lineage.

Chillicote, Sr., commits suicide in despair over his drinking, causing his daughter, Maggie May, to become a teetotaler. Roger Chillicote, Jr., a rebellious young writer, refuses to take the pledge, for he is a young man determined to defy convention and family wishes. All of Roger's later attempts to control his drinking, first by limiting his consumption, then by periodic abstinence, lastly by teetotaling, are failures. He is hereditarily hooked, driven mad, and, at last, confined to an insane asylum.

Pow Tarleton, the head of the second family, is an active spokesman in Tammany Hall politics and a fierce opponent of

---

[3] Upton Sinclair, pp. 328–29.

prohibition, both in speech and practice. The final passage of the Eighteenth Amendment leads him to a defiant drunken spree that results in a stroke, confining him to bed for the rest of his life. Tarleton's enfeeblement forces his son Kip to manage the family's small hotel. Kip reacts to his own father's drinking by becoming, like Maggie May, a confirmed nondrinker.

When Roger, Jr., comes to New York, he lives in Kip's hotel, and Maggie May visits repeatedly as she attempts to control Roger's drinking. The hotel becomes insolvent, Kip obtains a job as a caretaker on an estate, and he and Maggie May marry. Their happiness, however, is shattered by omnipresent alcohol. They discover that the estate is being used for rum-running, and after a bootlegger is murdered, Kip chooses to testify before the law and thus loses his job. His search for work leads him, almost inevitably, to the prohibition service.

Because Kip has rejected alcohol, he has always been regarded as a social misfit and even been made the butt of jokes at chic parties. Now, when he enters the prohibition service, he discovers he must drink at speakeasies to obtain evidence. Despite the fact that he finds liquor repugnant, he becomes intoxicated in the line of duty. He immediately develops an addiction to drink which can only be controlled by complete abstinence. In an attempt to find a job which does not involve drinking, Kip requests a transfer to more dangerous work and this transfer leads to his death while raiding a gangster distillery.

Kip's murder by bootleggers brings Maggie May to the forefront of the novel. Whereas the other female characters in *The Wet Parade* are ineffectual and cringing, Maggie May carries the author's torch through her strength of character and prohibitionist zeal. She finds herself driven to become a temperance lecturer. And, in order to make her talks convincing, she makes specific references to the drunkards in her own household and thus shocks her relatives. This bold honesty demonstrates the difference between Maggie May and her own timid society, which hides any discussion of alcoholism out of shame. She is capable of sacrificing all family honor in order to destroy drink.

Maggie's initial intention is to speak only to children so that the next generation will not be cursed. But her development, from a family-oriented teetotaler into a partisan political activist, is taken forward when she is introduced to the radical Dr. Craven, who opens up to her the political and social background of the prohibition fight. Craven claims that alcohol is a poison and so should be regulated by government. He reasons that the prohibitionists must separate their cause from religion and unite it with the socialist movement; he argues that the forces of capitalism are behind the "Wets," who seek repeal because of the huge profits available from legalized liquor. Craven further asserts that socialism would improve living conditions and free the working people from reliance on liquor as an escape from the evil system.

Craven also advocates contraception for women, claiming that such knowledge and devices are illegal only because church groups oppose birth control. Maggie May accepts his argument that private morality is above the law and begins to advocate birth control while devoting her energies to the prohibition movement. (In *The Wet Parade* Sinclair never resolves the implied moral contradiction here, for, historically, the Wets made the same essential claim—that the private right to drink was infringed upon by organized groups attempting to convert *their* personal morality into public law. This contradiction suggests that Sinclair was uncertain of how to integrate his own convictions on civil liberties with his strong opposition to alcohol.) Craven's arguments turn Maggie May into a socialist and revolutionary. The death of Kip brings her to champion Carrie Nation's position that women should physically attack speakeasies. She claims that this is the only possible response to a lawless political and social system.

Sinclair's novel thus advocates revolutionary violence in order for the people of America to regain control of the Constitution. Quite the contrary, the movie *The Wet Parade* shows people confused about their wishes and attitudes toward alcohol. By default, those in power must make the decisions for them.

In the brief time between the writing of the novel and the release of the film version in 1932, public opinion had shifted steadily toward repeal of the Eighteenth Amendment. Even such strange bedfellows as Democratic presidential candidate Franklin Roosevelt and *the* Republican studio, MGM, found themselves agreeing on repeal.

MGM's *The Wet Parade* portrays the evils of drink primarily in terms of a separate class: alcoholics. Liquor is simply bad for a certain segment of the population who cannot consume it moderately and thus become addicted. Jerry, a minor and corrupt character in the novel, becomes in the film a man who drinks but remains moderate and gentlemanly, in contrast to his friend, Roger, Jr. Such a character permits the filmmaker, Victor Fleming, to portray alcohol as a neutral substance, dangerous only to certain types of people.

The film's supposedly neutral position on the Eighteenth Amendment is shown up by the cynical manner in which prohibition enforcement is portrayed. Roger, Jr.'s mistress (Myrna Loy in a blonde wig) opens a night club, which attracts an elegant crowd to its well-appointed room. The singers and dancers are lighthearted and the audience decorously dressed. Then comes the raid. Kip's fellow agent, played by Jimmy Durante, is disguised as a foreign ambassador who suddenly removes his comic beard, makes a few crude jokes, and then orders his men into action. This results in confusion among the guests and much violence against property as the raiders smash the glassware, the liquor, and the bar. The effect of this scene is to make the viewer regard prohibition agents as people who disrupt harmless and essentially positive social gatherings in rather barbaric ways. (This scene is contrasted with an earlier example of inefficiency, where Kip and his fellow agent are spotted attempting to get evidence in a working-class bar and are comically roughed up by the customers and the bartenders, while a policeman watches.)

The film undercuts the arguments of the prohibitionists for stricter law enforcement by showing that government agents approach their work frivolously, that their tactics are antisocial, and that the entire process is like a game. Also, the film softens consideration of the way in which the wealthy finance bootlegging and profit from it. Indeed, the only scene that reflects any aspect of Sinclair's concern has one of the leading bootleggers talking to his criminal cohorts and then moving to the next room to meet with the wealthy backers of his proposed syndicate. (But even then, the financiers protest against violence, thereby separating themselves from the dangerous lower-class criminals.)

Other alterations in the film serve to strengthen the case *against* prohibition. For example, in the movie Kip's father does not die; worse, he is driven insane from drinking poisonous bootleg and kills his wife when she attempts to stop his drinking. Roger, Jr., does not lose *his* sanity in the film but is made blind by drinking the same illegal stuff. These sequences show that it is the existence of prohibition which forces poisonous liquor to dominate the marketplace and insure alcoholism.

Kip's experiences as a prohibition agent are radically altered in the film. Kip is not killed; rather, in the time-honored Hollywood tradition, his comic fellow agent is shot and killed. Nor does Kip become addicted to alcohol because he must drink on the job. The effect of his service, rather, is to disillusion him with the entire process of enforcement and raise doubts about his own abilities to maintain the law. He notes that many of the drinkers in the saloons he attempts to close are under age and that it is prohibition which has brought about this loosening of social rules.

At the end of the film, Kip goes to the hospital and embraces his wife and newborn child while wondering aloud about the failure of the law. He states that before the child grows up, "They'll have it all figured out." This reference to a vague governmental "they" suggest the way in which the film eventually presents the alcohol question as something too complex for individual solution. Maggie May can only chime in, "I hope and pray you're right."

This comment indicates another incredible distortion by MGM of Upton Sinclair's purposes. It is Maggie May who, above all, loses the strength of character that make her the center of the novel. She now adheres to traditional patterns of female submissiveness. Her concern about drinking in the film is confined to those around her family, as when she attacks her father's friends for imbibing at his funeral. But she qualifies the attack by stating that she is mainly opposed to their partaking of alcohol in her home. She uses feminine wiles rather than argument on Roger when attempting to limit his consumption, and when she is at a party given after prohibition becomes law, she objects not to the serving of liquor, but to the fact that it is Roger who is drinking (and this does not anger her as much as the fact that he has taken a mistress). When the film ends, she lies in bed holding her baby. Despite everything, she is the picture of contented motherhood, with only benign hopes for the future.

The film does give some attention to the political system, predictably, from a position very much hostile to the socialism of Upton Sinclair. The film suggests (and not critically) that the system is beyond the wishes and control of individuals and propelled by mysterious rulers following their own destinies. For example, the film focuses at first on the character of Kip's father, who is an ardent Democrat. He delivers a speech favoring the election of Wilson, and his major arguments are that Wilson will keep the country out of war and allow freedom of choice in drinking. His speech is followed by a speech by a Republican who makes exactly the same promises. At the conclusion of the rally, the audience moves to a saloon where one of the party men begins to dispense drinks to all. The scene suggests that both political parties use speech and drink to confuse the issues and the constituency. Further evidences of this point of view abound in later sequences.

Election night is presented as a welter of noise and drunkenness, with voters unable to determine who is winning or losing. The next day, when Wilson's election is finally determined, his supporters dance in belief that he will keep them out of war, but a montage of men marching and planes and ships moving off to battle clearly reinforces the notion of political duplicity. (And from Republican MGM, in an election year, this must be seen as a not-so-gratuitous introduction of the old idea that it's the Democrats who always start wars.) The prohibitionists, too, are presented as opportunists who play on patriotic sentiment in wartime to implement their cause. Their political maneuvering is supported when the film shows a group of soldiers in the trenches expressing dismay that they will be unable to get a drink, if they are lucky enough to survive the war.

Regardless of the origin of these political games, the film is consistent in showing not only that the American people are never consulted, but that they accept passively the decisions of the political system. When reporting the ratification of the Eighteenth Amendment, the film presents the vote visually, in terms of large block letters. As the names of the ratifying states move ominously toward the audience, punctuated by the sound of a judicial gavel, the overall image gives no sense whatsoever of democratic participation in this process.

It is this mystification of government that most radically alters the political themes of Sinclair's novel. The cynicism of the film destroys the populist vision of a knowledgeable and powerful people arising to overthrow the interests that control and manipulate their society. The entirely different tones and themes are not accidental, though. Despite Mary Sinclair's report that Irving Thalberg intended the film to be neutral on the question of prohibition, it seems clear that the film seeks passivity in its audience and urges that the powers of government be allowed to resolve problems in God-like isolation. Needless to say, such attitudes meshed very nicely with attitudes prevalent among MGM's tycoon management.

It seems completely consistent with Louis B. Mayer and Thalberg's class interests that the film portrays wealthy men, who support organized bootlegging, as naive about the violence of such organizations; and upperclass drinkers, except for several unwieldy alcoholics, as able to handle their liquor—something the lower classes are incapable of doing. (Further, the portrayal of an enervated homebound Maggie May, and the film's stress on motherhood, reflect Mayer's well-known enthusiasm for such a view of women's "proper" role.)

The politics of the film carefully load the question against Democrats, vesting Wilson with responsibility not only for World War I but, at a slight remove, for prohibition itself. Once this link is established, no further mention is made of political administrations, so that the three Republicans, Harding, Coolidge, and

Hoover, escape any possible blame for prohibition violations. Mayer's intense advocacy of Hoover undoubtedly influenced these decisions.[4]

In fact, the manipulation of Sinclair's ideas by MGM did not end with *The Wet Parade*. In 1934, when Sinclair ran his ill-fated EPIC (End Poverty in California) campaign for governor of the state on a platform of taxing the rich, Thalberg had MGM prepare a "newsreel" depicting hoboes riding trains into the state in order to be ready to share in Sinclair's promised welfare plans. This film, credited with aiding the defeat of Sinclair, is probably Thalberg's most cynical manipulation of film and audience, but it clearly derives from the kind of world view evident in MGM's adaptation of *The Wet Parade*.[5]

[4] For Mayer's social and political attitudes see Bosley Crowther, *Hollywood Rajah* (New York: Holt, Rinehart & Winston, 1960).

[5] Thalberg's involvement in the E.P.I.C. campaign and his cynical attitude toward politics is recounted in Bob Thomas, *Thalberg: Life and Legend* (Garden City, N.Y.: Doubleday, 1969), pp. 268–270.

For Whom the Bell Tolls (1940)
Ernest Hemingway

The "Unmaking" of a Political Film

BY CONSTANCE POHL

Shortly after fighting broke out in Spain in 1936, Ernest Hemingway traveled to the front lines to collaborate with director Joris Ivens on the film *The Spanish Earth*. Hemingway wrote and narrated this documentary supporting the Loyalists in their war against the Franco-led Fascists. Following a tour of the United States with the movie to raise funds for Loyalist ambulances, Hemingway returned to Spain as a foreign correspondent. His news dispatches from the battlefield reiterated a single theme, "the necessity of opposing the rise of fascism in Europe before Hitler and Mussolini precipitated another world war." [1]

Hemingway brought all his prestige to bear in the fight against Fascism, delivering the following statement at the Writers Congress of 1937:

> . . . a writer's problem does not change. It is always how to write truly and having found what is true, to project it in such a way that it becomes part of the experience of the person who reads it. . . . Fascism is a lie told by bullies. A writer who will not lie cannot live and work under fascism. [2]

[1] Carlos Baker, *Ernest Hemingway, A Life Story* (New York: Scribner's, 1969), p. 332.
[2] Ibid., p. 314.

As the world war against Fascism approached, Hemingway wrote *For Whom the Bell Tolls* in 1940 about the civil war between the Loyalists and the Fascists, drawing upon his own experiences on the battlefields of Spain. Hemingway followed his own credo. The enduring value of *For Whom the Bell Tolls* lies in Hemingway's commitment to truth in recording the resistance to Fascism. Some thirty years afterward Fidel Castro paid the novel the ultimate compliment when he noted that he learned some of his own tactics from the book's descriptions of guerilla fighting in the Spanish mountains. This acknowledgment would have pleased Hemingway.

Produced at the height of the American war effort against Fascist Germany and Italy in 1942, the Paramount Pictures screen version of *For Whom the Bell Tolls* is in many ways a scrupulously faithful adaptation of Hemingway's novel. There are no "additional scenes" in Dudley Nichols's screenplay, and much of the original dialogue is retained. Moreover, the three-hour-long technicolor film, released in 1943, follows events in the book closely. Set in the mountains of Spain, *For Whom the Bell Tolls* recounts the sabotage of a bridge as part of a Loyalist offensive against Franco's forces. The story begins on the first day of the mission as Robert Jordan, the American volunteer working behind enemy lines, contacts the guerilla band which is to assist him on this dangerous mission. The narrative continues as the band, led by a woman, Pilar, prepares for the assignment; Jordan falls in love with Maria, a young girl sheltered by the unit; and a neighboring band is massacred by a Fascist patrol. On the morning of the attack, Jordan and his people sabotage the bridge with inadequate weapons, while Jordan's courier is prevented from reaching the Loyalist commander in time to have the doomed offensive called off. The story ends as a wounded Jordan lies in wait for the enemy soldiers and his own certain death, after having first made sure that Maria escapes with the few surviving guerillas.

If the film adheres to the sequence of events in the novel, including retention of the "unhappy" ending, why was Hemingway so angered that he wished never to see the release version? The answer was inadvertently supplied by Adolph Zukor, then head

Robert Jordan (Gary Cooper) finds out about Loyalist Spain from
Maria (Ingrid Bergman) and Pilar (Katina Paxinou). *For Whom the
Bell Tolls* (1943)

of Paramount, who bragged of *For Whom the Bell Tolls,* winner of three Academy Awards: "It is a great picture, without political significance. We are not for or against anybody." [3]

In a classic case of Hollywood's sins of omission, the Paramount adaptation systematically excludes all aspects of the novel that deal with politics. The movie largely disregards Hemingway's long and complicated flashbacks, some of which occupy whole chapters, and concentrates only on the present-tense action of the mission itself. Yet it is in the flashbacks that Hemingway explains the issues behind the war, giving in Carlos Baker's words, "a persuasive demonstration of what men and women were willing to die for." [4]

Maria's monologue about her treatment by the Franco forces is the only film scene based on information gleaned from a Hemingway flashback. The camera focuses on Ingrid Bergman's face as she tells her harrowing story. But there is no shift in time as in the novel to dramatize what happened. In the book, Maria's slowly built tale of the murder of her parents and her ensuing rape by Fascist soldiers is rendered with painful, hypnotic vividness, and is as "real" to the reader as the blowing of the bridge. In the film however, the scene is important not because of its condemnation of the Fascists, but because Ingrid Bergman's Maria is making herself vulnerable to Gary Cooper's Robert Jordan. As an advertising blurb excerpted from a *Time* magazine review aptly put it, the star-studded movie is "a story of love and ideals set against the backdrop of the Civil War."

Hemingway attempted to set the whole historical scene, including Soviet participation in the Spanish Civil War. He devoted an entire chapter of the novel to Jordan's remembrances of Gaylords, the Madrid hotel which served as headquarters for the Russian contingent. Its principal figures are described by Jordan as among the most talented combatants: Golz is "the best general he had served under" and "Gaylords was the place you needed to complete your education. It was there you learned how it was really done instead of how it was supposed to be done."

Gaylords is not in the movie, and it is hardly surprising that

[3] James Agee, *Agee on Film* (New York: Beacon, 1964), p. 49.
[4] Baker, op. cit., p. 371.

Paramount declined to praise the Soviets' action in the war (even though they were soon to be our World War II allies). But the film of *For Whom the Bell Tolls* also ignores the contributions of non-Communist Loyalists. No direct expression of the political goals and sentiments of the guerillas is allowed. At best, there are only several statements that can be considered even vaguely partisan: Pilar's exclamation, when challenging Pablo for leadership of the band, "I am for the Republic," and Robert Jordan's reply when asked why he came to Spain, "A man must fight for what he believes in." *What* Jordan believes in is not indicated here, leaving the viewer free to insert any ideal with which he or she feels comfortable; Pilar's reference to the Republic could just as easily apply to the American Republican Party for all that is explained in the film. Ernest Hemingway specifically attacked Dudley Nichols's script on these two points. Nichols did not "begin to explain Jordan's willingness to die for the Republican cause." Moreover, the screenplay "had failed utterly in communicating the power of Pilar's political convictions in uniting the whole guerilla band." [5]

Why fight the war? In the novel, there are a number of explanations. In an interior monologue, Jordan says, "If the Republic lost it would be impossible for those who believed in it to live in Spain." Elsewhere he exclaims, "I believe in the people and their right to govern themselves as they wish." Of the fighting of the International Brigades, he says, "They had fought with the true comradeship of the revolution." Jordan comes to share their fervor: ". . . You fought . . . for all the poor in the world, against all tyranny, for all the new world you had been educated into." And Anselmo, the aging Loyalist guerilla whom Jordan most respects, expresses in simple, eloquent language his feelings about privilege and property:

I would make the [proprietors] work each day as we have worked in the fields and as we work in the mountains with the timber, all the rest of their lives. So they would see what a man is born to. That they should sleep where we sleep. That they should eat

[5] Ibid.

as we eat. But above all that they should work. Thus they would learn.

The movie dispenses with causes for the war. There are no such words as "revolution" or "comradeship," no criticisms of economic and social inequality—only the neutral word "Republic." And the almost-missing word: Fascism. As James Agee reported:

> When f-sc-sts are actually mentioned, the one time they are, the context makes it clear that they are just Italians who, in company with German Nazis and those dirty Russian Communists, are bully-ragging each other and poor little Spain, which wants only peace and quiet. . . . Mr. Nichols's original script is fairly riddled with the word fascist. The release script and the production prefer the word nationalist.[6]

Agee thus gives Dudley Nichols more credit for integrity than Hemingway wished to extend. But his remembrance of Gary Cooper/Jordan's one pointed reference to Fascism is slightly distorted. Jordan actually says, "The Nazis and Fascists are just as much against democracy as they are against Communism, and they're using your country as a proving ground for the war machinery—their tanks and dive bombers and stuff like that." And this is the single remaining speech in the film which seems to derive from an earlier script by Nichols which was, in turn, closer to the political intent of Hemingway. What is completely absent from the movie of *For Whom the Bell Tolls* are references to Fascism as an *internal* political force in Spain. The partisans of the Republic never explain their "Nationalist" enemies, nor do the costume uniforms worn by the adversary army in the film carry any distinctive, identifying marks.

The true and startling reason for this lack of specificity in the movie was the actual interference in the production by the Fascists themselves—by representatives of the victorious Franco government. An editorial in *The Nation* on December 19, 1942, made the scandal public:

[6] *The Nation*, July 24, 1953.

Recently, Hollywood stories have it, the State Department stepped in and advised Paramount to submit the film to a representative of the Franco dictatorship for his approval. The result was that certain scenes were reshot; so at the present moment two versions of them exist, one more or less representing Mr. Hemingway's intentions and the other representing Franco's view of what an American author should have written.

The initiative from the State Department proceeded from a logical desire to keep Franco's Spain neutral during the European war. Yet, as *The Nation* went on to explain, the State Department's wishes were met by a Paramount front office only too happy to oblige:

> After the final preparation of the shooting version of the script there were constant attempts on the part of Paramount big shots to tone down the story. Their intention was to insure that the "Bell" should be a wholly abstract film dealing with a saboteur's exploits in some mythical Ruritania. The words Spanish, Republic, fascist, democracy, and so forth were not to be heard.

But what if a forthright script had slipped past the State Department, Franco's representatives, and the front office at Paramount as well? Leading man Gary Cooper, Hemingway's close friend, was committed to a film adhering to the novel. (He cared little in 1942–43 about the novel's pro-Communist stance, although he was later to be a "friendly witness" before the House Un-American Activities Committee.) Ultimately, Cooper had minimal control. *For Whom the Bell Tolls* was destined for the hands of rabidly reactionary producer and director Sam Wood (who allegedly wrote a clause into his will making his daughter eligible for inheritance only upon signing of an anti-Communist oath, and who would be himself a vigorous and extremely "friendly" witness before HUAC).

Prior to *For Whom the Bell Tolls,* Wood had provided an indication of his sympathies; he had frustrated Hemingway's attempts to get a Hollywood job for his comrade from the Civil War, Gustave Duran, because Wood was, as Carlos Baker expressed it, "ultra-sensitive to the Red menace." [7] Knowing Wood's political disposition, Hemingway wanted someone else to make the movie. Donald Friede, Hemingway's literary advisor, tried to persuade David Selznick to buy the novel from Paramount and appoint Howard Hawks, another Hemingway friend, as director. The plan came to nought. (Hawks did end up, later on, making *To Have and Have Not* at Warners in 1944 from a Jules Furthman-William Faulkner script. Interestingly, that film also greatly altered the political intent and content of a Hemingway novel[8].)

For Whom the Bell Tolls remained with Sam Wood. And what remained of Hemingway's novel was a tale of tragic romance, not of tragic war. With the controversy of the Spanish Civil War literally cut from the film, the only dispute raised concerned the love scenes: these gave the movie a reputation for daring defiance of the Motion Picture Code. Ingrid Bergman and Gary Cooper shown together in a sleeping bag was considered a bold step toward a more sophisticated treatment of sex on the screen. What better way to distract the viewer from history and politics than with sex? In this respect, *For Whom the Bell Tolls* was a harbinger of many films to come.

[7] Ibid., p. 368.

[8] Editors' note. For a discussion of the adaptation of *To Have and Have Not*, see William Rothman's essay elsewhere in this volume.

The Fountainhead (1943)
Ayn Rand

Ayn Rand in the Stockyard of the Spirit

BY KEVIN MC GANN

Ayn Rand was born of prosperous parents in St. Petersburg in 1905 and stayed in Russia through the 1917 Revolution. Her only available biography, written by disciple Barbara Brandon, indicates that she saw the new Leninist Russia as a monstrous victory for "mediocrity," where "men's souls grew shabbier and pettier each dreary year." Before Rand departed for the United States in 1925, her mother urged her to tell America that "Russia is a huge cemetery, and that we are all dying slowly." *The Fountainhead* (1943), railed against the dragon forces of boorish "collectivisim" and conventional aesthetic standards in *this* country as concerned citizen Rand determined to save America from "dying" as well.

In this 754-page tome, Howard Roark, an architect-genius, persists in designing great buildings without sacrificing an inch of his integrity to the inevitably compromising demands of professional peers, opinion-makers, the public taste, and his clients: "I don't build to have clients; I have clients so I can build," he asserts. Throughout the book he is implicitly compared with pusillanimous Peter Keating, college roommate and then fellow architect, whose overriding desire for commercial success makes him willing to accommodate anyone who promises to further his career.

The general principle upon which the book is based—that the

mass of mankind is talentless, without creativity or originality, and bitterly jealous of those few who are different—is manifested most strongly in the character of Ellsworth Toohey (sounds like "all's-worth-hooey"), an architectural critic for a mammoth newspaper chain. Through his highly influential intellectual position, Toohey hypocritically manipulates public opinion in the direction of "selflessness," which, through Ayn Rand's inverted rhetoric, becomes a kind of meek mindless drift toward that ideological arch-villain, "collectivism." As a critic, Toohey creates nothing. "I deal in the stockmarket of the spirit," he cynically boasts at one point in the book, "and I sell short."

The first premise of Rand's philosophy—that everyone is ultimately selfish—is demonstrated in all three figures (Toohey, Keating, and Roark); but only one, Roark, also has "character," and the author's endorsement of his values places him far from the middling crowd, separating him from the spineless Keating and pitting him against the traitorous Toohey. The dialectic battle between a fantasy version of individualism—Roark—and a satanic version of the cooperative spirit—Toohey—culminates when Roark purposely dynamites a public-works housing project he designed because its architectural "integrity" has been compromised by the Toohey clique.

Between these forces are two other characters in *The Fountainhead* who, because they lack the courage to defend Roark's brilliant architecture before the rabble, masochistically bend their efforts to ruin it. Gail Wynand, the powerful Hearst-like publisher of Toohey's column, is an isolated cynic who at first tries to corrupt Roark to validate his own pessimism about human nature. Failing at that, and smitten finally by a glimpse of Roark's moral determination and idealistic faith ("I feel as if I found that honesty was possible . . . he is my youth."), Wynand throws his whole reputation into defending the young architect in his newspapers. The attempt at a personally redemptive crusade comes too late. Rand presents Wynand as a case study of the potentially enlightened capitalist-entrepreneur, but she makes him pay for his tardy patronage. Toohey subverts his organization and Wynand is stripped of his wealth, his wife, and—in the film of *The Fountainhead*—his life.

Like Wynand whom she married, Dominique Francon is a bitter example of approach-avoidance ambivalence. She is the daughter of a "successful" architect, but she despises her father's conventional mediocrity and secretly loves Roark. Her characterization is perhaps the most interesting aspect of the book. She makes a pact with Toohey to destroy Roark, argues publicly that his work ought to be banished (because it is "too good" for the people), tries to convince him to settle down (he refuses to be domesticated), and then succumbs to living with him. She is by turns the destroyer, the seducer, the disciple, and finally an ally. The passionate relationship is in reality a struggle for dominance; when she realizes she cannot win the struggle over Roark, she is compelled to love him.

The novel starts with Roark's expulsion from architectural school for refusing to follow "traditional" ideas. He takes work with the only man he admires, Henry Cameron, a despairing genius meant to recall Frank Lloyd Wright's mentor and predecessor, Louis Sullivan. And even if historical parallels do not go very deep, there is resemblance in their iconoclasm and visionary stance between Roark and Wright. Thus Ayn Rand's visual instructions at the beginning of her *Fountainhead* screenplay for Warner Brothers:

> Among present day architects, it is the style of Frank Lloyd Wright —and ONLY of Frank Lloyd Wright—that must be taken as a model for Roark's buildings. Wright holds a unique position with the general public—even the people who cling to traditional architecture and hate modernism of the concrete-and-steel-pipe school —love and admire Roark's work. This is extremely important to us, since we must make the audience admire Roark's buildings.[1]

Refusing commissions which would call for him to compromise the integrity of his conceptions with classical gewgaw, Roark goes broke. He works as a laborer in a quarry (where he first meets Dominique) until Roger Enright, another self-made worthy, sees his own spirit of independence in Roark's designs

---

[1] Rand's screenplays for the Warner Brothers' 1949 production are maintained in the United Artists collection at the State Historical Society, University of Wisconsin at Madison.

and offers him carte blanche to build the Enright House. Roark's success, though, is muted by growing public resentment, fostered by Toohey, against his unorthodoxy.

Up to this point Peter Keating had served as a choral voice urging "compromise." Now he comes to Roark seeking help—as he had always done in school. He wants Roark to solve his own problem of designing a sound but appealing low-income housing project on a short budget. Roark agrees to help on condition that, though Keating will get the credit, *nothing* of Roark's perfect plans will be changed by "intellectual second-handers." Predictably, changes are made. When Roark dynamites the project, Wynand's newspaper fails to hold out against the public outcry. Dominique throws in with Roark, Toohey's plans collapse, and, after an essay-length courtroom self-defense by Roark ("There is no collective mind," he maintains), Rand's enlightened jury acquits him. Dominique and Roark live happily ever after. Toohey, like a temporarily repulsed evil spirit, moves on to another newspaper, there quietly to harvest weaker souls.

By 1962 *The Fountainhead* had sold nearly half a million copies in hardcover and over a million in paperback, and it continues today to move on bookstore shelves. Although it has all the characteristics of pulp fiction, including flood-tide length and watery content, *The Fountainhead* is, of course, much more than a potboiler about the personal traumas behind the lives of busy architects. It is actually an "idea" novel, however crude or obvious, about fiercely opposing political ideologies. It is an overheard version of an internal American cultural debate between individualism and collectivism. (In the film, a simple lighting design makes this dialectic theme clear: the two primary antagonists, Toohey and Roark, are each first introduced in back-silhouette, before we see their faces, as if behind these representative men are "shadow-worlds" of ideology locked in struggle.) In articulating this struggle, Rand speaks simultaneously to the highest aspirations and the deepest suspicions of the culture, precipitating the broadly based, though mostly unspoken, acceptance of her work.

Part of *The Fountainhead*'s success is due to the way in which it includes its reader in a disenfranchised "elect." It appeals to the romantic sense of alienation and superiority, asking the reader to identify with an elite still sensitive to aesthetic "integrity" and tortured by the low-brow conventional mediocrity of a small-minded society. It has the bitterness of the "outsider" and offers a hero who is determined enough to overcome these obstacles. (Ayn Rand's own favorite modern literary personage is Mickey Spillane's extra-determined Mike Hammer.) This country, *The Fountainhead* seems to say, does not lack True Believers but rather something or someone to believe in: a Howard Roark, a moral absolutist and fervent crusader amidst the ugly spiritual malaise. Perceived by some as "radical" because its values—the emphasis on individualism, the romantic faith in the efficacy of an idea over all practical obstacles, grim moral purity—belong to an earlier, pioneer stage of economic development in a capitalist culture, it is ultimately an attack on present society from the regressive Right Wing.

In 1943 Warner Brothers bought the screen rights to *The Fountainhead* and hired Ayn Rand to do the screenplay. Several revised scripts were presented before filming started in 1948 under the direction of King Vidor. Despite the book's extreme length, not too much is lost in the adaptation; several minor characters are dropped, speeches are reduced to their essential thought, and scenes which functioned as thematic reiteration are excised. King Vidor could add, of course, his distinctive cinematic signature, but Rand had complete control over the script and final approval for all changes.

Ironically, the "integrity" of the character of Dominique (Patricia Neal) is compromised by Ayn Rand herself in order to suit the public moral taste and the Hollywood formula. In the novel Dominique initially conspires with Toohey to destroy Roark. In the film her attempts to destroy Roark (Gary Cooper) are more sympathetically motivated by a desire to protect him. In the book her cynicism and self-hatred are dramatized by her actually marrying Keating, whom she detests, whereas the film offers a more morally palatable "engagement." When Dominique turns finally to Roark at the end of the book, she purposely publicizes her adulterous relationship with him in order to force Wynand (whom she married after Keating) to divorce her. In the film Wynand (Raymond Massey) is simply eliminated by suicide. The book also graphically details the illicit sexual relationship between Dominique and Roark, which the movie skirts.

The single most interesting change between the novel and the final film script occurs in the film judge's instruction to the jury. In weighing the evidence, he asks them to make an important distinction:

> Further, you are instructed that the extent of the monetary loss suffered by the owner is not a matter to be considered by you. The liability of the defendant for any financial loss is a question to be considered in a civil suit. You are concerned here only with a criminal action.

No such distinction is made in the book or in previous scripts. (The final script indicates considerable rewriting over the summer of 1948, and the change in the judge's speech is the very last revision.) Apparently someone in Warner Brothers' corporate headquarters could not endorse Rand's extreme interpretation of private property—that because Roark "owned" the idea, he therefore "owned" the building and should have control over its fate; and that therefore he is "not guilty" on all charges, including financial liability. In the movie Roark is judged "not guilty" of a criminal violation but may still have to pay for the property damage. This moot change still did not satisfy the more righteous who saw the film. As Bosley Crowther wrote in the *New York Times*, July 9, 1949, "We ask by what moral reasoning his act can be justified? . . . If all were excused such transgressions, then society would indeed be in peril!" Even King Vidor, the director, was bothered by the tempered conclusion:

> I liked the film but hated the ending. I thought it was ridiculous to have a fellow blow up a building because they changed some of the facade. I went to Jack Warner and said, "If you make a cut in this picture and I burn it are you going to forgive me?" and he said, "Well, we won't but the judge might." [2]

[2] Peter Greenberg, "War, Wheat, and Steel: An Interview With King Vidor," *Sight and Sound*, vol. 37, no. 4, Autumn, 1968, p. 197.

Always eager to discuss his most personal projects like *The Big Parade* (1925), *The Crowd* (1928), *Hallelujah!* (1929), and *Our Daily Bread* (1934), Vidor devotes all of one sentence in his autobiography to *The Fountainhead*. But he and Ayn Rand were not *that* far apart, as evidenced by Vidor's own testimony when asked (though years later) if he agreed with Rand's philosophy:

> Not to the point of arrogance. I do believe firmly that all inspiration, our life and everything, comes to us directly, rather than having to go through any institutional or orthodox channels, and to this degree I believe that I'm in direct communication with God or whatever you want to call it. So it was compatible with what I believe.[3]

The emphasis here is on what Raymond Durgnat has called Vidor's "transcendentalism," a direct intuition of truth.[4] Roark, shunning orthodoxy in favor of creative originality, is also directly inspired.

Roark's fight to convert the public and the architectural world to his thinking is really an expression of the romantic's egocentric attempt to force reality to accord with his private perceptions, and this too was compatible with Vidor, and even with his understanding of filmmaking. "Something about the lens is very akin to the human consciousness which looks out at the universe. 'I am a camera'—we are all cameras," he has said. "And in *The Fountainhead,* the solipsistic idea, the integrity, the divinity almost, of the artist, is another theme which I've always been interested in; that the whole universe springs from the individual —what he's conscious of, that's reality; what he is not conscious of doesn't exist." [5] (At one point in the film, Toohey asks Roark what he thinks of him. When he tells Toohey, "But I don't think of you," it is not bravado, but daringly forthright solipsism—King Vidor's thematic preoccupation.)

[3] Ibid.
[4] Raymond Durgnat, "King Vidor: Part II," *Film Comment,* vol. 9, no. 5, September-October 1973, pp. 29–35.
[5] Richard Schickel, *The Men Who Made the Movies* (New York: Atheneum, 1975), p. 158.

Howard Roark (Gary Cooper) sits on the raw material that will bring his architectural concepts to life. *The Fountainhead* (1949)

Vidor had wanted Bogart for the role. But there is uncanny accuracy in Warner's casting Gary Cooper as Howard Roark, whether he is remembered as *Sergeant York* (1941) or, earlier, *The Virginian* (1929). If in the former we discover Roark's individualism and private conscience combined with deadly determination, in the latter we are able to seek Roark for what he really is, the perfect image of the Western hero: isolated, driven by a morally pure inner code, the man who forces the Western woman to arrive at *his* way of thinking, absolutely uncompromising. Roark always draws straight, and his buildings never lie. One of the Warner's "consulting architects" who helps ruin the design of the housing project is, in fact, the familiar unshaven face of a B-grade Western thug, the hireling for crooked business interests. Holding a pointer over a mock-up of the building, he says, "Hmmm, we gotta have some kinna—trimmins— over the entrance," and smashes it down. "Aw, what's the use of talking," he says again, "let's go to work," and gleefully crumbles the entire building. (As in any frontier crusade, it is fairly easy to tell the White Hats from the Black Hats.)

Roark, the Westerner, is also a powerful figure of sexual fantasy. The rhetoric of the film suggests that two people cannot be lovers unless both are equal individuals, but the plot and imagery tell another story. Dominique first meets Roark, a prince in disguise, when he is working on her father's quarry in Connecticut, and her first "knowledge" of him occurs when she is awakened from restless sleep by far-off dynamiting in the quarry. Roark is identified with force, and her erotic instincts are stirred by it. He is the man with the chisel, the man with the air hammer; she lures him to her bedroom on a pretext and tries to seduce him ("Would you like to make some extra money?"), but he chooses instead to return that night and—as she admits later in the book —rape her.[6] The shots in the quarry, which are the most beauti-

---

[6] The rape occurs in the novel on p. 230, but not until p. 729 are we informed (off-hand) of just what happened, in steamy, best-seller prose: "She fought like an animal. But she made no sound. She did not call for help. She heard the echoes of her blows in a gasp of his breath, and she knew that it was a gasp of pleasure. . . ."

—Ayn Rand, *The Fountainhead*
(New York & Indianapolis: Bobbs-Merrill, 1943), pp. 230–31.

ful in the film in their use of sunlight, open spaces, and large, architecturally arranged blocks of marble, also set the stage for a sexual struggle of wills. He is "below" her, covered with sweat, proletarian dust, and bulging sinews; she stands above, a riding whip in her hand, distant but aroused, dressed in a simple white blouse and black pants. She tries to tame and exploit him but feels the attraction of his force. He overpowers her brutally, but she knows that this is good and right, she is never to forget the delicious pain, bonded to him by her humiliation. "It's the things that we want or admire that enslave us," she says later, "and I'm not easy to bring into submission." "That depends on the strength of your adversary," Roark retorts.

The equation of sex with pain and humiliation, and of that with pleasure, goes to the core of the sadomasochistic characterization of Dominique. Typical of her is this line: "If it gives you pleasure to know that you are breaking me down, I'll give you greater satisfaction. I love you, Howard Roark." Her relationship with Keating (Kent Smith) is a self-punishing attempt to avoid disillusionment, as is her loveless marriage to Wynand. She destroys objects of art she admires, just as she originally tries to destroy Roark. She is attracted to Roark although she knows that he will purposely violate her defenses, psychologically and physically, making her even more vulnerable. All of this psychological drama culminates (as it began) in the final dynamiting, which Dominique witnesses with a mixture of erotic pleasure and anguish.

When Roark blows up his own best building, he does it through moral strength (better dead than red?). But Dominique does not have the emotional strength to endure his inevitable public crucifixion, and so ,either out of self-pity or self-hatred, attempts suicide, only to be reborn a changed woman. In the incredible Freudian denouement, she happily climbs Roark's tower, his newest and most potent architectural achievement.

Dominique's crisis of conscience, the central personal drama of the film, is inextricably intertwined with its political implications. Such "female crises" are not cinematically unique. At about the same time that Rand was writing her book, Frank Capra directed *Mr. Deeds Goes to Town* (1936) and *Meet John Doe*

(1941), which presented Gary Cooper as an idealistic outsider hero who throws himself against institutionalized hypocrisy and corruption. And in both Capra films, the women, Jean Arthur and Barbara Stanwyck, are initially hostile to the male, interested in him only as a curiosity, a Don Quixote figure. As familiarity grows, however, their repressed hopes and idealism are quickened by Cooper's indomitable determination. For Dominique, who is more neurotic than the women in Capra's films, the cycle of self-hatred and desire for vengeance dominates her psyche. Yet even Dominique finally confesses her betrayal and joins with the crusader. In all three films the cynical women undergo traumatic conversion experiences, because they cannot ultimately deny their heartfelt desire for the Good.

The difference in the films, however, indicate the opposite ideologies of the authors or directors. In the Capra films the hero's determination at first comes from nonconformity expressed as boyish innocence and naivete, though it is soon more indignant, whereas in the Rand-Vidor film, from the beginning, it comes from manly strength and a hard-nosed conception of Self. Unlike Capra's hero—one of the "folk," vulnerable and sensitive, likely to get hurt—Roark begins as a rock and ends as a rock. The most striking difference between the politics of Frank Capra and Ayn Rand is in their conception of the public, and the fundamental argument is over the nature of human nature. For Capra, consonant with his conservative populism, the films end with jubilant social salvation, a conclusion that is anathema to Rand. Although she professes great faith in the economic system of her adopted country, she has little respect or affection for its populace. But as the tortuous relationships in both versions of *The Fountainhead* demonstrate, respect and affection are difficult, trying, confusing concepts for their proudly selfish author.

ROBERT ALDRIDGE has taught English and Drama at Mississippi State University, the University of Wisconsin, and currently Kirkwood Community College in Cedar Rapids, Iowa. His doctoral dissertation is on the plays of Paul Green.

SERAFINA KENT BATHRICK taught American Film at the University of Wisconsin, Madison, where she is completing a dissertation on the ideology of everyday family life in the Hollywood film, 1945–1950.

JAMES F. BEATON teaches nineteenth- and twentieth-century literature at Wellesley College and is at work on a book about fable elements in Victorian social and cultural history.

MARK BEZANSON is a filmmaker who also teaches film and English at Somerset County College in New Jersey.

PETER BRUNETTE is an Assistant Professor of English at George Mason University in Virginia. He has published articles and interviews in *Cineaste, Film Comment, Film Quarterly,* and the *Washington Post,* and he writes regularly for the *Chronicle of Higher Education.*

RUSSELL CAMPBELL was founder and editor of *The Velvet Light Trap* at the University of Wisconsin and is now writing a dissertation on the Film and Photo League at Northwestern University. He is the author of *Photographic Theory for the Motion Picture Cameraman* and *Practical Motion Picture Photography* (both 1970).

336

LESLIE CLARK taught film at Livingston College, Rutgers University, and the University of California, Santa Barbara, and is an Associate Editor of *Jump Cut*.

E. PAULINE DEGENFELDER taught film and English at Lake Erie College and Lakeland Community College (Ohio) and Fitchburg State College and Assumption College (Massachusetts) before assuming her current post as Coordinator of English for the Worcester, Massachusetts, Public Schools. She has published in *Style, American Quarterly,* and *Western Humanities Review*.

STEVEN DIMEO received a Ph.D. from the University of Utah and resides in Hillsboro, Oregon, where he edits *Transition, The Literary Magazine for a World of Change*. He has published in *Riverside Quarterly* and the *Journal of Popular Culture*.

WILLIAM K. EVERSON teaches in the Cinema Studies Department, New York University, and is the coauthor of *The Western from Silents to the Seventies* (1973) and many other books on film. During World War II he became, at age fourteen, Publicity Director of Renown Pictures Corporation in England.

BRANDON FRENCH is an Assistant Professor of English at Yale University and Curator of the Yale College of Classic Films. Her independently produced film, *Brandy in the Wilderness* (1969) won prizes at Ann Arbor and Cannes. She is writing a book on women and the movies for Frederick Ungar Publishing Co.

DOUGLAS GOMERY teaches film history and criticism in the Department of Mass Communication at the University of Wisconsin, Milwaukee. He has published articles in *Screen,* the *Quarterly Review of Film Studies, Cinema Journal,* and in several anthologies about the history of the American film industry.

SIDNEY GOTTLIEB is Assistant Professor of English at Sacred Heart University in Bridgeport, Connecticut, where he edits the *George Herbert Journal*. He is also a teacher of karate and leader of Heavy Trucking, a central New Jersey rock band.

MOLLY HASKELL is film critic for *New York* magazine and author of *From Reverence to Rape: The Treatment of Women in the Movies* (1974). She also has written for *Ms., Viva, Film Comment,* and has contributed many articles to the *Village Voice*.

JOSEPH HELLER is the author of *Something Happened* (1974).

Stuart M. Kaminsky teaches film history in the Division of Film, Northwestern University, Evanston, Illinois. He is the author of *American Film Genres* (1974), *Ingmar Bergman: Essays in Criticism* (1975), new volumes on John Huston and William Wyler, and two detective novels.

Michael Klein is an Assistant Professor of film and English at Livingston College, Rutgers University. He has written criticism for *Film Quarterly, Cineaste,* and *The Velvet Light Trap,* and is currently preparing an anthology on the British novel and the movies for Frederick Ungar Publishing Co.

Norman Mailer satirized Hollywood in *The Deer Park* (1955) and then gave the movies a second look in *Marilyn* (1973).

Kevin McGann did graduate work in English at the University of Delaware and the University of Wisconsin and is currently employed by the city of Madison, Wisconsin.

Patrick McGilligan is film and music editor of the *Boston Real Paper* and author of *Ginger Rogers* (1975) and *James Cagney: The Actor as Auteur* (1975). He is completing a book on Karl Armstrong, jailed in Wisconsin for blowing up the Army Math Research Center in 1969.

Robert L. Nadeau is Assistant Professor of English and American Studies at George Mason University. He has published critical studies of William Melvin Kelley and Djuna Barnes and is working on a book-length study of William Faulkner.

Constance Pohl has taught at Livingston College, Rutgers University, and Hofstra University while preparing her doctoral dissertation on *King Lear* for the University of Wisconsin, Madison. A free-lance journalist, she has written for *Seven Days* and reported for WBAI-FM in New York City.

Robert C. Rosen is Assistant Professor of English at William Patterson College (N.J.). He is a member of the Editorial Group responsible for the *Radical Teacher* and has contributed to *Jump Cut.*

William Rothman received his Ph.D. in philosophy from Harvard University. He taught Cinema Studies at New York University and is presently Research Associate and Lecturer in Visual and Environmental Studies at Carpenter Center, Harvard University.

Gary Seigal is currently completing his doctoral work at Rutgers

University and is teaching English at Mission College in San Fernando, California.

MICHAEL STERN has taught film at Wesleyan University in Connecticut and Columbia University, where he is completing his doctoral work. He is coauthor of several books of Americana, including *Road Food* with Jane Stern.

ROBERT TAYLOR is an arts editor for the *Boston Globe* and offers, pseudonymously, a regular column of literary satire in *The Atlantic Monthly*.

WILLIAM WALLING is Professor of English at University College, Rutgers University, specializing in the English Romantics, the novel, and film. His latest book, *The Romantic Image* (Yale University Press, 1978), concerns literature and the visual arts.

PAUL WARSHOW attended Reed College and Columbia University and he has an M.A. in Communications from Stanford University. He has published cinema and literary criticism in *Film Quarterly* and *Commentary* and taught film at the University of California, Santa Barbara.

ROBIN WOOD teaches film at York University, Toronto, and has written book-length studies of Arthur Penn, Howard Hawks, Ingmar Bergman, Claude Chabrol, and Alfred Hitchcock. His articles appear regularly in *Film Comment* and *Movie*, and his latest book is *Personal Views: Explorations in Style* from Gordon Fraser, London.

THE EDITORS

GERALD PEARY is Assistant Professor of English and Film at Livingston College, Rutgers University, and is the author of *Rita Hayworth* (1976) and coeditor of *Women and the Cinema* (1977) and *The Classic American Novel and the Movies* (1977). His articles and reviews have appeared in *Film Comment, The Velvet Light Trap, Jump Cut,* and *Film Heritage,* and he writes regularly for the Boston *Real Paper*.

ROGER SHATZKIN is Instructor of English and Film at University College, Rutgers University. He is coeditor of *The Classic American Novel and the Movies* (1977). His articles and reviews on film and literature have appeared in *Society, The Velvet Light Trap, Rolling Stone,* and the *Journal of Jazz Studies*.

SOURCES FOR FILMS LISTED
IN FILM CREDITS AND FILMOGRAPHY

AB
Audio Brandon Films
  (Macmillan)
34 MacQuesten Parkway South
Mount Vernon, New York 10550
(914) 664-5051
  or
1619 North Cherokee
Los Angeles, California 90028
(213) 463-0357
  or
Branch offices in Oakland,
Dallas, and Brookfield, Illinois

ARG
Argosy Film Service
1939 Central Street
Evanston, Illinois 60201
(312) 491-9090

BUD
Budget Films
4590 Santa Monica Blvd.
Los Angeles, California 90029
(213) 660-0187

CIV
Cinema 5-16mm.
595 Madison Avenue
New York, New York 10022
(212) 421-5555

CON
Contemporary/McGraw Hill
  Films
Princeton Road
Hightstown, New Jersey 08520
(609) 448-1700
  or
828 Custer Avenue
Evanston, Illinois 60202
(312) 869-5010
  or
1714 Stockton Street
San Francisco, California 94133
(415) 362-3115

CWF
Clem Williams Films, Inc.
2240 Noblestown Road
Pittsburg, Pennsylvania 15205
(412) 921-5810
  or

Branch offices in Atlanta,
Chicago, and Houston

FI
Films Incorporated
4420 Oakton Street
Skokie, Illinois 60076
(312) 676-1088
or
440 Park Avenue South
New York, New York 10016
(212) 889-7910
or
5625 Hollywood Boulevard
Hollywood, California 90028
(213) 466-5481
or
Branch offices in Atlanta, Boston,
Salt Lake City, and San Diego

GRO
Grove Films
196 West Houston Street
New York, New York 10014
(212) 242-4900

HUR
Hurlock Cine World, Inc.
13 Arcadia Road
Greenwich, Connecticut 06870
(203) 637-4319

ICS
Institutional Cinema Service
915 Broadway
New York, New York 10010
(212) 673-3990

ILL
University of Illinois
Visual Aids Service
Div. of University Extension
704 S. Sixth Street
Champaign, Illinois 61820
(217) 333-1360

IVY
IVY Film
165 West 46th Street
New York, New York 10036
(212) 765-3940

JAN
Janus Films
745 Fifth Avenue
New York, New York 10022
(212) 753-7100

KPF
Kit Parker Films
Box 227
Carmel Valley, California 93924
(408) 659-4131

MMA
Museum of Modern Art
11 West 53rd Street
New York, New York 10019
(212) 956-4205

MOD
Modern Sound Pictures
1402 Howard Street
Omaha, Nebraska 68102
(402) 341-8476

MOG
Mogull's
235 West 46th Street
New York, New York 10036
(212) 757-1414

MOT
Mottas Films
1318 Ohio Avenue N.E.
Canton, Ohio 44705
(216) 494-6058

NYF
New Yorker Films
43 West 61st Street
New York, New York 10023
(212) 247-6110

PNX
Phoenix Films
470 Park Avenue South
New York, New York 10016
(212) 684-5910

RBC
rbc Films
933 N. LaBrea Avenue
Los Angeles, California 90038
(213) 874-7330

ROA
Roa's Films
1696 N. Astor Street
Milwaukee, Wisconsin 53202
(414) 271-0861

SEL
Select Film Library
115 West 31st Street
New York, New York 10001
(212) 594-4500

SWA
Swank Motion Pictures
201 S. Jefferson Avenue
St. Louis, Missouri 63166
(314) 534-6300
            or
393 Front Street
Hempstead, New York 11550
(516) 538-6500
            or
6767 Forest Lawn Drive
Hollywood, California 90068
(213) 851-6300
            or
Branch offices in Braintree,
Massachusetts; Chicago;
Washington, D.C.; and
Houston

TFC
"The" Film Center
915 12th Street, N.W.
Washington, D.C. 20005
(202) 393-1205

TWY
Twyman Films
321 Salem Avenue
Dayton, Ohio 45401
(513) 222-4014

UA
United Artists Sixteen
729 Seventh Avenue
New York, New York 10019
(212) 575-3000

UF
United Films
1425 South Main
Tulsa, Oklahoma 74119
(918) 583-2681

UNI
Universal Sixteen
445 Park Avenue
New York, New York 10022
(212) 759-7500
    or
2001 South Vermont Avenue
Los Angeles, California 90007
(213) 731-2151
    or
Branch offices in Atlanta,
Chicago, and Dallas

USF
U.S. Film Office
230 Park Avenue
New York, New York 10017
(212) 689-5859

WCF
Westcoast Films
25 Lusk Street
San Francisco, California 94107
(415) 362-4700

WHO
Wholesome Film Center
20 Melrose Street
Boston, Massachusetts 02116
(617) 426-0155

ZIP
Zipporah Films
54 Lewis Wharf
Boston, Massachusetts 02110
(617) 742-6680

NOTE: For reasons of space this is a selected list of distributors, chosen by regional representation. For more complete information on film rental sources, see James L. Limbacher, ed., *Feature Films on 8mm and 16mm,* 5th ed. N.Y.: R. R. Bowker, 1977 and Kathleen Weaver, ed., *Film Programmer's Guide to 16mm Rentals,* 2nd ed. Berkeley, Calif.: Reel Research, 1975.

Film leasing arrangements change frequently. Since this list was compiled, we have noted the following changes: Much of the Contemporary/ McGraw Hill feature film catalog has been taken over by Corinth Films, Inc., 410 East 62nd Street, New York, New York 10021 (212-421-4720); Swank Motion Pictures has assumed distribution of Warners films made after 1950 and previously available from Warners Non-Theatrical Division.

FILM CREDITS

CODE: P: Production Company/Producer (when pertinent); R: Releasing-Distribution Company (when different from Production Co.); D: Director; Sc: Screenplay; Ph: Photography (c: color; ws: wide-screen); M: Music; C: Cast; (RENTAL SOURCE[S]).* Films are listed in order of discussion in this volume.

Tobacco Road (1941). P: Twentieth Century-Fox/Darryl F. Zanuck. D: John Ford. Sc: Nunnally Johnson, adapted from stage play by Jack Kirkland. Ph: Arthur C. Miller. M: David Buttolph. C: Charley Grapewin, Marjorie Rambeau, Gene Tierney, William Tracy, Elizabeth Patterson, Dana Andrews, Slim Summerville, Ward Bond, Grant Mitchell, Zeffie Tilbury. (AB, KPF, BUD, SEL, SWA, UF, WCF, WHO)

Lonelyhearts (1959). P: Dore Schary. R: United Artists. D: Vincent J. Donehue. Sc: Dore Schary, based on Nathenael West novel and play by Howard Teichmann. Ph: John Alton. M: Conrad Salinger. C: Montgomery Clift, Robert Ryan, Myrna Loy, Dolores Hart, Maureen Stapleton, Frank Maxwell, Jackie Coogan. (UA)

They Shoot Horses, Don't They? (1969). P: ABC/Irwin Winkler, Robert Chartoff. R: Cinerama Releasing. D: Sydney Pollack. Sc: James Poe, Robert E. Thompson. Ph(c/ws): Philip H. Lathrop. M: John Green. C: Jane Fonda, Michael Sarrazin, Susannah York, Gig Young, Red Buttons, Bonnie Bedelia, Michael Conrad, Bruce Dern. (FI)

The Tarnished Angels (1957). P: Universal/Albert Zugsmith. D: Douglas Sirk. Sc: George Zuckerman. PH(ws): Irving Glassberg.

* See pp. 340–343 for key to abbreviations used.

344

M: Frank Skinner, Joseph Gershenson. C: Rock Hudson, Robert Stack, Dorothy Malone, Jack Carson, Robert Middleton, Alan Reed, Chris Olsen, Troy Donahue. (UNI))

The Treasure of the Sierra Madre (1948). P: Warners. D/Sc: John Huston. Ph: Ted McCord. M: Max Steiner. C: Humphrey Bogart, Walter Huston, Tim Holt, Bruce Bennett, Barton MacLane, Alfonso Bedoya. (UA)

Of Mice and Men (1940). P: Hal Roach/Lewis Milestone. R: United Artists. D: Lewis Milestone. Sc: Eugene Solow. Ph: Norbert Brodine. M: Aaron Copland. C: Burgess Meredith, Betty Field, Lon Chaney, Jr., Charles Bickford, Roman Bohnen, Bob Steele, Noah Beery, Jr., Leigh Whipper. (USF)

To Have and Have Not (1944). P: Warners/Howard Hawks. D: Howard Hawks. Sc: Jules Furthman, William Faulkner. Ph: Sid Hickox. M: Franz Waxman. C: Humphrey Bogart, Lauren Bacall, Walter Brennan, Dolores Moran, Hoagy Carmichael, Walter Molnar, Sheldon Leonard, Marcel Dalio. (UA)

The Big Sleep (1946). P: Warners/Howard Hawks. D: Howard Hawks. Sc: Leigh Brackett, William Faulkner, Jules Furthman. Ph: Sidney Hickcox. M: Max Steiner. C: Humphrey Bogart, Lauren Bacall, John Ridgely, Martha Vickers, Dorothy Malone, Peggy Knudsen, Regis Toomey, Charles Waldren, Elisha Cook, Jr. (UA)

The Day of the Locust (1975). P: Jerome Hellman. R: Paramount. D: John Schlesinger. Sc: Waldo Salt. Ph(c): Conrad Hall. M: John Barry. C: Karen Black, Donald Sutherland, William Atherton, Burgess Meredith, Richard A. Dysart, Billy Barty, Jackie Haley (FI)

The Grapes of Wrath (1940). P: Twentieth Century-Fox/Darryl F. Zanuck. D: John Ford. Sc: Nunnally Johnson. Ph: Gregg Toland. M: Alfred Newman. C: Henry Fonda, Jane Darwell, John Carradine, Charley Grapewin, Dorris Bowdon, Russell Simpson, O. Z. Whitehead, John Qualen. (FI)

The Heart Is a Lonely Hunter (1968). P: Warners-Seven Arts. D: Robert Ellis Miller. Sc: Thomas C. Ryan. Ph: James Wong Howe. M: David Grusin. C: Sondra Locke, Alan Arkin, Laurinda Barrett, Stacy Keach, Jr., Chuck McCann, Biff McGuire, Percy Rodriguez, Cicely Tyson, Jackie Marlowe. (AB, BUD, CON, CWF, ICS, TWY, WCF, WHO)

Native Son (1951). P: James Prades, Walter Gould. R: Classic Pictures. D: Pierre Chenal. Sc: Richard Wright, P. Chenal; dialogue—R. Wright. Ph: A. V. Meray. M: John Elhert. C: Richard Wright, Jean Wallace, Nicholas Joy, Gloria Madison, Charles Cane, Jean Michael, Willa Pearl Curtis, Don Dean. (−)

In This Our Life (1942). P: Warners/Hal B. Wallis. D: John Huston. Sc: Howard Koch. Ph: Ernie Haller. M: Max Steiner. C: Bette Davis, Olivia de Havilland, George Brent, Dennis Morgan, Charles Coburn, Frank Craven, Billie Burke. (UA)

The Human Comedy (1943). P: MGM/Howard Estabrook. D: Clarence Brown. Sc: Howard Estabrook. Ph: Harry Stradling. M: Herbert Stothart. C: Mickey Rooney, James Craig, Frank Morgan, Fay Bainter, Marsha Hunt, Van Johnson, Donna Reed, Ray Collins. (FI)

All the King's Men (1949). P: Columbia/Robert Rossen. D/Sc: Robert Rossen. Ph: Burnett Guffey. M: Morris Stoloff. C: Broderick Crawford, John Derek, Joanne Dru, John Ireland, Mercedes McCambridge, Sheppard Strudwick, Ralph Dumke, Ann Seymour, Raymond Greenleaf. (AB, BUD, CON, CWF, ICS, SWA, TFC, WCF, WHO)

Intruder in the Dust (1949). P: MGM/Clarence Brown. D: Clarence Brown. Sc: Ben Maddow. Ph: Robert Surtees. M: Adoph Deutsch. C: David Brian, Claude Jarman, Jr., Juano Hernandez, Porter Hall, Elizabeth Patterson, Charles Kemper, Will Geer, David Clark. (FI)

The Naked and the Dead (1958). P: RKO. R: Warners. D: Raoul Walsh. Sc: Denis and Terry Sanders. Ph(c/ws): Joseph LaShelle. M: Bernard Hermann. C: Aldo Ray, Cliff Robertson, Raymond Massey, Lili St. Cyr, Barbara Nichols. (BUD, UF)

The Man with the Golden Arm (1955). P: United Artists/Otto Preminger. D: Otto Preminger. Sc: Walter Newman, Lewis Meltzer. Ph: Sam Leavitt. M: Elmer Bernstein. C: Frank Sinatra, Eleanor Parker, Kim Novak, Arnold Stang, Darren McGavin, Robert Strauss, John Conte, Doro Merande. (−)

The Old Man and the Sea (1958). P: Warners/Leland Hayward. D: John Sturges. Sc: Peter Viertel. Ph(c): James Wong Howe. M: Dmitri Tiomkin. C: Spencer Tracy, Felipe Pazos, Harry Bellaver. (CON, CWF, ICS, TWY, WCF)

Night of the Hunter (1955). P: United Artists/Paul Gregory. D: Charles Laughton. Sc: James Agee. Ph: Stanley Cortez. M: Walter Schumann. C: Robert Mitchum, Shelley Winters, Lillian Gish, Evelyn Varden, Peter Graves, Billy Chapin, James Gleason. (UA)

The Last Hurrah (1958). P: Columbia/John Ford. D: John Ford. Sc: Frank Nugent. Ph: Charles Lawton, Jr. C: Spencer Tracy,

Jeffrey Hunter, Dianne Foster, Pat O'Brien, Basil Rathbone, Donald Crisp, James Gleason, Edward Brophy, John Carradine, Willis Bouchey, Basil Ruysdael, Ricardo Cortez, Wallace Ford, Frank McHugh. (AB, ARG, BUD, CON, CWF, TWY, WCF, WHO)

Lolita (1962, Gr. Britain). P: Seven Arts/Anya/Transworld. R: MGM. D: Stanley Kubrick. Sc: Vladimir Nabokov. Ph: Oswald Morris. M: Nelson Riddle. C: James Mason, Sue Lyon, Shelley Winters, Peter Sellers, Diana Decker, Marianne Stone. (FI)

Breakfast at Tiffany's (1961). P: Paramount. D: Blake Edwards. Sc: George Axelrod. Ph: Franz Planer. M: Henry Mancini/"Moon River" lyrics—Johnny Mercer. C: Audrey Hepburn, George Peppard, Patricia Neal, Buddy Ebsen, Martin Balsam, Villalonga, John McGiver, Alan Reed, Dorothy Whitney, Stanley Adams, Mickey Rooney. (FI)

Rabbit, Run (1970). P: Warners/Howard B. Kreitsek. D: Jack Smight. Sc: Howard B. Kreitsek. Ph(c/ws): Philip Lathrop. M: Sonny Burke. C: James Caan, Anjanette Comer, Jack Albertson, Melodie Johnson, Carrie Snodgrass, Henry Jones, Carmen Mathews. (SWA)

Catch-22 (1970). P: Paramount. D: Mike Nichols. Sc: Buck Henry. Ph(c): David Watkin. M: John Hammell. C: Alan Arkin, Martin Balsam, Richard Benjamin, Art Garfunkel, Jack Gilford, Bob Newhart, Anthony Perkins, Paula Prentiss, Martin Sheen, Jon Voight, Orson Welles, Charles Grodin, Buck Henry. (FI)

One Flew Over the Cuckoo's Nest (1975). P: Fantasy Films. R: United Artists. D: Milos Forman. Sc: Lawrence Hauben, Bo Goldman. Ph(c): Haskell Wexler, Bill Butler, William Fraker. M: Jack Nitzsche. C: Jack Nicholson, Louise Fletcher, Brad Dourif, William Redfield, Will Sampson, Marya Small. (UA)

Little Big Man (1970). P: Cinema Center Films. R: National General. D: Arthur Penn. Sc: Calder Willingham. Ph(c/ws): Harry Stradling, Jr. M: John Hammond, Jr. C: Dustin Hoffman, Faye Dunaway, Martin Balsam, Richard Mulligan, Chief Dan George, Jeff Corey, Amy Eccles. (SWA)

Slaughterhouse-Five (1972). P: Universal-Vanadas/George Roy Hill-Paul Monash Productions. D: George Roy Hill. Sc: Stephen Geller. Ph(c/ws): Miroslav Ondricek. M: Glenn Gould. Editor: Dede Allen. C: Michael Sacks, Ron Leibman, Eugene Roche, Sharon Gans, Valerie Perrine, John Dehner. (CWF, SWA, UNI)

Deliverance (1972). P: Warners/Elmer Enterprises/A John Boorman Film. D: John Boorman. Sc: James Dickey. Ph(c): Vilmos Zsigmond. M: Eric Weissberg. C: Jon Voight, Burt Reynolds, Ned Beatty, Ronny Cox, Bill McKinney, Herbert "Cowboy" Coward, James Dickey. (SWA)

The Wet Parade (1932). P: MGM. D: Victor Fleming. Sc: John L. Mahin. Ph: George Barnes. C: Dorothy Jordan, Lewis Stone, Neil Hamilton, Emma Dunn, Robert Young, Walter Huston, Jimmy Durante, Wallace Ford, Myrna Loy. (FI)

For Whom the Bell Tolls (1943). P: Paramount/Sam Wood. D: Sam Wood. Sc: Dudley Nichols. Ph(c): Ray Rennahan. M: Victor Young. C: Gary Cooper, Ingrid Bergman, Akim Tamiroff, Katina Paxinou, Vladimir Sokolof, Arturo de Cordova, Joseph Calleia, Mikhail Rasmuny, Fortunia Bonanova. (SWA, TWY)

The Fountainhead (1949). P: Warners. D: King Vidor. Sc: Ayn Rand. Ph: Robert Burks. M: Max Steiner. C: Gary Cooper, Patricia Neal, Raymond Massey, Kent Smith, Robert Douglas, Henry Hull, Ray Collins, Jerome Cowan. (UA)

Film Adaptations of American Novels, 1930–1975

The sheer number of novels made into films and the fact that the literary and cinematic "canon" is invariably in flux has forced us to make this a very "selected," if eclectic, listing. Our general principle has been to include those novels and films we think will be of immediate interest to film and literary scholars, to archivists and librarians. At present, there are no comprehensive reference guides for filmed adaptations, although the eventual completion of the American Film Institute Catalogues may help fill that gap. In the meantime, further information can be culled from A. G. S. Enser, *Filmed Books and Plays 1928–1974*, London: Andre Deutsch, 1975 (though Enser's reliance on British publishing sources and dates of film release creates some problems); Richard B. Dimmit, *A Title Guide to the Talkies*, 2 vols., Metuchen, N.J.: Scarecrow Press, 1970, 1971, 1973, supplemented by Andrew A. Aros, *A Title Guide to the Talkies, 1964–1974*, Scarecrow Press, 1977; *The American Film Institute Catalogue of Motion Pictures, Feature Films 1960–1970*, ed. by Richard P. Krafsur, 2 vols., N.Y.: R. R. Bowker, 1976; *The New York Times Film Reviews 1913–1968*, 6 vols., N.Y.: Arno, 1970, and the four subsequent volumes covering 1969–70 (Arno, 1971), 1971–72 (1973), 1973–74 (1975), 1975–76 (1977); *Contemporary Authors: A Bio-Bibliographical Guide to Current Authors and Their Works*, 69 vols. to date, Detroit: Gale Research Co.

Not every novel written by the authors listed that has been adapted for the screen appears here. We have not listed any "television movies" made from American novels; though this has become a trend documentation on these films is difficult to obtain. Nor have we included "novelizations."

The release date and releasing companies reflect American distribution; foreign films are listed by their American titles. An asterisk (*) indicates that an author is listed in the Filmography in *The Classic American Novel and the Movies* for novels written prior to 1930. Finally, if no rental source is indicated, this does not mean that the film is positively unavailable, only that current reference sources had no listings (see note at end of "Sources for Films Listed in Film Credits and Filmography").

The first listing (I) is alphabetical by author; the second (II) is alphabetical by film title. Both include cross references when novel and film titles differ.

I / *By Author*

Author—Title	Film Version: Title (if changed) Production or Releasing Company, Release Date Director (d)	Rental Source(s)
AGEE, James (1901–55)		
A Death in the Family (1957)	*All the Way Home* Paramount, 1963 (d) Alex Segal	FI
ALGREN, Nelson (1909–)		
The Man with the Golden Arm (1949)	United Artists, 1956 (d) Otto Preminger	—
A Walk on the Wild Side (1956)	Columbia, 1962 (d) Edward Dmytryk	AB, BUD, CON, CWF, ICS, MOD
ANDERSON, Edward (1905–)		
Thieves Like Us (1937)	*They Live By Night* RKO, 1949 (d) Nicholas Ray	FI
	United Artists, 1974 (d) Robert Altman	UA

Author—Title	Film Version: Title (if changed) Production or Releasing Company, Release Date Director (d)	Rental Source(s)
ARMSTRONG, William H. (1914–) *Sounder* (1969)	20th Century-Fox, 1972 (d) Martin Ritt	FI
BAKER, Dorothy (1907–68) *Young Man with a Horn* (1938)	Warners, 1950 (d) Michael Curtiz	AB, ARG, WHO
BAKER, Elliott (1922–) *A Fine Madness* (1964)	Warners, 1966 (d) Irving Kershner	AB, BUD, CWF, ICS, MOD, MOT, SWA, TWY, UF
BARTH, John (1930–) *The End of the Road* (1958)	Allied Artists, 1970 (d) Aram Avakian	HUR

BENCHLEY, Nathaniel (1915–   )

The Off-Islanders (1961)

The Russians Are Coming,
The Russians Are Coming
United Artists, 1966
(d) Norman Jewison

UA

BENCHLEY, Peter (1940–   )

Jaws (1974)

Universal, 1975
(d) Steven Spielberg

UNI

BENSON, Sally (1900–72)

Meet Me in St. Louis (1942)

MGM, 1944
(d) Vincente Minnelli

FI

BERGER, Thomas (1924–   )

Little Big Man (1964)

National General, 1970
(d) Arthur Penn

SWA

BEZZERIDES, A[lbert] I[saac] (1908–   )

Long Haul (1938)

They Drive By Night
Warners, 1940
(d) Raoul Walsh

UA

BLATTY, William Peter (1928–   )

The Exorcist (1973)

Warners, 1974
(d) William Friedkin

SWA

Author—Title	Film Version: Title (if changed) Production or Releasing Company, Release Date Director (d)	Rental Source(s)
Thieves Market (1949)	*Thieves Highway* 20th Century-Fox, 1949 (d) Jules Dassin	FI
BLOCH, Robert (1917–) *Psycho* (1959)	Paramount, 1960 (d) Alfred Hitchcock	CWF, TWY, UNI
BOYLE, Kay (1903–) *Avalanche* (1944)	PRC, 1946 (d) Irving Allen	IVY
BRACKETT, Leigh (1915–78) *The Tiger Among Us* (1957)	*13 West Street* Columbia, 1962 (d) Philip Leacock	MOD

BRADBURY, Ray (1920–)
Fahrenheit 451 (1953)

Fr. 1966
(d) Francois Truffaut

AB, CWF, MOD, ROA,
SWA, TWY, UNI, WCF

BRADFORD, Richard
Red Sky at Morning (1968)

Universal, 1971
(d) James Goldstone

CWF, SWA, TWY, UNI

BRAND, Max [Frederick Faust]
(1892–1944)
Destry Rides Again (1930)

Universal, 1932
(d) Ben Stoloff

UNI

Universal, 1939
(d) George Marshall

SWA, TWY, UNI

Destry
Universal, 1954
(d) George Marshall

UNI

Author—Title	Film Version: Title (if changed) Production or Releasing Company, Release Date Director (d)	Rental Source(s)
Brown, Harry [Peter M'Nab] (1917–)		
A Walk in the Sun (1944)	20th Century-Fox, 1945 (d) Lewis Milestone	BUD
The Stars in Their Courses (1960)	*El Dorado* Paramount, 1967 (d) Howard Hawks	—
Brown, Joe David (1915–76)		
Addie Pray (1971)	*Paper Moon* Paramount, 1973 (d) Peter Bogdanovich	FI
Brown, Will C. [C. Scott Boyles, Jr.] (1905–)		
The Border Jumpers (1955)	*Man of the West* United Artists, 1958 (d) Anthony Mann	UA

BRYANT, Peter [Peter Bryan George]
(1924–　)

Red Alert (1958)

*Dr. Strangelove, or: How I
Learned to Stop Worrying
and Love the Bomb*
Columbia, 1964
(d) Stanley Kubrick .... SWA

BUCK, Pearl (1892–1973)

The Good Earth (1931)
MGM, 1937
(d) Sidney Franklin .... FI

The Dragon Seed (1942)
MGM, 1944
(d) Jack Conway .... FI

BURDICK, Eugene (1918–65) and
Harvey WHEELER (1918–　)

Fail-Safe (1962)
Columbia, 1964
(d) Sidney Lumet .... AB, ARG, BUD, CWF,
KPF, MOD, ROA, SEL,
SWA, TWY, UF, WCF,
WHO

Author—Title	Film Version: Title (if changed) Production or Releasing Company, Release Date Director (d)	Rental Source(s)
* BURNETT, W[illiam] R[iley] (1899–)		
Iron Man (1930)	*The Iron Man* Universal, 1931 (d) Tod Browning	UNI
	Universal, 1951 (d) Joseph Pevney	UNI
The Dark Command (1938)	*Dark Command* Republic, 1940 (d) Raoul Walsh	IVY
High Sierra (1940)	Warners, 1941 (d) Raoul Walsh	UA
	Colorado Territory Warners, 1949 (d) Raoul Walsh	UA
	I Died a Thousand Times Warners, 1955 (d) Stuart Heisler	—

Nobody Lives Forever (1943)   Warners, 1946   (d) Jean Negulesco   UA

The Asphalt Jungle (1949)   MGM, 1950   (d) John Huston   FI

   The Badlanders   MGM, 1958   (d) Delmer Daves   FI

   Cairo   MGM, 1962   (d) Wolf Rilla   FI

   Cool Breeze   MGM, 1972   (d) Barry Pollack   FI

Captain Lightfoot (1954)   Universal, 1955   (d) Douglas Sirk   UNI

BUSCH, Niven (1903–)

Duel in the Sun (1944)   Selznick, 1946   (d) King Vidor   AB, BUD, MOT, ROA, SEL, TWY, UF, WHO

Author—Title	Film Version: Title (if changed) Production or Releasing Company, Release Date Director (d)	Rental Source(s)
CAIN, James M. (1892–1977)		
The Postman Always Rings Twice (1934)	*Ossessione* Ital., 1942 (d) Luchino Visconti	AB
	MGM, 1946 (d) Tay Garnett	FI
Serenade (1937)	Warners, 1956 (d) Anthony Mann	—
Mildred Pierce (1941)	Warners, 1945 (d) Michael Curtiz	UA
Double Indemnity (1943)	Paramount, 1944 (d) Billy Wilder	UNI

CALDWELL, Erskine (1903–)

Tobacco Road (1932)   20th Century-Fox, 1941 (d) John Ford   AB, BUD, KPF, MOD, MOT, ROA, SEL, SWA, TFC, TWY, UF, WCF, WHO

God's Little Acre (1933)   United Artists, 1958 (d) Anthony Mann   UA

CAPOTE, Truman (1924–)

Breakfast at Tiffany's (1958)   Paramount, 1961 (d) Blake Edwards   FI

In Cold Blood (1966)   Columbia, 1967 (d) Richard Brooks   SWA

CARLINO, Lewis John (1932–)

The Brotherhood (1968)   Paramount, 1968 (d) Martin Ritt   FI

CASPARY, Vera (c. 1899–)

Laura (1943)   20th Century-Fox, 1944 (d) Otto Preminger   FI

Author—Title	Film Version: Title (if changed) Production or Releasing Company, Release Date Director (d)	Rental Source(s)
CHANDLER, Raymond (1888–1959)		
The Big Sleep (1939)	Warners, 1946 (d) Howard Hawks	UA
	United Artists, 1978 (d) Michael Winner	UA
Farewell, My Lovely (1940)	*The Falcon Takes Over* RKO, 1942 (d) Irving Reis	FI
	Murder, My Sweet RKO, 1944 (d) Edward Dmytryk	FI
	Avco-Embassy, 1975 (d) Dick Richards	SWA
The High Window (1942)	*The Brasher Doubloon* 20th Century-Fox, 1947 (d) John Brahm	FI

The Lady in the Lake (1943) — MGM, 1946 (d) Robert Montgomery — FI

The Little Sister (1949) — *Marlowe* MGM, 1969 (d) Paul Bogart — FI

The Long Goodbye (1954) — United Artists, 1973 (d) Robert Altman — UA

CHANSLOR, Roy (1899–1964)

Johnny Guitar (1953) — Republic, 1954 (d) Nicholas Ray — IVY

The Ballad of Cat Ballou (1956) — *Cat Ballou* Columbia, 1965 (d) Elliott Silverstein — AB, ARG, BUD, CWF, ICS, MOD, MOT, ROA, SEL, SWA, TFC, TWY, UF, WHO

CHASE, Borden (1900–71)

Blazing Guns on the Chisholm Trail (1948) — *Red River* United Artists, 1948 (d) Howard Hawks — UA

Author—Title	Film Version: Title (if changed) Production or Releasing Company, Release Date Director (d)	Rental Source(s)
CLARK, Walter van Tilburg (1909–71)		
The Ox-Bow Incident (1940)	20th Century-Fox, 1943 (d) William Wellman	FI
The Track of the Cat (1949)	*Track of the Cat* Warners, 1954 (d) William Wellman	—
CLAVELL, James (1942–)		
King Rat (1962)	Columbia, 1965 (d) Bryan Forbes	AB, ARG, BUD, CWF, MOD, ROA, SWA, TWY, WCF, WHO
COATES, Robert M. (1897–1973)		
Wisteria Cottage (1948)	*Edge of Fury* United Artists, 1958 (d) Irving Lerner	YA
COBB, Humphrey (1912–)		
Paths of Glory (1935)	United Artists, 1957 (d) Stanley Kubrick	UA

CONDON, Richard (1915–   )

The Manchurian Candidate (1959)   United Artists, 1962   UA
                                     (d) John Frankenheimer

COZZENS, James Gould (1903–   )

The Last Adam (1933)   *Dr. Bull*
                     Fox, 1933   FI
                     (d) John Ford

By Love Possessed (1957)   United Artists, 1961   UA
                            (d) John Sturges

CRICHTON, Michael (1942–   )

The Andromeda Strain (1969)   Universal, 1971   CWF, SWA, TWY, UNI
                              (d) Robert Wise

The Terminal Man (1972)   Warners, 1974   SWA
                          (d) Mike Hodges

DeVRIES, Peter (1910–   )

Tunnel of Love (1954)   MGM, 1958   FI
                     (d) Gene Kelly

Author—Title	Film Version: Title (if changed) Production or Releasing Company, Release Date Director (d)	Rental Source(s)
Let Me Count the Ways (1965)	*How Do I Love Thee?* ABC, 1970 (d) Michael Gordon	FI
The Cat's Pajamas and Witch's Milk (1968)	*Pete 'n' Tillie* Universal, 1972 (d) Martin Ritt	CWF, UNI
DICKEY, James (1923–　)		
Deliverance (1970)	Warners, 1972 (d) John Boorman	SWA
DIDION, Joan (1934–　)		
Play It As It Lays (1970)	Universal, 1972 (d) Frank Perry	UNI
DOCTOROW, E. L. (1931–　)		
Welcome to Hard Times (1960)	MGM, 1967 (d) Burt Kennedy	FI

Di Donato, Pietro (1911–)
Christ in Concrete (1939)

Give Us This Day
General Film, 1949
(d) Edward Dmytryk
new release, 1978   —

Douglas, Lloyd C. (1877–1951)
The Robe (1942)

20th Century-Fox, 1953
(d) Henry Koster   FI

Drought, James (1931–)
The Gypsy Moths (1964)

MGM, 1969
(d) John Frankenheimer   FI

Drury, Allen (1918–)
Advise and Consent (1959)

Columbia, 1962
(d) Otto Preminger   AB, ARG, BUD, CWF,
                                                    MOT, SEL, SWA, WHO

Edmonds, Walter D. (1903–)
Drums Along the Mohawk (1936)

20th Century Fox, 1939
(d) John Ford   FI

Author—Title	Film Version: Title (if changed) Production or Releasing Company, Release Date Director (d)	Rental Source(s)
ELKIN, Stanley (1930–)		
The Bailbondsman (in *Searches and Seizures*, 1973)	*Alex and the Gypsy* 20th Century-Fox, 1976 (d) John Korty	FI
FARRELL, Henry		
What Ever Happened to Baby Jane? (1960)	Warners, 1962 (d) Robert Aldrich	AB, ARG, BUD, MOD, MOT, ROA, SEL, SWA, TFC, UF, WCF, WHO
Such a Gorgeous Kid Like Me (1967)	Fr., 1973 (d) Francois Truffaut	SWA
FARRELL, James T. (1904–)		
Studs Lonigan (1935)	United Artists, 1960 (d) Irving Lerner	UA

FAST, Howard (1914–   )

Spartacus (1952) — Universal, 1960 / (d) Stanley Kubrick — TWY, UNI

* FAULKNER, William (1897–1962)

Sanctuary (1931) — *The Story of Temple Drake* Paramount, 1933 / (d) Stephen Roberts — —

Sanctuary/Requiem for a Nun (1951) — *Sanctuary* 20th Century-Fox, 1961 / (d) Tony Richardson — AB, ICS, MOD

Pylon (1935) — *The Tarnished Angels* Universal, 1957 / (d) Douglas Sirk — UNI

The Hamlet (1940) — *The Long Hot Summer* 20th Century-Fox, 1958 / (d) Martin Ritt — FI

Intruder in the Dust (1948) — MGM, 1949 / (d) Clarence Brown — FI

Requiem for a Nun (1951)—see Sanctuary

The Reivers (1962) — National General, 1969 / (d) Mark Rydell — SWA

Author—Title	Film Version: Title (if changed) Production or Releasing Company, Release Date Director (d)	Rental Source(s)
FEARING, Kenneth (1902–61)		
The Big Clock (1946)	Paramount, 1948 (d) John Farrow	UNI
* FERBER, Edna (1887–1968)		
Cimarron (1930)	RKO, 1931 (d) Wesley Ruggles	FI
	MGM, 1960 (d) Anthony Mann	FI
Come and Get It (1935)	Goldwyn, 1936 (d) Howard Hawks	AB, BUD
Saratoga Trunk (1941)	Warners, 1945 (d) Sam Wood	—
Giant (1950)	Warners, 1956 (d) George Stevens	AB, BUD, CWF, ICS, SEL, TFC, WCF, WHO

Ice Palace (1958)

Warners, 1960
(d) Vincent Sherman   SWA

FINNEY, Jack

The Body Snatchers (1955)

Invasion of the Body Snatchers
Allied Artists, 1956
(d) Don Siegel   IVY
New release, 1978

* FITZGERALD, F. Scott (1896–1940)

Tender Is the Night (1934)

20th Century-Fox, 1962
(d) Henry King   FI

The Last Tycoon (1941)

Paramount, 1976
(d) Elia Kazan   FI

FUCHS, Daniel (1909–)

Low Company (1937)

The Gangster
Allied Artists, 1947
(d) Gordon Wiles   HUR

GANN, Ernest K. (1910–)

Island in the Sky (1944)

Warners, 1953
(d) William Wellman   —

Author—Title	Film Version: Title (if changed) Production or Releasing Company, Release Date Director (d)	Rental Source(s)
The High and the Mighty	Warners, 1954 (d) William Wellman	—
GARDNER, Leonard *Fat City* (1969)	Columbia, 1972 (d) John Huston	SWA
GARFIELD, Brian (1939–) *Death Wish* (1972)	Paramount, 1974 (d) Michael Winner	FI
GLASGOW, Ellen (1874–1945) *In This Our Life* (1941)	Warners, 1942 (d) John Huston	UA
GOLDMAN, William (1931–) *Soldier in the Rain* (1960)	Allied Artists, 1963 (d) Ralph Nelson	HUR

No Way to Treat a Lady (1964)	Paramount, 1968 (d) Jack Smight	FI
GOODIS, David (1917–67) *Dark Passage* (1946)	Warners, 1947 (d) Delmer Daves	UA
Nightfall (1947)	Columbia, 1956 (d) Jacques Tourneur	ICS, TFC
Down There (1956)	*Shoot the Piano Player* Fr., 1960 (d) Francois Truffaut	JAN
GOULD, Lois *Such Good Friends* (1972)	Paramount, 1972 (d) Otto Preminger	FI
GREENBERG, Joanne (originally as Hannah Green) *I Never Promised You a Rose Garden* (1964)	New World Pictures, 1977 (d) Anthony Page	—

Author—Title	Film Version: Title (if changed) Production or Releasing Company, Release Date Director (d)	Rental Source(s)
GREENLEE, Sam (1930–)		
The Spook Who Sat by the Door (1969)	United Artists, 1973 (d) Ivan Dixon	UA
GRESHAM, William Lindsay (1909–62)		
Nightmare Alley (1946)	20th Century-Fox, 1947 (d) Edmund Goulding	FI
GRUBB, Davis (1919–)		
Night of the Hunter (1953)	United Artists, 1955 (d) Charles Laughton	UA
GUTHRIE, A[lfred] B[ertram], Jr. (1901–)		
The Big Sky (1947)	RKO, 1952 (d) Howard Hawks	FI

The Way West (1949)

United Artists, 1967
(d) Andrew V. McLaglen

UA

These Thousand Hills (1956)

20th Century Fox, 1959
(d) Richard Fleischer

FI

HALL, Oakley (1920–   )

Warlock (1958)

20th Century-Fox, 1959
(d) Edward Dmytryk

FI

The Downhill Racers (1963)

Downhill Racer
Paramount, 1969
(d) Michael Ritchie

FI

HAMILTON, Donald (1916–   )

The Wrecking Crew (1960)

Columbia, 1968
(d) Phil Karlson

AB, ARG, BUD, CWF, ICS,
ROA, SWA, TFC, TWY,
UF, WCF, WHO

HAMMETT, Dashiell (1894–1961)

The Maltese Falcon (1930)

(*The Dangerous Female*)
Warners, 1931
(d) Roy del Ruth

UA

Author—Title	Film Version: Title (if changed) Production or Releasing Company, Release Date Director (d)	Rental Source(s)
	Satan Met a Lady Warners, 1936 (d) William Dieterle	UA
	Warners, 1941 (d) John Huston	UA
The Glass Key (1931)	Paramount, 1935 (d) Frank Tuttle	—
	Paramount, 1942 (d) Stuart Heisler	UNI
The Thin Man (1934)	MGM, 1934 (d) W. S. Van Dyke	FI
HARRIS, Mark (1922–)		
Bang the Drum Slowly (1956)	Paramount, 1973 (d) John Hancock	FI

HATCH, Eric (c. 1902–73)
My Man Godfrey (1935)

Universal, 1936
(d) Gregory La Cava

BUD, KPF, UNI, WCF

HAWLEY, Cameron (1905–69)
Executive Suite (1952)

MGM, 1954
(d) Robert Wise

FI

HEGGEN, Thomas (1919–49)
Mr. Roberts (1946)

Warners, 1955
(d) John Ford/Mervyn LeRoy

AB, ARB, BUD, MOD,
MOT, ROA, TFC, TWY,
WCF, WHO

HELLER, Joseph (1923–   )
Catch-22 (1961)

Paramount, 1970
(d) Mike Nichols

FI

* HEMINGWAY, Ernest (1899–1961)
To Have and Have Not (1937)

Warners, 1944
(d) Howard Hawks

UA

Author—Title	Film Version: Title (if changed) Production or Releasing Company, Release Date Director (d)	Rental Source(s)
	The Breaking Point Warners, 1950 (d) Michael Curtiz	UA
For Whom the Bell Tolls (1940)	Paramount, 1943 (d) Sam Wood	SWA, TWY
The Old Man and the Sea (1952)	Warners, 1957 (d) John Sturges	AB
Islands in the Stream (1970)	Paramount, 1977 (d) Franklin J. Schaffner	
HERLIHY, James Leo (1927–)		
All Fall Down (1960)	MGM, 1962 (d) John Frankenheimer	FI
Midnight Cowboy (1965)	United Artists, 1969 (d) John Schlesinger	UA

HERSEY, John (1914–   )

A Bell for Adano (1944)
20th Century-Fox, 1945
(d) Henry King
FI

The War Lover (1959)
Columbia, 1963
(d) Philip Leacock
AB, ARG, CWF, WHO

HIGGINS, George V. (1939–   )

The Friends of Eddie Coyle (1972)
Paramount, 1973
(d) Peter Yates
FI

HIGHSMITH, Patricia (1921–   )

Strangers on a Train (1950)
Warners, 1951
(d) Alfred Hitchcock
SWA

Once You Kiss a Stranger
Warners, 1969
(d) Robert Speer
—

The Blunderer (1954)
Enough Rope
Fr., 1965
(d) Claude Autant-Lara
AB

The Talented Mr. Ripley
Purple Noon
Fr., 1961
(d) René Clement
AB

Author—Title	Film Version: Title (if changed) Production or Releasing Company, Release Date Director (d)	Rental Source(s)
Ripley's Game (1974)	*The American Friend* Ger., 1977 (d) Wim Wenders	NYF
HIMES, Chester (1909—)		
The Heat's On (1960)	*Come Back, Charleston Blue* Warners, 1972 (d) Mark Warren	AB, ARG, CWF, ICS, MOD, TFC, TWY, WCF, WHO
Cotton Comes to Harlem (1964)	United Artists, 1970 (d) Ossie Davis	UA
HOBSON, Laura Z. (1900—)		
Gentleman's Agreement (1947)	20th Century-Fox, 1947 (d) Elia Kazan	FI
HODGINS, Eric (1899–1971)		
Mr. Blandings Builds His Dream House (1946)	RKO, 1948 (d) H. C. Potter	FI

HOOKER, Richard
M*A*S*H* (1968) — 20th Century-Fox, 1970 (d) Robert Altman — FI

HUGHES, Dorothy B. (1904–)
The Fallen Sparrow (1942) — RKO, 1943 (d) Richard Wallace — FI

Ride the Pink Horse (1946) — Universal, 1947 (d) Robert Montgomery — UNI

In a Lonely Place (1947) — Columbia, 1950 (d) Nicholas Ray — SWA, WCF

HUIE, William Bradford (1910–)
The Revolt of Mamie Stover (1951) — 20th Century-Fox, 1956 (d) Raoul Walsh — FI

The Americanization of Emily (1959) — MGM, 1964 (d) Arthur Hiller — FI

HUMPHREY, William (1924–)
Home from the Hill (1958) — MGM, 1960 (d) Vincente Minnelli — FI

Author—Title	Film Version: Title (if changed) Production or Releasing Company, Release Date Director (d)	Rental Source(s)
HUNTER, Evan (1926–)		
The Blackboard Jungle (1954)	MGM, 1955 (d) Richard Brooks	FI
[as Ed McBain		
Strangers When We Meet (1958)	Columbia, 1960 (d) Richard Quine	ICS, MOD
King's Ransom (1959)]	*High and Low* Japan, 1963 (d) Akira Kurosawa	JAN
A Matter of Conviction (1959)	*The Young Savages* United Artists, 1961 (d) John Frankenheimer	UA
Last Summer (1968)	Allied Artists, 1969 (d) Frank Perry	HUR
HURST, Fannie (1889–1968)		
Back Street (1931)	Universal, 1932 (d) John M. Stahl	UNI

Imitation of Life (1933)

Universal, 1941
(d) Robert Stevenson — UNI

Universal, 1961
(d) David Miller — UNI

Universal, 1934
(d) John M. Stahl — UNI

Universal, 1959
(d) Douglas Sirk — CWF, UNI

JACKSON, Shirley (1919–65)
The Haunting of Hill House (1959)

The Haunting
MGM, 1963
(d) Robert Wise — FI

JACKSON, Charles Reginald (1903–68)
The Lost Weekend (1944)

Paramount, 1945
(d) Billy Wilder — CWF, TWY, UNI

JENKINS, Dan
Semi-Tough (1972)

United Artists, 1977
(d) Michael Ritchie — UA

Author—Title	Film Version: Title (if changed) Production or Releasing Company, Release Date Director (d)	Rental Source(s)
JOHNSON, Dorothy M. (1905–) *The Hanging Tree* (1957)	Warners, 1959 (d) Delmer Daves	—
JONES, James (1921–77) *From Here to Eternity* (1951)	Columbia, 1953 (d) Fred Zinnemann	AB, ARG, BUD, CWF, MOD, ROA, SEL, TFC, TWY, UF, WCF, WHO
Some Came Running (1957)	MGM, 1958 (d) Vincente Minnelli	FI
The Thin Red Line (1962)	Allied Artists, 1963 (d) Andrew Marton	HUR
KANTOR, MacKinlay (1904–) *Glory for Me* (1945)	*The Best Years of Our Lives* Goldwyn/RKO, 1946 (d) William Wyler	AB, BUD, TWY, WHO

KAZAN, Elia (1909–)

America, America (1962)   Warners, 1963
                                (d) Elia Kazan   SWA

The Arrangement   Warners, 1969
                                (d) Elia Kazan   AB, BUD, CWF, SEL

KEROUAC, Jack (1922–69)

The Subterraneans (1958)   MGM, 1960
                                (d) Ranald MacDougall   FI

KERSH, Gerald (1911–68)

Night and the City (1946)   20th Century-Fox, 1950
                                (d) Jules Dassin   FI

KESEY, Ken (1935–)

One Flew Over the Cuckoo's Nest (1962)   United Artists, 1975
                                (d) Milos Forman   UA

Sometimes a Great Notion (1966)   (retitled *Never Give an Inch*)
                                Universal, 1972
                                (d) Paul Newman   CWF, SWA, TWY, UNI

Author—Title	Film Version: Title (if changed) Production or Releasing Company, Release Date Director (d)	Rental Source(s)
KEYES, Daniel (1927–)		
Flowers for Algernon (1966)	*Charly* ABC, 1968 (d) Ralph Nelson	FI
KNEBEL, Fletcher (1911–) and Charles BAILEY (1929–)		
Seven Days in May (1960)	Paramount, 1964 (d) John Frankenheimer	FI
KNOWLES, John (1926–)		
A Separate Peace (1959)	Paramount, 1972 (d) Larry Peerce	FI
L'AMOUR, Louis (1908–)		
Hondo (1953)	Warners, 1955 (d) John Farrow	—

Heller with a Gun (1954)

Heller in Pink Tights
Paramount, 1960
(d) George Cukor

FI

LARNER, Jeremy (1937–   )
Drive, He Said (1964)

BBS, 1971
(d) Jack Nicholson

RBC

LAWTON, Harry (1927–   )
Willie Boy (1960)

Tell Them Willie Boy Is Here
Universal, 1970
(d) Abraham Polonsky

CWF, SWA, TWY, UNI

LEDERER, William J. (1912–   ) and
Eugene L. BURDICK (1918–65)
The Ugly American

Universal, 1963
(d) George Englund

AB, CWF, SWA, UNI,
WCF

LEE, Harper (1926–   )
To Kill a Mockingbird (1960)

Universal, 1962
(d) Robert Mulligan

CWF, SWA, TWY, UNI

Author—Title	Film Version: Title (if changed) Production or Releasing Company, Release Date Director (d)	Rental Source(s)
LE MAY, Alan (1899–)		
The Searchers (1954)	Warners, 1956 (d) John Ford	SWA
The Unforgiven (1957)	United Artists, 1960 (d) John Huston	UA
LEONARD, Elmore (1925–)		
Hombre	20th Century-Fox, 1967 (d) Martin Ritt	FI
LEVIN, Ira (1929–)		
A Kiss Before Dying (1953)	United Artists, 1956 (d) Gerd Oswald	UA
Rosemary's Baby (1967)	Paramount, 1968 (d) Roman Polanski	FI
The Stepford Wives (1972)	Columbia, 1975 (d) Bryan Forbes	SWA

LEVIN, Meyer (1905–)
  Compulsion (1956) — 20th Century-Fox, 1959 (d) Richard Fleischer — FI

* LEWIS, Sinclair (1885–1951)
  Ann Vickers (1933) — RKO, 1933 (d) John Cromwell — —

  Cass Timberlane (1945) — MGM, 1947 (d) George Sidney — FI

LOCKRIDGE, Ross (1914–48)
  Raintree County (1948) — MGM, 1957 (d) Edward Dmytryk — FI

McCARTHY, Mary (1912–)
  The Group (1963) — United Artists, 1966 (d) Sidney Lumet — UA

McCOY, Horace (1897–1955)
  They Shoot Horses, Don't They? (1935) — ABC, 1969 (d) Sidney Pollack — FI

  Kiss Tomorrow Goodbye (1948) — Warners, 1950 (d) Gordon Douglas — —

Author—Title	Film Version: Production or Releasing Company, Release Date Director (d)	Rental Source(s)
McCullers, Carson (1917–67)		
The Heart Is a Lonely Hunter (1940)	Warners-7 Arts, 1968 (d) Robert Ellis Miller	AB, BUD, CWF, ICS, MOD, ROA, TWY, WCF, WHO
Reflections in a Golden Eye (1941)	Warners, 1967 (d) John Huston	AB, ARG, BUD, CWF, MOD, UF
The Member of the Wedding (1946)	Columbia, 1952 (d) Fred Zinnemann	AB, SWA
MacDonald, John D. (1916–)		
The Executioners (1958)	*Cape Fear* Universal, 1962 (d) J. Lee Thompson	UNI
MacDonald, Ross [Kenneth Millar] (1915–)		
The Moving Target (1949)	*Harper* Warners, 1966 (d) Jack Smight	AB, ARG, BUD, CWF, ICS, SWA, TFC, TWY, WCF, WHO

The Drowning Pool (1950)
Warners, 1975
(d) Stuart Rosenberg
SWA

McGIVERN, William P. (1927–   )
The Big Heat (1953)
Columbia, 1953
(d) Fritz Lang
AB, BUD, SEL, WCF

Odds Against Tomorrow (1957)
United Artists, 1959
(d) Robert Wise
UA

McGUANE, Thomas (1940–   )
The Sporting Club (1968)
Avco-Embassy, 1971
(d) Larry Peerce
AB

Ninety-Two in the Shade (1973)
United Artists, 1975
(d) Thomas McGuane
UA

McMURTRY, Larry (1936–   )
Horseman, Pass By (1961)
Hud
Paramount, 1963
(d) Martin Ritt
FI

Leaving Cheyenne (1963)
Lovin' Molly
Columbia, 1974
(d) Sidney Lumet
SWA

The Last Picture Show (1966)
BBS, 1971
(d) Peter Bogdanovich
RBC, SWA

Author—Title	Film Version: Title (if changed) Production or Releasing Company, Release Date Director (d)	Rental Source(s)
MAILER, Norman (1923–)		
The Naked and the Dead (1948)	Warners, 1958 (d) Raoul Walsh	BUD, UF
An American Dream (1965)	Warners, 1966 (d) Robert Gist	SWA
MAINWARING, Daniel (1902–) [as Geoffrey Homes]		
Build My Gallows High (1946)	*Out of the Past* RKO, 1947 (d) Jacques Tourneur	FI
MALAMUD, Bernard (1914–)		
The Fixer (1966)	MGM, 1968 (d) John Frankenheimer	FI

MANKIEWICZ, Don M. (1922–   )

Trial (1955)
MGM, 1955
(d) Mark Robson
FI

MARCH, William (1893–1954)
[William Edward March Campbell]

The Bad Seed (1954)
Warners, 1956
(d) Mervyn LeRoy
MOG, SWA

MARQUAND, J[ohn] P[hillips] (1893–1960)

The Late George Apley (1937)
20th Century-Fox, 1947
(d) Joseph L. Mankiewicz
FI

H. M. Pullman, Esq. (1941)
MGM, 1941
(d) King Vidor
FI

MATHESON, Richard (1926–   )

I Am Legend (1954)
The Last Man on Earth
American International, 1964
(d) Sidney Salkow
AB, BUD, IVY, ROA, SEL, UF, WCF

The Omega Man
Warners, 1971
(d) Boris Sagal
CWF, ROA, TFC, WHO

Author—Title	Film Version: Title (if changed) Production or Releasing Company, Release Date Director (d)	Rental Source(s)
	The Last Man on Earth New World, 1974 (d) Robert Fuest	FI
The Shrinking Man (1956)	*The Incredible Shrinking Man* Universal, 1957 (d) Jack Arnold	CWF, SWA, TWY, UNI
METALIOUS, Grace (1924–64)		
Peyton Place (1956)	20th Century-Fox, 1957 (d) Mark Robson	FI
Return to Peyton Place (1959)	20th Century-Fox, 1961 (d) Jose Ferrer	FI
MICHENER, James A. (1907–)		
Tales from the South Pacific (1947)	*South Pacific* Todd-AO, 1958 (d) Joshua Logan	BUD, CWF, MOT, WCF

Return to Paradise (1951)	United Artists, 1953 (d) Mark Robson	UA
The Bridges at Toko-Ri (1953)	Paramount, 1954 (d) Mark Robson	FI
Sayonara (1954)	Warners, 1957 (d) Joshua Logan	AB, TWY, WCF
Hawaii (1959)	United Artists, 1966 (d) George Roy Hill	AB, UA
MILLER, Arthur (1915–) *The Misfits* (1961)	United Artists, 1961 (d) John Huston	UA
MILLER, Henry (1891–) *Tropic of Cancer* (1934, U.S. 1961)	Paramount, 1970 (d) Joseph Strick	—
Quiet Days in Clichy (1965)	Denmark, 1970 (d) Jens-Jorgen Thorsen	GRO
MILLER, Warren (1921–66) *The Cool World* (1959)	Wiseman Film Co., 1964 (d) Shirley Clarke	ZIP

Author—Title	Film Version: Title (if changed) Production or Releasing Company, Release Date Director (d)	Rental Source(s)
MITCHELL, Margaret (1900–49)		
Gone With the Wind (1936)	MGM, 1939 (d) Victor Fleming	FI
MORLEY, Christopher (1890–1957)		
Kitty Foyle (1939)	RKO, 1941 (d) Sam Wood	FI
MOTLEY, Willard (1912–65)		
Knock on Any Door (1947)	Columbia, 1949 (d) Nicholas Ray	AB, BUD, CWF, ICS, ROA, SWA, WCF
Let No Man Write My Epitaph (1958)	Columbia, 1960 (d) Philip Leacock	—
NABOKOV, Vladimir (1899–1977)		
Laughter in the Dark (1938)	Gr. Br., 1969 (d) Tony Richardson	UA

Lolita (1955)

MGM, 1962
(d) Stanley Kubrick

FI

NATHAN, Robert (1894–   )
Portrait of Jennie (1940)

Selznick, 1948
(d) William Dieterle

AB

NAUGHTON, Edmund (1926–   )
McCabe (1959)

McCabe and Mrs. Miller
Warners, 1971
(d) Robert Altman

SWA

NEIDER, Charles (1915–   )
The Authentic Death of Hendry Jones
(1956)

One-Eyed Jacks
Paramount, 1961
(d) Marlon Brando

FI

NICHOLS, John (1940–   )
The Sterile Cuckoo (1965)

Paramount, 1969
(d) Alan Pakula

FI

Author—Title	Film Version: Title (if changed) Production or Releasing Company, Release Date Director (d)	Rental Source(s)
NORDHOFF, Charles Bernard (1887–1947) and James Norman HALL (1887–1951)		
Mutiny on the Bounty (1932)	MGM, 1935 (d) Frank Lloyd	FI
	MGM, 1962 (d) Lewis Milestone	FI
Hurricane (1936)	*The Hurricane* Goldwyn, 1937 (d) John Ford	AB, BUD, TWY
O'CONNOR, Edwin (1918–68)		
The Last Hurrah (1956)	Columbia, 1958 (d) John Ford	AB, ARG, BUD, CWF, WCF, WHO
O'HARA, John (1905–70)		
Butterfield 8 (1935)	MGM, 1960 (d) Daniel Mann	FI

Pal Joey (1940)	Columbia, 1957 (d) George Sidney	AB, ARG, BUD, CWF, ROA, SEL, WHO
A Rage to Live (1949)	United Artists, 1965 (d) Walter Grauman	UA
Ten North Frederick (1955)	20th Century-Fox, 1958 (d) Philip Dunne	FI
From the Terrace (1958)	20th Century-Fox, 1960 (d) Mark Robson	FI
OLSEN, Theodore V. (1932–　)		
The Stalking Moon (1965)	National General, 1969 (d) Robert Mulligan	—
Arrow in the Sun (1969)	*Soldier Blue* Avco-Embassy, 1970 (d) Ralph Nelson	AB, CWF, UF
PERRY, George Sessions (1910–56)		
Hold Autumn in Your Hands (1941)	*The Southerner* United Artists, 1945 (d) Jean Renoir	BUD, IVY

Author—Title	Film Version: Title (if changed) Production or Releasing Company, Release Date Director (d)	Rental Source(s)
PONICSAN, Daryl (1938–)		
The Last Detail (1970)	Columbia, 1973 (d) Hal Ashby	SWA
Cinderella Liberty (1973)	20th Century-Fox, 1973 (d) Mark Rydell	FI
PORTER, Katherine Ann (1890–)		
Ship of Fools (1962)	Columbia, 1965 (d) Stanley Kramer	AB, ARG, BUD, CON, CWF, ICS, KPF, ROA, SWA, TFC, TWY, UF, WCF, WHO
PORTIS, Charles (1933–)		
True Grit (1968)	Paramount, 1969 (d) Henry Hathaway	FI
PUZO, Mario (1920–)		
The Godfather (1969)	Paramount, 1972 (d) Francis Ford Coppola	FI

QUEEN, Ellery [Frederick Dannay (1905–   ) and Manfred Lee (1905–1971)]

Ten Days' Wonder (1948)	Fr., 1971 (d) Claude Chabrol	FI

RAND, Ayn (1905–   )

The Fountainhead (1943)	Warners, 1949 (d) King Vidor	UA

RAWLINGS, Marjorie K. (1896–1953)

The Yearling (1938)	MGM, 1946 (d) Clarence Brown	FI

RICHTER, Conrad (1890–1968)

The Sea of Grass (1937)	MGM, 1947 (d) Elia Kazan	FI
The Light in the Forest (1953)	Disney, 1958 (d) Herschel Daugherty	AB, CWF, FI, ROA, SWA, TWY

ROBBINS, Harold (1912–   )

A Stone for Danny Fisher (1952)	*King Creole* Paramount, 1958 (d) Michael Curtiz	AB, BUD, UF

Author—Title	Film Version: Title (if changed) Production or Releasing Company, Release Date Director (d)	Rental Source(s)
The Carpetbaggers (1961)	Paramount, 1964 (d) Edward Dmytryk	FI
	Nevada Smith Paramount, 1966 (d) Henry Hathaway	FI
Where Love Has Gone (1962)	Paramount, 1964 (d) Edward Dmytryk	FI
The Adventurers (1969)	Paramount, 1970 (d) Lewis Gilbert	—
The Betsy (1971)	Allied Artists, 1978 (d) Daniel Petrie	HUR
ROBERTS, Kenneth (1885–1957)		
Northwest Passage (1937)	MGM, 1940 (d) King Vidor	FI

	Frontier Rangers MGM, 1959 (d) Jacques Tourneur	—
Lydia Bailey (1947)	20th Century-Fox, 1952 (d) Jean Negulesco	AB, MOG, SEL, WCF
ROIPHE, Anne (1935–　) *Up the Sandbox* (1970)	National General, 1972 (d) Irving Kershner	SWA
ROSSNER, Judith (1935–　) *Looking for Mr. Goodbar* (1975)	Paramount, 1977 (d) Richard Brooks	—
ROTH, Philip (1933–　) *Goodbye, Columbus* (1959)	Paramount, 1969 (d) Larry Peerce	FI
Portnoy's Complaint (1969)	Warners, 1972 (d) Ernest Lehman	SWA
RUARK, Robert C. (1915–65) *Something of Value* (1955)	MGM, 1957 (d) Richard Brooks	FI

Author—Title	Film Version: Title (if changed) Production or Releasing Company, Release Date Director (d)	Rental Source(s)
SALE, Richard (1911–)		
Not Too Narrow, Not Too Deep (1936)	*Strange Cargo* MGM, 1940 (d) Frank Borzage	FI
The Oscar (1963)	Embassy, 1966 (d) Russell Rouse	ILL
SAROYAN, William (1908–)		
The Human Comedy (1943)	MGM, 1943 (d) Clarence Brown	FI
SCHAEFER, Jack (1907–)		
Shane (1949)	Paramount, 1953 (d) George Stevens	FI
Company of Cowards (1957)	MGM, 1964 (d) George Marshall	—
Monte Walsh (1963)	National General, 1970 (d) William Fraker	BUD, SWA, WCF

	AB, BUD, MOT, SWA, WCF, WHO
SCHULBERG, Budd (1914–)	
The Harder They Fall (1947)	
Columbia, 1956	
(d) Mark Robson	
SETON, Anya (1916–)	
Dragonwyck (1944)	
20th Century-Fox, 1946	
(d) Joseph L. Mankiewicz	FI
Foxfire (1951)	
Universal, 1955	
(d) Joseph Pevney	UNI
SHAW, Irwin (1913–)	
The Young Lions (1948)	
20th Century-Fox, 1958	
(d) Edward Dmytryk	FI
Two Weeks in Another Town (1960)	
MGM, 1962	
(d) Vincente Minnelli	FI
SHULMAN, Irving (1913–)	
The Amboy Dukes (1947)	
City Across the River	
Universal, 1949	
(d) Maxwell Shane	UNI

Author—Title	Film Version: Title (if changed) Production or Releasing Company, Release Date Director (d)	Rental Source(s)
SHULMAN, Max (1919–)		
Rally Round the Flag Boys! (1957)	20th Century-Fox, 1958 (d) Leo McCarey	FI
*SINCLAIR, Upton (1878–1968)		
The Wet Parade (1931)	MGM, 1932 (d) Victor Fleming	FI
SMITH, Betty (1904–72)		
A Tree Grows in Brooklyn	20th Century-Fox, 1945 (d) Elia Kazan	AB, ARG, BUD, CWF, FI, ROA, SEL, TWY, UF, WCF, WHO
SOUTHERN, Terry (1924–) and Mason HOFFENBERG		
Candy (1958)	ABC, 1968 (d) Christian Marquand	

The Magic Christian (1959)   Commonwealth Unlimited, 1970   AB, BUD, IVY, UF, WCF
                                      (d) Joseph McGrath

SPILLANE, Mickey (1918–   ) [Frank
Morrison]

I, the Jury (1942)   United Artists, 1953   AB, ROA, UF
                                      (d) Harry Essex

My Gun Is Quick (1950)   United Artists, 1957   UA
                                      (d) George White/Phil Victor

Kiss Me, Deadly (1952)   United Artists, 1955   UA
                                      (d) Robert Aldrich

The Girl Hunters (1962)   Gr. Br., 20th Century-Fox, 1968   AB, IVY
                                      (d) Roy Rowland

STEINBECK, John (1902–68)

Tortilla Flat (1935)   MGM, 1942   FI
                                      (d) Victor Fleming

Of Mice and Men (1937)   United Artists, 1939   USF
                                      (d) Lewis Milestone

The Grapes of Wrath (1939)   20th Century-Fox, 1940   FI
                                      (d) John Ford

The Moon Is Down (1942)   20th Century-Fox, 1943   FI
                                      (d) Irving Pichel

Author—Title	Film Version: Title (if changed) Production or Releasing Company, Release Date Director (d)	Rental Source(s)
The Red Pony (1937)	Republic, 1949 (d) Lewis Milestone	IVY
	Phoenix, 1974 (d) Robert Totten	PNX
The Wayward Bus (1947)	20th Century-Fox, 1957 (d) Victor Vicas	FI
The Pearl (1947)	Mexico, 1948 (d) Emilio Fernandez	AB
East of Eden (1952)	Warners, 1955 (d) Elia Kazan	AB, ARG, BUD, CON, CWF, ICS, KPF, ROA, SEL, SWA, TWY, UF, WHO
STONE, Irving (1903–)		
Lust for Life (1934)	MGM, 1956 (d) Vincente Minnelli	FI
The Agony and the Ecstasy (1961)	20th Century-Fox, 1965 (d) Carol Reed	FI

STONE, Robert (c. 1937–)

A Hall of Mirrors (1967)
W.U.S.A.
Paramount, 1970
(d) Stuart Rosenberg — FI

Dog Soldiers (1974)
Who'll Stop the Rain?
United Artists, 1978
(d) Karel Reisz — UA

STOUT, Rex (1886–1975)
Fer-de-Lance (1934)
Meet Nero Wolfe
Columbia, 1936
(d) Herbert Biberman — (No. Dist.)

The President Vanishes (1934)
Paramount, 1934
(d) William Wellman — MMA, UNI

SUSANN, Jacqueline (1921–74)
Valley of the Dolls (1966)
20th Century-Fox, 1967
(d) Mark Robson — FI

The Love Machine (1969)
Jacqueline Susann's The Love Machine
Columbia, 1971
(d) Jack Haley, Jr. — AB, BUD, CWF, SEL, UF

TEVIS, Walter S.
The Hustler (1959)
20th Century-Fox, 1961
(d) Robert Rossen — FI

Author—Title	Film Version: Title (if changed) Production or Releasing Company, Release Date Director (d)	Rental Source(s)
The Man Who Fell to Earth (1963)	Cinerama V, 1976 (d) Nicholas Roeg	CIV
THORP, Roderick (1936–) *The Detective* (1966)	20th Century-Fox, 1968 (d) Gordon Douglas	FI
TIDYMAN, Ernest *Shaft* (1970)	MGM, 1971 (d) Gordon Parks	FI
TRAVEN, B. (1890–1969) [Berick Traven Torsvan] *The Treasure of the Sierra Madre* (1935)	Warners, 1948 (d) John Huston	UA
TRAVER, Robert (1903–) [John D. Voelker] *Anatomy of a Murder* (1958)	Columbia, 1959 (d) Otto Preminger	AB, ARG, BUD, CWF, ICS, ROA, SWA, TFC, WCF, WHO

TRUMBO, Dalton (1905–76)
Johnny Got His Gun (1939)

Cinemation, 1971
(d) Dalton Trumbo

SWA

UPDIKE, John (1932–)
Rabbit, Run (1960)

Warners, 1970
(d) Jack Smight

SWA

URIS, Leon (1924–)
Battle Cry (1953)

Warners, 1955
(d) Raoul Walsh

AB, BUD, TWY, UF, WCF

The Angry Hills (1955)

MGM, 1959
(d) Robert Aldrich

FI

Exodus (1958)

United Artists, 1960
(d) Otto Preminger

UA

Topaz (1967)

Universal, 1969
(d) Alfred Hitchcock

CWF, SWA, TWY, UNI,
 WCF

VIDAL, Gore (1925–)
Myra Breckenridge (1968)

20th Century-Fox, 1970
(d) Michael Sarne

FI

Author—Title	Film Version: Title (if changed) Production or Releasing Company, Release Date Director (d)	Rental Source(s)
VONNEGUT, Kurt, Jr. (1922–)		
Slaughterhouse-Five, or The Children's Crusade (1969)	Universal, 1972 (d) George Roy Hill	CWF, SWA, UNI
WALLACE, Irving (1916–)		
The Chapman Report (1960)	Warners, 1962 (d) George Cukor	—
The Prize (1962)	MGM, 1963 (d) Mark Robson	FI
The Man (1964)	Paramount, 1972 (d) Joseph Sargent	AB, BUD, FI, UF, WHO
The Seven Minutes (1969)	20th Century-Fox, 1971 (d) Russ Meyer	FI
WALLANT, Edward (1926–62)		
The Pawnbroker (1961)	Landau, 1964 (d) Sidney Lumet	AB

WAMBAUGH, Joseph (1937–)
  The New Centurions (1971)

Columbia, 1972
(d) Richard Fleischer

SWA

WARREN, Robert Penn (1905–)
  All the King's Men (1946)

Columbia, 1949
(d) Robert Rossen

AB, ARG, BUD, CON, CWF, ICS, SWA, WCF, WHO

  Band of Angels (1955)

Warners, 1957
(d) Raoul Walsh

—

WEBB, Charles (1939–)
  The Graduate (1963)

Avco-Embassy, 1967
(d) Mike Nichols

AB, BUD, CWF, ICS, ROA, TWY, UF, WCF, WHO

WELLES, Orson (1915–)
  Mr. Arkadin (1954)

Gr. Br., 1955
(d) Orson Welles

CON

WEST, Jessamyn (1907–)
  Friendly Persuasion (1945)

Allied Artists, 1956
(d) William Wyler

HUR

Author—Title	Film Version: Title (if changed) Production or Releasing Company, Release Date Director (d)	Rental Source(s)
WEST, Nathanael (1903–40)		
Miss Lonelyhearts (1933)	*Advice to the Lovelorn* 20th Century, 1933 (d) Alfred Werker	—
	Lonelyhearts United Artists, 1958 (d) Vincent J. Donehue	UA
The Day of the Locust (1939)	Paramount, 1974 (d) John Schlesinger	FI
WESTLAKE, Donald E. (1933–)		
[as Richard Stark *The Hunter* (1963)]	*Point Blank* MGM, 1967 (d) John Boorman	FI
[as R. Stark *The Jugger* (1965)]	*Made in USA* Fr., 1966 (d) Jean-Luc Godard	

The Hot Rock (1970)

  20th Century-Fox, 1972 FI
  (d) Peter Yates

Cops and Robbers (1972)

  United Artists, 1972 UA
  (d) Aram Avakian

WILDER, Robert (1901–74)
Written on the Wind (1945)

  Universal, 1951 UNI
  (d) Douglas Sirk

WILLIAMS, John A. (1925–)
Night Song (1961)

  Sweet Love, Bitter
  Film 2 Associates, 1968 AB
  (d) Herbert Danska

WILLINGHAM, Calder (1922–)
End as a Man (1947)

  The Strange One
  Columbia, 1957 —
  (d) Jack Garfein

WILSON, Sloan (1920–)
The Man in the Gray Flannel Suit (1955)

  20th Century-Fox, 1956 FI
  (d) Nunnally Johnson

WINSOR, Kathleen
Forever Amber (1944)

  20th Century-Fox, 1947 —
  (d) Otto Preminger

Author—Title	Film Version: Title (if changed) Production or Releasing Company, Release Date Director (d)	Rental Source(s)
WOLFERT, Ira (1908–)		
Tucker's People (1943)	*Force of Evil* Warners, 1948 (d) Abraham Polonsky	IVY
WOOLRICH, Cornell (1903–68) [Cornell George Hopley-Woolrich]		
The Bride Wore Black (1940)	Fr., 1967 (d) Francois Truffaut	UA
Black Alibi (1942)	*The Leopard Man* RKO, 1943 (d) Jacques Tourneur	FI
[as William Irish *Phantom Lady* (1942)]	Universal, 1944 (d) Robert Siodmak	UNI
[as W. Irish *It Had to Be Murder* (1942)]	*Rear Window* Paramount, 1954 (d) Alfred Hitchcock	—
The Black Angel (1943)	Universal, 1946 (d) Roy William Neill	—

[as W. Irish
  Deadline at Dawn (1944)]

RKO, 1946
(d) Harold Clurman   FI

[as George Hopley
  Night Has a Thousand Eyes (1945)]

Paramount, 1948
(d) John Farrow   UNI

[as W. Irish
  Waltz into Darkness (1947)]

Mississippi Mermaid
Fr., 1969
(d) Francois Truffaut   UA

I Married a Dead Man (1948)]

No Man of Her Own
Paramount, 1950
(d) Mitchell Leisen   —

Wouk, Herman (1915–)
  The Caine Mutiny (1951)

Columbia, 1954
(d) Edward Dmytryk

AB, ARB, BUD, CWF,
KPF, ROA, SWA, TFC,
TWY, UF, WCF, WHO

Marjorie Morningstar (1955)

Warners, 1958
(d) Irving Rapper   USF (lease)

Youngblood Hawke (1962)

Warners, 1964
(d) Delmer Daves   AB, ARG

Wright, Richard (1908–60)
  Native Son (1940)

Classic Pictures, 1951
(d) Pierre Chenal   —

II / By Film Title *

Adventurers, The (1970)
  Harold Robbins
Advice to the Lovelorn (1933)
  Nathanael West
  Miss Lonelyhearts
Advise and Consent (1962)
  Allen Drury
Agony and the Ecstasy, The (1965)
  Irving Stone
Alex and the Gypsy (1976)
  Stanley Elkin
  The Bailbondsman
All Fall Down (1962)
  James Leo Herlihy
All the King's Men (1949)
  Robert Penn Warren
All the Way Home (1963)
  James Agee
  A Death in the Family
America, America (1963)
  Elia Kazan
American Dream, An (1966)
  Norman Mailer
American Friend, The (1977)
  Patricia Highsmith
  Ripley's Game
Americanization of Emily, The
  (1964)
  William Bradford Huie
Anatomy of a Murder (1959)
  Robert Traver
Andromeda Strain, The (1969)
  Michael Crichton
Angry Hills, The (1959)
  Leon Uris
Ann Vickers (1933)
  Sinclair Lewis

Arrangement, The (1969)
  Elia Kazan
Asphalt Jungle, The (1950)
  W. R. Burnett
Avalanche (1946)
  Kay Boyle
Back Street (1932, 1941, 1961)
  Fannie Hurst
Bad Seed, The (1956)
  William March
Badlanders, The (1958)
  W. R. Burnett
  The Asphalt Jungle
Band of Angels (1957)
  Robert Penn Warren
Bang the Drum Slowly (1973)
  Mark Harris
Battle Cry (1955)
  Leon Uris
Bell for Adano, A (1945)
  John Hersey
Best Years of Our Lives, The
  (1946)
  MacKinlay Kantor
  Glory for Me
Betsy, The (1978)
  Harold Robbins
Big Heat, The (1953)
  William P. McGivern
Big Sky, The (1952)
  A. B. Guthrie, Jr.
Big Sleep, The (1946, 1978)
  Raymond Chandler
Big Clock, The (1948)
  Kenneth Fearing
Black Angel, The (1946)
  Cornell Woolrich

---

* See Filmography I for further information on both films and authors. Book title given only if it differs from film title.

Blackboard Jungle, The
   (1955)
   Evan Hunter
Brasher Doubloon, The (1947)
   Raymond Chandler
   The High Window
Breakfast at Tiffany's (1961)
   Truman Capote
Breaking Point, The (1950)
   Ernest Hemingway
   To Have and Have Not
Bride Wore Black, The (1967)
   Cornell Woolrich
Bridges at Toko-Ri, The (1954)
   James A. Michener
Brotherhood, The (1968)
   Lewis John Carlino
Butterfield 8 (1960)
   John O'Hara
By Love Possessed (1961)
   James Gould Cozzens
Caine Mutiny, The (1954)
   Herman Wouk
Cairo (1962)
   W. R. Burnett
   The Asphalt Jungle
Candy (1968)
   Terry Southern [and Mason
   Hoffenberg]
Cape Fear (1962)
   John D. MacDonald
   The Executioners
Captain Lightfoot (1955)
   W. R. Burnett
Carpetbaggers, The (1964)
   Harold Robbins
Cass Timberlane (1947)
   Sinclair Lewis
Cat Ballou (1965)
   Roy Chanslor
   The Ballad of Cat Ballou
Catch-22 (1970)

   Joseph Heller
Chapman Report, The (1962)
   Irving Wallace
Charly (1968)
   Daniel Keyes
   Flowers for Algernon
Christ in Concrete (1978)
   Pietro di Donato
Cimarron (1931, 1960)
   Edna Ferber
Cinderella Liberty (1973)
   Darryl Ponicsan
City Across the River (1949)
   Irving Shulman
   The Amboy Dukes
Colorado Territory (1949)
   W. R. Burnett
   High Sierra
Cool Breeze (1972)
   W. R. Burnett
   The Asphalt Jungle
Come and Get It (1936)
   Edna Ferber
Come Back, Charleston Blue
   (1972)
   Chester Himes
   The Heat's On
Company of Cowards (1964)
   Jack Schaefer
Compulsion (1959)
   Meyer Levin
Cool World, The (1964)
   Warren Miller
Cops and Robbers (1973)
   Donald E. Westlake
Cotton Comes to Harlem (1970)
   Chester Himes
Dark Command (1940)
   W. R. Burnett
   The Dark Command
Dark Passage (1947)
   David Goodis

Forever Amber (1947)
    Kathleen Winsor
Fountainhead, The (1949)
    Ayn Rand
Foxfire (1955)
    Anya Seton
Friendly Persuasion (1956)
    Jessamyn West
Friends of Eddie Coyle, The
    (1973)
    George V. Higgins
From Here to Eternity
    (1953)
    James Jones
From the Terrace (1960)
    John O'Hara
Frontier Rangers (1959)
    Kenneth Roberts
    Northwest Passage
Gangster, The (1947)
    Daniel Fuchs
    Low Company
Gentleman's Agreement (1947)
    Laura Z. Hobson
Giant (1956)
    Edna Ferber
Girl Hunters, The (1963)
    Mickey Spillane
Give Us This Day (1949)
    Pietro di Donato
    Christ in Concrete
Glass Key, The (1935, 1942)
    Dashiell Hammett
Godfather, The (1972)
    Mario Puzo
God's Little Acre (1958)
    Erskine Caldwell
Gone With the Wind (1939)
    Margaret Mitchell
Good Earth, The (1937)
    Pearl Buck
Goodbye, Columbus (1969)

    Philip Roth
Graduate, The (1967)
    Charles Webb
Grapes of Wrath, The (1940)
    John Steinbeck
Group, The (1966)
    Mary McCarthy
Gypsy Moths, The (1969)
    James Drought
H. M. Pullman, Esq. (1941)
    J. P. Marquand
Hanging Tree, The (1959)
    Dorothy M. Johnson
Harder They Fall, The (1947)
    Budd Schulberg
Harper (1966)
    Ross Macdonald
    The Moving Target
Haunting, The (1963)
    Shirley Jackson
    The Haunting of Hill House
Hawaii (1966)
    James A. Michener
Heart Is a Lonely Hunter, The
    (1968)
    Carson McCullers
Heller in Pink Tights (1960)
    Louis L'Amour
    Heller with a Gun
High and Low (1963)
    Ed McBain [Evan Hunter]
    King's Ransom
High and the Mighty, The (1954)
    Ernest K. Gann
High Sierra (1941)
    W. R. Burnett
Hombre (1967)
    Elmore Leonard
Home from the Hill (1960)
    William Humphrey
Hondo (1955)
    Louis L'Amour

Richard Matheson
I Am Legend
Last Picture Show, The (1971)
Larry McMurtry
Last Summer (1969)
Evan Hunter
Last Tycoon, The (1976)
F. Scott Fitzgerald
Late George Apley, The (1947)
J. P. Marquand
Laughter in the Dark (1969)
Vladimir Nabokov
Laura (1941)
Vera Caspary
Leopard Man, The (1943)
Cornell Woolrich
Black Alibi
Let No Man Write My Epitaph (1960)
Willard Motley
Light in the Forest, The (1958)
Conrad Richter
Little Big Man (1970)
Thomas Berger
Lolita (1962)
Vladimir Nabokov
Lonelyhearts (1958)
Nathanael West
Miss Lonelyhearts
Long Goodbye, The (1973)
Raymond Chandler
Long Hot Summer, The (1958)
William Faulkner
The Hamlet
Looking for Mr. Goodbar (1977)
Judith Rossner
Lost Weekend, The (1945)
Charles Reginald Jackson
Love Machine, The (1971)
Jacqueline Susann
Lovin' Molly (1974)

Larry McMurtry
Leaving Cheyenne
Lust for Life (1956)
Irving Stone
Lydia Bailey (1952)
Kenneth Roberts
M*A*S*H* (1970)
Richard Hooker
McCabe and Mrs. Miller (1971)
Edmund Naughton
McCabe
Made in USA (1966)
Richard Stark [Donald E. Westlake]
The Jugger
Magic Christian, The (1970)
Terry Southern
Maltese Falcon, The (1931, 1941)
Dashiell Hammett
Man, The (1972)
Irving Wallace
Man of the West (1958)
Will C. Brown
The Border Jumpers
Man in the Gray Flannel Suit, The (1956)
Sloan Wilson
Man Who Fell to Earth, The (1976)
Walter S. Tevis
Man with the Golden Arm, The (1956)
Nelson Algren
Manchurian Candidate, The (1962)
Richard Condon
Majorie Morningstar (1958)
Herman Wouk
Marlowe (1969)
Raymond Chandler
The Little Sister

Meet Me in St. Louis (1944)
  Sally Benson
Meet Nero Wolfe (1936)
  Rex Stout
  Fer-de-Lance
Member of the Wedding, The
    (1952)
  Carson McCullers
Midnight Cowboy (1969)
  James Leo Herlihy
Mildred Pierce (1945)
  James M. Cain
Mr. Arkadin (1955)
  Orson Welles
Mr. Blandings Builds His Dream
    House (1948)
  Eric Hodgins
Mr. Roberts (1955)
  Thomas Heggen
Misfits, The (1961)
  Arthur Miller
Mississippi Mermaid (1969)
  William Irish [Cornell
    Woolrich]
  Waltz into Darkness
Moon is Down, The (1943)
  John Steinbeck
Monte Walsh (1970)
  Jack Schaefer
Murder, My Sweet (1944)
  Raymond Chandler
  Farewell, My Lovely
Mutiny on the Bounty (1935,
    1962)
  Charles Bernard Nordhoff and
    James Norman Hall
My Gun Is Quick (1957)
  Mickey Spillane
My Man Godfrey (1936)
  Eric Hatch
Myra Breckenridge (1970)
  Gore Vidal

Naked and the Dead, The (1958)
  Norman Mailer
Native Son (1951)
  Richard Wright
Nevada Smith (1966)
  Harold Robbins
  The Carpetbaggers
Never Give an Inch, see
    Sometimes a Great Notion
New Centurions, The (1972)
  Joseph Wambaugh
Night and the City (1950)
  Gerald Kersh
Night Has a Thousand Eyes
    (1948)
  George Hopley [Cornell
    Woolrich]
Night of the Hunter (1955)
  Davis Grubb
Nightfall (1956)
  David Goodis
Nightmare Alley (1947)
  William Lindsay Gresham
Ninety-Two in the Shade (1975)
  Thomas McGuane
No Man of Her Own (1950)
  William Irish [Cornell
    Woolrich]
  I Married a Dead Man
No Way to Treat a Lady (1968)
  William Goldman
Nobody Lives Forever (1946)
  W. R. Burnett
Northwest Passage (1940)
  Kenneth Roberts
Odds Against Tomorrow (1959)
  William P. McGivern
Of Mice and Men (1939)
  John Steinbeck
Omega Man, The (1971)
  Richard Matheson
  I Am Legend

Once You Kiss a Stranger (1969)
  Patricia Highsmith
  Strangers on a Train
One-Eyed Jacks (1961)
  Charles Neider
  *The Authentic Death of
    Hendry Jones*
One Flew Over the Cuckoo's Nest
  (1975)
  Ken Kesey
Oscar, The (1966)
  Richard Sale
Ossessione (1942)
  James M. Cain
  *The Postman Always Rings
    Twice*
Out of the Past (1947)
  Daniel Mainwaring
  Build My Gallows High
Ox-Bow Incident, The
  (1943)
  Walter van Tilburg Clark
Pal Joey (1957)
  John O'Hara
Paper Moon (1973)
  Joe David Brown
  Addie Pray
Paths of Glory (1957)
  Humphrey Cobb
Pawnbroker, The (1965)
  Edward Wallant
Pearl, The (1948)
  John Steinbeck
Pete 'n' Tillie (1972)
  Peter DeVries
  *The Cat's Pajamas and Witch's
    Milk*
Peyton Place (1957)
  Grace Metalious
Phantom Lady (1944)
  William Irish [Cornell
    Woolrich]

Play It As It Lays (1972)
  Joan Didion
Point Blank (1967)
  Richard Stark [Donald E.
    Westlake]
  The Hunter
Portnoy's Complaint (1972)
  Philip Roth
Portrait of Jennie (1948)
  Robert Nathan
*Postman Always Rings Twice,
  The* (1946)
  James M. Cain
President Vanishes, The (1934)
  Rex Stout
Prize, The (1963)
  Irving Wallace
Psycho (1960)
  Robert Bloch
Purple Noon (1961)
  Patricia Highsmith
  The Talented Mr. Ripley
Quiet Days at Clichy (1970)
  Henry Miller
Rabbit, Run (1970)
  John Updike
Rage to Live, A (1965)
  John O'Hara
Raintree County (1957)
  Ross Lockridge
Rally Round the Flag Boys! (1958)
  Max Shulman
Rear Window (1954)
  William Irish [Cornell
    Woolrich]
  It Had to Be Murder
Red Pony, The (1949, 1974)
  John Steinbeck
Red River (1948)
  Borden Chase
  *Blazing Guns on the Chisholm
    Trail*

Red Sky at Morning (1970)
Richard Bradford
Reflections in a Golden Eye
(1967)
Carson McCullers
Reivers, The (1969)
William Faulkner
Return to Paradise (1953)
James A. Michener
Return to Peyton Place (1961)
Grace Metalious
Revolt of Mamie Stover, The
(1956)
William Bradford Huie
Ride the Pink Horse (1947)
Dorothy B. Hughes
Robe, The (1953)
Lloyd C. Douglas
Rosemary's Baby (1968)
Ira Levin
Russians Are Coming, The
Russians Are Coming, The
(1966)
Nathaniel Benchley
The Off-Islanders
Sanctuary (1961)
William Faulkner
Sanctuary/Requiem for a Nun
Saratoga Trunk (1945)
Edna Ferber
Satan Met a Lady (1936)
Dashiell Hammett
The Maltese Falcon
Sayonara (1957)
James A. Michener
Sea of Grass, The (1947)
Conrad Richter
Searchers, The (1956)
Alan LeMay
Semi-Tough (1977)
Dan Jenkins

Separate Peace, A (1972)
John Knowles
Serenade (1956)
James M. Cain
Seven Days in May (1964)
Fletcher Knebel and Charles
Bailey
Seven Minutes, The (1971)
Irving Wallace
Shaft (1971)
Ernest Tidyman
Shane (1953)
Jack Schaefer
Ship of Fools (1965)
Katherine Anne Porter
Shoot the Piano Player (1960)
David Goodis
Down There
Silken Affair, The (1957)
Robert L. Taylor
Slaughterhouse-Five (1972)
Kurt Vonnegut, Jr.
Slaughterhouse-Five, or the
Children's Crusade
Soldier Blue (1970)
Theodore V. Olsen
Arrow in the Sun
Soldier in the Rain (1963)
William Goldman
Some Came Running (1958)
James Jones
Something of Value (1957)
Robert C. Ruark
Sometimes a Great Notion
(1972)
Ken Kesey
Sounder (1972)
William H. Armstrong
South Pacific (1958)
James A. Michener
Tales from the South Pacific

I / Covering Film Adaptations of Individual American Novels, 1930–1975

Alpert, Hollis. "Fitzgerald, Hollywood, and *The Last Tycoon*," *American Film*, 1, No. 5 (March 1976), pp. 8–14.

Appel, Alfred, Jr. "The End of the Road: Dark Cinema and *Lolita*," *Film Comment*, 10, No. 5 (September-October 1974), pp. 25–31.

Armour, Robert. "*Deliverance*: Four Variations of the American Adam," *Literature/Film Quarterly*, 1, No. 3 (Summer 1973), pp. 280–285.

Atkins, Thomas R. "Ray Bradbury: The Illustrated Man" [*Fahrenheit 451*], *Sight and Sound*, 43, No. 2 (Spring 1974), pp. 96–100.

Baxter, John. "The Oldest Hero: *The Last Hurrah*," *The Cinema of John Ford*. New York: A. S. Barnes, 1971, pp. 154–161.

Bergen, Candice. "What I Did Last Summer" [*The Group*], *Esquire*, 64 (December 1965), pp. 234–237+.

Biskind, Peter. "*They Live by Night* by Daylight," *Sight and Sound*, 45, No. 4 (Autumn 1976), pp. 218–222.

Birdsall, Eric R. and Fred H. Marcus. "Schlesinger's *Midnight Cowboy*: Creating a Classic," *Film and Literature: Contrasts in Media*, Ed. by Fred H. Marcus. Scranton, Pa.: Chandler Publishing, 1971, pp. 178–190.

Bluestone, George. "The Fire and the Future" [*Fahrenheit 451*], *Film Quarterly*, 20, No. 4 (Summer 1967), pp. 3–10.

Bluestone, George. *Novels into Film* [*The Grapes of Wrath, The Ox-Bow Incident*]. Berkeley: University of California Press, 1966 (reprint of 1957 ed.).

Bobrow, Andrew. "John Schlesinger and *The Day of the Locust*," *Filmmakers Newsletter*, 8, No. 9 (July 1975), pp. 28–32.

Bowles, Stephen E. "*The Exorcist* and *Jaws*," *Literature/Film Quarterly*, 4, No. 3 (Summer 1976), pp. 196–214.

Brackett, Leigh, William Faulkner, and Jules Furthman. "*The Big Sleep*—Screenplay," *Film Scripts One*. Edited by George P. Garrett, et al. New York: Appleton, 1971, pp. 137–329.

Brackett, Leigh. "From *The Big Sleep* to *The Long Goodbye* and More or Less How We Got There." *Take One*, 4, No. 1 (Jan. 1974), pp. 26–28.

Bradbury, Ray. "Film in the Space Age" [*Fahrenheit 451*], *American Cinematographer*, 48, No. 1 (January 1967), pp. 34–35+.

Braudy, Leo. "Catch 8½" [*Catch-22*], *On Film*, 1 (1970), pp. 88–90.

Braudy, Leo. "The Difficulties of *Little Big Man*," *Film Quarterly*, XXV, No. 1 (Fall 1971), pp. 30–33.

Brenton, Guy. "Two Adaptations" [*All the King's Men, Tucker's People/Force of Evil*], *Sequence*, 12 (Autumn 1950), pp. 33–36.

Burrows, Michael. *John Steinbeck and His Films*. New York(?): Primestyle, 1970.

Byron, Stuart. "*The Exorcist:* Part of a Phenomenon?" *Film Comment*, 10, No. 3 (May-June 1974), pp. 33–35.

Byron, Stuart. "Martyr Complexes" [*One Flew Over the Cuckoo's Nest*], *Film Comment*, 12, No. 4 (July-August 1976), pp. 29–30.

Callenbach, Ernest. "*The Old Man and the Sea*," *Film Quarterly*, XII, No. 2 (Winter 1958), pp. 45–46.

Capote, Truman. "Truman Capote Reports on the Filming of *In Cold Blood*," *The Saturday Evening Post*, 241 (June 13, 1968), pp. 62–65.

Chelminski, R. "Cotton Cashes In" [*Cotton Comes to Harlem*], *Life*, 69 (August 28, 1970), pp. 58–61.

Childs, James. "Interview with John Hancock" [*Bang the Drum Slowly*], *Literature/Film Quarterly*, 3, No. 2 (Spring 1975), pp. 109–116.

Combs, Richard. "*The Last Tycoon*," *Sight and Sound*, 46, No. 2 (Spring 1977), p. 124.

Cooper, Duncan. "A Second Look—*Spartacus*," *Cineaste*, VI, No. 3 (1974), pp. 30–31.

Corliss, Mary and Charles Silver. "Hollywood Under Water—Elia Kazan on *The Last Tycoon*," *Film Comment*, 13, No. 1 (January-February 1977), pp. 40–44.

Crain, Mary Beth. "*The Ox-Bow Incident* Revisited," *Literature/Film Quarterly*, 4, No. 3 (Summer 1976), pp. 240–248.

Davis, John. "The Tragedy of *Mildred Pierce*," *The Velvet Light Trap*, No. 6 (Fall 1972), pp. 27–30.

Dawson, Jan. "R. Altman Speaking" [*The Long Goodbye*], *Film Comment*, 10, No. 2 (March-April 1974), pp. 40–41.

Degenfelder, Pauline. "Sirk's *The Tarnished Angels* and *Pylon* Re-created," *Literature/Film Quarterly*, 5, No. 3 (Summer 1977), pp. 242–251.

Delpino, Louis. "Transliterations: Joseph Strick's *Tropic of Cancer*," *Film Heritage*, 6, No. 1 (Fall 1970), pp. 27–29.

Dempsey, Michael. "*Deliverance*/Boorman-Dickey in the Woods," *Cinema* (Calif.), 8, No. 1 (Spring 1973), pp. 10–17.

Dempsey, Michael. "Robert Altman: The Empty Staircase and the Chinese Princess" [*The Long Goodbye, M*A*S*H*, Thieves Like Us*], *Film Comment*, 10, No. 5 (September-October 1974), pp. 10–17.

Dempsey, Michael. "They Shaft Writers Don't They?—James Poe Interviewed" [*They Shoot Horses, Don't They?*], *Film Comment*, 6, No. 4 (Winter 1970–71), pp. 65–73.

Desilets, E. Michael. "*The Long Goodbye:* A Novel into Film," *Filmograph*, IV, No. 2 (3rd Quarter, 1974), pp. 23–25.

Drury, Alan. "Based on the Novel, *Advise and Consent*," *McCall's*, 89 (July 1962), pp. 12+.

Ephron, Nora. "Yossarian Is Alive and Well in the Mexican Desert: Production of *Catch-22*," The *New York Times Magazine* (March 16, 1969), pp. 30–31+.

Erens, Patricia. "Sidney Pollack: The Way We Are" [*They Shoot Horses, Don't They?* and *Three Days of the Condor/Six Days of the Condor*], *Film Comment*, 11, No. 5 (September-October 1975), pp. 24–29.

Eyles, Allen. "*The Maltese Falcon*," *Films and Filming*, 11, No. 2 (November 1964), pp. 45–50.

Fadiman, Regina K. *Faulkner's* Intruder in the Dust: *Novel Into Film*. Knoxville: University of Tennessee, 1978.

Farber, Stephen. "Coppola and *The Godfather*," *Sight and Sound*, 41, No. 4 (Autumn 1972), pp. 217–223.

Farber, Stephen. "*The Exorcist:* A Unique Freak Show," *Film Comment*, 10, No. 3 (May-June 1974), pp. 32, 34.

Farber, Stephen. "*Goodbye, Columbus*," *Film Quarterly*, XXII, No. 1 (Fall 1969), pp. 34–38.

Farber, Stephen. "The Monster Marathon" [*They Shoot Horses, Don't They?*], *Cinema* (Calif.), 6, No. 1 (1970), pp. 10–15.

Farrell, James T. "Cain's Movietone Realism" [*Mildred Pierce*], *Literature and Morality*. New York: Vanguard Press, 1947, pp. 79–89.

Flore, Robert L. "The Picaresque Tradition in *Midnight Cowboy*," *Literature/Film Quarterly*, 3, No. 3 (Summer 1975), pp. 270–276.

Folsom, James K. "*Shane* and *Hud:* Two Stories in Search of a Medium," *Western Humanities Review*, 24, No. 4 (Autumn 1970), pp. 359–372.

Foote, Horton. Screenplay: *To Kill a Mockingbird*. New York: Harcourt Brace, 1963.

"Franco in Hollywood" [*For Whom the Bell Tools*], *The Nation*, 155 (December 19, 1942).

Freiman, Ray. *Porgy and Bess* [*Porgy*]. New York: Random House, 1959.

French, Warren. Filmguide to *The Grapes of Wrath*. Bloomington: Indiana University Press, 1973.

Gerlach, John. "*The Last Picture Show* and One More Adaptation," *Literature/Film Quarterly*, 1, No. 2 (Spring 1973), pp. 161–166.

Gill, Brendan. "Novels Into Films: *Islands in the Stream*," *Film Comment*, 13, No. 2 (March-April 1977), pp. 44–45.

Gill, Brendan. "A Plague of Locusts." [*The Day of the Locust*], *Film Comment*, 11, No. 3 (May-June 1975), p. 43.

Gow, Gordon. "Pursuit of the Falcon" [*The Maltese Falcon*], *Films and Filming*, 20, No. 6 (March 1974), pp. 56–58.

Graham, Frank. "Man Behind $M^*A^*S^*H^*$," *Today's Health*, 48 (December 1970), pp. 24–27.

Grauman, Lawrence, Jr. "*Studs Lonigan*," *Film Quarterly*, XV, No. 4 (Summer 1962), pp. 60–61.

Gregory, Charles. "Knight Without Meaning?" [*The Long Goodbye*], *Sight and Sound*, 42, No. 3 (Summer 1973), pp. 155–159.

Gregory, Charles. "*The Long Goodbye*." *Film Quarterly*, XXVI, No. 4 (Summer 1973), pp. 46–48.

Griffith, Richard. *Anatomy of a Motion Picture* [*Anatomy of a Murder*]. New York: St. Martin's Press, 1959.

Guiles, Fred Lawrence. *Hanging Out in Paradise*. New York: McGraw-Hill, 1975.

Harvey, Stephen and Richard Corliss. "Outlaws, Auteurs and Actors" [*Thieves Like Us*], *Film Comment*, 10, No. 3 (May-June 1974), pp. 14–15.

Heinz, Linda and Roy Huss. "*A Separate Peace:* Filming the War Within," *Literature/Film Quarterly*, 3, No. 2 (Spring 1975), pp. 160–171.

Helpern, David. "At Sea with Steven Spielberg" [*Jaws*], *Take One*, 4, No. 10 (1975), pp. 8–12.

Henry, Buck. "Frantic Filming of a Crazy Classic" [*Catch-22*], *Life*, 68 June 12, 1970), pp. 44–48.

Hogue, Peter. "Hawks, Chandler and *The Big Sleep*." *Movietone News*, No. 57 (February 1978), pp. 12–16.

Houston, Beverle and Marsha Kinder. "*Rosemary's Baby*," *Sight and Sound*, 38 (Winter 1968–69), pp. 17–19.

Houston, Penelope. "*Shane* and George Stevens," *Sight and Sound*, 23, No. 2 (October-December 1953), pp. 71–75.

Isaacs, Neil D. "Unstuck in Time: *Clockwork Orange* and *Slaughter-house-Five*," *Literature/Film Quarterly*, 1, No. 2 (Spring 1973), pp. 122–131.

Jameson, Richard T. "People Who Need People," [*To Have and Have Not*], *Movietone News*, 40 (April 13, 1975), pp. 11–15.

Johnson, Albert. "*Studs Lonigan* and *Elmer Gantry*," *Sight and Sound*, 29, No. 4 (Autumn 1960), pp. 173–175.

Johnson, Nunnally. *The Grapes of Wrath*. In *Twenty Best Plays*. Ed. by John Gassner and Dudley Nichols. New York: Crown, 1943.

Jones, Dorothy. "William Faulkner: Novel Into Film" [*Intruder in the Dust*], The *Quarterly of Film, Radio and Television*, 8, No. 1 (Fall 1953), pp. 51–71.

Kawin, Bruce F. *Faulkner and Film*. New York: Frederick Ungar, 1977.

Kawin, Bruce. "A Faulkner Filmography," *Film Quarterly*, XXX, No. 4 (Summer 1977), pp. 12–21.

Kehl, D. G. "Steinbeck's 'String of Pictures' in *The Grapes of Wrath*," *Image*, 17, No. 1 (March 1974), pp. 1–10.

Knebel, Fletcher. "*Seven Days in May*: the Movie the Military Shunned," *Look*, 27 (November 19, 1963), pp. 90–95.

Kolker, R. P. "Night and Day" [*Thieves Like Us*], *Sight and Sound*, XLIII, No. 4 (Autumn 1974), pp. 236–239.

Kozloff, Max. "*In Cold Blood*," *Sight and Sound*, 37, No. 3 (Summer 1968), p. 148–150.

Kunert, Arnold R. "Ray Bradbury on Hitchcock, Huston and Other Magic of the Screen" [*Fahrenheit 451*], *Take One*, 3, No. 11 (1973), pp. 15–23.

Lambert, Gavin. "*Lonelyhearts*" [*Miss Lonelyhearts*], *Film Quarterly*, XII, No. 3 (Spring 1959), pp. 46–48.

Leff, Leonard J. "Quilts, Radios and Baseball Gloves: The Accessible World of *Thieves Like Us*," *Film Heritage*, 12, No. 2 (Winter 1976–77), pp. 31–38.

Lerner, Irving. "Breaking Down the Conventional Barriers" [*Studs Lonigan*], *Films and Filming*, 7, No. 7 (April 1961), pp. 18–19+.

Lerner, Max. "Cain in the Movies," *Public Journal: Marginal Notes on Wartime America*. New York: Viking, 1945, pp. 46–48.

Locke, Edwin. "Adaptation of Reality in *The Grapes of Wrath*," *Films*, 1, No. 2 (1940), pp. 49–55.

Lowry, Malcolm and Margerie Brenner Lowry. *Notes on a Screenplay for F. Scott Fitzgerald's* Tender Is the Night. Bloomfield Hills, Michigan, and Columbia, S.C.: Bruccoli Clark, 1976.

Lumet, Sidney. "Keep Them on the Hook" [*The Pawnbroker*], *Films and Filming*, 11, No. 1 (October 1964), pp. 17–20.

Lyons, Joseph. "*The Pawnbroker:* Flashback in the Novel and the Film," *Western Humanities Review*, 20 (1966), pp. 243–248.

Macklin, F. Anthony. "'Benjamin Will Survive . . .' Interview with Charles Webb" [*The Graduate*], *Film Heritage*, 4, No. 1 (Fall 1968), pp. 1–6.

McCormick, Ruth. "*One Flew Over the Cuckoo's Nest*," *Cineaste*, VII, No. 3 (Fall 1976), pp. 42–43.

McCreadie, Marsha. "*One Flew Over the Cuckoo's Nest:* Some Reasons for One Happy Adaptation," *Literature/Film Quarterly*, V, No. 2 (Spring 1977), pp. 125–131.

McKee, Mel. "*2001:* Out of the Silent Planet." *Sight and Sound*, 38 (Autumn 1969), pp. 204–207.

McMurtry, Larry. "McMurtry on the Movies: O Ragged Time Knit Up Thy Ravell'd Sleeve" [*Ragtime*], *American Film*, II, No. 3 (December-January 1977), pp. 4–5.

Merryman, Richard. "Cinematic Assault" [*The End of the Road*], *Life*, 67 (November 7, 1969), pp. 64–72,

Meyer, Nicholas. *The* Love Story *Story*. New York: Avon, 1971.

Miller, Henry. "*Tropic of Cancer* Revisited," *Playboy*, 17, No. 6 (June 1970), p. 133+.

Moffat, Ivan. "Script Extract—*Tender Is the Night*," *Films and Filming*, 8, No. 7 (April 1962), pp. 18–19+.

Murphy, Kathleen. "Blues for Mr. Chandler," [*The Long Goodbye*], *Movietone News*, 29 (January-February 1974), pp. 1–6.

Murphy, Richard. ". . . And Why We Were Compelled to Put Frost on the Cake" [*Compulsion*], *Films and Filming*, 5, No. 8 (May 1959), pp. 19+.

Murray, Edward. "*In Cold Blood:* The Filmic Novel and the Problem of Adaptation," *Literature/Film Quarterly*, 1, No. 2 (Spring 1973), pp. 132–137.

Nabokov, Vladimir. *Lolita: A Screenplay*. New York: McGraw-Hill, 1975.

Naremore, James. "John Huston and *The Maltese Falcon*." *Literature/ Film Quarterly*, 1, No. 3 (July 1973), pp. 239–250.

Nelson, Joyce. "*Mildred Pierce* Reconsidered," *Film Reader*, 2 (January 1977), pp. 65–70.

Nelson, Joyce. "*Slaughterhouse-Five:* Novel and Film," *Literature/Film Quarterly*, 1, No. 2 (Spring 1973), pp. 149–153.

Oliver, Bill. "*The Long Goodbye* and *Chinatown:* Debunking the Private Eye Tradition," *Literature/Film Quarterly*, 3, No. 3 (Summer 1975), pp. 240–248.

Pellow, G. Kenneth. "The Transformation of *The Sterile Cuckoo*," *Literature/Film Quarterly*, 5, No. 3 (Summer 1977), pp. 252–257.

Pendo, Stephen. *Raymond Chandler on Screen: His Novels Into Film*. Metuchen, N.J.: Scarecrow Press, 1976.

Phillips, Gene. "*The Day of the Locust:* John Schlesinger Interviewed," *Film Comment*, 11, No. 3 (May-June 1975), pp. 40–42.

Phillips, Gene. "Faulkner and the Film: Two Versions of *Sanctuary*," *Literature/Film Quarterly*, 1, No. 3 (Summer 1973), pp. 263–273.

Place, Janey. "*The Grapes of Wrath:* A Visual Analysis," *Film Comment*, 12, No. 5 (September-October 1976), pp. 46–51.

Potter, Vilma Raskin. "*The Autobiography of Miss Jane Pittman:* How to Make a White Film from a Black Novel," *Literature/Film Quarterly*, 3, No. 4 (Fall 1975), pp. 371–375.

Pratley, Gerald. "*The Fixer*." In *The Cinema of John Frankenheimer*. New York: A. S. Barnes, 1969.

Preminger, Otto. "*The Cardinal* and I," *Films and Filming*, 10, No. 10 (November 1963), pp. 11–12.

Pulliam, Rebecca. "*The Grapes of Wrath*," The *Velvet Light Trap*, No. 2 (August 1971), pp. 3–7.

Puzo, Mario. *The* Godfather *Papers and Other Confessions*. New York: G. P. Putnam's Sons, 1972.

Quart, Barbara and Leonard Quart. "*The Last Tycoon*," *Cineaste*, VII, No. 4 (Winter 1976–77), pp. 45–46.

Reisman, Phillip, Jr. "All the Way Home" [*A Death in the Family*]. In *Creative Arts: Four Representative Types*. Ed. by Rod Sheratsky. New York: Globe Books, 1968.

Roberts, Marguerite and Jane Murfin. *Dragon Seed*. In *Best Film Plays 1943–1944*. Ed. by John Gassner and Dudley Nichols. New York: Crown, 1945.

Rossen, Robert. *All the King's Men*. In *Three Screenplays*. New York: Doubleday, 1972, pp. 3–108.

Roud, Richard. "The Empty Streets" [*The Member of the Wedding*], 26, No. 4 (Spring 1957), pp. 191–195.

Safer, Elaine B. " 'It's the Truth Even If It Didn't Happen': Ken Kesey's *One Flew Over the Cuckoo's Nest*," *Literature/Film Quarterly*, 5, No. 2 (Spring 1977), pp. 132–141.

Samuels, Charles S. "How Not to Film a Novel" [*Fat City, Deliverance*], *The American Scholar*, 42, No. 1 (Winter 1972–73), pp. 148–154.

Sarris, Andrew. "*Giant*," *Film Culture*, 2, No. 4 [10] (1956), pp. 23–24.

Schulberg, Budd. "Why Write It When You Can't Sell It to the Pictures?" [*On the Waterfront*], The *Saturday Review*, 38, No. 36 (September 3, 1955), pp. 5–6+.

Sharples, Win. "The Art of Filmmaking: An Analysis of *Slaughterhouse-Five*," *Filmmakers Newsletter*, 6, No. 1 (November 1972), pp. 24–28.

Silver, Alain. "Robert Aldrich's *Kiss Me Deadly*," *Film Comment*, 11, No. 2 (March-April 1975), pp. 24–30.

Sirkin, Elliott. "*The Group*," *Film Comment*, 8, No. 3 (September-October 1972), pp. 66–68.

Shivas, Mark. "Preminger and *Advise and Consent*," *Movie*, 2 (September 1962), pp. 26–30.

Slesinger, Tess and Frank Davis. *A Tree Grows in Brooklyn*. In *The Best Film Plays*. Ed. by John Gassner and Dudley Nichols. New York: Crown, 1946.

Slesinger, Tess and Talbot Jennings et al. *The Good Earth*. In *Twenty Best Film Plans*. Ed. by John Gassner and Dudley Nichols. New York: Crown, 1943, pp. 875–950.

Stone, Judy. *The Mystery of B. Traven* [*The Treasure of Sierra Madre*]. Los Altos, California: William Kaufmann, 1977.

Strawn, Lynda. "Conversation with John Boorman" [*Deliverance*], *Action*, 7, No. 6 (November-December 1972), pp. 3–5.

Strick, Philip. "*Slaughterhouse-Five*." *Sight and Sound*, 41, No. 4 (Autumn 1972), pp. 232–233.

Sturhahn, Larry. "The Making of *One Flew Over the Cuckoo's Nest*," *Filmmakers Newsletter*, 9, No. 2 (December 1975), pp. 26–31.

Taradash, Daniel. "Into Another World" [*From Here to Eternity*], *Films and Filming*, 5, No. 8 (May 1959), pp. 9, 33.

Thegze, Chuck. "'I See Everything Twice.' An Examination of *Catch-22*," *Film Quarterly*, XXIV, No. 1 (Fall 1970), pp. 7–17.

Trotti, Lamar. *The Ox-Bow Incident*. In *Best Film Plays 1943–44*. Ed. by John Gassner and Dudley Nichols. New York: Crown, 1945.

Truffaut, Francois. "The Journal of *Fahrenheit 451*," *Cahiers du Cinema in English*, 5 (1966), pp. 10–22; 6 (December 1966), pp. 10–23; 7 (November-January 1967), pp. 8–19.

Turner, John W. "*Little Big Man*. The Novel and the Film: A Study of Narrative Structure," *Literature/Film Quarterly*, 5, No. 2 (Spring 1977), pp. 154–163.

Van Wert, William. "Phillip Marlowe: Hardboiled to Softboiled to Poached" [*The Little Sister, The Long Goodbye*], *Jump Cut*, 3 (September-October 1974), pp. 10–13.

Wald, Jerry. "Screen Adaptation" [*From Here to Eternity*], *Films in Review*, 5 (February 1954), pp. 62–67.

West, Jessamyn. "Hollyood Diary: Filming *Friendly Persuasion*," The *Ladies' Home Journal*, 73 (November 1956), pp. 70–71+.

Wexman, Virginia Wright. "The Transfer from One Medium to Another: *The Maltese Falcon* From Fiction to Film." *Library Quarterly*, 15, No. 1 (January 1975), pp. 46–55.

Wilder, Billy and Charles Brackett. *The Lost Weekend*. In *The Best Film Plays of 1945*. Ed. by John Gassner and Dudley Nichols. New York: Crown, 1946.

Wilder, Billy and James M. Cain. *Double Indemnity*. In *The Best Film Plays of 1945*. Ed. by John Gassner and Dudley Nichols. New York: Crown, 1946.

Willson, Robert F., Jr. "*Deliverance* from Novel to Film: Where is Our Hero?" *Literature/Film Quarterly*, 2, No. 1 (Winter 1974), pp. 52–58.

Willson, Robert F., Jr. "Which Is the Real *Last Picture Show?*" *Literature/Film Quarterly*, 1, No. 2 (Spring 1973), pp. 167–169.

Wolfe, Gary K. "*Dr. Strangelove, Red Alert*, and Patterns of Paranoia in the 1950's," *Journal of Popular Film*, V, No. 1 (1976), pp. 57–67.

Wood, Robin. "Shooting *Little Big Man*." In *Arthur Penn*. New York: Praeger, 1969, pp. 118–133.

Wood, Robin. "To Have (Written) and Have Not (Directed)," *Film Comment*, 9, No. 3 (May-June (1973)), pp. 30–35.

Yacowar, Maurice. "*The Roman Spring of Mrs. Stone*." In *Tennessee Williams and Film*. New York: Frederick Ungar, 1977.

Zito, Stephen. "*Dog Soldiers:* Novel Into Film," *American Film*, II, No. 10 September 1977), pp. 8–15.

Zlotnick, Joan. "*The Day of the Locust*—Comparing John Schlesinger's Film and Nathanael West's Novel," *Filmograph*, V, No. 1 (2nd Quarter, 1976).

Editors' Note. For anthologized reviews of individual films made from American novels, consult the title listing in Richard Heinzkill's *Film Criticism: An Index to Critics' Anthologies* (Metuchen, N.J.: Scarecrow Press, 1975).

II / General Entries

Althusser, Louis. *For Marx*. Trans. by Ben Brewster. London: Penguin, 1969.

Armes, Roy. *Film and Reality: An Historical Survey*. London: Penguin, 1974.

Arnheim, Rudolf. *Film as Art*. Berkeley: University of California Press, 1966.

Asheim, Lester. "From Book to Film." Four articles in *Hollywood Quarterly*, 5, No. 3 (Spring 1951), pp. 289–304; 5, No. 4 (Summer 1951), pp. 334–349; 6, No. 1 (Fall 1951), pp. 54–68; 6, No. 3 (Spring 1952), pp. 258–273.

Balazs, Bela. *Theory of Film*. New York: Dover, 1971.

Barthes, Roland. *Elements of Semiology/Writing Degree Zero*. Boston: Beacon, 1968.

Barthes, Roland. *Mythologies*. New York: Hill and Wang, 1972.

Bazin, Andre. *What Is Cinema?* Vol. I. Trans. by Hugh Gray. Berkeley: University of California Press, 1967.

Bazin, Andre. *What Is Cinema?* Vol. II. Trans. by Hugh Gray, Berkeley: University of California Press, 1971.

Bellour, Raymond. "The Unattainable Text," *Screen* 16, No. 3 (Autumn 1975), pp. 19–28.

Benjamin, Walter. "The Work of Art in the Age of Mechanical Reproduction," *Illuminations*. Ed. by Hannah Arendt. New York: Harcourt Brace, 1968.

Bergman, Ingmar. "Film Has Nothing to Do with Literature." Introduction to *Four Screenplays of Ingmar Bergman*. Trans. by Lars Malmstrom and David Kushner. New York: Simon and Schuster, 1960.

Bodeen, DeWitt. "Films and Edith Wharton," *Films in Review,* XXVIII, No. 2 (February 1977), pp. 73–82.

Bond, Kirk. "Film as Literature," *Bookman,* 84 July 1933), pp. 188–189.

Brunette, Peter and Gerald Peary. "Tough Guy: James M. Cain Interviewed," *Film Comment,* 12, No. 3 (May–June 1976), pp. 50–57.

Burch, Noel. *The Theory of Film Practice.* New York: Praeger, 1973.

Buscombe, Edward. "Dickens and Hitchcock," *Screen,* II, Nos. 4–5 (1970), pp. 97–114.

Cahiers du Cinema, 185 (December 1966), issue devoted to novels and film.

Cavell, Stanley. *The World Viewed: Reflections on the Ontology of Film.* New York: Viking, 1971.

Cohen, Keith. "Novel and Cinema: Dynamics of Literary Exchange," *Film Reader* (Northwestern University), 2 (January 1977), pp. 42–51.

Cohen, Mitchell S. "Odd Jobs and Subsidies: Nathanael West in Hollywood," *Film Comment,* 11, No. 3 (May–June 1975), pp. 44–46.

Connor, Edward. "Of Time and the Movies," *Films in Review,* 12, No. 3 (March 1961), pp. 131–143.

Corliss, Richard. *Talking Pictures—Screenwriters in the American Cinema 1927–1973.* Woodstock, New York: The Overland Press, 1974.

Dardis, Tom. *Some Time in the Sun.* New York: Scribner's, 1976.

de Saussure, Ferdinand. *Course in General Linguistics.* Trans. by Wade Baskin. New York: McGraw-Hill, 1966.

Durgnat, Raymond. "This Damned Eternal Triangle," *Films and Filming,* 11, No. 3 (December 1964), pp. 15–19.

Durgnat, Raymond. "The Mongrel Muse," *Films and Feeling.* Cambridge, Mass.: MIT Press, 1971, pp. 13–30.

Eagleton, Terry. *Marxism and Literary Criticism.* Berkeley: University of California Press, 1976.

Eco, Umberto. *A Theory of Semiotics.* Bloomington: Indiana University Press, 1976.

Edel, Leon. "Novel and Camera," *The Theory of the Novel: New Essays.* Ed. by John Halperin. New York: Oxford Press, 1974.

Eidsvik, Charles. "Soft Edges: The Art of Literature, the Medium of Film," *Literature/Film Quarterly,* II, No. 1 (Winter 1974), pp. 16–21.

Eidsvik, Charles. "Toward a 'Politique des Adaptations,'" *Literature/ Film Quarterly*, III, No. 3 (Summer 1975), pp. 255–263.

Eisenstein, Sergei. "Dickens, Griffith, and the Film Today," *Film Form.* Ed. by Jay Leyda. New York: Harcourt, Brace, 1949.

Eisenstein, Sergei. *Film Sense.* Ed. by Jay Leyda. New York: Harcourt Brace, 1957.

Eisenstein, Sergei. "Lessons from Literature," *Film Essays and A Lecture.* Ed. by Jay Leyda. N.Y.: Praeger, 1970.

Enser, A.G.S. *Filmed Books and Plays.* Revised edition. Kent, England: Andre Deutsch, 1975.

Fiedler, Leslie. "The Death and Rebirth of the Novel." In *The Theory of the Novel: New Essays.* Ed. by John Halperin. New York: Oxford University Press, 1974, pp. 189–209.

Fell, John L. *Film and the Narrative Tradition.* Norman, Oklahoma: University of Oklahoma Press, 1974.

French, Philip. "All the Better Books," *Sight and Sound,* 36, No. 1 (Winter 1966–67), pp. 38–41.

Geduld, Harry M., ed. *Authors on Film.* Bloomington, Indiana: Indiana University Press, 1972.

Godfrey, Lionel. "It Wasn't Like That in the Book," *Films and Filming,* 13, No. 7 (April 1967), pp. 12–16.

Hartley, Dean Wilson. "'How Do We Teach It?' A Primer for the Basic Literature/Film Course," *Literature/Film Quarterly,* 3, No. 1 (Winter 1975), pp. 60–68.

Hauser, Arnold. "The Film Age," *The Social History of Art.* Trans. by Stanley Goodman. New York: Knopf, 1951, pp. 927–959.

Jensen, Paul. "Film Noir—The Writer: Raymond Chandler and the World You Live In," *Film Comment,* 10, No. 6 (November-December 1974), pp. 18–26.

Kael, Pauline. "Notes on Heart and Mind," *Deeper into Movies.* Boston: Little Brown and Co. 1973, pp. 230–238.

Kagan, Norman. *Cinema of Stanley Kubrick.* New York: Grove Press, 1975.

Kanin, Garson. "Way Out West: Nathanael West in Locust Land," *American Film,* I, No. 5 (March 1976), pp. 54–59.

Katz, John. "An Integrated Approach to the Teaching of Film and Literature," *Screen,* 11, Nos. 4–5 (August-September 1970), pp. 55–60.

Knight, Arthur. "Hemingway into Film," The *Saturday Review* (July 29, 1961), pp. 33–34.

Koch, Stephen. "Fiction and Film: A Study for New Sources," The *Saturday Review* (December 27, 1969), pp. 12–14.

Kracauer, Siegfried. *Theory of Film.* New York: Oxford University Press, 1960.

Lambert, Gavin. *On Cukor.* New York: Capricorn Books, 1973.

Langer, Susanne K. "A Note on Film," *Feeling and Form.* New York: Scribners, 1953, pp. 411–415.

Latham, Aaron. *Crazy Sundays: F. Scott Fitzgerald in Hollywood.* New York: Viking Press, 1971.

Lewis, Sinclair and Dore Schary. *Storm in the West.* New York: Stein and Day, 1963.

Lillich, Richard B. "Hemingway on the Screen," *Films in Review,* 10 (April 1959), pp. 208–218.

Lindsay, Vachel. *The Art of the Moving Picture.* New York: Macmillan, 1952.

MacShane, Frank. "Raymond Chandler and Hollywood," *American Film,* I, No. 6 (April 1976), pp. 62–69; No. 7 (May 1976), pp. 54–60.

McConnell, Frank. "Film and Writing: The Political Dimension," *Massachusetts Review,* 13, No. 4 (Autumn 1972), pp. 543–562.

Madden, David. "James M. Cain and the Movies of the Thirties and Forties," *Film Heritage,* II, No. 4 (Summer 1967), pp. 9–25.

Magny, Claude-Edmonde. *The Age of the American Novel: The Film Aesthetic of Fiction Between the Two Wars.* Trans. by Eleanor Hochman. New York: Frederick Ungar, 1972.

Mailer, Norman. "A Course in Film Making," *New American Review,* 12, New York: Simon and Schuster, 1971, pp. 200–241.

Martin, Jay. *Nathanael West—The Art of His Life.* New York: Farrar, Strauss and Giroux, 1970.

Marx and Engels on Literature and Art: A Selection of Writings. Ed. by Lee Baxandall and Stefan Morawski. St. Louis: Telos, 1973.

Mason, Ronald. "The Film of the Book," *Film,* 16 (March-April 1958), pp. 18–20.

Mast, Gerald and Marshall Cohen, eds. *Film Theory and Criticism.* New York: Oxford University Press, 1974.

Mayersberg, Paul. "The Great Rewrite," *Sight and Sound,* 36, No. 2 (Spring 1967), pp. 72–77.

Metz, Christian. *Film Language: A Semiotics of the Cinema.* Trans. by Michael Taylor. New York: Oxford University Press, 1974.

Monaco, James. *How to Read a Film.* New York: Oxford University Press, 1977.

Moreno, Julio L. "Subjective Cinema: And the Problem of Film in the First Person," The *Quarterly of Film, Radio and Television*, 7, No. 4 (Summer 1953), pp. 341–358.

Munden, Kenneth. "Sinclair Lewis and the Movies," *Cinema Journal*, XII, No. 1 (Fall 1972), pp. 46–56.

Munsterberg, Hugo. *The Film: A Psychological Study*. New York: Dover Press, 1969.

Murray, Edward. *The Cinematic Imagination: Writers and the Motion Pictures*. New York: Frederick Ungar, 1972.

Nathan, Robert. "A Novelist Looks at Hollywood," *Hollywood Quarterly*, 1, No. 2 (1945), pp. 146–147.

Nichols, Bill, ed. *Movies and Methods*. Berkeley: University of California Press, 1977.

Nicoll, Allardyce. "Literature and the Film," *English Journal*, 26 (January 1937), pp. 1–9.

Nolan, William F. *John Huston—King Rebel*. Los Angeles: Sherbourne Press, 1965.

Ortman, Marguerite G. *Fiction and the Screen*. Boston: Marshall Jones, 1935.

Panofsky, Erwin. "Style and Medium in the Moving Pictures," *Critique*, 1, No. 3 (January–February 1947).

Peary, Gerald. "Selected Sound Westerns and Their Novel Sources," *The Velvet Light Trap*, 12 (Spring 1974), pp. 15–19.

Peary, Gerald and Roger Shatzkin. *The Classic American Novel and the Movies*. New York: Frederick Ungar, 1977.

Perkins, V. F. *Film as Film*. London: Penguin, 1972.

Phelps William Lyon. "Stories I'd Like to See Screened," *The Movies on Trial*. Ed. by William J. Perlman. New York: MacMillan, 1936, pp. 92–98.

Pingaud, Bernard. "The Aquarium," *Sight and Sound*, 32, No. 3 (Summer 1963), pp. 136–139.

Pratt, Theodore. "From the Novel by . . . ," *Atlantic Monthly*, 175 (March 1945), pp. 114–119.

Purdy, Strother B. "Can the Novel and the Film Disappear?" *Literature/Film Quarterly*, II, No. 3 (Fall 1974), pp. 237–255.

Read, Herbert. "Towards a Film Aesthetic," *Cinema Quarterly*, 1, No. 4 (Summer 1933), pp. 197–202.

Richardson, Robert. *Literature and Film*. Bloomington, Indiana: Indiana University Press, 1969.

Riesman, Evelyn. "Film and Fiction," *Antioch Review*, 17 (Fall 1957), pp. 353–363.

Roud, Richard. "Novel Novel; Fable Fable?" *Sight and Sound,* 31 (Spring 1962), pp. 84–88.

Ruhe, Edward. "Film: The 'Literary' Approach," *Literature/Film Quarterly,* 1, No. 1 (January 1973), pp. 76–83.

Schneider, Harold W. "Literature and Film: Marking Out the Boundaries," *Literature/Film Quarterly,* 3, No. 1 (Winter 1975), pp. 30–44.

Schulberg, Budd. "The Hollywood Novel," *American Film,* I, No. 7 (May 1976), pp. 28–32.

Seldes, Gilbert. "Vandals of Hollywood," The *Saturday Review* (October 17, 1936), pp. 3–4.

Sherman, William David. "David Goodis: Dark Passage," *Sight and Sound,* 38, No. 1 (Winter 1968–69), p. 41.

Sobchack, Vivian C. "Tradition and Cinematic Allusion," *Literature/Film Quarterly,* 2, No. 1 (Winter 1974), pp. 59–65.

Solomon, Maynard, ed. *Marxism and Art: Essays Classic and Contemporary.* New York: Vintage, 1973.

Sontag, Susan. "A Note on Novels and Films," *Against Interpretation.* New York: Dell, 1972, pp. 245–250.

Thorp, Margaret. "The Motion Picture and the Novel," *American Quarterly,* 3, No. 3 (1951), pp. 195–203.

Trotsky, Leon. *Literature and Revolution.* Ann Arbor: University of Michigan Press, 1960.

Tudor, Andrew. *Theories of Film.* New York: Viking, 1974.

Van Wert, William. "Adaptations," *Guidebook to Film.* Ed. by Ronald Gottesman and Harry M. Geduld. New York: Holt, Rinehart, 1972, pp. 30–35.

Wagner, Geoffrey. *The Novel and the Cinema.* Cranbury, N.J.: Fairleigh Dickinson University Press, 1975.

Warshow, Robert. *The Immediate Experience.* New York: Atheneum, 1964.

Weinberg, Herman G. "Novel into Film," *Literature/Film Quarterly,* 1, No. 2 (April 1973), pp. 99–102.

Weisman, E. "Literature and Film Art," *Soviet Cinema.* Ed. by Alexander Yakovlevich Arosev. Moscow: Voks, 1935, pp. 77–88.

Williams, Raymond. *Marxism and Literature.* New York: Oxford University Press, 1977.

Wollen, Peter. *Signs and Meaning in the Cinema.* Revised edition. Bloomington, Indiana: Indiana University Press, 1972.

Wollen, Peter, ed. *Working Papers on the Cinema: Sociology and Semiology.* London: British Film Institute, 1969.

INDEX